Literary Theory's Future(s)

Literary
Theory's
Future(s)

Edited by
Joseph Natoli

University of Illinois Press
Urbana and Chicago

© 1989 by the Board of Trustees of the University of Illinois
Manufactured in the United States of America
1 2 3 4 5 C P 5 4 3 2 1

This book is printed on acid-free paper.

Library of Congress Cataloging-in-Publication Data

Literary theory's future(s) / edited by Joseph Natoli.
    p. cm.
   Includes bibliographies and index.
   IBSN 0-252-01599-1 (cloth:alk. paper). — ISBN 0-252-06049-0 (paper:
alk. paper)
    1. Literature—History and criticism—Theory, etc. I. Natoli,
Joseph P., 1943-
PN441.L488 1989   88-31742
801'.95—dc19   CIP

Contents

Acknowledgments

My needs in concocting this collection and seeing it through were filled first of all by its contributors, our efforts complemented by a host of competent readers and competent dialogists, especially William Tyrrell, Mark Edmundson, Daniel Kinney, Michael Levenson, Jerome J. McGann, Austin Quigley, Richard Rorty, Gustavo Pellon, Evan Watkins, René Girard, Roger Meiners, David M. Harmon, Neal Bruss, Jim Merod, and Stanley Fish. An essential dialogics has been supplied for the last year through my involvement with Provost David Scott's Council to Review Undergraduate Education at Michigan State University. I here earned my sense of the practicality and the politics of theory in the curriculum, in the classroom, and in the university, and came to see cultural critique's place in supplementing the ever-narrowing focus of undergraduate education. In helping me "translate" and "export" between alternative word-processing universes, I thank Peter Cookingham, Barbara Sagraves, Jon Harrison, Kriss Ostrom, Amy Washburn, Brian Borst, and especially Janice Clark, to whom I owe my beginnings in such universes, and Bill Wheeler and Duane Gliwa for their advice and assistance. I am indebted to Ann Lowry Weir, senior editor at the University of Illinois Press, for grasping this project—both *Tracing* and *Future(s)*—so immediately and completely. Beyond categories is my debt to Elaine Natoli for helping me meet deadlines, for helping me see life without deadlines. Both *Tracing Literary Theory* and *Literary Theory's Future(s)* finally came to be through the encouragement of Lawrence Farese, who died two days before *Tracing* was released. In memory of his courage in seeing always beyond the Panopticon, I dedicate both collections.

JOSEPH NATOLI

Prefacing *Future(s)*/Meditating
on One Future

Prefacing *Future(s)*

The shape of this collection—the selection of certain
authors, discourses, and issues—attempts to capture a tracing of
the future, of what we each live with, in a markedly original,
ideocratic way. When one contrasts a discourse on the future with
a discourse on the past, the past comes forth as a determining
record—even if that record can only express indeterminacy regarding what was "really there." For all its real imbrication in the
present, the future can never offer us any record at all. If tracing
a present/past relationship is a tricky business (see the Preface to
Tracing Literary Theory) because it sets out to reflect a reality that
has different faces, the tracing of a present/future dialogic goes on
in the domain of "magic realism."[1]

But even the art of selection within such a domain has its
roots in notions of the future that are interwoven with the ways
we shape ourselves in the present, as well as by considerations as
to what political and rhetorical patterns in that tapestry should be
brought forth. While this collection needs *Tracing Literary Theory*
as a supplementary text only in the Derridean sense that all texts
claiming to be autotelic cry out for supplementation, the shape of
Tracing affected the shape—the pattern and the privileged voices—
of this present collection. A great deal in *Tracing* retains center
stage here, but within the altered setting of a present/future dialogic.
But a number of the essays in *Tracing*—A. C. Goodson's essay on

structuralism in the moment of Bakhtin, Herman Rapaport's re-presencing of phenomenology, Carolyn Allen's advocacy of a feminist critique not obedient to postmodernism but both scribing and enacting a cultural critique, and Gregory Colomb's prophetic treatment of semiotics—already achieve a clear dialogic of present/future as well as present/past. My thought from the beginning was that, unless theory could be presented as interpenetrating and interconnecting with time—past, present, and future—as well as with other discourses, any tracing would be only partial. *Tracing Literary Theory* needed supplementation, although quite clearly an endless chain of supplementation confounds a desire to achieve closure, to render for the reader a smooth, polished surface. Alongside such a philosophical imbroglio there is always a political/rhetorical urgency—brawl rather than aporia—to script what we hope to one day enact.

I shall presently meditate upon a role for literary theory within cultural critique, one in which literary theory is conflated and yet retains its identity while being part of a cultural critique. Indeed, the essays in this collection themselves to various degrees perform such a cultural critique. It is not cultural critique's dialogic of present/future that is the "privileged presence" in this collection, however, but literary theory's. The future of an emerging cultural critique captures more than literary theory, extends to a number of heterogeneous discourses that, like literary theory, trespass against disciplines and departments. The tracing of literary theory's own relationship with other discourses in this collection and in *Tracing Literary Theory* points to an homology of the theory "carnival" and cultural critique, hopes to underwrite a dialogic between the two, and implicitly underwrites supplementation rather than metamorphosis. I conceive a tracing of literary theory as being not only what is needed in a political/rhetorical sense at the moment, but also as a rich ground from which a pervasive political/rhetorical, worldly/academic compact of literary theory and cultural studies can be effected. We are fast moving toward a way to find an identity for cultural critique, toward a climate similar to the one that fostered a tracing of literary theory. How that tracing will be shaped still awaits what is yet to be scripted/enacted on many levels.

Therefore I would describe as precipitous my own attempt—
softened as a meditation—to inscribe a future for a literary theory
transformed into a cultural critique without losing its identity as
a *literary* critique. This meditation is not itself a cultural critique
but is intent on finding a way toward it. This parallels what David
Bohm sees as the plight of modern physics in hoping to reveal an
implicate order, an order of interconnectedness and interpenetra-
tion, from within a physics that first must be transformed before
it can become the means toward transformation.[2] My own meditation then proceeds neither through a *rapprochement* of theoretical conflicts and difficulties nor into a thoroughgoing critique
of prevailing systems. In short, while both systematizing and cri-
tiquing fall back at the first sign of the incommensurable, medi-
tating plows ahead.

Literary studies is not now instituted so that it can follow my
meditative scripting of its future. I cannot endorse that future that
lies so readily at hand, that in effect dissolves the scope of theory.
In many ways all the essays in this collection seek to bring their
voices out of a dilemma in which they are threatened with being
either dissolved within an entrenched orchestration or excluded as
what Michel Serres calls "notes played in the seventh chord."[3] And
this vision of a future for a literary theory neither dissolved within
nor excluded by, and yet *with*, a cultural critique can be seen as
a magical jump out of a present context for literary theory. All of
the following essays concoct futures for theory, but they do not
inscribe upon the reader a steady, relentless progress toward cultural critique. For the most part they arrest my own meditative
rush and draw the reader into dimensions of theory that have been
and must not be missed. Indeed, they draw the reader away from
clean, magical jumps into grandiose signifiers and back to the
murky present entanglements of literary theory. There is, then, a
rushing toward an expanded identity for literary theory (marked
by my own meditation) and a deceleration (created by the ensuing
essays) that enables the reader to observe the scene more closely,
to scrutinize the ways and whys of a variety of presents and futures
of what I have called the theory "carnival." This is the sort of
tension, of disequilibrium, that undermines the smooth, polished
surface of our "collective" discourse, yet remains faithful to my

intent here and in *Tracing Literary Theory* to trace a dialogic of imbricated voices within an imbricated time and to do that (necessarily) in seventh chords.

Because of such varied presents and futures, I must defer to the moment of reading itself a "prefacing" that should reveal a consensus in regard to what we talk about when we talk about literary theory's future. What each writer perceives to be his or her relationship with the present and the future is interwoven with the futures they urge, or seek to inscribe, or hope to deter us from. What each reader finally interprets as unison or dissonance is therefore not in the editor's hands but in the reader's own, though admittedly the essays themselves are set on affecting what a reader has already necessarily conceived as his or her own entente with the future and what it holds for literary theory.

There is, then, a mutually held "will to affect," a belief, as Susan Horton expresses it in her essay, "in the importance of the exertion of will and purpose over present and future, against and instead of more intellection and problematization of that term." No bargaining with the future in the present would take place if one did not first believe that we could, here and now, affect the future. In the same fashion, no collaboration concerning future theory would ensue if there was not already in place a workable bargaining between present and future. Indeed, without going through the throes of "scripting" that bargaining, it could only be "workable" as a point of departure.

In using the words "already necessarily conceived" I have already revealed my own entente with the future, my own view that we all live with some sense of the future activated or driven by the present. Living in the present with a sense of having no future, a future like a blank wall, is yet living with some sense of the future (albeit, in this case, we would have a psychopathology). In those instances where a schizoid state has been reached, where we seem to be approaching two opposing futures at the same time, the urge to either endorse or censure is strongest. And in this view, while futures are present and yet future, conceived but not enacted, a tracing of futures present becomes essential. Among other matters in the present, literary theory now foresees both its own continuance and its own end.

The movement of *Literary Theory's Future(s)* is toward a representation of literary theory and its interrelationships with other matters—discourses, practices, and institutions. But this is true only in the sense that we move from a focus on individuals—Lacan, de Man, and Girard—to broader considerations of the discourses of science, history, and politics, and finally to even broader considerations of cultural community, cultural critique, and the institution of literature. Literary theory is given a wider and wider staging. We begin with close-ups of faces, of authors who create discourses, and next replace them with the discourses that create authors, and finally, replace those with discourses about both. It is my belief, however, that the actual nature of literary theory confounds any such gradual progression of broad cultural entanglements. When literary theory is considered as being imbricated with the work of Lacan, we are immediately overlapping everything that the entire collection considers under the rubric of "literary theory" with a psychoanalytic approach that bears all the richness of psychoanalysis's dialogue with Western culture. The same holds true for the imbrication of literary theory and the work of René Girard. Girard's intention, in William Johnsen's view, "means nothing less . . . than to make good on the dream of a hypothesis that ultimately accounts for the generation of all cultural forms." And in considering the legacy of Paul de Man, Richard Barney positions de Man's work at a crucial moment: "De Man's doubtful and ironic study of language . . . is only too appropriate in the context of this American culture of suspicion." From the very beginning this collection reveals literary theory in all the diversity of its cultural indebtedness so that its relation to cultural critique appears as neither presumptuous nor suicidal. The voices of Lacan and Girard have been selected because they remain voices that we in the present have to a great extent deferred. Ellie Ragland-Sullivan and William Johnsen argue, respectively, for a present confrontation with the work of Lacan and Girard, the necessary first step toward any future that they can help inscribe. And who would argue with the view that, although Paul de Man has gained a level of hearing within literary theory so far denied to Girard and Lacan, it is de Man's work for which we now concoct no future? These three have been selected not because their work will necessarily be the *prima materia* of the future, but because they hang perilously in the present, and there are those who fear that such a present state of affairs imperils the future of theory.

In the same fashion, science, history, and politics are not being presented as the only discourses with which future theory should be concerned. Rather, their present situation has led to their being foregrounded in this collection. I believe literary theory is at the threshold of its relationship with science. Edward Davenport's view is that, although literary theory has developed a very attractive body of discourses, it can begin to learn from them only if it finds "ways to criticize and test them, and thus to learn about them and from them." Here a politics of inquiry, an amalgam of Karl Popper and Thomas Kuhn, is recommended.

David Gorman notes a shift in theoretical directions revealed in key terms. While an earlier generation had deployed terms such as *text, discourse, rhetoric, signifier, code, reading,* and *writing,* a later generation mobilized *history, society, politics, ideology, power, the body, material culture.* Indeed, we are acutely aware in the present of the need to historicize (a need Gorman interrogates) and to politicize (which, in Michael Clark's view, often involves "naming" rather than "acting"). Rather than preaching a "New Historicism," Gorman considers three areas of history/ theory intersection—philology, social action, and genealogy— which he first explores in the work of Edward Said. In doing so he succeeds in filling many of those gaps neglected in the present enthusiasm regarding our need to historicize. He re-shapes the present lineaments of history/theory and thus, I believe, re-shapes its future lineaments as well. Michael Clark also steps back from the present rush in the name of politics and theory and scrutinizes a position somewhere between "the simpler forms of nominalism and materialism that pervade most political readings of literary texts today." This sort of wide-angle viewing enables him to note that "politics has become aestheticized" to the point where politicized literary theories may "be well on the way to restoring the literary text to a world that no longer exists."

Perhaps, because literary theory is itself a site of transdisciplinary relations, we should expect some agitation to develop. But Susan Horton's essay in the last section of the collection does not restrict itself to any one turmoil or to the defense of any one theory voice. Her own vigilant auto-critique is revealed in her opening comments: ". . . the only way I have been able to map the terrain of our future is by letting my experience of trying to provide that mapping do three things: first, interrogate the notion of 'future' itself; second, not write 'about' that 'future' so much as participate in what Ulmer calls its *scripting*, helping to actualize what I pretend only to describe; and, finally, letting my own experience of trying to script that future stand in synecdochically for the moment in which I believe we may all be secret sharers." In this fashion Horton works conscientiously toward evoking "not a specific program so much as my own longing, desire for a better and more genuinely communal future, and my own will to bring that about." Her essay "scripts" a desire that grounds the entire collection, and a will that can inscribe in the present a future that we will one day enact.

Meditating on One Future

Compared to an article by Daniel Bell in a recent issue of *Daedalus*, "The World and the United States in 2013," the title *Literary Theory's Future(s)* seems decidedly less significant, certainly more claustrophobic.[4] Nevertheless, my meditation here is initiated by the belief that the subject of theory's future, protestations aside, is significant. The future of theory matters because it is, at its very best, moving toward claiming its place within and alongside a broad cultural critique of what we believe, what we intend, what we practice—what we are. This critique has the capacity to problematize what otherwise might be construed as the "right moves" for all of us.

 I realize how closely this desire to draw us back from what we might otherwise consider to be "right moves" parallels Matthew Arnold's desire, expressed almost immediately in *Culture and Anarchy*, to draw his readers back by the force of culture from what they might consider to be the "right moves." I cannot confess to bowing to Arnold's notion of culture or anarchy, or to the reason and will of God which chaperones the former. However, the sense of urgency of *Culture and Anarchy* has been inherited today by what has been called the Conservative Counter-Reformation (what Irving Howe has called a "partial counter-revolution"). The urgency of that rush to re-illuminate a fading sweetness and light in

the old building—because of Foucault I cannot think of this building as anything but Bentham's Panopticon—compels an equal and
opposite rush to consolidate the "Reformation." For me, that is
a consolidation toward cultural critique, an alliance formed not
under the gaze of those Presences that Arnold could summon nor
as straight-arrow directed toward human perfectability as Arnold
conceived it: "It is in making endless additions to itself, in the
endless expansion of its powers, in endless growth in wisdom and
beauty, that the spirit of the human race finds its ideal."[5]

Theory makes "citational" a panopticon of reason and authority. It reveals that light is not always from the center, that the
Sun itself is ambivalent, both resplendent in its visibility and
chthonian in its invisibility. The signifiers "unity" and "difference"
(or, in the current curricula debate, "integration" and "specialization") mirror not a diversity that world and discourse reveal,
but a monologism arising from "the current of unifying and cen-
tralizing centripetal forces of verbal and ideological life"—what
William Spanos in his critique of the Harvard core curriculum
identifies as "the perennial panoptic effort of Western Man to
perpetuate his will to power over being."[6]

Foucault brilliantly seizes upon the idea of Bentham's Panopticon, the prison employing the circle with a fixed center and
light, to speak of a panopticism which Spanos describes as "the
pervasively inscribed impulse to re-form deviants, eccentrics, idlers,
invalids, etc., in the name of the normalizing anthropomorphic
Logos."[7] The power of the panopticon is behind the lens, if you
will, and not in the field of observation. "Although the universal
juridicism of modern society," Foucault writes, "seems to fix limits
on the exercise of power, its universally widespread panopticism
enables it to operate, on the underside of the law, a machinery
both immense and minute." This "invisibility" of power itself to
the eye of those in the panoptic circle effects an insidious relationship between power and the surveilled. The panoptic "architectural apparatus should be a machine for creating and sustaining
a power relation independent of the person who exercises it; in
short, that the inmates should be caught up in a power situation
of which they are themselves the bearers."[8]

In his effort to position critical practice specifically within
"sets of discursive and institutional formations that are parts of

larger constellations of cultural and political power," Paul Bové finds Kant's claims regarding providential nature and reason as ultimately leading to a culture "conceived as the space of human priority and fulfillment." In this distinguished, highly privileged role, culture becomes "a regulative concept, along with a subsidiary set of concepts and practices—will to knowledge, science, instrumental reason, the leading intellectual—that, among others, delimit humanistic and critical discourse up to the present time." Such optimism serves neither culture nor humanism, since it "nullifies critical practice, submerging it, in turn, in the role of 'police man' guarding against barbarism and other threats to the preserved rational order. Critique becomes quietistic. It cannot be either active negation or the positive projection of alternatives. It merely discriminates and externalizes while serving what it and its masters take to be the 'rational order.'"[9] This system of surveillance, of observing closely (the panopticon is also that cross-bred microscope/telescope that makes use of light) that takes place within the center tower of a constraining, normalizing, anthropomorphic logos, endorses only those differences that can never be different "in the view" of that center of surveillance.

This observing tower at the center represents a persistent attempt in the West to fix "being as *presence*," which, according to Derrida, typifies Western metaphysics: "The whole history of the concept of structure . . . must be thought of as a series of substitutions of center for center, as a linked chain of determinations of the center. Successively, and in a regulated fashion, the center receives different forms or names. The history of metaphysics, like the history of the West, is the history of these metaphors and metonymies. Its matrix . . . is the determination of being as *presence* in all the senses of this word."[10]

But viewing from the center can be displaced with scrutiny from the periphery as any individual eye casts the light of its own being outward. Although you would expect the monologism of the Sun to prevail, the panoptic eying that we have presently in theory consists of a diversity of discourses regarding theory's future, most prominently: that theory has reached its end; that theory should end; that when theory detracts us from a pedagogical discourse and a practice of literary studies, it should be resisted; that theory should move on to an acceptance of the political-historical-social horizon as primary in culture and therefore primary for itself; that theory should move on to a cultural critique that privileges no particular voice but heterology ("a term that inserts itself between two other parallel coinages, *raznojazycie,* heteroglossia or diversity of languages, and *raznogolosie,* heterophony or diversity of [individual] voices"[11]). Here in this last suggestion—which I prefer—culture, like time at any given moment, is what theory at its most expansive has shown it to be—not culture in the Kantian sense of taste, sensibility, or cultivation, but culture in the broader sense of a common style revealed in actual practices such as religion, philosophy, politics, psychiatry, law, language, art, or science, but not excluding, within these discourse practices, institutions, objects, the material culture. The *real* is not subsumed under the *word.*[12]

A panoramic eying of culture, extending it to a Vichian rather than Kantian eying, is paralleled by an equal panoramic eying of literary theory. Theory, like culture, is more than what academic departments allow in line with interdepartmental detente. Gerald Graff expands the viewing field appropriately: "Contrary to the stipulation of recent pragmatist arguments 'Against Theory,' literary theory may but need not be a *system* or *foundational discourse* that aims to 'govern' critical practice from some outside metaphysical standpoint . . . it is at least as legitimate, and more in line with normal usage, to think of literary theory not as a set of systematic principles, necessarily or a founding philosophy, but simply as an inquiry into assumptions, premises, and legitimating principles and concepts."[13]

Such an inquiry is, one hopes, not lost in a babble of discourse heterology—a telling description of cultural critique. My view is that literary theory, composed in the present of a great throng of voices, has affirmed—has even made brilliant use of—its expanded and contracted identities. Our special realizing of unity gives top honors to acts of subsuming, to the commensurable; supposedly diverse and diverging identities will lose themselves on the road to a simple and elegant omniscience. This doesn't seem to happen either in us, in Nature, or in our culture, despite our efforts. I suggest that the matter of identity and its loss in regard to literary theory won't survive the scrutinizing, the self-reflexivity, of theory itself. What follows this loss of identity is a loss of a center, of a power base. Of course, for many, the chaos of literary theory itself is evidence of what's left when we fail to uphold a traditional identity of literary studies. That identity severs literary studies, purely for identity's sake, from all extra-literary discourses.

Any effort to see the future as in a fluid, interpenetrating relation with the present and the past, to see a discourse as also being in the same sort of fluid, interpenetrating relation with other discourses, to thus de-center "eying" itself from a panoptic post, won't reveal a "social analysis" from the center but will reveal one that is nevertheless significant. Significant not only in the attempt to enrich our conversation regarding cultural critique—a critique emerging both from the heterology of culture itself and from the heterology of discourse—but also, through that attempt, to reveal the slippage in prime-time conversations that have gone on and still go on. Richard Johnson, a historian, provides us with a renewal of cultural studies itself and with a plea to move forward: "There are lots of half-way houses, many of them serviceable workshops for cultural study, but the *direction* of movement, to my mind, has to be out, and away, and into more dangerous places."[14] To pursue the discourse of literary theory toward cultural critique is, to my mind also, a significant enterprise. But it is also crucial to observe a concern. This concern is expressed in theory's own embodiment of diverse ways in which experience is realized, and in its concern for the politics of privilege attendant to any realizing. If the status of the real can be achieved solely by simply recording—present, past, and future—the experiential scenarios in which reality reveals itself, there is no escape from whatever identity has already been "realized."

Theory's context at this moment is developing a mounting inability to "identify" it. Nor is theory's metamorphosis to cultural critique a sure bet, since the struggle of theory to construct a variety of experiences as real occurs within a context that has lost its memory of having experienced them as real. There is, then, in the absence of such memory, no present "identifying frame" for what theory is shaping as its eventual identity. No identity for anything or anyone can exist if the means of identification must arise from within a context that has forgotten how to identify those means.

Within this context it matters *only hermetically* if the "cosmic textualism" that prevails at Brown's Center for Modern Culture and Media "is not," in the words of Stanley Fish, "something that is so foundational it has taken over all other activities," or that, in the absence of a foolproof plan to recover the author's "real intentions," not only literary theory but also associated efforts should cease to exist.[15] It matters *only hermetically* that theory has yet failed to uncover the relationship between intellectual practices and cultural domination that obscures social reality and thereby advances capitalist hierarchies and the power of the state.

Some part of this whole matter is theoretical—a revisiting of the Panopticon's foundational structure. But the attempt here is not to demolish the voice of Foucault and "center" that of Derrida or to reject Habermas in favor of Gadamer, Ricoeur instead of Lacan, Rorty and not Bakhtin, Gramsci and not Croce, Adorno and not Benjamin, Lentricchia and not de Man, almost everybody and just not Heidegger. Or Sartre, or Husserl. Or Frye, Richards, Brooks, Tate, Vivas. Or—what is most dramatic—some unearthed voice, like Bakhtin's or Burke's, which in the furor of a new theory "season" takes center stage. It is revealing that a feminist critique in its most expansive form as cultural critique continues a dialogue with theory while yet privileging the heterology of its total discourse. In other words, feminist theorists are involved not simply in the de-struction or deconstruction of "abstract system[s] of normative forms" or the politics of "Passing Theories," but in a cultural diversity whose utterances and discourses interpenetrate and interconnect. Within this rich, intense social life such utterances and discourses can neither be resolved nor rendered context-less nor bracketed nor endlessly deferred.

When theory acts as if its utterances and discourses comprise "an abstract system" and "not a concrete heterological opinion on the world," it abides by that frame of mutual comprehension established by panopticism.[16] It replaces interconnectedness and resemblance with the dogmatism of its own theoretical/critical activity, a state of affairs that Max Stirner's (here unearthed) brand of deconstruction rejects through a simple assertion of the context of his own individuality: "I am neither the champion of a thought nor the champion of thinking: for 'I,' from whom I start, am not a thought, not do I consist in thinking. Against me, the unnameable, the realm of thoughts, thinking, and mind is shattered."[17] When we expand Stirner's "own" to include not only the individual but all worldly contextual harmonies with which theory has to deal, it is clear that no presently construed identifying frame exists for it, or for the cultural critique that heterology implies. Thus it matters only hermetically to me, to my meditation, that I end it by invoking an ontological dimension of cultural critique—citing Heideggerian being—while invoking the cultural materialism of Foucault and here acknowledging the value of deconstruction to stand, within cultural critique, as a "rigorous examination of all . . . pretension to closure and discreteness in order to show how such claims work to disguise the material forces of culture. . . ."[18] The internal force of a dialogic within cultural critique must enact its own identity and not simply wait to be identified while fulfilling the expectations of a Prevailing Truth.

Theory as it exists now in the United States, within academe, awaits an uncertain future. It sits unobserved in a classroom within a context that is centered in a reality and that promotes a "well-made" experiencing of that reality, which Derrida in his Cornell address defines as a context of modern technoscience "built both on the principle of reason and what remains hidden in that principle."[19] Unless we can come within the sight of "humanistic education" *without being transformed into an agreement with it,* I doubt we'll get a hearing for any interrogation of "theoretical energies that promote the long-repressed analysis of *class struggle* as it approaches, and in extremely guarded or covert form circulates through, humanistic education."[20] "There is a double gesture here," Derrida said at his Cornell lecture, "a double postulation: to ensure professional competence and the most serious tradition of the university even while going as far as possible, theoretically and practically, in the most directly underground thinking about the abyss beneath the university. . . ."[21]

Committed to the pursuit of a privileged experiencing of reality, academe cannot sponsor theory's difference, its transgression of academe's foundational identity. Committed to interrogating the reality of experiences, theory pursues an interrogation of our present academe's own special experiencing of reality. Derrida asserts that this sort of interrogation "appears unsuitable and thus unbearable to certain university professionals in every country who join ranks to foreclose or censure it by all available means."[22] Not only does a certain precariousness therefore result from the "social analysis," the brand of "eying" that we bring to a consideration of the future of theory or cultural critique, but a certain precariousness in making such a "social analysis" involves the reality of the ways we have already realized our experiencing of what now comes under our "eying." "If the police is always waiting in the wings," Derrida writes, "it is because conventions are by essence violable and precarious, *in themselves* and by the fictionality that constitutes them, even before there has been any overt transgression, in the 'first sense' of *to pretend.*"[23]

Literary theory did not begin in the streets, nor is it likely ever to work up a "public guise." Its move toward cultural critique goes on within academe. It is doubtless difficult for a cultural critique to retreat from the "real world" of hardball politics and entrepreneurial power, to back off and publish from a tenured spot for an academic coterie. The lack of worldliness threatens to enervate any self-respecting cultural critic. This sort of reaction buys into a scene without seeming to upset the hidden dualisms it contains: world vs. academe, theory vs. social practice—in short, the academic myth exploded by Lentricchia. What is seen as a retreat behind the walls of academe is a retreat underwritten by the realizing of such conflicts. It is an especially pernicious realizing, since it sets many of us off in pursuit of a "real role" within our culture and causes us to think of critique and life within academe as a retreat or a dead end.

Perhaps, for those who foresee that one day we all should be "registering for rooms in the motel of the state," this present dangling of academe is hard to live with. While the Conservative Counter-Reformation yearns for *illo tempore* and despises those who are roadblocks to such a return, Marxist-socialists champ at the bit that keeps them powerless, incapable of realizing a future amalgam of power and people. I lean more toward accepting the world in its parts, with no template in hand for past or future unity.

Such a cultural critique does not have its eye on a past or future place but on the varied realizing of experiences that lead to, for instance, the conservative experience of a real past and the Marxist experience of a real future. What is threatened is an intended unity that demands a certain kind of separation, or a pan-optic eying of unity and difference. And it is cultural critique set to work within its worldly part—academe—that does the threatening, because it not only problematizes our present educational enterprises but also assumes a place within the same.

Although academe is inevitably of the world and infused with the agenda of its culture, it demonstrates no "worldliness," lost as it is in a schizoid way of seeing. One side of its face observes and laments its own worldless condition, while the other side observes the supposititious condition of the world itself. "Nothing appears more difficult, in the present age of theory," Mark Krupnick writes, "than the recovery of the old, unself-conscious conviction of the world's actuality." But Krupnick, for one, remains optimistic: "Certainly criticism needs to move worldwards. . . . Despite misgivings, however, one welcomes the new, more worldly criticism. It has been forty years since the New York intellectuals provided America with its last important body of social-cultural criticism written from the point of view of unspecialized men and women of letters. . . . With the exhaustion of the recent wave of aesthetic formalism, academic critics have the opportunity now to retrieve the mainline American tradition of cultural criticism."[24]

When Krupnick's cultural critique (basically a culture of journalism moving via literary theory toward cultural critique) is expanded to include sociology, media and communication studies, linguistics and history, we receive conflicting reports as to how they are faring. J. Hillis Miller is quoted in the *Chronicle of Higher Education* as stating that the interdisciplinary ferment "is taking place in what has been called the 'hidden university'—study groups, symposia, conferences, and institutes that are outside of departments."[25] Richard Johnson states that "cultural studies is now a movement or a network" possessing such an entrenched academic status ("Cultural studies is now a widely taught subject") that "unless we are very careful, students will encounter it as an orthodoxy."[26] The disagreement here—cultural studies has or lacks an academic identity—can, of course, be tracked to the unreliability of the signifier "cultural studies." Johnson's definition is grounded in Marxist critique, but, in recognizing the wider terrain involved, he points to that uncertainty, that lack of place to which Miller attests: "Cultural studies has been marked out, in the British context, for its concern with 'theory,' but the intimacy of the connection with philosophy has not been obvious until recently. Yet there is a very close cousinhood between epistemological problems and positions (e.g., empiricism, realism, and idealism) and the key questions of 'cultural theory' (e.g., economism, materialism, or the problem of culture's specific effects). Again, for me, a lot of roads lead back to Marx, but the appropriations need to be wider ones."[27]

When we combine the Marxist concern for social relations, power, and differences with theory's "focus on referentiality as a problem rather than as something that reliably and unambiguously relates a reader to the 'real world' of history, of society, and of people acting within society on the stage of history," we are basically extending our concept of cultural studies toward heteroglossia and self-reflexivity.[28] Will this marriage hold? Not in Terry Eagleton's view, if theory's self-reflexivity leads to renouncing the "urge to totalize and legitimate itself," a renouncing advocated by postmodernism. Social critique is impossible here, "since there is not any total to be criticized. We are always caught up in one narrative or another, and can never catapult ourselves to some metalinguistic vantage point beyond them."[29]

Does a failure to make an unambiguous contact with the "real world" subvert the construction of a political critique of such a world? The matter is crucial. Eagleton neatly points to what is at stake: "The Nicaraguans and the African National Congress, it would appear, have not yet been told about the epistemological illusions of metanarrative."[30] Feminist critique, perhaps the most effective contemporary thrust toward cultural critique, joins with Marxist critique in its "disenchantment" with postmodernism: "Seen from one angle, feminism, with its commitment to material change, has nothing in common with postmodernism and its preoccupation with language and the free play of signifiers. Indeed, many feminist critics view such a connection on a scale ranging somewhere from distracting to pernicious."[31] Carolyn Allen goes on, however, to trace feminism's intersections with certain voices contributing to the chorale of literary theory (namely, semiotics and psychoanalysis), voices that one can associate with literary theory's proven capacity to make wider appropriations than can be associated with a postmodernism (a term that relates to a sensibility best discerned in opposition to "what went on before"). We are sent backward to modernism.

When we act on our concern for extricating all that has been going on under the name of theory from the term "postmodernism," we discover that they are not identical. Neither literary theory nor cultural critique is represented by postmodernism, but postmodernism (especially in the constructive way leading to positive critique as hoped for by Paul Bové) is a voice within both. It serves to distinguish the problematizing Now from a past unproblematized confrontation of the problematic, a confrontation described as the modern temper.[32] A Marxist-based cultural critique can make appropriations beyond itself, into literary theory, without venturing into cultural relativism, without losing the cutting edge. This descent into cultural relativism—a plethora of narratives whose unreality one either suffocates within or rises above through the imposition of an equally unreal metanarrative—haunts the troublesome signifier of cultural critique when it is expanded to include, as I am doing, the equally troublesome signifier of literary theory.

Post-structuralist theory's depiction of indeterminacy lying right at the heart of every discourse's encounter with the world, its importance in any description of "postmodernism," brings us precisely to that state of affairs that a Conservative Counter-Reformation seeks to nip in the bud. Restricting our focus to theory's future place as cultural critique within academe, it is quite clear, in this Counter-Reformation view, that expanded open-endedness translates into more of that uncritical, unprofessional proliferation of courses—horizontal distribution models without coherence, unity, or continuity, and urging "relevance"—of the "virulent Sixties."[33] But it is equally clear that a narrowly conceived view of theory and of cultural critique—one as simply post-structuralist or postmodern, the other as simply neo-Marxist—is at the root of the problem.

In arguing that cultural critique is *more* than such conservatism is capable of imagining, I am also saying that if there is fear and trembling here, there should be *more*. I will not argue that cultural critique has its own unity or continuity unperceived by the present master discourse, that it moves toward a future utopian master discourse. Cultural critique expands beyond and through the lines of demarcation that every discourse, every voice, so conscientiously constructs; in so doing, it calls into question the impress of competing, disrupting voices that it somehow holds, and yet cannot hold, if it mirrors the open-endedness of a living culture itself.

This bit of identifying (identifiable, perhaps, within Feyerabend's dream) would surely ice the cockles of any heart set on reclaiming our cultural legacy (especially in the form of E. D. Hirsch's long list in an Appendix). What results from all this openness, these appropriations outside the Panopticon, the urging of an "unidentifiable" body of cultural critique? It leads to transgression not only in light of what is presently entrenched on all levels of discourse, practice, and institutionalization, but also through its confrontation with renewed centripetal currents bearing a tradition of unity and coherence.

Cultural critique threatens to crack the panoptic lens. In truth, it could only be visualized as a cultural critique *after* the lens was cracked. What is being "countered" in the present "Counter-Reformation" is the insolence of prior anarchic voices who traduced, curricularly speaking, the entrenched voices of linear continuity and progress, of sure and steady erection skyward from the center. In its spread horizontally, cultural critique violates the notion of such vertical growth, which science—though not, for instance, the holographic paradigm of David Bohm—supports. Cultural critique violates that generation of identity which a conservatism especially authorizes.

At the same time, this cultural critique generates space, within which difference is brought into our view. E. D. Hirsch's program of cultural literacy (a "body of information that literate people do know, and if you don't know it you're disadvantaged") which he conveniently presents as a list, reveals the level of crisis.[34] The basic building blocks of Hirsch's list hark back to Harvard's 1978 Core Curriculum Report—which attempts to ground itself not on a hierarchical ordering of knowledge (which every Harvard faculty member whose own special discourse was "de-privileged" would object to) but on "distinctive ways of thinking that are identifiable and important" (which every Harvard faculty member would be free to define as being reflected in his or her own special discourse).

The thrust of a present Conservative Counter-Reformation is toward desperate support of a unity, an identity, a monologism that has always promised real unity but has only succeeded in delivering desperation.

The buttressing of a harmonizing humanism, the buttressing of both academic specialization and integration by the voice of reason, the buttressing of identity within the academic setting are all agenda items of a Conservative Counter-Reformation. Likewise, they are perennial priorities of the Panopticon. Only an "eying" from off center has managed to connect our assertions about what is "really there" to the context of seeing itself, and thus to problematize such assertions. The "really there" that comes into focus within academe is full of identity and unity, the kind of identity and unity that a cultural critique exposes as being free of diversity and difference.

Critique displaces a lust for a power base, a lust for identity through the rules of the game: the discovery, maintenance, and furtherance of a specialized domain. This identity via specialization leads, as I have suggested, to a disconnectedness and isolation so complete that unreality is the result. While each discipline pursues an identity based upon the development of a unique metier, that identity only becomes identifiable if, in its pursuit of being different, it does not violate the overall panoptic seeing. In spite of its excruciating differentiation of its subject matter, a discipline obsession, to achieve identity *in the eyes of academe*, must exclude difference. Since a panoptic seeing excludes what is not observable from its centered perspective, difference is automatically, reflexively cast out. Instead of being recognized, it appears as absence.

The diversity that is explored by academic specialization cannot ever be realized *as* diversity, because the difference at the root of diversity's identity is always a gap and not a connection, an absence and not a presence. When we turn to movements toward unity, the same difficulties arise. Synthesizing and integrating, subsuming and incorporating what has been so zealously identified as a distinct province—a department—as an entity complete and worthy of academic institutionalization must be seen as a destructive act. Academic integration is unrealized not only because its panopticism has already excluded difference, but also because specializations must retain the power bases of what they assume to be their separate identities. The groundwork of a panoptic eying is raw politics.

Yet it remains true that, this *de facto* political unity and diversity aside, academe is indeed a multitude of severed specializations that remain foreign to each other precisely because of difference—an unobserved, unacknowledged, excluded difference. A centered monologism aspires to identity but cannot grant it. The integration of a cultural critique does not subsume individual identities or transmute them into a unified realizing. A dynamic issuing from real difference resubmits diversity each time unity is proposed; this dynamic delineates the physiognomy of the whole. In contrast, discriminating and differentiating conducted under the panoptic gaze can only endorse an integration and a specialization already circumscribed by that gaze. Cultural critique offers other places from which to gaze. This seeing differently will initiate our release from being "only instruments," as Paul Bové writes, "of a history we rarely try to question or to understand."[35]

It is one thing to press toward an imposed unity; it is quite another to perceive the necessity of mirroring the whole, of capturing that chorale of voices already present. The urgency is not only coming from the center. At the periphery, however, the concerns are necessarily "marginal" concerns. While a will-to-power crisis of a premier technological society exercises the center, marginal seeing is exercised by the efforts of a cultural Counter-Reformation to re-etch the monologism of the prevailing discourses and practices of that society. And this society is in a situation to "profit" more from critique, from the creation of a critical counter-memory, than from frenetic directives as to how we can trace ourselves back to an originating *logos*. The resuscitation of a consciousness that seeks the "standardization of the anthropocentric idea of man as measure, that is, of the measure of man as will to power"—which is what William Spanos sees in the Harvard Report—has disastrous effects: "Ontologically, such an educational program is implicated in the perennial panoptic effort of Western man to perpetuate his will to power over being—the will to power that has not only alienated being, but, as the increasing evidence of ecological imbalance suggests, transformed its energies into a retaliatory, indeed, demonic force."[36]

Surely our future appropriations toward cultural critique must be away from this demonic force. But is this just an eying from the margins, which, like all eying from the margins, ends up with a frenetic account of a demonic force? The question behind this question has to do with cultural critique's "promise to deliver," its promise that it can give us an influential critique because it represents the diversity of society itself, and not because it ousts from the center the dominant discourse. Cultural critique cannot master its centrifugal currents in the decisive manner of the Panopticon, and therefore it cannot create the requisite pattern that Richard Rorty finds necessary: "The method is to redescribe lots and lots of things in new ways, until you have created a pattern of linguistic behaviour which will tempt the rising generation to adopt it, thereby causing them to look for appropriate new forms of non-linguistic behaviour—e.g., the adoption of new scientific equipment or new social institutions."[37]

If the heterology of cultural critique produces no challenging pattern, how can the rising generation bring down the prevailing tower at the center and erect their own pattern of panoptic seeing in its place? How can literary theory hope to move toward even greater appropriations of other discourses if it is not only incapable of being identified but cannot, out of its own diversity, secure an identity identifiable to that diversity?

Literary theory needs to make wider appropriations because voices in the world have already been involved, as can only disingenuously be denied by academe. Bakhtin's concept of *raznorecie*, which Todorov translates as *heterology*, points out the role of difference operating within both utterance and discourse. This heterology arises naturally from social diversity, but just as a single state constrains such social diversity, there exist forces "correlative to all power, to institute a common language (or rather a speech)."[38] Bakhtin considers a centripetal force toward unification—both on the societal level and the discourse level—in a manner not to incite censorship: "The common language is never given but in fact always ordained, and at every moment of the life of the language it is opposed to genuine heterology. But at the same time, it is perfectly real as a force that overcomes this heterology; imposes certain limits upon it; guarantees a maximum of mutual comprehension; and becomes crystallized in the real, though relative, unity of spoken (daily) and literary language, of 'correct' language."[39] However, this opposition to heterology parallels in many ways the monologism of our Conservative Counter-Reformation. Discourses themselves variously further both centripetal and centrifugal forces: "The periods in which the novel flourishes are periods of weakening central power."[40]

Thus the statement that discourse has always already been carrying on a pre-institutionalized, pre-curricular relationship is grounded in Bakhtin's notion of the utterance. In seeking to reflect this basic heterology of society and discourse, cultural critique is therefore not abandoning difference. Rather than perceive difference strictly in the ultimate service of omniscience, that which must through method be reduced to a smooth, polished surface of elegant simplicity, cultural critique holds difference as fundamental, the whole (rather than unity) being its telos. On the other hand, because it parallels social diversity and discourse diversity, cultural critique can never be lost within that maze of difference that assails the panoptic conscience as it envisions anarchy on the societal level and a return to the '6os on the academic level. "The difference is part of the thing itself," Michel Serres writes, "and perhaps it even produces the thing. Maybe the radical origin of things is really the difference, even though classical rationalism damned it to hell. In the beginning was the noise."[41] Levels of harmony in discourse and society have, at various times, been reached at the cost of silenced voices. Continuity has been retained at the cost of people and ideas "discontinued," closure achieved in the name of unity, not of the whole.

We are far enough along to respond to Rorty's view of how a critique should be made. Only the contradictory nature of an unsuppressed heterology that maintains that discourses are irreducibly diverse serves to prevent the construction of a panoptic monologism. Rorty's "Passing Theory" conversation is designed to drown out rational critique, even the reupholstered Habermas version. All such critiques based on a metanarrative must face a pragmatics of generating a majority view. Within this pragmatics a conversation holds sway, a vocabulary reaches "entrenchment": this, in turn, leads to changes in practices and institutions. Thus Rorty describes, and at the same time confirms, the panopticon of surveillance empowered by a will to power that already holds sway.

The steps toward interrupting this conversation seem to be present in Rorty's pragmatics but in fact do not extend beyond the voice of the majority. Difference must be reidentified in line with the dominant conversation, or it must seek to overthrow such dominance through the assertion of its own conversation. Perhaps these cycles serve to describe, from a bourgeois liberal vantage point, what has actually occurred in the history of bourgeois capitalism. This is not, then, a story of how critique succeeds in finding a place for itself, but a history of how dominant conversations have succeeded in holding their places.

To hold a place dominant in the present involves holding onto a firm sense of that place dominant in the past, either the dominance of the revolutionary moment or the dominance of a fixed *ancien régime*. An urgent directive of a Conservative Counter-Reformation is, as I have said, a nostalgia for past unity. In what is this unity of *illo tempore* rooted? Our nostalgia for the unity of discourse must give way to the use of the diversity of discourse. Discourse is not insinuated in unity, in nostalgia, but in another discourse. To see this insinuation, especially within academe, we can easily take up Bakhtin again. Besides literary discourse, Bakhtin includes in a "general typology of discourses" the following: "In observing social life, we can easily isolate, outside of the artistic communication already discussed, the following types: 1. the communication of *production* (in the factory, in the shop, in the kolkhoz, etc.); 2. the communication of *business* (in offices, in social organizations, etc.); 3. familiar [*bytovoe*] communication (encounters and conversations in the street, the cafeteria, at home, etc.); and finally 4. *ideological* communication in the precise sense of the term: propaganda, school, science, philosophy, in all their varieties."[42]

Richard Johnson, defining cultural studies, says, "For me cultural studies is about the historical forms of consciousness or subjectivity, or the subjective forms we live by, or, in a rather perilous compression, perhaps a reduction, the subjective side of social relations." He accepts a diversity of social practices as a cultural studies domain, a range as broad as Bakhtin's. But while Johnson is concerned with how these forms of culture can be studied, Bakhtin's heterology of discourses "arises spontaneously from social diversity."[43] There is therefore an intercrossing between the practices of a diverse culture and the means of studying the diversity of that culture. The discourses of cultural critique are both product and process, have both nominalistic and realistic guises.

I am not advocating that cultural critique ignore the voice of rational method, nor am I asserting that, if we abandon a panoptic eying of the ordering of discourse, a pertinent critique will burst forth from the ensuing anarchy. On the other hand, I don't see reason as a cohort of Arnoldian "culture," mobilized against anarchy (and here anarchy means "merely doing as one likes"). Spanos lays this "disinterested humanistic discourse of Matthew Arnold" right in the middle of the Panopticon, the "disciplinary meta-physical paradigm."[44] But neither Kant's "moral gift" nor Arnold's "culture" make it logical for us to believe that it is reason that keeps each of us from merely doing as we like, or that reason keeps power from merely doing what it likes. It is not reason but stupendous rhetoric that casts power into an image of its own devising and then binds each of us to that image. The anarchy of a broadly based critique within which reason is set up and mobilized differently enables us to try on and contrast the shapes of reason, shapes that appear through the courtesy of, and through the agency of, their perceptual frames. Reason has established and supported closure any number of times in the past. I have been representing a cultural critique that is allied to anarchy and therefore most naturally set on problematizing a reason set up solely as an instrument of closure.

Anarchy is nothing more than a mirroring of this heterology; within cultural critique, it is the dialogism of discourses that tempers Paul Feyerabend's stereotypic view of anarchy as "anything goes."[45] But Feyerabend points to the intersection of science's rational method (mere rhetoric, in Feyerabend's view) with that of other discourses—religion, myth, magic—and contributes to that deflation of science's sacrosanct status, a deflation associated with Kuhn, Harré, Foucault, and Bachelard, for instance. Because of its rhetorical guise, science is in league with other discourses, such as history, sociology, and anthropology. But one always has the feeling with Feyerabend that this league—what I have been calling cultural critique—is much more of a rebellion against rational, scientific method than a construction toward an effective realizing of the experiences of human mind, society, and science interacting.

Whereas Feyerabend's anti-method position seems to leave him (rather like the devotee turned savagely against his devotion) with nothing but an ill-formed sense of anarchy, cultural critique's dialogic method works to displace the privileging of a scientific method through the heterology of discourse and of society itself. Anarchy is defined not as "anything goes now that science is proven mortal," but as the "chance, risk, anxiety, and even disorder" that consolidates the pieces we already have and already privilege. Such a dialogism accommodates the fact that, while Serres's parasite "is responsible for the growth of the system's complexity, such a parasite stops it."[46]

Our eying has brought us back to the point of impasse: at the center of a privileged realizing of the experience of complexity is harmony, equilibrium, a classical rationalism. "Can we rewrite the system," Serres asks, "in the way Leibnitz understood the term, not in the key of preestablished harmony but in what he called seventh chords?" Perhaps a cultural critique is just such a rewriting in seventh chords, "with the waves and shocks on the line in mind."[47]

It is the burden of the present and the future to construct a theory/strategy by which cultural critique appropriates beyond the level of Marxist, feminist, deconstructive, semiotic, psychoanalytic, pragmatic, hermeneutic discourse. It appropriates science and the materialist culture, as well as those levels of worldly discourse that go on in the street, the office, and the media. To construct in seventh chords involves cultural critique's displacement of science's monologistic path to a Golden Age omni-science as well as of "the perennial panoptic effort of Western man to perpetuate his will-to-power over being," an effort presently grounding an urgent agenda of a Conservative Counter-Reformation.[48]

Marginal stories today tend to take us back to demonic force. They are not all simply academic stories. The ones in the street, the ones that have fought their way into the public sphere—feminist critique, social ecology—disclose demonic force as our cultural *prima materia*. Does the possession reside in the eye, the *mal d'occhio*, of the viewer? Since, in a world lost in identity and difference, the province of eying resemblance is left to marginal discourse, perhaps those on the margins are the only ones possessed. Foucault identifies two such visionaries for us, the poet and the madman: "At the fringes of a knowledge that separates beings, signs, and similitudes, and as though to limit its power, the madman fulfills the function of *homosemanticism*: he groups all signs together and leads them with a resemblance that never ceases to proliferate. The poet fulfills the opposite function: his is the *allegorical* role; beneath the language of signs and beneath the interplay of their precisely delineated distinctions, he strains his ears to catch that 'other language,' the language, without words or discourse, of resemblance. The poet brings similitude to the signs that speak it, whereas the madman loads all signs with a resemblance that ultimately erases them. They share, then, on the outer edge of our culture . . . a marginal position. . . . Between them there has opened up a field of knowledge in which, because of an essential rupture in the Western world, what has become important is no longer resemblances but identities and differences."[49]

Such an eye for resemblance is part of cultural critique's utopianism. It reminds us that we are not involved with an ontic task, one in which the process of existing, of being, is static and objective and subject to our olympian critique. To eye resemblance is to perplex the panoptic eying of being apart from the world. Such panoptic eying privileges the Horatian maxim that urges continuity and connection. Continuity and connection count because a panoptic eying has already circumscribed the frame within which they can count. It is this state of affairs within which identity and difference rear their heads.

Cultural critique's ontological interrogation does not go on within a cycle of systematization and critique of systematization, within the movements of continuity and connection, within the frame rendered by a panoptic eying. Instead, it carries on at the level of revealing being to itself, a level where critique is that Heideggerian saying which leads to the "presencing of being."[50]

NOTES

1. Joseph Natoli, ed., *Tracing Literary Theory* (Urbana: University of Illinois Press, 1987).
2. David Bohm, *Wholeness and the Implicate Order* (Boston: Routledge & Kegan Paul, 1980).

3. Michel Serres, *The Parasite,* trans. Lawrence R. Schehr (Baltimore: Johns Hopkins University Press, 1982), p. 13.

4. Daniel Bell, "The World and the United States in 2013," *Daedalus* 116: 3 (Summer 1987): 1.

5. Matthew Arnold, "Sweetness and Light," in *Culture and Anarchy* (Ann Arbor: University of Michigan Press, 1965), p. 94.

6. William V. Spanos, "The End of Education: The Harvard Core Curriculum Report and the Pedagogy of Reformation," *boundary 2* 10: 2 (Winter 1982): 25.

7. Ibid., p. 3.

8. Michel Foucault, "Panopticism," in *Discipline and Punish: The Birth of the Prison* (New York: Vintage Books, 1979), pp. 223, 201.

9. Paul Bové, "Critical Negation: The Function of Criticism at the Present Time," in his *Intellectuals in Power: A Genealogy of Critical Humanism* (New York: Columbia University Press, 1986), pp. 240, 251.

10. Jacques Derrida, "Structure, Sign, and Play," in *The Languages of Criticism and the Sciences of Man,* ed. Richard Macksey and Eugenio Donato (Baltimore: Johns Hopkins University Press, 1970), p. 249.

11. Mikhail Bakhtin, quoted in Tzvetan Todorov, *Mikhail Bakhtin: The Dialogical Principle* (Minneapolis: University of Minnesota Press, 1984), p. 56.

12. While I will appropriate the enterprise of critique as Foucault considers it, I believe Aronowitz's observation regarding Foucault's sense of word and thing, of what I call the material culture as opposed to the discursive culture, is apt. See Michel Foucault, "What Is Enlightenment?" in *The Foucault Reader,* ed. Paul Rabinow (New York: Pantheon Books, 1984), p. 46; Stanley Aronowitz, *The Crisis in Historical Materialism* (New York: Praeger, 1981), p. 318. Vico's sense of culture as a correspondence between social practices and a symbolism constructed to express them parallels Foucault's own project. And his notion of *fantasia* or imagination discloses this correspondence in a fashion that resembles Foucault's poet's eye for resemblance. See, especially, Donald Phillip Verene, *Vico's Science of Imagination* (Ithaca: Cornell University Press, 1981). For a correspondence between image and practice in the path of culture theory initiated by Vico, see Murray Bookchin, *The Modern Crisis* (Philadelphia: New Society, 1986), p. 59.

13. Gerald Graff, *Professing Literature: An Institutional History* (Chicago: University of Chicago Press, 1987), p. 252.

14. Richard Johnson, "What Is Cultural Studies Anyway?" *Social Text* 6: 1 (Winter 1986/87): 42–43.

15. Quoted in the *Chronicle of Higher Education*, October 7, 1987, p. A15.
16. Bakhtin, quoted in Todorov, *Mikhail Bakhtin*, pp. 56–57.
17. Max Stirner, *The Ego and His Own* (New York: Libertarian Book Club, 1963), p. 146.
18. John Carlos Rowe, "Surplus Economies: Deconstruction, Ideology, and the Humanities," in *The Aims of Representation: Subject/Text/History*, ed. Murray Krieger (New York: Columbia University Press, 1987), p. 139.
19. Jacques Derrida, "The Principle of Reason: The University in the Eyes of Its Pupils," *Diacritics* 13 (Fall 1983): 10.
20. Jim Merod, *The Political Responsibility of the Critic* (Ithaca: Cornell University Press, 1987), p. 14.
21. Derrida, "The Principle of Reason," p. 17.
22. Ibid.
23. Jacques Derrida, "Limited Inc abc. . . .," trans. Samuel Weber, *Glyph* 2 (Baltimore: Johns Hopkins University Press, 1977), p. 250.
24. Mark Krupnick, "The Two Worlds of Cultural Criticism," in *Criticism in the University*, ed. Gerald Graff and Reginald Gibbons (Evanston: Northwestern University Press, 1985), p. 168.
25. Quoted in the *Chronicle of Higher Education*, October 7, 1987, p. A15.
26. Johnson, "What Is Cultural Studies Anyway?," pp. 38, 40.
27. Ibid., p. 39.
28. J. Hillis Miller, "Presidential Address 1986: The Triumph of Theory, the Resistance to Reading, and the Question of the Material Base," *PMLA* 102: 3 (May 1987): 283.
29. Terry Eagleton, "Awakening from Modernity," *TLS*, February 20, 1987, p. 194.
30. Ibid.
31. Carolyn Allen, "Feminist Criticism and Postmodernism," in Natoli, ed., *Tracing Literary Theory*, p. 279.
32. See Paul Bové, "The Ineluctability of Difference: Scientific Pluralism and the Critical Intelligence," in *Postmodernism and Politics*, ed. Jonathan Arac (Minneapolis: University of Minnesota Press, 1986). In fact, everything Bové says about "postmodernism" I attribute to "cultural critique." See especially his responses to those who argue that literary criticism shouldn't be dragged into the "discourse arena" (pp. 5–6). For recent attempts to pinpoint "postmodernism," see Ihab Hassan, "Making Sense," and Berel Lang, "Postmodern in Philosophy: Nostalgia for the Future, Waiting for the Past," both in

Literature and the Question of Philosophy, ed. Anthony J. Cascardi (Baltimore: Johns Hopkins University Press, 1987), pp. 331–32n1.

33. Association of American Colleges, *Integrity in the College Curriculum: A Report to the Academic Community* (Washington D.C., 1985).
34. Quoted in the *Chronicle of Higher Education,* August 5, 1987, "English Teachers Favor Emphasis on How to Read." Ashley Montague thirty years ago presented long lists of questions designed to separate the New Calibans from the Cultured Man; see *The Cultured Man: An Inquiry into Our Cultural Status* (New York: World, 1958).
35. Bové, *Intellectuals in Power,* p. 77.
36. Spanos, "The End of Education," p. 25.
37. Richard Rorty, "The Contingency of Language," *London Review of Books,* 17 April 1986, p. 4.
38. Bakhtin, quoted in Todorov, *Mikhail Bakhtin,* p. 57.
39. Ibid., pp. 57–58.
40. Ibid., p. 58.
41. Serres, *The Parasite,* p. 13.
42. Bakhtin, quoted in Todorov, *Mikhail Bakhtin,* p. 57.
43. Johnson, "What Is Cultural Studies Anyway?," pp. 43, 45.
44. Spanos, "The End of Education," p. 4.
45. See Paul Feyerabend, *Against Method* (Atlantic Highlands, N.J.: Humanities Press, 1975).
46. Serres, *The Parasite,* p. 14.
47. Ibid., p. 13.
48. Spanos, "The End of Education," p. 25.
49. Michel Foucault, *The Order of Things* (New York: Random House, 1970), pp. 49–50.
50. Martin Heidegger, "Words," in *On the Way to Language,* trans. Peter D. Hertz (New York: Harper & Row, 1971), p. 155.

VOICES: DEFERRED

ELLIE RAGLAND-SULLIVAN

The Eternal Return of
Jacques Lacan

The format of Jacques Lacan's oral presentations to over-flow audiences of international intellectuals and would-be analysts made it easy to remember him, but almost as easy to repress the degree of his impact on contemporary theories. At the Television conference held in New York in April 1987, where Lacan's *Télé-vision* was screened with English subtitles, Jacques-Alain Miller, the editor of Lacan's Seminars, described Lacan's words as some-times sounding as if they emanated from inside you.[1] Another effect of Lacan's words was to anger those who felt mystified by them, inspiring some listeners to forget this strange man. Psychoanalysis, of course, takes forgetting seriously as a sign that there may be something one does not want to know. But what could Lacan have said that one might not want to know? He said that every person's language and desire emanate from an unconscious whose knowl-edge is both Real and true. Lacan also said that truth is person-specific, the repressed part of what one does not want to know. By contrast, the Real is what we are used to. It is a place of radical loss containing a knot of signifiers that cannot be idealized because they are not symbolized or assimilated, even in unconscious knowledge.[2]

That Lacan's thought is both repressed and suspended in the contemporary American scene of theory and criticism might seem surprising. Many theorists will say with some certainty that they have already "done" Lacan. But to those who work with Lacan's teaching—a few here, and thousands in other countries—Lacan's impact has barely been felt yet. His dense and diffuse teaching has only begun to be clarified and explained since his death in 1981. Until then, those who followed Lacan's Seminars were engaged with him in the shaping of a radical new way of thinking about thinking. In a 1986 interview with Jacques-Alain Miller, the French newspaper *Le Matin* said to Miller: "Lacan had a reputation for being hermetical. It turns out that we find ourselves in the presence of a thought that is perfectly accessible or, better yet, in the process of being created."[3] Miller's response reveals that the post-structuralist American Lacan is not the Lacan known in France or in other countries where Lacan's texts have been studied for two and three decades. If Lacan is to have the impact he deserves in the United States, it is essential to dive into the imbroglio and argue for his role in shaping current cultural critique as well as theory. At the very least, readers should be aware that much critique of Lacan comes from the failure of present discourses to grapple with the complexities of his work and density of his style, as well as from a resistance to making sense of his valorization of lack as a Real presence in being and representation.

Generally speaking, Lacan's texts have been transmitted in the United States under four guises: 1) Lacan *qua* author of the *Écrits* (1966); 2) the Lacan of a few published Seminars; 3) the Lacan re-presented by "eclectic derivationists," and 4) the Lacan of polemicists who attack him either openly or covertly. The last group includes Parisian intellectuals—some relatively unknown in France—who have fought their battles regarding Lacan's rereading of Freud through their own books and as professors in American universities. For the third and fourth groups, Lacan's texts, as well as the *context* of the furor and intellectual renovations surrounding his radical theories, are missing. Thus the question of where to begin in approaching (or introducing) Lacan pervades the whole of his reception in North America. On the one hand, of the thirty-six lectures and papers that Lacan presented from 1932 on, many published in the *Écrits* (1966), only nine have been translated into English.[4] Yet Lacan dated his *official* teaching from 1953, when he gave his first public Seminar at the Saint Anne Psychiatric Hospital. By the 1960s, says Catherine Clément in her *Vies et légendes de Jacques Lacan* (1981), the Seminars had become intellectual and social happenings: a theater of the unconscious in which intellectuals from all disciplines gathered at the École Normale Supérieure, where Lacan's Seminars had moved.[5] In 1968 Lacan left that institution to hold his Seminars at the Law School adjacent to the Sorbonne and the Panthéon.[6] In 1980 he dissolved the École Freudienne and discontinued his Seminars.[7]

Another way to characterize Lacan's work is by periods of teaching. Jacques-Alain Miller has noted three periods. At Saint Anne from 1953 to 1963 Lacan elaborated on the ideas he had been developing since the 1920s. Between 1964 and 1974 he set forth his most widely diffused and characteristic concepts at the École Normale Supérieure. From 1974 to 1980 Lacan developed his mathematical topology and reworked at length his earlier conceptions of an order he called the Real.[8] This teaching appears and reappears on the American scene with a haunting aura, similar to the camera-shutter-like operation of the unconscious as Lacan described it. It opens briefly, only to close back on its moment of insight with a click of the apparatus: "suture."

Lacan's published texts (as well as some black market transcriptions and tapes) are now in the hands of the many, although he is officially represented by the Department of Psychoanalysis at Paris VIII (Saint-Denis), by the École de la cause Freudienne (which succeeded the École Freudienne), and by the Fondation du champ Freudien. The impact of Lacan within and outside France has been characterized by problems, controversies, and lawsuits over matters of attribution, possession, and interpretive mandates.[9] Since Lacan spoke to thousands but had little interest in publishing his own words (much publication was redefined by him as *poubellication*, a word he invented to describe that which fills up garbage cans), he insured that the problem of transcribing his oral text into a written one would be fraught with competitions and complications. Yet, beginning in 1951, when Lacan gave his first Seminars in his apartment, his pupils wanted to publish his Seminars in some form. Lacan resisted, insisting that the stenographically transcribed copies of his lectures were not publishable. But in 1973 Lacan chose Jacques-Alain Miller as editor for his Seminars. That author/editor relationship is reputed to have worked smoothly until Lacan's death, when many who had approved of or even praised Miller's work with Lacan began to denigrate both the work and the relationship.

In the 1986 *Le Matin* interview Miller explained how Lacan prepared his Seminars, giving us some idea why Lacan did not view the taped results as ready for publication:

> He arrived at his seminar each week with numerous pages of notes; there were sentences, schemas, and references that most of the time did not constitute a coherent text, so that during the two hours of the lecture there was an activity of creation. One can assume that he followed one path or the other, depending on the reactions of his audience and as a function of the difficulties or the zest he felt in making a given point. He often said himself that he only used a part of the notes he prepared. The next seminar picked up at the point where he had left off, but obviously the work during the week displaced the original intention, the former purpose. We don't, therefore, have a reading, but an improvisation that had been worked on, prepared by a long period of reflection, solicitous of its audience and designed for it. Many things are therefore simply referred to and not fully worked through . . . but they remain extremely suggestive.[10]

In *Entretien sur le séminaire* (1985) Miller told François Ansermet that, from 1951 to 1973, various efforts were made at publishing Lacan's oral teaching. J. B. Pontalis prepared two or three résumés that appeared in the *Bulletin de psychologie*. M. Safouan presented a résumé of *L'Éthique* that Lacan did not consider definitive. J. Nassif published résumés of *La Logique du fantasme*. C. Conté drafted a long article on *L'Identification*. Miller said that, while countless plagiarisms were available as easily recognizable adaptations of Lacan's teaching, the many students (such as those mentioned above) who wanted to valorize Lacan did not seek to make his name disappear. Yet Miller was alone among the students in suggesting that the richness of Lacan's style and the vitality and power of his words not be "junked" in favor of résumés of his Seminar, or articles or books about the Seminar. "I proposed to Lacan," Miller said to Ansermet, ". . . to make a book of the Seminar, which would respect the *découpage* into lessons." In 1973, in a bid to prove his point, Miller asked Lacan if he could edit *Séminaire* XI, the first one he had attended in 1964. When he returned with the results of his work some months later, Lacan accepted his *preuve par la parole* and asked Miller to be the official editor of the Seminar, the person he trusted to put order into his "lecture notes."[11]

When *Le Matin* asked Miller about his work on *L'Éthique de la psychanalyse*, the first Seminar to appear since Lacan's death, he answered: "I worked from those [the typed versions] exactly as I did when he was alive. His death did not interrupt that work, that desire."[12] One notes with interest that the officially edited versions of Lacan's Seminars are described as *établi* by Miller. But, as one may have guessed, *établi* means more here than a form of editing or mediation. In the *Entretien*, Ansermet asked Miller about the scope of his role in "establishing" Lacan's Seminar. Miller answered that despite the "higher bid" mentality that has appeared, depicting the stenographs as original texts, Lacan remained firm in his conviction that he did not want those versions to become written texts. Miller's way of editing the Seminar was the one that convinced Lacan. In *L'Entretien* Miller revealed to Ansermet that their work was a collaborative one, as had been apparent to those in Paris from 1964 until Lacan's death. "I can tell you, furthermore, that from the moment of my establishing the first Seminar, Dr. Lacan had the idea that we sign together. . . . He thought the part that I brought to it [the Seminar] justified a double signature. I refused . . . but having already cosigned the contracts of editorship with Lacan [before this refusal], I legally have the status of co-author." Ansermet asked Miller just how Lacan had characterized Miller's input. "Lacan once said . . . that I put his Seminar in my own French, and that that pleased him," said Miller. Yet Miller's own view of working on the Seminars is that he erases himself by bending to the rationality of Lacan's thought. This is also a demand for clarity, Miller says, for bringing out the lineaments from which it becomes possible to establish the text. But the bigger question concerns how to put into writing the vitality and power of an oral teaching that was always in process, always changing as Lacan moved on. Miller told Ansermet that his final reference point in establishing the Seminar is always Lacan's *Écrits*.[13]

In 1973 *Séminaire* IX (1964) appeared; in 1975 *Séminaire* I (1953–54) as well as *Séminaire* XX (1972–73); in 1978 *Séminaire* II (1954–55); in 1981 *Séminaire* III (1955–56); and in 1987 *Séminaire* VII (1959–60). Some of the other *Séminaires* have appeared in *Ornicar?*, as have selections. Pirated copies of various Seminars, as well as taped versions, abound. If one reads French, it is not difficult to find the Seminars of Jacques Lacan. That the pirated editions are full of errors is obvious to anyone who has followed the careful development of Lacan's major arguments. Nonetheless, *Stécriture* went to court to argue for the right to publish their versions of the Seminars, arguing that Lacan's oral teaching belongs to everyone. The court found in favor of Miller and has since ruled in another similar case, using *Miller* v. *Stécriture* as a precedent. On this same issue of who the teaching belongs to, Miller answered Ansermet in 1985, "To no one." "This teaching is not the property of any group, no more the École de la Cause Freudienne, to which I belong, than to any other group. Jacques Lacan's Seminar has always been published without bearing any institutional mark of any sort. It is there to take its place in the analytic community, and beyond. Having said that, I know that it is around these Seminars that work groups constitute themselves ... gatherings of people who seek to know."[14] We are left with the impression that the Seminars "belong" to anyone willing to undergo the rigors of reading them and trying to work from them.

Evidence of the influence of Lacan's teaching was apparent in the United States as early as 1965, in René Girard's *Desire, Deceit and the Novel,* where the triangulation of desire is a major concept; and in *The Language of the Self* (1968), where Girard's pupil Anthony Wilden translated Lacan's "Rome Discourse," including an essay on it, with extensive notes and bibliography.[15] But most of Lacan's texts are not available in English, thus complicating matters for interested parties. To make things even more confusing, Lacan's texts keep appearing in an uneven way, leading to confusion about who said what when and to whom. Indeed, this *Fort! Da!* appearance of Lacan's work has the same disquieting effect as does his style, where pronouncements continually double back on themselves, posing questions that may be answered twenty years later, or perhaps never answered at all. Lacan's teaching evolved as a new way of thinking about how mentality and identity are constituted. It is not surprising that this teaching is a play of certainty and uncertainties, rather than a neat series of clearcut resolutions. Moreover, Americans are still not aware of the degree to which Lacan influenced post-structuralist thinkers and writers who never credit him. In a 1987 column entitled "Post-Structuralism: An Often-Abstruse French Import Profoundly Affects Research in the United States," Karen J. Winkler quotes Harvard professor Barbara Johnson as saying, "Many of the perspectives that seemed new in the 1970's have taken hold so that people are saying things—about reading conflict of meaning in a text, or about the problems of intention in writing—that derived from the work of Derrida or Barthes, without even realizing where they came from."[16] Ironically, those Americans who have read Derrida, Barthes, and others but who have not read Lacan's Seminars (or *Ornicar?*) do not realize that Derrida and Barthes often write things derived from Lacan's oral teaching—perhaps without themselves realizing where they came from.

In the 1980s books began to appear telling Americans how to read Lacan. John Muller, a clinical psychologist, and William Richardson, a philosopher and analyst, believe we will not be able to understand Lacan until all of his texts have appeared. (They insinuate the same in *The Purloined Poe.*) In *Lacan and Language: A Reader's Guide to Écrits* (1982) these authors take a tentatively interpretive footnote and outline approach to the nine translated *Écrits*. Yet, when one reads the articles these men have written on Lacan, each has a clear idea of what Lacan means. Richardson tends to equate Lacan with Heidegger.[17] Muller reads Lacan through the eyes of "self" psychology, trying to turn him into an American product.

Jane Gallop, in *The Daughter's Seduction* and *Reading Lacan*, is largely responsible for the post-structuralist feminist Lacan in vogue in the United States. Gallop has continually cited Luce Irigaray and has used Derridean strategies and arguments purportedly to illuminate Lacan. In her hands Lacan becomes, as Irigaray, Hélène Cixous, and Jacques Derrida have claimed, a "phallocrat." Using deconstructive method, Gallop sets up binary oppositions in order to knock them down, thereby claiming to destroy hierarchies in order to question Lacan's authority, his supposed discourse of mastery, although Lacan's teaching and clinical practice are themselves critiques of a master discourse: one that mistakes the visible for the whole of cause and effect. By playing down differences of any sort—here, between the masculine and feminine—feminist critics such as Gallop have failed to address

Lacan's powerful idea that culture itself arises out of interpretations and representations of the difference between the sexes. So perplexing and problematic is the anatomical difference between boys and girls and the myths surrounding it—the only clear difference between the genders when they are young—that cultures derive social practice, myth, and ideology in interpretation of the "third term," the difference itself.[18]

That American literary criticism and feminism have been interested in Jacques Lacan makes sense. Literature and psychoanalysis have always been coupled, and psychoanalysis began as a questioning of what causes "feminine" suffering. Yet neither of these aspects of Lacan—his value for literary criticism or his rethinking of the feminine and masculine—has been seriously taken up by post-structuralism. Although a vast array of articles can be found in which efforts are made to "apply" Lacan to literary and film texts, generally speaking American critics and feminists think Lacan has been succeeded by Jacques Derrida in a linear progression of insight and applicability.[19] Lacan uses language to refer to things outside discourse; to truth, the Real, the unconscious, which are not subsumed by Derridean Writing. Insofar as post-structuralism does not wish to link its practice to anything outside irreducible dualities, Lacan's knots, circles, and graphs, his topological efforts to diagram how the unconscious functions, become proof for Lacoue-Labarthe and Jean-Luc Nancy, for example, that Lacan is caught in his own circle(s), which are simply systems to be deconstructed by those philosophers who know how to cut up systems. As Juliet Flower MacCannell has argued, some people may laugh at Lacan's efforts at proof of an unconscious lack that constitutes meaning by the effects of the signifier itself; but they have not stopped to consider that he might actually have discovered a structure (an ordering), without being a partisan of the process of structuring such "structure."[20]

What Lacan has discovered is that the signifier and the signified do not reside at the same place, do not follow each other linearly, and that in the space between them there is a division in the subject that creates the subject as a paradox. That is, speech, writing, or perception occurs at the same time that these acts erase knowledge of their inscription elsewhere: in an Other discourse. The post-structuralist assumption that everyone is always already framed by the frame of his or her linguistic presentations or rhetorical strategies does not allow for the unconscious subject of desire or the Real. If post-structuralism can reduce all phenomena to language effects, it can dismiss the problems posed by memory, fantasy, dreams, literary language, enigmatic desire, psychotic language, the whys of sexual difference, the opacity of language, the "true" nature of time (timing), the mysteries of aggression. Post-structuralist assumptions that equate representations to figural tropes can only do so by leaving out any consideration of a link between language and causality.

Josué V. Harari wrote in 1979 that the term "post-structuralist" was itself problematic, raising geographical and philosophical difficulties regarding the nature of delimitation and of epistemology. Harari's collected essays, *Textual Strategies: Perspectives in Post-Structuralist Criticism*, reflect the mood of the late 1970s, in contrast to the structuralist-dominated theory of the 1960s and early '70s.[21] Although many have attempted to define post-structuralism and proponents have been named, it is generally synonymous with the thought and methods of Jacques Derrida, and it is principally an American (not a French) phenomenon. Insofar as Lacan, Derrida, and Foucault all criticized the closure in the classical conceptualization of the linguistic sign as described by Saussure, they have been uncritically lumped together as post-structuralists and, more recently, as semioticians. But semiotics—a study of sign systems—has most particularly evolved as a multidisciplinary effort to actually save the classical sense of the Saussurean sign, in which form refers to an idea or coded meaning, or in a broader sense to discourse theory in its various modes. In the 1980s post-structuralists talk about the loss of origins, the decentered subject, the floating signifier, the incompleteness of language, and the framing of texts. Semioticians, Marxists, and feminists have joined hands with proponents of deconstruction in an effort to disturb the bourgeoisie.

In the 1987 *Chronicle of Higher Education* column on post-structuralism Lacan is nonetheless considered a post-structuralist linked to Derrida, Barthes, and Foucault. Yet throughout his life Lacan was a practicing psychiatrist and psychoanalyst. In May 1984 Jacques-Alain Miller told an audience made up principally of literary critics that Lacan had not written for them. Moreover, he astonished those who had come to a conference on "The Reception of Post-Structuralism in Francophone and Anglophone Canada" by saying that "post-structuralism" was not a word used in France.[22] If labels must be assigned, Lacan had considered himself a topological structuralist, not a linguistic or an anthropological one. As this idea has grown—that Lacan might not be a post-structuralist—reactions have differed markedly. Many who think Derrida has brought us into the future, and who equate post-structuralism with deconstruction, have so reversed history they think Lacan "copied" Derrida!

The historian Martin Jay, of the University of California at Berkeley, has quoted Jacques Derrida thus: "In 1984, Jacques Derrida noted that, as far as deconstruction was concerned, post-structuralism was 'stronger in the United States then anywhere else.' Moreover, he said in that interview, which was published in the journal *Critical Exchange* in 1985, 'Something has happened in the United States which is not a simple translation or importation of something European.'"[23] Yet, as one who has read Lacan's Seminars and other writings, I would agree with Juliet MacCannell that "a case could certainly be made for Lacan's claim that everything in Derrida is already in his work; Derrida, despite *La Facteur de la vérité,* has followed a career path that has taken him quite literally down Lacan's 'track,'" retreading Hegel and Kant in *Glas* in the light of Lacan's attempt to counter Oedipus with Antigone; emphasizing metonymy in the work on Edmund Jabés; writing on the irreducibility of metaphor and the sun in *La Mythologie blanche;* and listening more closely to the ear of the Other. "The question is whether he has traveled this 'track' in an opposing direction."[24] Certainly, most post-structuralist critics think Derrida has gone in the opposite direction, taking us beyond Lacan, beyond Freud (although the post-structuralist critical tendency is to go backward and cite Freud, carefully avoiding Lacan).

Lacan poses a major problem for contemporary thought by asking whether there might just be a "universal": structured as One minus. We thought we had gotten rid of all that, and Lacan returns with one more version of the unconscious, including maps of how unconscious formations are structured (ordered), thus giving rise to subject-ivity and to culture. But Lacan's picture of the unconscious as an absence whose effects are present does not culminate in elements that are characteristic of post-structuralist thought: pluralism, rejection of hierarchies, and denials that anything is decidable. MacCannell concludes that Derrida uses Lacan as a starting point for breaking out of the impasses, the closed circles of the signifier, and into another way of framing the sign. While she credits Lacan with uncovering the power of metaphor, she credits Derrida with radicalizing the dissymmetry of metaphor and metonymy, enabling himself to conclude that metaphor is irreducible.[25] Lacan sees metonymy as the by-product of metaphor, its effects revealing that knowledge, desire, and truth come from somewhere else: the Other of unconscious memory.

The postmodern critic Gregory Ulmer steers away from Lacan to argue that pedagogy learns from Freud about invention, about the way Freud carried styles and languages (art, dreams, folklore, etc.) into science, but not about the theory and practice of psychoanalysis or an asymmetrical Other. "What is psychoanalysis," he asks, "but the frame by means of which our aesthetic culture has intervened in a society committed to science, a fact that most of the important theorists of psychoanalysis readily admit? To learn from Freud, then, we should not repeat his discovery, at least not repeat psychoanalysis."[26] One wonders why "the important theorists of psychoanalysis" would believe we should not repeat Freud's discovery? Indeed, many theorists of psychoanalysis are in the process of unveiling just what the discovery of an unconscious might mean. For if the subject is structured by the signifier—made up of oppositions that work by substitution to re-present it for an other signifier—then psychoanalysis can never *not* repeat its discovery: that the unconscious repeats. Precisely those *styles* that Ulmer uses to teach his student about invention are on the side of metaphor, which Lacan equated with language itself; that is, language as the enunciated (*énoncé*) subject of grammar whose roots lie in the myths and lore that constitute acquired language in an unconscious signifying chain. The subject of enunciation (*énonciation*) is, on the contrary, the speaking subject, the unconscious subject of desire who "tells" a single truth in myriad forms: the absence of a natural sexual *rapport*. Lacan argued that discourse— a social tie or a link between those who speak—always refers itself to the signifier for sexual difference around which subjects organize their desire, responses to power, their use of knowledge, and the movement of their speech, all attached to primordial objects of desire. Lacan taught that metaphor works by substitutions that permit a functioning of ego and desire by displacement means. But metonymy demarcates the limits (or *jouissance*) of a particular ego or discourse, meeting metaphor at the *littoral*, the point where coast and sea join before receding.[27]

This is a strange notion. Why should anyone accept it? If one wants to find a theoretical way of understanding Lacan's notion that metonymy is on the side of the unconscious and desire, it might help to consider the example given by Stuart Schneiderman in an essay entitled "Affects." Precisely at the point of praxis which Lacan defined as "a concerted human action, whatever it may be, which places man in a position to treat the real by the symbolic" there arises the issue of where desire (metonymy) and metaphor (any double structure) meet. That is, unconscious desire is recognizable as what is not affect (a metaphorical construct such as the ego), or any other substitutive constellation. In Socrates' *Philebus,* Schneiderman says Socrates demonstrates just how desire and affect are opposed to each other. If one is hungry and then imagines himself to be full, Socrates asks where the image of fullness comes from. Says Schneiderman,

> He asserts that it must come from memory, which for us [Lacanians] means that it comes from elsewhere. It is not an expression of the bodily affective states; in fact, the image which represents the desire realized is precisely the contrary of the affective state. You might say that the desire is in dialectical opposition to the affect, remembering, of course, that this example is not chosen for its theoretical rigor. The reason for choosing it is that it permits you to see that desire is in a relation of contiguity with affective states, that it is not related by similarity or resemblance. Desire is not just some other kind of appetite. So desire is Other to whatever state one is subjectively conscious of. Being Other it is also enigmatic.[28]

The 1987 *Chronicle* column views Lacan as one who said our unconscious life is shaped like and by language; that the Oedipus complex is inscribed in our psyche by the linguistic construction of male and female; that meaning is unstable; that infants perceive themselves in a mirror as coherent and self-governing individuals; that infants pass from this imaginary stage to a symbolic phase in which inconsistencies in language begin to disrupt a stable sense of identity. Having reduced Lacan to these (mostly incorrect) statements, Winkler concludes that "portions of Lacan's work seem to aspire to science and system."[29] Clearly, it is problematic to use the word "science" in discussing Lacan. According to Jacques-Alain Miller, "The analyst is there to say that what you believe you are saying by chance is, as a matter of fact, perfectly determined, has a reason, has a cause. And that, we may say, is the scientific inspiration of psychoanalysis. From my viewpoint the scientific inspiration of psychoanalysis is this: psychoanalysis . . . pushes the principle of causality to the extreme, the principle of causality being that nothing happens without a reason."[30]

Equally problematic is a reductionist attribution of a literalist mirror-stage to Lacan. His 1936 article on "The Mirror Stage as Formative of the Function of the I" became a logically inferred moment in the constitution of an Imaginary identity, body and being, by the early 1940s.[31] But even in the 1936 article Lacan clarifies that he is not talking about a mirror per se. (For instance, sight-impaired people would also experience a mirror stage.) Rather, he refers to the identificatory/perceptual mimicry of human infants. Yet both Donald Winnicott and Heinz Kohut took the 1936 idea of the mirror literally. In an article entitled "Memories of Jacques Lacan (1901–1981)" the French-Canadian psychoanalyst M. Dongier writes, "Today, I must confess that I have undoubtedly more balanced views regarding his [Lacan's] theory, if not his practice, than 20 years ago: then I was put off by his rhetoric, hyperboles, frustrating allusions, neologisms, sarcasms, mannerisms, his knowingly and purposefully torturous and obscure style. . . . I believe we should not dismiss him with a few sentences as I did then."[32] As pointed out by Kerrigan (1983), Dongier goes on, Lacan remained ignored by the English-speaking psychoanalytic intelligentsia until the late 1970s. Kohut published *The Analysis of the Self* in 1971, describing at length the "mirror transference" and narcissistic mirroring and not mentioning Lacan's work presented at the 13th International Psychoanalytic Congress, held at Marienbad in 1936. Winnicott alludes to Lacan's article only twice, briefly, in his book *Playing and Reality* (1971).[33] Kernberg develops theories on narcissism that owe a debt to Lacan and never mentions him, as late as 1975.[34]

Paul de Man released the word "theory" into the literary

canon, saying that, if we want to know about the originary text, we are resisting theory.[35] Lacan (like Freud) says we resist, but not that we resist theory. We resist truth or the Real. We resist knowing that our desire and language are not our own but are already imposed on us by alien voices, gazes, myths, aspirations, expectations and desires, and in reference to a primordial mothering, a linguistically imposed mother's desire, and a signifier for a Father's name that we did not choose. For Lacanians, theory is itself resistance if it refuses to consider the notion that individuals do not have altogether free choice. I would even risk arguing that Lacan is himself the Other of much recent American theory and criticism. Surprisingly, Americans who describe themselves as "doing" Lacan show little, if any, interest in the work of those Europeans who have been doing him in both theory and practice for decades.[36]

If one were to rethink only the notion of resistance or theory, or *le sujet supposé savoir*, not to mention countless others, one would be working with a very different Lacan than the one regularly cited in American journals where, for example, resistance to theory has become "resistance to questioning ideology." Such articles argue that teachers and ideology *should* be rejected when they place themselves in any role of mastery. Basing this imperative on his reading of Lacan, Gregory Jay says (in "The Subject of Pedagogy"), "Teachers are imposters."[37] Yet Lacan did not equate resistance with transference, or teaching with the master discourse. Both grammatical language and the ego constitute resistance in Lacan's eyes, the major resistance being a subject's resistance to knowing that his or her unconscious desire constitutes an intentionality. From a Lacanian viewpoint—one in which the only subject is the subject of unconscious desire, and the only *savoir* every person's supposition that he or she knows something—a teacher's unconscious desire subjectivizes any theory or material taught.[38] *Savoir* then is inhabited by a division in the subject, a division that shows up as myriad kinds of aphanisis (fading). Moreover, fading occurs between orders that chain themselves around the hole in the Other that Lacan called the Real. Any critic who thinks Lacan's reflections on the unconscious, or beyond the unconscious, are self-reflexive has missed the point. For Lacan, "self" is a fantasy, an illusion, a *semblance* anchored to others by identificatory relations, language, and desire. To undo the "subject of certainty"—insofar as it is the ego—as Gregory Jay suggests, would also require one to take into account what Lacan taught about the dangers of such work. Unraveling the ego is death work, work to be approached with great caution, as any analyst should know, lest a psychosis or suicide be triggered.

Yet teachers usually confront students whose assumptions (ideologies, egos, illusions) are minimally questioned. Thus Lacan believed psychoanalysis could be taught as such—not just as a training for analysts, or as something that offered a few techniques we could use to break down ignorance. Indeed, the use of the word "ignorance" by contemporary American critics seems to borrow less from Lacan than from the traditional meaning, where "one does not know something." Lacan spoke of three passions: love, hate, and ignorance. In his reworking, ignorance equals belief or assumptions. One is not ignorant of something; rather, one clings to one's assumptions with a passion, lest anxiety subvert the certainties by which one tries to keep the unconscious at bay. In 1971 Lacan spoke of ignorance as the correlate of *savoir*, pointing out that in Buddhism ignorance is thought to be a passion that can perhaps be balanced by meditation. Lacan's interest here is neither in passion nor in meditation, but in the intimate link between ignorance and knowing.[39] Dismantling fixed ideas or the free-associational flow of fantasies is also a matter of teleology. When anyone aims to disturb another, one ought to know why, and what the means and consequences are, because dismantling ideas runs into what Lacan called "the ethics of psychoanalysis," where one had best use judgment to balance desire.

In my reading of Lacan any purported post-structuralist affinities actually obscure the differences between that trend and his ideas. Indeed, Lacan says that an Other desire inhabits every subject, as does *das Ding* or the Real that he names the *objet a* (primordial objects of desire, causes of desire, the drives; the excess *jouissance* of desire that comes to the place of whatever *lacks* in the unclosed universe of discourse that *causes* the subject to desire in the first place). In this sense the *objet a* is the *point de capiton* where language, desire, and fantasy meet to continually fill in a void in representation, making unconscious activity an ongoing oscillation between being and no-thingness. We see that Lacan differs from any post-structuralist who sees in the noumenal only ambiguity, opacity, or the undecidable. The noumenal or *das Ding* is, of course, undecidable in part. But Lacan's interest is in the enigmatic or undecoded part that speaks anyway, or writes itself on the body, sometimes as a symptom. That part can always be studied as an *objet a*, itself heterogeneous.

In a 1980 article in *Encyclopedia Universalis* Jacques-Alain Miller points out that Lacan resides in the line of structuralist thinkers that includes Saussure, Lévi-Strauss, and Roman Jakobson. On the other hand, beyond the affinities, Miller says that Lacan was most radically a structuralist in the sense that psychoanalysis operates at the join between structure and subject. And in a third sense, Miller says, Lacan did not belong to the structuralists at all, for their structure was coherent and complete, while his concept of structure is of an ordering that is always paradoxical and uncompleted.⁴⁰ By "structure" Lacan meant a logical ordering of desire that appears in the way a person's language moves, in the uses one makes of language and knowledge, in one's relationship to power. But such structure can only be read or decoded retroactively in light of the ontology or set of "believed self-descriptions." These point to a given subject structured, in terms of gender difference, into a mythology of self or identity, and in reference to an unconscious positioning whose coordinates are the signifier of a Father's Name and its correlative, a mother's desire. It is not that Lacan fetishized childhood, as one might believe by literalizing his mirror stage; rather, he envisioned childhood as structured around desires and myths that do not disappear merely because a person ages. Moreover, these desires and myths are repeated and fixed in a way that can cause an adult to suffer from messages that remain active but have no apparent purpose in adult life. Indeed, such structure remains hidden (and denied) by the system of language and by the ego that believes itself to be unified.

For Lacan, loss—objects lost to memory—lives at the heart of being as a palpable agent that materializes subject-ivity (mind and identity). It is not, then, the organic biological "material" that causes human response. The subject operates from a logic of the signifier, not from a body per se. So the Real appears as enigmatic meaning on the body. Jacques-Alain Miller has called response, decision, and choice three formations of the Real. Here one learns about the unconscious, not just *in* language, but in terms of what

Lacan called a timing that emanates from the Other, and not as a random thing.[41] This timing points to the Real of structure where the limits of desire concern *jouissance* and the Real Father as desiring. If one considers the possibility that all ideologies (political ones or self beliefs) function to deal with a fundamental lack in humanness, circumscribed by a particular *jouissance,* it becomes easier to see why one future direction emanating from Lacan's teaching is political. Perhaps one can imagine an approach in which the politics of the personal—What is your desire? To what timing are you enslaved?—could be extended to a consideration of group politics. One could seek the key signifiers in an ideology, listen for founding myths, and organize group activity around an understanding that both lack and desire motivate power, for good or for bad. That is, any drive to unify, resolve, or totalize risks falling into the trap of reification of a leader, a group of ideals, or a set of beliefs. Once moral superiority is assigned to a position, one risks the total-itarianism of the left or right. However, Slovenian Marxists who are currently working with and from Lacan's teaching tell us that they have had to refute classical revolutionary doctrine.[42] If one goes to the psychoanalytic view and accepts Lacan's idea that truth is on the side of desire, in dialectical opposition to the Real or the death drive (the unsymbolized or negative kernel of *jouissance* at the heart of being), then one grasps that *Realpolitik* is not "reality" (true versus false consciousness), but the negativity that links ideals to death in an often desperate attempt to save a set of ideals that stand in—unconsciously—for the representation of an ideal Father's Name. Here affect opposes desire in a *jouissance* whose limits are that of group fervor, organized around an ideology pronounced for or against some Father's Name.[43]

But to rethink the relationships between desire and justice is complex. In "Kant avec Sade" Lacan posed opposite poles in trying to answer the question of what to do with desire when its law is the law of love or recognition (Imaginary politics).[44] Lacan's proposition that nothing can be stated in conscious life that has not already been repeated elsewhere sutures logical discourse by making lack a part of the structure itself. But since humans do not readily recognize this somewhere else, conscious-life endeavors are based on *méconnaissance*. Lacan's view of the unconscious differs

49

profoundly from the Derridean idea that the unconscious is just linguistic and can be "sounded out" down to noises. In Derrida's idea, language comes after the fact as a repetition derived from a rehearsal. For Lacan, the *a priori* is lost because it has to do with desire, and because "It" repeats itself in-conscious life as if its "origins" were natural or spontaneous. In Jacques-Alain Miller's words, *suture* is defined as "the general relation of lack to the structure of which lack is an element."[45] In Lacan, lack becomes protean desire, taking many forms—primordial objects, mother's desire, father's desire—but none to be confused with meta-structure. In this sense, desire falls outside the academic arena of consciousness-bound discourse and generalized postulates.[46]

The Lacan I have just described belongs to the world of psychoanalysis, not that of philosophy or psychology. Indeed, Lacan's idea of the signifier extends as far as the realm of psychosis, where the signifier does not represent something for an other. In schizophrenic speech, language functions *as if,* in reference to nothing ascertainable. For Lacan the *as if* points to the concrete genesis of speech and ego, not to a brain dysfunction. The psychotic speaks the Other *as if* others were not to be taken into account.[47] In psychosis the ego collapses into the metonymical graveyard of pre-castration *jouissance,* where suffering arises from inadequate individuation: not-good-enough-metaphor. In psychosis the three orders that Lacan represents by a Borromean knot—Real, Symbolic, and Imaginary—lack the signifier for the Father's Name and become unknotted.[48] The signifier for the Father's Name has already been foreclosed in early life, and when its absence is adequately challenged later, an only apparently unified ego or grammar can cave in on itself, as if into a black hole.[49] One way of describing psychosis might be as the eradication of "border anxiety," although paranoid psychotics live at the limits of the Other, where both gaze and voice make the superego an omnipresence of Real effects and constant threats, producing anxiety.

In creating a strange new epistemology describing how and from where we know, Lacan offers a bizarre language that tends to put off those who have not learned to speak it. While American analysts and some schools of literary criticism are still concerned about making a separation between feelings and mind, Lacan taught that language structures feelings, giving them the shape of person-specific meaning. Yet the only affect Lacan privileged in the clinic or in analytic theory was anxiety, because its object is the *objet a:* that which falls from the Other as if essentialized.[50] This is the same object Lacan delineated as causing desire and named in "The Subversion of the Subject and the Dialectic of Desire in the Freudian Unconscious" (1960): the breast, the feces, the voice, the gaze, the phoneme, the (imaginary) phallus, the urinary flow, the nothing.[51] This seems an unlikely list, unless one sees that these particular objects are valorized primordially in subject constitution, and that throughout life they build up matrices of meaning where desire and anxiety will generally interface with affects. Moreover, they weld subject structure both diachronically and synchronically so that one need not rely on memory or well-made fantasies to talk about a link between past and present life. Rather, the *objet a* links consciousness to the history of the subject, placing the subject as "the being of a fall" in the space of the "therefore" in the "I think, therefore I am."[52] Such theories reveal why early Lacanians such as Anthony Wilden repudiated Lacan because of his hermeticism, declaring themselves instead on the side of communications theory, information systems, artificial intelligence, Marxism, cognitive psychology, brain research, and so on—any of which is "supposed" to represent an advance in understanding the nature of meaning over any theory of meaning developed by Lacan.[53] Yet Lacan's influence is not so easy to shake off, as Wilden demonstrates in *Man and Woman, War and Peace: The Strategist's Companion.* In a section called "In the Penal Colony: The Body as the Discourse of the Other" he argues that sexual differences "are not the result of genes, innate tendencies, hormone balances, anatomy, brain differences, or 'masculine' or 'feminine.'" Rather, these differences are unconscious. More than this Wilden does not say.[54]

In his preface to Anika Lemaire's book *Jacques Lacan* (1970) Lacan says that Freud was fortunate not to have had the university pack at his heels, for the university gang behaves oddly toward *him.* "The good use [Lemaire] has made of academic sources inevitably lacks what oral tradition will designate for the future: texts faithful in pillaging me, but never deigning to pay me back. Their interest will be that they transmit what I have said literally; like the amber which holds the fly so as to know nothing of its flight."[55]

By opening the doors of psychoanalysis to those from many disciplines, Lacan not only reversed their tradition of closing the doors to all but themselves, but he also changed the concept of what one can do with psychoanalysis. If one can teach it to anyone, then psychoanalysis must be seen as a "way of thinking" about being and non-being. In the clinic, it works with the problems of one person. In the forum, it works to dismantle unquestioned assumptions by the mere fact that the subject matter in question is individual truth and desire, as well as the question of how collectivities arise out of the structuration of singular subjects around one difference: the sexual one. One point at which Lacan's teachings can go beyond in the 1990s is in our acknowledgment of the forum. The first seduction Lacan's theory offers usually concerns the idea that each person's *parole* is informed by the Symbolic, both its language and its institutions. The second-level seduction, one to which film theory particularly has succumbed, was a recognition that the lover's discourse emanated from Imaginary identifications. But American film theory and literary criticism have read Lacan very partially in the 1970s and '80s. Critics tended to fuse language itself—as a system of codes and conventions—with identificatory relations, thus believing that one could make films (or critique films) by equating control with an assimilation of convention to identification. In this scenario, critics thought they could assess why certain shots would make people cry, others make them laugh, and so on. One ended up with an aesthetics of affect, where affects were not problematized and where the camera was reified, if not deified.

In the 1990s no one who reads Jacques Lacan, or who follows Miller's clarification of his teaching, can dismiss the Real, for that dimension points to something beyond—not only to the unconscious that works us, but also to something beyond the aesthetic. In the Seminar *Les Non-dupes errent* (1973–74) Lacan said that the Real is what makes us ask, "Where is this unconscious *savoir* situated?"[56] The analytic discourse makes us aware of a kind of *savoir* unlike any other preceding in history, says Lacan, and makes us consider that *it* is contingent. But contingent on what? Lacan answers his own question. The discourse emanating from the unconscious is contingent on what it opposes: the impossible or the Real. But how can one imagine a Real except as *supposé*? The answer, Lacan said, is that double binds point to something beyond themselves, something that causes the problem in the first place, even if that something is an unoccupied or unsymbolized position. The knot that Lacan used, a Borromean knot, was a pedagogical device meant to depict intersections in subject-ivity. Lacan described the Real as that in the knotting of the two—the Imaginary and the Symbolic—which makes a third. This idea supposes an experiential basis to mathematical topology, because for him the number, like the knot, is Real. That is, Lacan's knot is neither figural nor metaphorical.

But why does the Real constitute a third element? Lacan justifies his answer from his axiom: there is no sexual relation. The relation between the two sexes must be interpreted because the difference itself presents a symbol in nature whose existence is a question mark for people. Cultural (or individual) interpretations give rise to mythologies about men and women, while always leaving Woman on the side of the Real: that which cannot be pinned down to one unconscious representation. The masculine symbol for difference necessitates an interpretation of its visibility that ends up somehow equating that symbol with interpretation (the word) and with a sense of its being something extra (the imaginary phallus). Beyond the twoness of the Imaginary and Symbolic (the symbol and the word interpreting difference), Lacan thought Woman was associated with something beyond the Imaginary and Symbolic, with the Real.[57]

In the 1990s, feminist theory must grapple with Lacan's idea of why an anatomical difference could make such a difference. Post-structuralist feminisms have blamed oppression on patriarchy without worrying about how or why patriarchy came to be. This hermeneutic approach to feminist issues has kept women from making their knowledge about gender difference work to explain the forces that subvert the best efforts of women and men to change, despite themselves. One can change laws and conventions, but actual equality eludes women. A Lacanian politicization of knowledge would reveal not only that labels fix people, and that discourse is allied with power, but would also show the ego as resistant to change and would explain why aggression arises in the first place out of a dialectic concerning difference. Certainly theories abound, but none as innovative as Lacan's. Lacan sees the ego as blocking unconscious desire, and aggression as the obverse face of thwarted (ego) narcissism. Moreover, this dialectical movement is characteristic of *all* subjects, not just neurotic ones. Lacan is almost perverse in telling us that the neurotic knows more than a normative subject, the normative being the one in any culture who speaks a closed discourse. (This is not necessarily a male discourse, or a discourse of power; it is, rather, that use of language whose goal is to shut out any intimation of the unconscious, of a source of desire or knowledge from Elsewhere.) Normative men caricature the stereotypes of masculinity in a given culture, and normative women caricature social conventions of femininity.[58] The normative refers to mastery over disturbances arising from the unconscious.

If Lacan is correct, one is dealing with something quite awesome: unconscious desire of an Other as the *necessity* behind human intentionality. The Catch-22 is that "It" eludes us, playing at the edge of a hole "in-consciousness." We are confronted with this paradox, applicable to the personal or the cultural: unsymbolized (Real) does not mean unwritten. In Lacan's words, when one tries to question the unconscious in a place, this *où* (or *vel*) is something in the Real, and the place is a writing, an *articulation écrite*. Only in that can something witness the Real.[59]

But by "writing" Lacan does not mean the inscription of literal letters, although they do play a role. By *écrit* he said he meant a *savoir supposé sujet*; something that gives a materiality (density, motion, and weight) to language and lies between the written and spoken. We see that suture of the unconscious goes in altogether a different direction for Lacan than it does for a post-structuralism where one has two alternatives; either deconstruct Language, or forget about trying to decide upon the undecidable. Today film theory has reduced suture to cut/take. Referring to his first article on suture in the 1970s, Jacques-Alain Miller has reformulated his thinking in the 1980s: " 'Suture' had the function in its time of qualifying the relationship of the subject and the signifier in Lacan. Suture [is] this relationship which enables the subject to be represented by a signifier." Yet, when talking about unconscious phenomena, the subject cannot represent anything to himself, for "there is a kind of 'blackout' of the subject as the subject of conscious representation."[60] Perhaps this is a less obscure way of saying, as did Lacan, that the subject is not there where it is thinking.

Lacan taught analysts in training to study the *objet a*, which supports the constant movement of fantasies (an ever-moving flow of free associations), by linking it to desire. Moreover, Lacan's *objet a* is *das Ding*, the kernel of the Real at the heart of *la chose freudienne* (unconscious truth). So we have language *causing effect* as it ebbs and flows around a hole in representations. Lemaire called the *objet a* "the pivot around which every turn of phrase unfolds in its metonymy." Yet desire, like language, only seems to be full because it aims at some object. Lacan's Real takes us onto the terrain where aphanisis itself has meaning. Still, post-structuralists generally counter Lacan's contentions regarding an unconscious subject by saying, "Yes, but everything comes through language."

In the American critical/theoretical scene it is generally not appreciated that Lacan has not been theoretically supplanted by those younger dissidents and critics who came after him. Such an error in logic regarding Freud is, indeed, what Lacan's career was about. Yet Lacan's "return to Freud" was in no way a return to the same reading of Freud that had been done by those who followed Freud. On the contrary, Lacan aimed to go back to the moment of Freud's demise and read him differently. This reading always puts the Freud we know a bit off balance, turns him askew. American critics have tended to dismiss Lacan (and to return to Freud), or to blame Lacan for distorting things. In 1970 Lacan said: "When, beginning with the structure of language, I formulate metaphor in such a way as to account for what he [Freud] calls condensation in the unconscious, and I formulate metonymy in such a way as to provide the motive for displacement, they become indignant that I do not quote Jakobson (whose name would never have been suspected in my gang—if I had not pronounced it). But when they finally read him and notice that the formula in which I articulate metonymy differs somewhat from Jakobson's formula in that he makes Freudian displacement depend upon metaphor, then they blame me, as if I had attributed my formula to him."[61]

Several things stand out in Lacan's statement. One particularly interesting thing is his effort to account for or explain the primary-process condensation that Freud named but could not account for.

A second point of interest in Lacan's reshaping is the idea that metaphor resides in the unconscious. This point of view removes him entirely from the post-structuralist camp regarding what metaphor might be. If metaphor is a substitutive use of the language, images, and desires that operate unconscious *savoir,* then metaphor *cannot* be equated with representations or with the figural. On the other hand, metonymy, in Lacan's reworking, refers to the something lacking that would cause a signifying chain to work substitutively in the first place. These notions alone explode the idea that language works narratively, linearly, if indeed it does stand in for something else. Although post-structuralist interest in language followed Lacan's early comments on the errors in Saussure's notion of sign function, one can see that post-structuralists have remained on the side of consciousness. In 1986 Jacques-Alain Miller told an audience of biologically oriented psychologists and psychiatrists that the material of things is language, loads of it. He went on to say that metaphor and metonymy are materials ingrained in language as a logic, while language's sound patterns are object matters.[62] But they are ingrained in language as primary-process laws operating conscious perception, the interaction being that of the Imaginary, Symbolic, and Real, knotted by the signifier for the Father's Name.

Jean Laplanche disagreed with Lacan over the issue of the unconscious, arguing as late as 1972 that primary process is indeed primary (i.e., innate) and is itself the regulator of secondary process (language). Lacan argued the reverse: the unconscious is the outcome of language; language is not the natural product of an unconscious already in place.[63] It is easy to see why Laplanche's work on psychoanalysis has been embraced by American post-structuralists, who have called Laplanche the only great French Freudian, claiming that Laplanche teaches us that Lacan is a "post-structuralist after all."[64] In Laplanche's direction, Jacques Derrida has made the text—Writing, Language—the condition of itself.[65]

Much current American critical theory has been shaped by those individuals who attended Lacan's Seminars but came away with negative reactions or misconceptions.[66] One misunderstanding of Lacan that MacCannell perpetuates concerns his concept of metaphor as it relates to primary and secondary process: "For Lacan, metaphor is an impoverished mode dependent on a lack of reality, of meaning. But it presents itself in the mode of excess, of surplus value: it always signifies *more* than it says. This surplus is fictitious, a cover-up for its essential negativity, its barrenness. In short, it is ideological in its culture work, extracting libidinal energy from the subject with the promise of productivity."[67]

Lacan says the opposite: metaphor makes both language and being possible; indeed, it makes language a kind of supplemental poetics. MacCannell has confused Lacan's idea that libidinal energy is extracted from the subject by desire, which is on the side of metonymy, with metaphor. While psychologists and object-relations theorists (among others) reify the ego, the mother, the self, the fantasy, etc., as prime movers of libidinal energy, Lacan pinpointed a hole in the Other that he called the Real. Throughout life humans try to reify objects around this hole made up of lost objects that coalesced to create it in the first place in order to eradicate any brush with unconscious *savoir* in the shape of anxiety or admissible doubt. Rather than dismiss what disappears—the wisps, the cuts, the edges of time—Lacan finds aphanisis in most human activities. In *L' Éthique de la psychanalyse* Lacan fascinates by proposing that the curious thing about the Heideggerean vase was not the hole in its middle, nor its utilitarian value, but that the vase itself was a creation shaped around a hole; an art object made for the purpose of covering over a fundamental hole in being, the paradox being the statement of something beyond the obvious.[68]

A decade before Harari's *Textual Strategies* there appeared a book entitled *The Structuralist Controversy: The Languages of Criticism and the Sciences of Man*.[69] Interestingly enough, only Roland Barthes and Jacques Derrida have essays in both volumes. Goldmann, Poulet, and Todorov appear in the 1970 volume, to be replaced ten years later by Foucault, Genette, and Serres. One could think of Lacan as having been bumped by his erstwhile pupil and analysand Gilles Deleuze. Deleuze and Guattari, now popular in the United States, argue in a Marcusian way for a society not marked by an Oedipal structure, which they equate to the "Holy Family" mentality of a capitalist bourgeoisie.[70] But Lacan's rethinking of Freud on the Oedipal complex did not lean toward a "Holy Family" solution to life's ills, or to society's. What counted for Lacan was that every subject is constituted by the social order she or he inhabits and, in turn, reconstitutes. Subjects are positioned in familial and cultural signifying chains by virtue of naming, identifying myths, an Other's desire. In turn, these effects produce causes that return as *objet a*.

Like the *objet a*, Lacan never disappears. Not only does he reappear through those who argue against him, or who use his ideas; he reappears as well in his own name as texts become available. We hear Jean-François Lyotard telling postmodernists that there are no metagames.[71] In the background one can hear Lacan quoting the Viennese mathematical circle of the 1920s, telling us that there is no metalanguage, that not only mathematicians but all thinkers are reduced to using minimal interpretive measures. Lacan chose to use little letters he called mathemes—because of the inseparability of his theories from language—to try to formalize our knowledge somewhat because *there is no metalanguage*. One sees the importance of trying to understand how structures function, of not being totally framed by the structure. Yet Lacan knew he could not find safety outside language or beyond desire. By using topology he rethought matters of time, form, and space by taking account of an unconsciousness *in* language. These theories are so far-reaching and radical that their impact can only grow as they are further elucidated.

Meanwhile, Deleuze and Guattari find their acknowledged mentors in Nietzsche and others. In "The Schizophrenic and Language," Deleuze argues that although there is some affinity between schizophrenic *portmanteau* words and some children's speech or certain literary texts, superficially analogous similarities give us no reason to believe that the problems involved are the same.[72] Having avoided the logician's error of picking disembodied examples of nonsense to prove a point, Deleuze uses a clinical viewpoint to examine surface versus depth displacement from one mode of organization to another, or the formation of a progressive and creative disorganization.[73] Lacan's theories on psychotic language clarify Deleuze's somewhat confused theory. In *Séminaire* III: *Les psychoses* (1955–56) Lacan taught that psychotic language appears when ego structure collapses and communicative coherence recedes. The metaphorical nature of language ceases to function; substitution stops. The ego falls into the building blocks that initially gave it distance from the subject of desire, and the drive of desire tries to re-sequentialize ideas around finding a new name: a new sexual identity ("the wife of God"), an ideal grandiosity ("Napoleon"), or a father's name supplied for the missing signifier. In psychosis, metaphor gives way to metonymical function. That is, the referential signifier already there simply repeats itself to the Other, but to no other. No surface versus depth structures are to be found in Lacan's theory of psychotic language, for all language—psychotic or otherwise—is always on the surface. Deleuze's use of surface versus depth is reminiscent of Noam Chomsky's deep and surface transformational grammar structures. This kind of binary thinking was, in Lacan's estimation, Imaginary thinking. Indeed, Lacan argued that Imaginary models draw upon the body itself to impose inside/outside distinctions on mind distinctions that falsify how thinking actually works.

But Deleuze did not stop at inside versus outside. Rather, his study of surface (or puerile) language serves as a focal point for arguing that such language is a microcosmic portrait of the true problem posed by language in its depth—the schizophrenic problem of suffering or death, and life. Comparing schizophrenic language to Lewis Carroll's *Alice Through the Looking Glass,* Deleuze argues that events differ radically from things and thus are sought not in depths, but at the surface, flattened in a front-to-back continuity.[74] But how does one separate events from things in memory? Is language not also an event, an act? And how can *any* language recount an event except in a substitutive structure, i.e., a referential one? In Lacan's teaching both ego and language function as metaphorical—doubled—structures. Language takes its knowledge from an unconscious signifying chain, and the ego takes its fictions from language and identificatory conjunctions. When metaphor ceases to be functional—desire/lack stopping as well—one does not see a surface versus depth projection. Rather, the nonsensical droning on of an unconscious signifying chain continues, with its links to others and to grammar broken, representing itself for the Other, reconstituting itself for no one.

Deleuze's study is not inspired by Lacan's teaching that language is materialized by the *objet a* which initially acts as an agent of separation, or as a part susceptible of perceptual separation from the body; separable because it exceeds the binary that disappears into obvious reversibilities. In turn, language and desire materialize the body always in reference to a call to an other: need and demand also play their roles.[75] Deleuze has drawn upon some of Lacan's arguments on the relationship of death to *jouissance,* or the unconscious suffering that does not wish the good of the sufferer. The point about psychotic suffering, however, is not, as Deleuze claims, that language itself becomes differently organized, but that language loses its symbolic organization to show its underside, palpably parasitical. The psychotic person has no Symbolic order distance from his Other, and indeed is playing dead near the hole in the Other. The problem for the analyst is to create borders for the psychotic so that life and substitutive desire can function again through the doubleness that the signifying process requires.

Deleuze demonstrates at the highest level of brilliance how problematic it can be to apply Lacan's theories, either to psychotic discourse or to literary discourse, when the critique is fundamentally divorced from what Stuart Schneiderman has called "The Other Lacan." This Other Lacan, the psychoanalyst, cannot be separated from the theorist. Schneiderman writes: "I would go so far as to say that any approach to Lacan that does not see his theory in its relationship to analytic practice is doomed to an irreducible obscurity and confusion."[76] Yet Deleuze does try to deal with the idea of structure, pointing out that "structuralism reminds us that form and content matter only within the original and irreducible structures in which they are organized."[77] But some who listened to the early Lacan left him on just such issues, creating a distinction between post-structuralist Lacanians and other Lacanians, leaving pending the issue of what structure is for Lacan.

How *does* one interpret the primordial and irrecuperable nature of primary structures? While Deleuze's Chomskyesque answer dead ends in a quasi-linguistic phenomenology, Derrida argues that, since the "primitive scene" is inscribed in repetition itself, its originary quality will always already be in question, be framed. Lacan separated the "Other scene" from repetition, which he linked instead to the Real (see *Seminar* XI, ch. 4). But Lacan, too, was always wary about interpreting the primordial period prior to coherent naming and then speaking, calling it an unfathomable world of poetic shimmer. Yet he understood, as a clinician, that it could not be dismissed. The issue of "matter," said Lacan, is the issue around which all ancient philosophy turns: "All Aristotelian philosophy must be thought—and it is for that reason that it is so difficult for us to think it—according to a mode which never omits that *mater* (*la matière*) is eternal, and that nothing is made from nothing."[78]

Perception itself is not a continuous or unified activity, if you believe Lacan. Moreover, perception is structured (i.e., ordered) from the start of life by the inscriptions of gazes, words, touches, etc., on the flesh, making a primordial lining of the subject that Lacan called "letters"—localized signifiers linked to the body. As language is acquired, alongside images, the unconscious is structured by Freud's *Vorstellungsrepräsentanz*—that which Lacan names the binary signifier; that which constitutes the central point of the *Urverdrängung* of what, from having passed into the unconscious, will always be the point of *Anziehung* [attraction] through which all other repressions will be possible, all the other similar passages in the *Unterdrückt*, of what has passed underneath as signifier. This is what is involved in the term *Vorstellung*.[79] The unconscious is structured "because *Vorstellungen* forever and from the beginning at the origin, have the character of a signifying structure."[80] We are not built up as chance machines, because effects—even if random—occur in a sequence, and the sequencing makes a difference: odds or evens.[81]

Where post-structuralists tend to see letters as things, sometimes playthings, or as larger units of discourse that speak mind, their strategies for disrupting institutions have aimed at undermining binary oppositions or institutional hierarchies. Lacan's efforts went in an Other direction—that of showing why mind works oppositionally in the first place; where hierarchies come from; and how those hierarchies subvert each other without any consciously intentional intervention. Lacan's teachings reverse Derrida, who stopped at metaphor and made metonymy the search to become metaphor. In this post-structuralist view, metonymy itself is totalizing, making a literary text "total metaphor."[82] Indeed, the text is said to be opened up and desedimented, to expose the trace from which it has grown. According to Christopher Norris in *The Deconstructive Turn*, Derrida's return to writing, to rhetoric and figural language—where all ideas are said to be formulated—can lead critics to unlooked for fictive possibilities in texts; it can also challenge the devaluation of language which has (supposedly) haunted philosophy from Plato to Husserl.[83] Where ambiguities, opacities, slipperiness, and gaps in discourse are a final point for Derrida, this was the place from which Lacan began to ask questions.

Unfortunately, today's theorists and their students often speak as if secondary sources had already said all there is to say about Lacan. Jonathan Culler claims that what Barbara Johnson has called "the transferential structure of all reading" has become an important aspect of deconstructive criticism.[84] Another commonplace idea is that *différance* "designates the impossible origin of difference in differing and of differing in difference."[85] In this worldview, events happen randomly, haphazardly. There is no beginning, thus no subject or structure. Having accepted this Derridean premise, it is but a small leap to view the unconscious as a myth or an invention after the fact (*Nachträglichkeit*), not unlike Voltaire's God. "The irreducibility of the 'effect of deferral,'" writes Derrida, "is no doubt Freud's discovery."[86] Texts, aftereffects, and re-created primal scenes have become the *Stoff* of American critical theory; but none of this work maps out the limits of the deferral, that enterprise on which Lacan spent over fifty years of his life. We know that Lacan had considerable effect on Derrida. One can imagine that in 1962–63, when he is said to have attended Lacan's Seminar on "Anxiety," Derrida was taken with Lacan's use of the *Unheimlich*, and with Lacan's theory that the voice comes from an Other place, its sonorities and words seeming to belong elsewhere.[87] In *The Purloined Poe* Muller and Richardson write that, despite his critical questions regarding Lacan's work, Derrida "felt that his best contribution to the entire problem at that time was the continued pursuit of his own work 'whether or not this work should encounter Lacan's and Lacan's—I do not at all reject the idea—more than any other today.'"[88]

But it is not only deconstructive post-structuralism that has read Lacan *à rebours,* or perhaps heard him through the ears of the unconscious (the only organ, says Lacan, that does not close its ears). Post-structuralist feminism has so distorted Lacan that one can only read the French feminist canon as an absence whose locus is Lacan. Such feminists furnish criticisms of psychoanalysis whose *raison d'être* is based on the idea that they have read, assimilated, and dismissed Lacan's body of work. Nonetheless, a major pattern emerging in feminist work by Luce Irigaray, Hélène Cixous, Alice Jardine, and others is the tendency to oppose Lacan to Derrida, either directly or by implication, *as if* the two had built their careers in mutual dialogue. In *Gynesis,* for example, Alice Jardine opens her text with six quotations, starting with Lacan and ending with Cixous. Lacan is quoted as saying, "Nothing can be said of woman." Derrida is third with "However—it is woman who will be my subject. Still, one might wonder whether that doesn't really amount to the same thing—or is it to the other."[89] Lacan has written woman off, according to Jardine. Derrida has equated woman to his subject, and then has suggested that she might be the same thing as the other. That is, the difference between man and woman makes no difference. One begins to get suspicious: Is feminism not based on the idea that the difference has been crucial in all historicized societies across time and space?

Lacan can be dismissed, Jardine asserts, because he has nothing to say about women. Yet Lacan's views are based on the premise that men essentialize Woman in order that she be the keeper of their fantasy of what truth is. Woman becomes, for men, the "dark-sided face of god." Why? Lacan argues that Woman has been saddled with this burden because no one unconscious symbol represents her as a specificity, as the penis symbolizes the link between male gender, otherness/difference, and culture (beyond the concrete of the mother's body into the language and law of the social). When one reads feminist criticisms of this theory, the misunderstanding is clear. It has not been grasped that Lacan is talking about how representational bases are put in place long before any meanings that confer power or privilege are grasped by subjects whose *savoir* is nonetheless built up out of sequential re-presentings of the visible world. Yet Jardine distinguishes her feelings about Derrida from her irritation with Lacan. "Derrida's politics of enunciation are of an entirely different color from those of Lacan—mostly because his work is on and about the politics of enunciation itself. That is always where Derrida's style lands first—on those places where people start showing their colors."[90] Jardine likes Derrida because she can *see* his point of origin. In Jardine's hands, Lacan's definition of the Other as the discourse of the unconscious—that which is asymmetrical and not readily visible to conscious knowing/seeing—becomes Derrida's The Text. Is this not contradictory? Derrida argues over and over that there is no original text because the point of origin is always already lost. Lacan argues that the only locatable origin is that point where each subject is the function of countable particularities, as the function of those countable signifiers (*les uns*) returning from the unconscious in a signifying chain.[91]

Lacan's starting point is the enigma posed by sexual difference. Woman has been written upon, spat upon, silenced, deified, reified, and dignified because she resides on the side of the Real: that which exceeds definition, simple symbolization, and ready enunciation. It sounds as if some feminists reject the unconscious that Freud and Lacan discovered through their work with the pain of female subjects. Are academic feminists so identified with the presence of the word that the void of specifically feminine suffering is not recognizable to them except as a sociological problematic—"Here *we* are, so where are Plato's sisters?" Has it been forgotten that women could only write or speak once they had attained sufficient credentials to enter a workforce, and when they had access to birth control? Moreover, such feminist criticism devalorizes those "normative" women who choose to play the role of "the hand that rocks the cradle." More troubling to me is the feminist rejection of Lacan's difference from Freud. Lacan discovered that there is everything to be learned about language and being from Woman who is a signifier, but is not represented by one unconscious symbol: no *the* in Woman. Is the acute awareness of emptiness and Otherness that is ours something we wish to jettison so quickly, rather than something to learn from/about?

Equally problematic is the feminist reading of Lacan as if he were Derrida (or Irigaray or Cixous, who work with Derrida). Lacan is not the only man to have female followers. Jane Gallop reads the Clément/Cixous debate (*La Jeune née*) regarding Freud's Dora case and opts for Cixous: "The symbolic is politically healthy; the imaginary is regressive. That is a classic Lacanian ethical hierarchy. But like all hierarchies, it can be oppressive. One of the effects of this hierarchy, of all hierarchies (Cixous suggests, pp. 115–17), is to support the valuation of men over women."[92] Because hierarchies are oppressive, Lacan challenged them in his thinking and teaching. He viewed the Symbolic as alienating, the cause of alienated desire, and combated the Imaginary and linguistic tendencies of binary oppositions to make global judgments (good versus bad / you versus me) with his three orders: The Real, Symbolic, and Imaginary linked in three circles like the Borromean knot. In a note to "Seminar of 21 January 1975," Jacqueline Rose and Juliet Mitchell emphasized Lacan's opposition to hierarchies: "More recently the theory of knots has been used to stress the relations which bind or link Imaginary, Symbolic and the Real, and the subject to each, in a way which avoids any notion of hierarchy, or any priority of one of the three terms." In *Scilicet* Lacan said, "These three terms: what we imagine as a form, what we hold as circular in language, and that which exists in relation both to the imaginary and to language, have led me to bring out the way in which they are linked together."[93]

Insofar as Lacan's three orders are linked together by the signifier of a Father's Name, correlative to a mother's desire, Lacan returned to the Oedipal complex, which then becomes a structure (an ordering) of being and knowing in relation to desire where language is an ornament of desire. The well-made sense of ideas and concepts becomes porous and indicative of sex, power, wounds, pleas when one turns a Lacanian ear to "scanning discourse." Indeed, books such as Paul Ricoeur's *De l'interprétation: essai sur Freud* (1965) become monuments to interpretation where Interpretation aims to become a metalanguage, a resolution or final word. Although Ricoeur said this book arose out of three lectures on Freud that he gave at Yale in 1961,[94] readers find themselves confronted with Ricoeur's Lacan, rather than Ricoeur's Freud. But as recently as 1983 this was not known. Joseph Smith and William Kerrigan declare, in the introduction to the collection of essays entitled *Interpreting Lacan*:

> Finally the boom began: an issue of *Yale French Studies* given over to the "French Freud" (1976) [*sic*]; the translation of Anika Lemaire's *Jacques Lacan* (1977). . . . Suddenly Lacan was the darling of English psychoanalytic chatter. What about *him*? And then he was dead. A major irony of this story lies in the fact that the most thoughtful arguments against Lacan's renovation of psychoanalysis were available in English before Lacan's own works. In *Freud and Philosophy* (1970) [a translation of Ricoeur's 1965 book], probably the finest contribution to psychoanalysis by a nonanalyst, Paul Ricoeur commences interpreting Freud with a defense of psychic energy

as a concept poised between biology and semantics, reducible to neither. . . . It may help to realize that what is really at stake in this section of *Freud and Philosophy* is Lacan: Ricoeur is interpreting the underpinnings of psychoanalysis in such a way that, much later in the argument . . . Lacan's linguistic unconscious can be discarded as an untenable distortion. . . . Although Lacan is at last available to us in English, questions like these may make him appear to be already behind us. The best minds have agreed upon his failings.[95]

And what about Ricoeur, a French philosopher who had been a translator of Husserl up until he began to heed the furor around Lacan in the 1950s? In the preface to his book on Freud, Ricoeur says that his book is on philosophy (not psychoanalysis) and aims to study "la consistance du discours Freudien." The word "consistency" will not be lost on anyone who no longer views discourse or language as consistent. Ricoeur goes on to stress that his book comes from his own reading of Freud, and that he has distanced himself from "new theoretical conceptions whose discussion would have distanced me from severe debate with the only founder of psychoanalysis [Freud]. That is why I treated Freud's work like a work henceforth closed, and renounce discussing the conceptions, either of dissidents become adversaries . . . or of students become dissidents . . . or of disciples become adversaries . . . or of disciples become creators—Melanie Klein, Jacques Lacan."[96] Yet, when Ricoeur wrote his book, Lacan (a psychoanalyst practicing since the 1930s) was unique in setting out radical and new readings of Freud in his Seminars, where symbol, representation, language, and energy were submitted to the innovative scrutiny that Ricoeur claims as his own interpretation of Freud.

In 1966 Michel Tort wrote a scathing attack on Ricoeur's book in *Les Temps Modernes* entitled "De l'interprétation ou la machine herméneutique." Having debunked the positivism in psychology, Ricoeur sets out in this book to argue for psychoanalysis, Tort writes.

> But it was not useful [for Ricoeur] to follow these psychologists into their conceptual swamps, only to open up onto evidence which, for being first, does not date any the less precisely from a certain Report of Jacques Lacan on the word [*parole*] and language (1953), where the place of psychoanalysis found itself established in a de-

finitive manner in the word and in language. Also, when P. Ricoeur declares in a note [p. 358], that one could draw from this Report [the "Discourse of Rome"] a critique *very close* to the one he is developing for the purpose of situating the place and object of psychoanalysis, he remains—one must say it here—a bit and even a lot beyond the truth. Because, it would not be difficult at all to admit it, it is even a justice to be rendered to psychoanalysis itself, to observe that *without exception* all the concepts which P. Ricoeur uses to define the exact problematic of Freudianism, all those where there is nothing to correct [pp. 353–64], are concepts elaborated from the appearance of the Report of J. Lacan, as one can assure oneself by referring to no. 1 of *La Psychanalyse* (now out of stock), pp. 81–160. And one can measure to what point the lack of these certain guidelines would have compromised P. Ricoeur's analysis, by holding in the other hand a text of the chapters written by him in "Le volontaire et l'involontaire" (1950) on the Freudian unconscious.[97]

Although Ricoeur claimed in 1983 that he had never attended Lacan's Seminars, MacCannell says otherwise.[98] In any case Michel Tort's "Exposé," carried on into a second issue of *Les Temps Modernes,* makes it clear that Ricoeur's careful reading of the Rome Discourse was a sufficient basis for his book; that, along with a comparison with his 1950 chapter, where the unconscious is little more than a *psyché-objet* and a *corps-objet*.[99] Yet any reading of Ricoeur's book—as well as his later one on metaphor, where he elaborates Lacan's notion of a split in metaphor itself—shows the lack of spirit and problematic opened up by Lacan. When Ricoeur cannot go beyond metaphor or symbol, he merely returns to History and Biology.[100] Lacan, meanwhile, has made of psychic energy a constellation of desire, knotted signifiers in the Real, and the Imaginary transference that motivates both desire and speech. Lacan developed the theory that because Freud had divorced *Wunsch* (wish) and *Begierde* (desire) from *Vorstellung* (representation), he ended up without a way to explain how energy was driven by the desire and transference relations that build up as complex layers of signifying chains from the start of life. For Lacan, biology is structured by meaning, instead of the reverse. Surely if Kerrigan and Smith had possessed these facts, they would have been less hasty in accusing Lacan of borrowing his ideas from Ricoeur.

While critics such as Malcolm Bowie in his book *Freud, Proust and Lacan* accept that desire links the subject to both metaphor and language, others still agree with Ricoeur and Derrida that metaphor and language have nothing to do with the subject *qua* subject. Meanwhile, Lacanian clinics treat psychosis by using Lacan's ideas on metaphor/metonymy to reconstitute the subject of language and unconscious desire.[101] In psychosis a nonsense language reveals that language functions mechanically when the Other is laid bare, stripped of the metaphorical movements of ego and grammatical displacements. In schizophrenic discourse, language functions as if for no one, as if there were no listener. Lacan hears such speech as a mechanical language underlying everyday coherent language that turns out to be meaningful to the degree that it can be decoded. But beyond clinical matters of psychotic pain and "cure" lies a theoretical issue. For Lacan, psychotic language proved that language has a function having nothing to do with communication and lying beyond metaphor. It fills a hole in the Other that threatens to engulf anyone who gets hooked on the void *per se* (such as in suicides or some hysterias). When the signifier functions as if for no one, this usually points to a problem around the prestige or authenticity of a proper name, sexual identity, and perhaps even whether or not the person is human. If Lacan is right, no future study of language can fail to take psychotic discourse into account. I would argue that the sterility and repetitious inanity of such language are the antithesis of the creative expansion some critics have thought to emulate psychotic language, such as that of James Joyce, or Lewis Carroll or Henry James (Derrida, Deleuze, Felman).[102] In these literary languages stretched to the breaking point we sometimes see the Real begin to function in conjunction with the other orders, while in psychosis Symbolic meaning resembles aphasic disorders rather than sheer enigma.

Lacan's theories on psychosis produce a jarring effect similar to his placing the Seminar on Poe's *Purloined Letter* at the start of his 1966 collection of *Écrits*. Language is always already there, he argued, offering up its glittering insights and memorable formulations for anyone who wants to construct a solid text from it. The point is powerful. Texts appear to speak truth because they mimic the language system itself, while speech flows away and thus seems valueless on its own. Its power lasts only while it is spoken; it is lauded today and forgotten tomorrow—unless it is written down and published. According to Lacan language can, however, be stolen—borrowed—in the Imaginary, where subjects identify their words with their names (narcissism and desire); in the Symbolic, where the word is law, linking voice to superego and ideal ego; and in the Real, where effects remain, split off from memory. Now that Lacan's words are appearing in texts, they will doubtless be judged alongside Freud's texts, and alongside the texts they spawned. We will read Lacan on the Real and rethink this theory in relation to political matters, art, and literary texts, not only as ideas germane to a clinical never-never-land. Lacan believed that truth comes from *lalangue,* that language which is "mine" (each person's); not *la langue* of grammar. *Lalangue* is the language of re-presentations filling a void. Thus Lacan made sense of non-sense: dreams, psychosis, mathematics, art, literary particularity, etc., and devised ways to teach his theories without disappearing into all the eclipses that keep us away from this void.

Paradoxically, Lacan fights contemporary formalisms (including post-structuralism, in my view) with his theories of the materiality of language and a logic of the signifier where form and content merge into desire as *cause and effect* of language acts. Lacan has rethought form, making of human subjects topological forms, and not just rhetorical topoi. I speak of form that goes beyond the epistemological, ontological, and aesthetic, that ends up including the mysteries that frame existence in the form that each person's identity quest(ion) takes. There is no unity of knowledge, being, or seeing between the world and the perceiver, Lacan taught. Even History is not an adequate way to object-ify who and what we are. While Derrida sees History as a "white mythology" whose origins are irrecuperable and whose end products are logocentric lies, Lacan taught that the contrast between the constancy of a literary work or historical interpretation and the ever-changing nature of the commentary it engenders puts History itself into question, narrowing the focus to the relationship of each person to the "letter" [*l'être*].[103] In *The Political Unconscious* Fredric Jameson declares that History is Lacan's Real.[104] But, if the Real is the unsymbolized that returns (if at all) as an enigmatic fragment, split off from knowledge of itself, the Real cannot be History. History, by definition, becomes Imaginary and Symbolic interpretations moving, perhaps, around the Real, but not sure how to take it into account.

Whereas hermeneutic criticsm relies on History and a semiotic concept of "a community of speakers," its accounts of the world as text, or text as world, remain imprisoned within the metaphysics of consciousness. Even Derrida stays locked within the *logos* that he must continually destroy in order to validate his theoretical method of viewing meaning as coinciding with language. Foucault adds power to the sign, affirming dimensions beyond. Lacan adds the structuring (materializing) impact of the objects of desire, the gaze, the voice, etc., as well as the omnipresence of the Real such that the sign is always susceptible of subversion, and always potentially open to effects radiating from the Other out of which Things always come, even if only obviously in dreams. Whereas Derrida claimed that his Sisyphean gesture is a political posture, to deconstruct or invent a Writing capable of disturbing institutions, Lacan's teaching politicizes every area it touches. If the unconscious makes all conscious acts and products Other than what they seem, then everything must be rethought. At the New York Television conference in 1987, Slavoj Zizek refuted the post-structuralist devalorization of freedom, the "you're already framed anyway" attitude, by asserting that freedom *is* the Real: that which cannot be idealized. A week later, Jacques-Alain Miller spoke on art, saying that art does not provide pleasure, as post-structuralists have argued since Roland Barthes began to speak of the pleasure of the text. Rather, said Miller, art provides *jouissance*, a satisfaction of unconscious drives: "Art is not a product of the unconscious (*pace* Surrealism), but rather that of the most civilizing urge. That, significantly, is sublimation—which is popularly confused with repression. For this reason, art can be said to 'respond' [but not correspond] to the unconscious."[105]

We can conclude, I hope, that the new Lacan—who is really an old Lacan only now being read—is quite different from Freud. In the second Yale collection on psychoanalysis Shoshana Felman argued, for example, that according to Freud "seeing is . . . above all *transferring*. And if . . . seeing is always reading, deciphering, *interpreting*, it is because reading is also transferring."[106] Yet Stuart Schneiderman argued in 1986, at an art talk sponsored by the Collective for Living Cinema, that looking and seeing are hardly synonymous: " 'Looking' implies a search. 'Seeing' implies taking something for granted. 'I see' means that the point is *already* understood. Artworks succeed in appropriating our gaze and casting it back at us. This, too, is an act of appropriation."[107] Moreover, transference is a response of love or hate elicited in interhuman reactions. We transfer to others what we are, as we appropriate something from them. Reading will include transference, then, but will not equal it, any more than seeing will equal reading or transferring. With Lacan we are neither in the text nor outside it, but at a third point of creation between the two. Poulet's, Heidegger's, and Derrida's "phenomenological" theories of reading will therefore not be compatible with Lacanian ones. Poulet argued that one consciousness could empty itself out to be replaced by another. Derrida argues that you can appropriate a text by deconstructing or reinventing its rhetorical strategies.

For Lacan, seeing and reading cannot be equated in any simple way. Seeing is, above all, connected to desire, which acquires its first structural significance when a child becomes aware of producing feces—a visible object—in response to an other's demand for this performance. With the awareness that this command performance requires giving, the act of giving is linked to seeing a product. But, along with giving, anxiety is born, in its connection with the desire to please.[108] Indeed, Lacan links the scopic drive to the early structural experience, where fantasies first begin to function as a free-associational shadow language that fills up the hole in the Other, and also to deal with the Other's desire.

Neil Hertz and Gilles Deleuze have argued that transference and repetition are more or less the same thing.[109] Transference and repetition are said to motivate (drive) texts. Moreover, repetition becomes translation of the same into varying generic modes. Derrida, de Man, and Freud are called upon most frequently as theoretical reference points for these ideas. But with Lacan, narrative—not to mention poetry, drama, and other literary genres—breaks out of linear modes. For him, repetition can never equal insight, where transference is seen as a complicity between reading and writing. Nor can transference equal the limits of a frame, because, beyond repetition, one finds the Real, truth, desire, and *jouissance*. By noting that there are gaps in language, Lacan shows that the gap is a hole in unconscious *savoir* that (de-)centers the subject variously on Imaginary, Symbolic, and Real planes at the same time. With Lacan, then, repetition is an ego function, one that closes off the horror involved in confronting a lack-in-being that makes contradiction truth-functional. The structure of desire—in the Imaginary, Symbolic, and Real—partakes of the alienation and death work that Lacan attributes to a resistant ego and an Other's desire that "live us" as if we were dead. One can see that it is easier for literary critics to reduce transference to repetition, to go in search of tracks in a text (book or culture) and then to state it (master it), than to map out a mother's unconscious desire in the three orders as it effects the identificatory constitution of one's subjectivity, always in reference to a father's desire functioning in these same orders. Lacan's inclusions are head-spinning and require the nauseating effort of thinking against what comes naturally in thinking: that binary oppositions reveal simple differences or merely obscure them through an Imaginary politics of the same (an identity error in logic).[110]

In *The World, the Text, the Critic* Edward Said warned against the "loyal devotion" Lacan might inspire. In *Marxism and Deconstruction* Michael Ryan scoffed at the idea of an Oedipal complex or structure, calling Lacan fundamentalist and conservative. Others tell us that narration is structured like a (subject in) language.[111] But Lacan goes another way, telling us that the unconscious subject of desire appears in language as something more than language, something at odds with language. By dismissing Lacan's repeated insistence that nothing is more Real than the symptom (*jouissance*) at the heart of being that an analysand drags into an analyst's office, many theorists continue to blame Lacan for such crimes as rigging Edgar Allan Poe's story, when Lacan's major point in using this tale is found in the game of odds and evens at the end of the French version—a crucial parenthesis with which no American critic has grappled, to my knowledge. Derrida says Lacan brutalized the text by forging an image of psychoanalytic allegory. By simply ruling out of bounds Lacan's point about his use of the Poe story—that *la chose freudienne*, or unconscious truth, appears in speech, and speaks dialectically to the lost part of a subject's story—Derrida plays the role of "postman of truth," implicitly rejecting the decades of work now connected with the Lacanian clinic where psychoses are being treated by Freud's "talking cure," not to mention the other beneficial advances of Lacan's clinical work. One can see the bind that American critics are in by having bought into intellectual battles transported here from elsewhere. Is it more important that Lacan may have brutalized a literary text by possibly forging an image of an "allegory" than that his literary allegory might, indeed, exemplify the way subjects exist as effects of letters (of desire) that circulate? In *Criticism and Social Change* Frank Lentricchia argued that Derrida's critique of ideologies of the sign in no way touches the real work signs must do in representing the world.[112]

It remains to be seen whether American theorists and critics will rise to the as yet unmet challenge of seriously studying Lacan's texts, or whether they will bother to reconsider Sherry Turkle's claim, in *Psychoanalytic Politics,* that those who have dismissed Lacan for being too intellectual, too abstract, too mathematical, or conversely not suitable for the clinic, might not take into account that "for Lacan mathematics is not disembodied knowledge. It is constantly in touch with its roots in the unconscious. This contact has two consequences: first, that mathematical creativity draws on the unconscious, and second, that mathematics repays its debt by giving us a window back to the unconscious."[113] It remains to be seen how seriously theorists will take Lacan's re-reading of Freud's *Beyond the Pleasure Principle,* where the death drive is not (as Freud thought) organic or biologistic, but corresponds to the alienation of subjects into an Other's repetitions and desires. John Miller writes in *Artscribe*:

> Lacan explicitly linked the figure of Aristotle's *automaton* to the repetition compulsion, the principal manifestation of the death drive. And so Lacan referenced, instead of Bergson, an Aristotelean primacy of change and non-identity of parts. We think not in consequence of the totality of the body, nor through an integral vitalism, but rather in consequence of language carving up the body so that the resultant lack drives the subject beyond itself. The subject, therefore, is not determined from outside, from elsewhere, but according to a fundamental absence; the *object petit a.* A lack or absence defies monitoring. This, then, would in one sense qualify or delimit the extreme reach of totalitarianism, which always seeks a palpable "something" to control.[114]

It remains to be seen whether Jacques-Alain Miller is right in saying, "One notes . . . that where [Lacan's] teaching has not been received, in the United States for example, despite the popularity [psychoanalysis] knew after the War, the infatuation with analysis is extinguished. If its interpretation is predetermined by norms that always borrow their definition from social ideals, analysis always loses its potency, and the *sujet supposé savoir,* essential to the functioning of the experience, is twisted from its 'own' configuration."[115] Will the American academy remain interested in psychoanalysis, especially if the American clinic is not? Given the current tendency to read Foucault, to reread Marx, are theorists not ready to investigate desire, the dark-sided face of power? Even if Lacan is correct in saying that no one desires to know what his or her conscious visions skew (but know anyway at some Real level), will we not finally be pushed to study in greater detail the structures that live us, rather than the structures we live by? Will Lacan—theoretician, teacher, clinician and healer—not come to be interrogated on issues of *jouissance* and ethics, the Real and the "true"?

NOTES

1. "Jacques Lacan: Télévision," dir. Benoît Jacquot, 1973, 120 mins., published in *October* 40, special issue ed. Joan Copjec (Spring 1987). *Télévision* trans. D. Hollier, R. Krauss, and A. Michelson.

2. Jacques Lacan, *Télévision* (Paris: Seuil, 1973), p. 22.

3. Interview with Jacques-Alain Miller by Jean-Paul Morel, *Le Matin,* Sept. 26, 1986, rpt. in *Newsletter of the Freudian Field* 1 (Spring 1987): 6.

4. Jacques Lacan, *Écrits: A Selection,* trans. Alan Sheridan (New York: Norton, 1977).

5. Catherine Clément, *Vies et légendes de Jacques Lacan* (Paris: Bernard Grasset, 1981), p. 171.

6. English-language texts on the controversies surrounding Lacan include Monique David-Ménard, "Lacanians against Lacan," *Social Text* 6 (Fall 1982): 86–111, and Sherry Turkle, *Psychoanalytic Politics* (New York: Basic Books, 1978). In French one can consult Jacques-Alain Miller, *La Communauté psychanalytique en France,* vol. I: *La Scission de 1953* and vol. II: *L'Excommunication* (Paris: Navarin éditeur, diffusion Seuil, 1984), and Élisabeth Roudinesco, *La Bataille de cent ans: Histoire de la psychanalyse en France, 1925–1985,* Vol. 2 (Paris: Seuil, 1986).

7. Jacques Lacan, "Letter of Dissolution," Guitrancourt, Jan. 5, 1980, trans. in *October* 40 (Spring 1987): 129–30.

8. The Fondation du Champ Freudien is a nonprofit network created by Jacques Lacan in February 1979 and presided over by Judith Miller since 1981. Its goal is the diffusion of Lacan's teachings on psychoanalysis. Its orientation is international. For further information regarding the Fondation, one may write to 31 rue de Navarin, 75009 Paris, France.

9. Gérôme Taillandier represents the group named Stécriture in an article in *Littoral* 13 (June 1984): 121–26. In "Quelques problèmes de l'établissement du séminaire de J. Lacan," Taillandier criticizes Jacques-Alain Miller's "establishment" of Lacan's texts but refuses to identify the sources on which he bases his accusations. É. Roudinesco negates many of Taillandier's accusations in *La Bataille*, when she details how the seminars were recorded. An "original inscription" existed beginning in 1953 in stenographed form, and on tape after 1968 (*La Bataille* 2:569). In December 1985 the Tribunal of Paris found against the Association Après, which had already published a bulletin reproducing a part of the seminar on "Le Transfert" under the name Stécriture. Miller was granted the status of legal and moral executor of the Seminar. (Reported in "Le procès du Séminaire," *L'Âne* 24 [Jan.-Mars 1986]: 55.)

10. *Newsletter of the Freudian Field* 1 (Spring 1987): 6. See also Jacques-Alain Miller, *Entretien sur le Séminaire*, with François Ansermet (Paris: Navarin éditeur, 1985), p. 15, and *Le Séminaire de Jacques Lacan, Livre* XI: *Les Quatre Concepts fondamentaux de la psychanalyse* (1964), texte établi par Jacques-Alain Miller (Paris: Seuil, 1973), pp. 251–54.

11. Miller, *Entretien*, pp. 15, 16.

12. *Newsletter of the Freudian Field* 1 (Spring 1987): 6.

13. Miller, *Entretien*, pp. 17, 18, 23.

14. Ibid., pp. 52–53.

15. René Girard, *Deceit, Desire and the Novel: Self and Other in Literary Structure*, trans. Yvonne Freccero (Baltimore: Johns Hopkins University Press, 1965). See also Anthony Wilden, *The Language of the Self* (Baltimore: Johns Hopkins University Press, 1968).

16. Karen J. Winkler, "Post-Structuralism: An Often-Abstruse French Import Profoundly Affects Research in the United States," *Chronicle of Higher Education*, Nov. 25, 1987, p. A9.

17. John P. Muller and William J. Richardson, eds., *The Purloined Poe: Lacan, Derrida, and Psychoanalytic Reading* (Baltimore: Johns

Hopkins University Press, 1988), p. x; Muller and Richardson, *Lacan and Language: A Reader's Guide to Écrits* (New York: International Universities Press, 1982); and see, for example, Richardson, "Psychoanalysis and the Being-question," in *Interpreting Lacan*, ed. Joseph H. Smith and William Kerrigan (New Haven: Yale University Press, 1983).

18. Jane Gallop, *The Daughter's Seduction* (Ithaca: Cornell University Press, 1982) and *Reading Lacan* (Ithaca: Cornell University Press, 1985). Jacques Lacan, "Ste Anne," trans. Denise Green, in *Polysexuality*, special issue of *Semiotext(e)* 4: 1 (1981): 208–18. See also Ellie Ragland-Sullivan, "Seeking the Third Term: Desire, the Phallus, and the Materiality of Language," in *Psychoanalysis and Feminism*, ed. Judith Roof and Richard Feldstein (Ithaca: Cornell University Press, forthcoming).

19. Shoshana Felman, *Jacques Lacan and the Adventure of Insight: Psychoanalysis and Contemporary Culture* (Cambridge: Harvard University Press, 1987). See also Michael Clark, *An Annotated Bibliography of Jacques Lacan* (New York: Garland Press, 1988).

20. Jean-Luc Nancy and Philippe Lacoue-Labarthe, *Le Titre de la lettre* (Paris: Galilée, 1973); Juliet Flower MacCannell, *Figuring Lacan: Criticism and the Cultural Unconscious* (Lincoln: University of Nebraska Press, 1986), p. 22.

21. Josué V. Harari, ed., *Textual Strategies: Perspectives in Post-Structuralist Criticism* (Ithaca: Cornell University Press, 1979).

22. Jacques-Alain Miller, "Introductory Remarks," at a conference called "The Reception of Post-Structuralism in Anglophone and Francophone Canada," May 10–13, 1984, University of Ottawa.

23. Martin Jay, quoted in Winkler, "Post-Structuralism," *Chronicle*, p. A7.

24. MacCannell, *Figuring Lacan*, p. 20.

25. Ibid., p. 174, n1.

26. Gregory Ulmer, "Textshop for Psychoanalysis: On De-Programing Freshmen Platonists," *College English* 49:7 (Nov. 1987): 768–69.

27. Jacques Lacan, "Lituraterre," *Ornicar?* 41 (Spring 1987): 5–13; appeared initially in *Littérature* (*Larousse*) 3 (1971).

28. Stuart Schneiderman, "Affects," *Acts of the Paris-New York Psychoanalytic Workshop: 1986* (New York: Schneiderman Press, 1987), pp. 7–8.

29. Winkler, "Post-Structuralism," *Chronicle*, p. A8.

30. Jacques-Alain Miller, "How Psychoanalysis Cures According to Lacan," *Newsletter of the Freudian Field* 1:2 (Fall 1987): 15.

31. Jacques Lacan, "The Mirror Stage as Formative of the Function of

the I as Revealed in Psychoanalytic Experience," in *Ecrits: A Selection*, trans. Sheridan, pp. 1–7.

32. M. Dongier, "Memories of Jacques Lacan (1901–1981)," unpublished paper. Dongier concludes: "Even dead, Lacan remains an open question . . ., not only as a French phenomenon, but at the international level as well. Was he only a sleight of hand, magician of the verb, or also a genial, creative scientist, contemporary socratist who has been maybe the first one to rediscover, expand and deepen Freud's work?"

33. Donald Winnicott, *Playing and Reality* (New York: Basic Books, 1971), pp. 111, 117.

34. Otto Kernberg, *Borderline Conditions and Pathological Narcissism* (New York: Jason Aronson, 1975), cited in Dongier, "Memories," p. 2.

35. Barbara Jones Guetti, review of *The Resistance to Theory* by Paul de Man, *South Atlantic Review* 52:4 (Nov. 1987): 110–14.

36. See the journals springing up internationally and inscribing themselves within the Freudian Field, as well as the International *Rencontres*.

37. Gregory Jay, "The Subject of Pedagogy: Lessons in Psychoanalysis and Politics," *College English* 49:7 (Nov. 1987): 786.

38. See *Le Séminaire de Jacques Lacan, Livre* XX: *Encore* (1972–73), texte établi par Jacques-Alain Miller (Paris: Seuil, 1975), esp. "A Jakobson," pp. 19–28. See also Ellie Ragland-Sullivan, "Psychoanalysis and Pedagogy: A Discourse of Love," forthcoming in *College English*, special issue ed. R. C. Davis.

39. Jacques Lacan, "Le Séminaire de Jacques Lacan: Le savoir du psychanalyste" (1971–72), 4 Nov. 1971, unpublished.

40. Jacques-Alain Miller, "Lacan (Jacques)," *Encyclopaedia Universalis* 18 (1980): 111.

41. Jean-Jacques Bouquier, Nathalie Charraud, Geneviève Morel, "Ella Sharpe, 1875–1947: L'Esprit de la lettre," *Ornicar?* 38 (Fall 1986): 138. See also Jacques Lacan, "Le Temps logique et l'assertion de certitude anticipée," *Écrits* (Paris: Seuil, 1966).

42. Milan Balazic, "Slovénie: un moment crucial," *L'Âne* 32 (Oct.–Dec. 1987): 45–46.

43. In "Affects" Stuart Schneiderman says: "Truth does not lie at the level of the affects; quite the contrary, the truth is the desire" (p. 7).

44. Jacques Lacan, "Kant avec Sade" (1962), *Écrits*, pp. 765–90.

45. Jacques-Alain Miller, "Suture (elements of the logic of the signifier)," *Screen* 18:4 (Winter 1977–78): 26.

46. Bernard Sichère, *Le Moment Lacanien* (Paris: Bernard Grasset, 1983), p. 42.
47. Jacques Lacan, *Le Séminaire de Jacques Lacan, Livre III: Les psychoses* (1955–56), texte établi par Jacques-Alain Miller (Paris: Seuil, 1981).
48. Russell Grigg, "The Function of the Father in Psychoanalysis," *Australian Journal of Psychotherapy* 5:2 (1986): 120.
49. Ellie Ragland-Sullivan, "Les Origines de la psychose: La 'Forclusion' lacanienne," in *Folie, Mystique et Poésie* (Québec: Collection Noeuds, 1988).
50. Jacques Lacan, "Introduction to the Names-of-the-Father Seminar," *October* 40 (Spring 1987): 82.
51. Jacques Lacan, "The Subversion of the Subject and the Dialectic of Desire in the Freudian Unconscious," in *Écrits: A Selection*, trans. Sheridan, p. 315.
52. *October/Ornicar?*, pp. 106–7.
53. Anthony Wilden, *System and Structure: Essays in Communication and Exchange* (London: Tavistock, 1972), pp. 5–6.
54. Anthony Wilden, *Man and Woman, War and Peace: The Strategist's Companion* (New York: Routledge & Kegan Paul, 1987), p. 217.
55. Anika Lemaire, *Jacques Lacan*, trans. David Macey (London: Routledge & Kegan Paul, 1977), pp. xiv–xv.
56. Jacques Lacan, "Le Séminaire de Jacques Lacan, Livre XXI: Les Non-dupes errent" (1974–75), 15 Jan. 1974, unpublished.
57. Ibid.
58. Lacan, *Télévision, October/Ornicar?*, pp. 44–45.
59. Lacan, "Les Non-dupes errent."
60. Jacques-Alain Miller, "A and a in Clinical Structures," *Acts of the Paris-New York Psychoanalytic Workshop: 1986*, pp. 16–17.
61. Lemaire, *Jacques Lacan*, p. xiv.
62. Jacques-Alain Miller, "How Psychoanalysis Cures According to Lacan," lecture given at Paris-Chicago Psychoanalytic Workshop, in *Newsletter of the Freudian Field* 1:2 (Fall 1987).
63. Lemaire, *Jacques Lacan*; see pp. 96–131.
64. Jonathan Culler, "On Deconstruction," Spring 1987 lecture, University of Florida, Gainesville.
65. Elizabeth Wright, *Psychoanalytic Criticism: Theory in Practice* (London: Metheun, 1984); see Ch. 8, "Post-structural Psychoanalysis: Text as Psyche."
66. MacCannell, *Figuring Lacan*, p. 24.
67. Ibid., p. 98.
68. Jacques Lacan, *Le Séminaire de Jacques Lacan, Livre VII: L'Éthique*

de la psychanalyse (1959–60), texte établi par Jacques-Alain Miller (Paris: Seuil, 1986), p. 145.

69. Richard Macksey and Eugenio Donato, eds., *The Structuralist Controversy: The Languages of Criticism and the Sciences of Man* (Baltimore: Johns Hopkins University Press, 1970).

70. Gilles Deleuze and Félix Guattari, *Capitalisme et schizophrénie: l'Anti-Oedipe* (Paris: Minuit, 1972).

71. Jean-François Lyotard, *The Postmodern Condition: A Report on Knowledge,* trans G. Bennington and B. Massumi (Minneapolis: University of Minnesota Press, 1984).

72. Gilles Deleuze, "The Schizophrenic and Language: Surface and Depth in Lewis Carroll and Antonin Artaud," in Harari, ed., *Textual Strategies,* p. 277. Deleuze's essay is taken from his book *Logique du sens* (Paris: Minuit, 1969), pp. 89–90.

73. Deleuze, "Schizophrenic," p. 278.

74. Ibid., p. 280.

75. Ellie Ragland-Sullivan, *Jacques Lacan and the Philosophy of Psychoanalysis* (Urbana: University of Illinois Press, 1986), pp. 69–89.

76. Stuart Schneiderman, *Returning to Freud: Clinical Psychoanalysis in the School of Lacan* (New Haven: Yale University Press, 1980), p. 9.

77. Deleuze, "Schizophrenic," p. 294.

78. Lacan, *L'Éthique,* p. 146.

79. Jacques Lacan, *Le Séminaire de Jacques Lacan, Livre XI: Les Quatre Concepts Fondamentaux* (1964), texte établi par Jacques-Alain Miller (Paris: Seuil, 1973), pp. 199–200.

80. Lacan, *L'Éthique,* p. 146.

81. Jacques Lacan, *Le Séminaire de Jacques Lacan, Livre II: Le Moi dans la théorie de Freud et dans la technique de la psychanalyse* (1954–55), texte établi par Jacques-Alain Miller (Paris: Seuil, 1978), pp. 207–27.

82. Peter Brooks, "Freud's Masterplot," *Yale French Studies* 55/56 (1977): 296.

83. Christopher Norris, *The Deconstructive Turn: Essays in the Rhetoric of Philosophy* (New York: Metheun, 1983).

84. "The transferential structure of reading, as deconstructive criticism has come to analyze it, involves a compulsion to repeat independent of the psychology of individual critics, based on a curious complicity of reading and writing," says Jonathan Culler in *On Deconstruction* (Ithaca: Cornell University Press, 1982), p. 272. Culler's many references are to Barbara Johnson's *The Critical Difference: Essays*

in the Contemporary Rhetoric of Reading (Baltimore: Johns Hopkins University Press, 1980).

85. Culler, *On Deconstruction,* p. 162.

86. Jacques Derrida, *L'Écriture et la différance* (Paris: Seuil, 1967), pp. 203, 303.

87. Jacques Lacan, "Le Séminaire de Jacques Lacan, Livre X: L'Angoisse," (1962–63), unpublished.

88. Muller and Richardson, *Purloined Poe,* p. 160.

89. Alice Jardine, *Gynesis: Configurations of Woman and Modernity* (Ithaca: Cornell University Press, 1985), p. 11.

90. Ibid., p. 178.

91. Jacques Lacan, "Seminar of 21 January 1975," in *Feminine Sexuality,* ed. Juliet Mitchell and Jacqueline Rose (New York: Norton, 1982), pp. 162–71.

92. Jane Gallop, "Keys to Dora," in *In Dora's Case: Freud—Hysteria—Feminism,* ed. Charles Bernheimer and Claire Kahane (New York: Columbia University Press, 1985), p. 219.

93. Mitchell and Rose, *Feminine Sexuality,* p. 171; Lacan, *Scilicet* 6/7 (1976): 56.

94. Paul Ricoeur, *De l'interprétation: Essai sur Freud* (Paris: Seuil, 1965), p. 7.

95. Joseph H. Smith and William Kerrigan, eds., *Interpreting Lacan* (New Haven: Yale University Press, 1983), pp. xiv–xv. Kerrigan says the boom began with an issue of *Yale French Studies* on "the French Freud," in 1976 (p. xiv). The correct date is 1972.

96. Paul Ricoeur, *Freud and Philosophy,* trans. Denis Savage (New Haven: Yale University Press, 1970), p. 8.

97. Michel Tort, "De l'interprétation ou la machine herméneutique," *Les Temps Modernes* 237 (Feb. 1966): 1461–93 and 238 (March 1966): 1629–52; 1472.

98. MacCannell, *Figuring Lacan,* p. 24. See also E. Roudinesco on Ricoeur, in *La Bataille de cent ans.*

99. Tort, *De l'interprétation,* p. 1472.

100. Paul Ricoeur, *La Métaphore vive* (Paris: Seuil, 1975). Although Lacan's contribution to *La Psychanalyse et sciences de l'homme* ("L'instance de la lettre dans l'inconscient ou la raison depuis Freud") was first delivered at the Sorbonne in 1957 and printed in the *Écrits* in 1966, Ricoeur uses Lacan's theory of a split in metaphor without ever referring directly to this essay. "Between philosophy and metaphor, an implication of a completely other kind comes to light, which connects them at the level of their hidden presuppositions rather than at that of their declared intentions" (p. 357).

Ricoeur attributes his theory to Nietzsche and calls it a "genealogical" way to interrogate philosophers. In footnote #2 he honors Lacoue-Labarthe and Jean-Luc Nancy and Sarah Kofman for their work on Nietzsche and metaphor, thereby allying himself with those thinkers who attack Lacan indirectly through Lacoue-Labarthe and Nancy, usually making some reference to their book on Lacan, *Le Titre de la lettre* (Paris: Galilée, 1973).

101. Malcom Bowie, *Freud, Proust and Lacan* (Cambridge: Cambridge University Press, 1987).

102. See Shoshana Felman, *La Folie et la chose littéraire* (Paris: Seuil, 1978); also Gregory Ulmer, "Sounding the Unconscious," in *Glassary* (Lincoln: University of Nebraska Press, 1986), pp. 23–113.

103. Jacques Lacan, "Jeunesse de Gide ou la lettre et le désir" (1958), *Écrits* (Paris: Seuil, 1966), p. 739.

104. Fredric Jameson, *The Political Unconscious* (Ithaca: Cornell University Press, 1981).

105. John Miller, "Jacques Lacan's Télévision," *Artscribe* 66 (Nov./Dec. 1987): 41.

106. Shoshana Felman, "Turning the Screw of Interpretation," *Yale French Studies* 55/56 (1977): 137.

107. John Miller, *Artscribe*, p. 41.

108. Jacques Lacan, "L'Angoisse," 12 juin 1963, unpublished.

109. Gilles Deleuze, *Différance et répétition* (Paris: PUF, 1968); see also Neil Hertz, "Freud and the Sandman," in Harari, ed., *Textual Strategies*, pp. 320–21.

110. Ragland-Sullivan, *Jacques Lacan and the Philosophy of Psychoanalysis*, pp. 110–29.

111. Edward Said, *The World, the Text, the Critic* (Cambridge: Harvard University Press, 1983); Michael Ryan, *Marxism and Deconstruction: A Critical Introduction* (Baltimore: Johns Hopkins University Press, 1982), p. 104; Robert Con Davis, in *MLN* 98:5 (Dec. 1983): 854–55.

112. Frank Lentricchia, *Criticism and Social Change* (Chicago: University of Chicago Press, 1983).

113. Sherry Turkle, *Psychoanalytic Politics: Freud's French Revolution* (New York: Basic Books, 1978), p. 247.

114. John Miller, *Artscribe*, p. 40.

115. Jacques-Alain Miller, *Entretien*, p. 59.

RICHARD A. BARNEY

Paul de Man and
the Legacy of Suspicion

> A statement of distrust is neither true nor false: it is rather
> in the nature of a permanent hypothesis.
> —Paul de Man[1]

> None suspected language more than Paul de Man.
> —Shoshana Felman[2]

Paul de Man's suspicion of language, which underlies
his untiring exposition of its elusive movements, insinuates itself
between the two poles of what Kierkegaard defines as "doubt"
and "irony." The doubting perceiver or subject, says Kierkegaard,
"is witness to a war of conquest in which every phenomenon is
destroyed, because the essence always resides behind the phenomenon." But with irony, "the subject constantly retires from the
field and proceeds to talk every phenomenon out of its reality in
order to save himself, that is, in order to preserve himself in his
negative independence of everything."[3] De Man is clearly no war-
rior in quest of essences, but when he says that truth is the "negative

A Prefatory Note: This essay was written before the recent news of Paul
de Man's contribution to anti-Semitic newspapers such as *Le Soir* during
the early 1940s. That revelation now puts an odd twist on my argument,
but to consider that fact in full would entail an entirely different essay.
Saving that discussion for another occasion, I have attempted instead, at
the end of this essay, to outline some general strategies for contending
with the problem of de Man's "collaborationist" past.

knowledge of error,"[4] he suggests what is his own kind of ironic doubt or doubtful irony. If error can be isolated and analyzed, then at least some measure of truth is required: de Man, for instance, often refers to the "true" rhetorical structure of texts. Such knowledge, however, is inevitably "negative knowledge," because it must avail itself of language, that medium whose tropological dimension enables the construction of descriptive statements at the same time that it also prevents them from acquiring full referentiality or truth. Ever aware of this difficulty, de Man writes with both aphoristic conviction and self-distancing irony about philosophy, literature, literary theory, and criticism.

This strange quality of de Man's work—what Barbara Johnson calls its "rigorous unreliability"[5]—creates the uncanny sense that perhaps it anticipates the ways other writers have responded to his arguments. That pattern suggests itself in the context of de Man's claim that a text (in this case, a commentary on de Man) can be considered as the structural and often thematic disfiguration of a proper name (here, "de Man") central to that text. When William Pritchard, for instance, implicitly portrays de Man as the high priest of a new form of critical occultation, might not that characterization emerge from the rubric that deconstruction is "de Manic"? In Frank Lentricchia's case, when he calls de Man the "godfather" of the Yale mafia, his discussion could very well issue from the Anglicized version of de Man's name: "the Man"—an underworld figure with tremendous, if not dangerous, authority.[6] These somewhat playful possibilities in fact pose serious exemplary instances that are momentarily chastening, for they indicate that no attempt to evaluate de Man's work—even sympathetically—can avoid some kind of (dis)figural misreading. With that in mind, I want to consider what has become of de Man's work since his death in 1983, and what consequences his deconstructive suspicion might have in the future.

The Problem of Reading

Although de Man's work is by no means synonymous with the development of deconstructive criticism in the United States, he was by far its most influential American practitioner. He began exploring such issues in essays written in the late 1960s and later published in *Blindness and Insight* (1971), but it was in *Allegories of Reading* (1979), a collection of pieces composed during the 1970s, that de Man articulated most cogently the nature of his approach. Though he always rejected the possibility that his arguments formed a coherent method, they have at least provided a powerful set of reading tactics and strategies.

In *Allegories of Reading*, de Man characterizes philosophical, political, and literary texts as the inevitable interference of rhetoric and grammar. In this view the rhetorical level of a text, its configuration of tropes and figures of speech, constitutes the grammatical level; and yet, because it follows its own unpredictable rules of patterning, rhetoric in the end disrupts the possibility of grammatical coherence, whose main features would be logicality and unambiguous reference. Since it participates in both processes, rhetoric is profoundly indeterminate, its function describable but never coming to rest. De Man approaches this problem in terms of *reading*, a process that pinpoints a text's (sometimes implicit) claims about the function of language, and then works away at crucial nodes of textual resistance that in turn undo those larger claims. But since this reading strategy itself must be enacted in language, it too is subject to the same analysis or displacement. As de Man puts it, "the paradigm for all texts consists of a figure (or a system of figures) and its deconstruction. But since this model cannot be closed off by a final reading, it engenders, in its turn, a supplementary figural superposition which narrates the unreadability of the prior narration. As distinguished from primary deconstructive narratives centered on figures . . . we can call such narratives to the second (or the third) degree *allegories*. Allegorical narratives tell the story of the failure to read whereas tropological narratives . . . tell the story of the failure to denominate" (*AR*, 205). Primary or first-degree deconstructions, then, present the possibility of genuine doubt, which in this case would get at the fundamental configurations of textual rhetoric. But this confidence must soon give way to the irony of allegory, which reveals—and temporarily removes itself from—the rhetorical error that accompanies deconstructive truth.

This two-part approach has largely characterized de Man's influence on his colleagues, students, and advocates,[7] and it helps distinguish between the perceived value of his work and Derrida's.

If Derrida seems to be the invidious philosopher who analyzes philosophical texts in literary critical fashion, then de Man is the critic who reformulates a vocabulary of philology for the purposes of linguistic description; if Derrida is the experimenter in seductive stylistics and new ways of writing, then de Man is the staunch theorist who persistently pursues a more circumscribed mode of reading; if Derrida poses as the playful speculator in textuality, then de Man is the exacting technician. Such a contrast is clearly overdrawn, since Derrida has his own kind of analytical rigor, and de Man also employs sudden leaps of argumentative logic, as well as hypothetical generalizations whose documentation appears less important than their heuristic value. It does help to suggest, however, why de Man's work has had an extremely strong appeal for American critics in departments of language and literature, which have historically had a strong affiliation with the disciplines of philology and linguistics.

The shock waves created by the recent news of de Man's political past have provoked an entirely different focus in the reception of his work; even before that shift, however, de Man's rhetorical approach has had to weather a new phase in the fortunes of post-structuralist or deconstructive thinking in the United States, a phase initiated in part by the dissolution of the so-called Yale School. Since de Man's unfortunate death in 1983, Barbara Johnson has moved to Harvard and J. Hillis Miller to the University of California at Irvine. Geoffrey Hartman, despite his enthusiastic forays in deconstruction, has declared his uneasiness with its tactics, espousing instead " 'saving the phenomena' of words."[8] Harold Bloom—who Hartman himself has said was "barely" a deconstructor—has recently been adamant in disclaiming any status as a deconstructionist.[9] Although the Yale critics did not actually compose a coherent "school" or intellectual front, they did constitute an institutional vanguard that served as the instigator and focus of heated debates about deconstructive practice in general. With that focal point gone, the controversy seems to have cooled, because opponents of deconstruction have had their say and are now turning their attention to other matters. Though there have been recent attacks by Nathan Scott and John Ellis,[10] M. H. Abrams seems to offer the most characteristic example: "Despite immersion in the deconstructive element of our time," he observes,

"I remain an unreconstructed humanist."[11] On the other hand, the discussion of deconstruction's merits has also abated, ironically enough, because of its institutional success. Deconstruction has now become an academic specialty, thereby gaining the accompanying institutional amenities: designated teaching positions, courses, and specially earmarked journals. With that gain, however, deconstruction is no longer a more or less troublesome outsider that captures everyone's attention, but instead a newcomer that must come to terms with its disciplinary goals and more isolated professional status.[12]

Even given this situation, de Man's work has continued to be actively published, read, and discussed. Two books have appeared posthumously, *The Rhetoric of Romanticism* (1984) and *The Resistance to Theory* (1986), and the University of Minnesota Press plans two more volumes of collected essays in the near future.[13] There is no better evidence of the tremendous impact de Man continues to have than the special issue of *Yale French Studies* entitled *The Lesson of Paul de Man* (1985), which contains twenty-nine contributions by various students, colleagues, and peers.[14] This volume has three main sections: the first is a selection of tributes offered at de Man's memorial service; the second, entitled "Reading de Man," consists of evaluations of his work; and the third, called "Reading with de Man," includes essays that analyze various texts with a de Manian perspective. It is a collection that is both moving and provocative, especially since it gathers together some of the most intelligent commentary on de Man's work.

The third and longest section of the volume is indicative of how de Man's approach might be used in the future. Despite the general high quality of these essays, however, they remain troubling because many of the contributors come extremely close to taking the de Manian process of reading for granted. Some seem to conclude, as does E. S. Burt, that de Man has provided a set of analytic instruments that can be systematically applied. Burt claims that de Man's treatment of autobiography "legitimates the study of autobiography [as] . . . the objective expression of a linguistic predicament," and has thus "made it possible to study autobiography with the rigor of a critical method."[15] (As if to underscore the fact that this conclusion can be assumed, Burt places it in a footnote.) Even those contributors who do not make such large claims for de Man tend to take his reading strategy as a given. This manifests itself partly by the fact that, in "reading with de Man," they make few, if any, comments concerning how his hypotheses are appropriate or in need of revision for their particular angle of attack. J. Hillis Miller is an exception to that general pattern, since he spends considerable time discussing his problematic relationship with de Man's work. But his essay is also particularly instructive because it presents a sophisticated and paradoxical version of the problem I have described. After considering the possibility of honoring de Man's memory and work by a vigorous return to read his essays, Miller suggests instead that perhaps the best way to honor de Man is by emulating his practice of a one-on-one confrontation with a text. Trying to apply or borrow from de Man's arguments, claims Miller, faces the "inevitability of falsifying de Man's work"; he advocates instead submitting to "the isolation of each act of reading," where "each critic in the work of reading is on his or her own, face to face with a text, alone with it, never so alone as at that moment."[16]

When Miller then turns to consider Wallace Stevens's poem "The Red Fern," he nevertheless finds there a textual configuration that is all too familiar. Miller finds that the poem's central metaphor of the sun renders interpretation "impossible" at two levels. First, it initiates a series of metaphors that indicate "the unsettling freedom of language from perception" (IM, 156). This interpretive disjunction, he argues, is followed by "the inability of the critic to read and draw lessons from his own act of reading": "The reader's insight into this first unreadability, the one at the level I have called interpretation, is powerless to prevent in the act of deconstruction it performs the repetition of the errors it denounces" (IM, 161). To be sure, Miller's reading of Stevens's poem bears the stamp of his own keen critical acumen and subtlety, but in effect, he has come around to the position he initially—or at least hypothetically—put aside. As he says himself in the concluding sentence, "Certainly my own procedures here would . . . confirm once more that 'impossibility of reading' which Paul de Man says should not be taken too lightly" (IM, 162).

Paradoxically, then, turning away from de Man ends up reaffirming his claims all the more. This is only possible, however, by a thoroughgoing objectification or phenomenalization of the deconstructive reading process. I do not want to argue with Miller about the entangled question of whether such aspects are in fact *in* a text, or whether they are produced by a deconstructive approach. The more important point is why Miller finds the objectification of reading so compelling, because he has continued to emphasize it in his more recent work. In Miller's presidential address to the MLA in 1986, for example, the stakes are extremely high, because Miller's aim is to persuade a diverse audience of professional readers that deconstruction has crucial value for the profession at large. He argues in powerful, nearly urgent tones that deconstruction has a critical role to play in the recent turn to historical, political, and institutional contexts. Miller supports that new focus, "but not," he says, "when it takes the form of an exhilarating experience of liberation from the obligation to read, carefully, patiently, with nothing taken for granted beforehand."[17] Since he suggests that deconstruction involves precisely such salutary attentiveness to what really happens in reading, this characterization is bracing, if not a bit uncanny. In these terms, deconstruction now provides a sober and constraining context in which the supposed newcomers—history, culture, politics—can proceed in provisional but responsible fashion. For Miller, then, rhetorical or deconstructive reading should be the first basis for shifting literary critical or theoretical attention to other areas. That is why he proposes as our first task the analysis of the figures of speech by which historical arguments establish the connective links between texts and their material contexts. Miller makes an eloquent case for the usefulness of rhetorical reading for historical study, but it is not clear that he must do so by insisting that deconstruction should be seen as the approach to reading that—in contrast with other self-promoting perspectives—takes "nothing . . . for granted beforehand."[18]

This difficulty is not only Miller's. De Man himself often had the tendency to make sweeping claims suggesting a systematic method or the obvious objectivity of the reading process. Despite that tendency, and the fact that his work as a whole exhibits remarkable consistencies, de Man was also acutely aware that general claims are only temporarily enabling, and he constantly scrutinized, emended, and made ironic his own proclivity for systematization or objectivization. He warns, for instance, that because it is such an entangled process, "reading can never be taken for granted."[19] In his discussion of Shelley's *Triumph of Life*, de Man concludes further that "reading as disfiguration . . . turns out to be historically more reliable than the products of historical archeology. To monumentalize this observation into a *method* of reading would be to regress from the rigor exhibited by Shelley which is exemplary precisely because it refuses to be generalized into a system" (*RR*, 123). Even here, however, de Man's endorsement of nonsystematic procedures sounds strongly formulaic. In other words, the point is not that Burt, Miller, or others get de Man wrong, or that they do not do what he did well enough, but that de Man's position with respect to method seems ambivalent. This issue is crucial because it touches on two developments in literary and theoretical study that will have much to say about the future of deconstruction. One, as Miller has already indicated, is the renewed interest in historical and political approaches to literature. The other is the response of philosophical pragmatism, the new theoretical kid on the block that claims to be a friend of deconstruction while also posing as its adversary. Before considering these areas, however, I want to endeavor a brief meditation on de Man's remarks concerning the limits of reading and language. His response to those limits can help clarify his relation to method, as well as situate the new claims for pragmatic or historical perspectives.

De Man and the Limits of Language

Derrida has astutely noted that de Man's work is "traversed by an insistent reflection on mourning, a meditation in which bereaved memory is deeply engraved" (*M*, 22). De Man's reflection on this human response to loss or deprivation—in short, the inevitable event of death—constitutes his own singular version of mournful contemplation. "Death," as he blankly puts it, "is a displaced name for a linguistic predicament" (*RR*, 81)—a predicament constituted by implacable limits to the construction of meaning, or by the irreparable disruption of semiotic reference to the world. De Man discerns this pattern particularly in those genres most strenuously attempting to contain mortality by means of consolation or renewal, especially the epitaph, elegy, autobiography, and Romantic lyric.

For de Man, the hallmark of such forms is the persistent and urgent anthropomorphization of what cannot in fact be reclaimed for human utility. Most frequently this gesture appears in the figure of prosopopoeia, "the fiction of an apostrophe to an absent, deceased, or voiceless entity, which posits the possibility of the latter's reply and confers upon it the power of speech" (*RR*, 75–76). Such a gesture is condemned to ultimate failure, however, even in terms of discursive continuity, because of what de Man calls "the deadly negative power invested" in tropes (*RR*, 247). That power is in large part due to the suspicion de Man shares with Walter Benjamin that language is in fact a *non*human mechanism that does not fully respond to authorial manipulation.[20] The vacillations of tropes are only the most obvious manifestation of that linguistic condition. While acknowledging that his own work is also subject to this rule of discursive Thanatos, de Man chooses a different response:

> Generic terms such as "lyric" (or its various sub-species, "ode," "idyll," or "elegy") as well as pseudo-historical period terms such as "romanticism" or "classicism" are always terms of resistance and nostalgia, at the furthest remove from the materiality of actual history. If mourning is called a "chambre d'éternel deuil où vibrent de vieux râles," [chamber of eternal mourning where the old deathrattle resonates] then this pathos of terror states in fact the desired consciousness of eternity and of temporal harmony. . . . True "mourning" is less deluded. The most *it* can do is allow for noncomprehension and enumerate non-anthropomorphic, non-elegiac, non-celebratory, non-lyrical, non-poetic, that is to say, prosaic, or better, *historical* modes of language power. (*RR*, 262)

Later in this essay I want to consider the implications of this passage in more detail. For the moment, it is striking that de Man is assured enough to declare that the perspectives of traditional historicism or elegiac mourning are remote from "the materiality of actual history," while of course his own hypotheses concerning the inaccessibility of referential knowledge must apply equally strongly to his own preference for prosaic stoicism.

This paradox, of course, is related to de Man's double gesture of doubt and irony, and it gives his work a curious fascination even for those who are not entirely convinced by his critical or theoretical conclusions. Readers come back to his texts again and again to watch his arguments play themselves out, even when they know in advance what the result of his discussion will be—that figural language will ensure the demise of coherent meaning, or that in addition even his own staunch analyses are subject to the same fate. De Man's arguments are consistently interesting and challenging, no matter what his topic, and this explains in part why even unpersuaded readers repeatedly return to consider them. But his focus on the mortality of language also resonates powerfully with what seems to be our late twentieth-century preoccupation with death in general—a preoccupation that takes many forms, the most predominant, perhaps, being our dread of nuclear annihilation. In the humanities, to cite only a few instances, we have witnessed the putative "death of the author," the "ends of man," the possibility of "nuclear criticism," Derrida's experiments with apocalyptic discourse, and, in another context, what J. H. Plumb calls the "death of the past."[21] In the culture at large, we protest death with the fervor of physical exercise and the rituals of diet, while also denouncing the threat of a nuclear blast. But our films, our media, and our literature have also fixed on the possibility of massive calamity—whether personal, ecological, or political—with manic (if not de Manic) fascination. The subculture of "new wave" and "hardcore" music is perhaps the most unsettling instance, because it not only celebrates the power of death, but brandishes it with visceral aggression.

De Man, of course, never explicitly related his work to any of these cultural phenomena, though (as in the case of Barthes, Derrida, and others) the concept of authorial intention was a casualty of his theoretical position. His focus on linguistic mortality does not merely pose another manifestation of a coherent cultural pattern, any more than it can be summarily attributed to his reflection, during the last years of his life, on his own impending death. De Man himself surmised that, even in his most obvious shifts in critical approach, he was probably only "restating, in a slightly different mode, earlier and unresolved obsessions" (*BI*, xii), and he was thoroughly familiar, from the very beginning, with the theme of death in the work of Sartrean existentialists and of Heidegger.[22] In any case, de Man's work has touched a mortal nerve in his readers, and, given the cultural scenario I have described, it will probably continue to do so in the future. De Man's analyses may be even more disturbing because they describe death not as the potential result of political antagonism combined with technological know-how, but as the consequence of a more pervasive human circumstance—an inexorable dependence on the machinations of language.

If our fate as speaking and writing subjects is always the fragmentary and the unreadable, why, from de Man's point of view, do we go on? In a sense, de Man could never answer this question satisfactorily: his answer to a great extent may simply be the fact that he wrote, and that he did so persistently, rather than what he said. But his work nevertheless suggests some possible responses. One, of course, is that we are always inmates in the prison-house of language, without the chance of a reprieve or even parole. As de Man repeatedly emphasizes, language consistently posits the goal of reference, logicality, and coherence: in that sense, we cannot *not* attempt to find truth or at least momentarily grasp meaning. Why then work in the discipline of language and literature, when the apparent life of those things—meaning or truth— is always and already fatally wounded? De Man's response is that traditional approaches have avoided for too long the indeterminacy of figural language, creating in its place the illusion of lyrical or historical continuity. He chooses instead salutary opposition. As he puts it, "it is better to fail in teaching what should not be taught than to succeed in teaching what is not true" (*RT*, 4). Similarly, deciding not to engage in literary theory because of its inherent limitations is as inconceivable, says de Man, as "rejecting anatomy because it has failed to cure mortality" (*RT*, 12). The struggle with language—challenging and exhilarating as it may be—is, like life, destined to the moment of final separation. The only alternative, however, would be to accept silence, nonmeaning, or death all the sooner by acquiescing, by not staying in the struggle.

This comes perilously close to portraying de Man as the courageous critic striving against all the odds, when in contrast he emphasizes unblinking, if not unperturbed, composure: "To read is to understand, to question, to know, to forget, to erase, to deface, to repeat—that is to say, the endless prosopopoeia by which the dead are made to have a face and a voice which tells the allegory of their demise and allows us to apostrophize them in our turn.

No degree of knowledge can ever stop this madness, for it is the madness of words. What *would* be naive is to believe that this strategy . . . can be a source of value and has to be celebrated or denounced accordingly" (*RR*, 122). Despite his apparent indifference, however, Shoshana Felman persuasively points out de Man's "self-denying pathos," his initial impulse for more traditional approaches to texts that he then stoically restrains and turns against itself.[23] Even in one of his last lectures, de Man confesses that he "unfortunately" has a proclivity for hermeneutic interpretation, which he then circumvents by way of deconstructive poetics.[24] This self-denial forms a paradoxical part of what might be called the pathos of methodological resistance. It constitutes not only de Man's resistance to tradition, as well as his ironic self-resistance with respect to the aporias of deconstruction, but also his resistance to the deleterious effects of temporality—its effacing process of change and dissolution. Hartman has remarked that de Man was a critic "who had the most resistance to time"; at its strongest, this impulse is what Derrida identifies as de Man's desire "to win time, to win over time, to deny it . . . but in a non-dialectical fashion."[25] As de Man himself admits, his own methodological claims concerning the "madness of words" are made "all the more pious by their denial of piety" (*RR*, 122). This pious resistance can best account for de Man's aphoristic bravura, his sweeping conclusions which, in the case of describing literary theory, would apply "at all times, at whatever historical moment one wishes to select" (*RT*, 12). Hence part of the legacy of de Man's penchant for analytical rigor—though presumably always subject to ironic displacement—is the tendency of Miller and his deconstructive counterparts to rely on general claims concerning the objective nature of reading.

Pragmatism, Rorty, and Deconstruction

Richard Rorty, one of pragmatism's foremost spokesmen, wants to consider de Man and other deconstructionists his "natural allies," though he remains critical of their tendency for programmatic assertions.[26] Rorty in fact has made only passing references to de Man in print, perhaps because he does not want to erode the support de Man's position can provide. He has, however, commented on de Man's work in various lectures and seminars, and his views also come to light in his remarks about "Derrideans" and "textualists."[27] Whatever Rorty's perspective on deconstruction, it is likely to carry considerable weight in the future, not only because pragmatism in general has captured the support of a growing number of critics—including Stanley Fish, Steven Knapp, Walter Benn Michaels, and Adena Rosmarin—but also because Rorty is extremely sympathetic to writers in the post-structuralist vein. Rorty has been especially appealing because of his facility in dealing with Continental philosophy, while also employing a straightforward clarity characteristic of the Anglo-American tradition.

Perhaps the best way to get at Rorty's opinion of de Man and American deconstruction is to start with his views on Derrida. For Rorty, Derrida's work falls into two distinct parts: on the one hand, there is the "good side" of Derrida, his attempt to leave behind the tradition of Western metaphysics by way of experimental writing, playful puns and neologisms, and enigmatic formulations. By deploying new ways of writing, claims Rorty, Derrida "is suggesting how things might look if we did not have Kantian philosophy built into the fabric of our intellectual life" (*CP*, 98; original emphasis removed). On the other hand, there is the "bad side" of Derrida where he succumbs to the temptation to outargue his philosophical forebears and establish something similar to fundamental rules of language or being. By deconstructing his predecessors and often claiming that there is a prior or "older" condition than they imagine for the advent of language— take, for instance, "iterability"—Derrida comes close to playing the old philosophical game of forming rock-bottom principles.

Rorty rejects the second trajectory of Derrida's work because he believes it will continue to prevent us from getting out from under the looming shadow of Western metaphysics. He asserts that the goals of epistemology—getting things right, demonstrating truth, and so forth—are not only unattainable but also uninteresting. He proposes instead that we try to imagine new ways of talking, and he suggests using the metaphors of conversation rather than argumentation, philosophical "narratives" rather than proofs, and edification rather than indoctrination in truth. Berel Lang has offered an intriguing analogy for avant-garde and postmodern writers that fits the Derridean tendency for philosophical one-upmanship: "Like the jiujitsu wrestler," he says, "they get strength for their throw from their opponent's rush."[28] For his part, Rorty is admonishing us in blunt pragmatic fashion: "Stop the wrestling! Let's try practical conversations rather than metaphysical athletics."

At first sight, de Man easily falls on the bad side of the Derridean spectrum. As we have already noted, de Man has a consistent tendency for general methodological claims, and he persistently focuses on what he calls the "epistemology of metaphor." Perhaps the greatest chasm between de Man's and Rorty's position appears in their view of language. For de Man, the tropes in a text both constitute and inhibit a larger network of fundamental assumptions that are often epistemological or metaphysical, despite an author's best intentions. Rorty retorts in good Wittgensteinian fashion that, as language users, we can in fact choose *not* to participate in such monolithic systems: "The [philosophical] attempt to find a closed and total vocabulary produced lots of great big binary oppositions which poets and essayists and novelists then proceeded to use as tropes. But one can use a trope perfectly well without taking seriously its claim to be part of such a vocabulary."[29]

This would seem to close the case on de Man until we look at Rorty's discussion of "weak textualists" and "strong textualists." The weak textualist, says Rorty, is "only a half-hearted pragmatist. He thinks that there really is a secret code and that once it's discovered we shall have gotten the text right. He believes that criticism is discovery rather than creation. . . . In fact he is just doing his best to imitate science—he wants a *method* of criticism." The strong textualist, in contrast, "doesn't care about the distinction between discovery and creation, finding and making. . . . He is in it for what he can get out of it, not for the satisfaction of getting something right." Like a good pragmatist, "he recognizes . . . that the idea of *method* presupposes that of a *privileged vocabulary*" (CP, 152; Rorty's emphasis). Although de Man's analytical rigor could well qualify him as a weak textualist, that possibility remains unclear. Much earlier in his discussion, Rorty mentions de Man only once as one among many "textualists" in general, but here he will only say that Bloom and Foucault are strong textualists, while refraining—out of tact, or tactics—to name *anyone* as a weak textualist. There is further room for doubt because in some ways de Man could in fact be considered a strong misreader in the terms Rorty describes. Like several of his New Critical predecessors, de Man rejects the pretensions of systematic science. His ironic suspicion, furthermore, is close to the strong textualist's lack of a distinction between discovery and creation: "A statement of distrust," says de Man, "is neither true nor false: it is rather in the nature of a permanent hypothesis" (*AR*, 150). And when he says that making meaning is in an epistemological sense finally arbitrary, the act of linguistic "imposition," de Man is talking very much like a strong textualist.[30] If pressed on this point, Rorty might reluctantly choose to say that de Man is really a weak textualist, though he dresses in strong textualist garb; Rorty's discussion, however, leaves de Man's position somewhat ambiguous.

It is probably not as important to decide the issue one way or the other as to note how de Man's ambivalent status is analogous to the dilemma Rorty finds in Derrida. For Rorty, the two sides of Derrida's work are mutually inextricable. On the one hand, if he sticks to deconstructing philosophical arguments, Derrida risks foundationalist thinking. But on the other, if he forgets philosophy and engages only in textual experimentation, his writing, says Rorty, "loses focus and point" (DC, 8–9). De Man seems similarly caught between making large claims about the nature of language, and simply employing rhetorical analyses because they produce persuasive results. He often describes his approach as a genuinely new way of analyzing the tropological working of texts, but he sometimes also suggests that 'in the end his own analyses must capitulate to the old categories of traditional thought.

This characterization of de Man and Derrida's work is overly schematic, but I think it pinpoints an area that will receive considerable discussion in the future. Jonathan Arac and Christopher Norris, for example, have already contended with Rorty's preference for Derrida's playful experimentation and rejection of epistemology. For Arac and Norris, Derrida retains the possibility of provisional representation and knowledge, which they consider crucial for historical and political analyses. Although Rorty himself is obviously interested in considering historical contexts and institutional practices, they argue that his view of Derrida's work will ultimately undermine useful historical or cultural approaches.[31] Cutting this knot one way or the other will obviously have far-reaching consequences for the way we practice philosophy, literary theory, or criticism in the near future. Since there are far too many possibilities for me to discuss here, I want merely to suggest one way we might consider Rorty's proposals for pragmatism.

It is important to point out that Rorty seems caught in a dilemma very similar to the one that plagues Derrida and de Man. That difficulty can be summed up as a problematic relationship with both the past and the future—a question, you might say, of whether or not to wrestle. Perhaps it is best exemplified by Rorty's use of the evaluative terms "interest" and "edification." When Rorty talks in terms of "interest," our decisions about the value of contending perspectives appear straightforward, if not casual. Since pragmatists, for instance, no longer find interesting the philosophical conversation that has been going on since Plato, says Rorty, "they would simply like to change the subject" (*CP*, xiv). It is a matter of shrugging one's shoulders and doing something else. When Rorty introduces the term "edification," however, the stakes become a great deal higher. Edification invokes concepts of embetterment, education, even the gradual accumulation of valuable accomplishments—all of which are implied when Rorty characterizes human history as a Hegelian *Bildungsroman* (*CP*, 91). To some extent, of course, the measure of edification, like that of interest, is *positional*: what is edifying now would not necessarily have been so in the past. But that does not defuse the strong implication—especially given Rorty's concern with the ethics of his position—that pragmatic edification should in some important sense be morally uplifting.[32] I think that imperative explains why Rorty takes his turn in wrestling with the philosophical tradition, for he too occasionally wants to say that his predecessors got it wrong. He does so, of course, not by claiming that Plato, Heidegger, or others got things wrong in terms of *epistemology*, but by asserting instead that they got things wrong—for us now, in the present—in terms of *edification*. This is a significant shift in the grounds for refuting one's forebears, but it can be an attempt to pin them down just the same. Rorty acknowledges this when he remarks that "we find Hegel, Nietzsche, Heidegger, Derrida, and pragmatical commentators on Derrida like myself jostling for the position of history's first really *radical* anti-Platonist. This somewhat farcical attempt to be ever more un-Platonic has produced the suspicion that, like so many windup dolls, the philosophers of this century are still performing the same tedious inversions which Hegel did to death in the *Phenomenology*" (DC, 11; Rorty's emphasis).

It is here, when he ironically deflates his own grandly conceived radicalism, that Rorty sounds the most like de Man. Like de Man, moreover, as well as Derrida, Rorty is caught between debunking the past once and for all and going about the more modest task of doing something new.[33] That similarity need not create an amorphous lump of their distinct—if not irreconcilable—positions. It does suggest, however, that, in attempting to evaluate the future possibilities of deconstruction or pragmatism, we can benefit by reexamining how their respective advocates contend, appropriate, or affiliate themselves with the past while keeping an eye toward the future. Fixing on that problem could help us decide, among other things, to what extent it might really be possible to overhaul our vocabulary in the thoroughgoing way Rorty recommends. It would mean, in short, renewing our commitment to reflect on the role of history and our place in it, not in terms of wholesale theories or demonstrations, but in terms of specific cases and local narratives. With that in mind, I want to turn to de Man's position with respect to historical writing, because that topic—in addition to the challenge of pragmatism—will no doubt be crucial in the future evaluation and extension of de Man's work.

The Resurgence of History

Almost from the beginning, de Man has been accused of being stubbornly ahistorical. Even when he seems receptive to the aim of writing history, his misgivings quickly seem to withdraw that possibility: in considering the work of young new scholars in the history of Romanticism, de Man says that their project is by no means "doomed from the start . . . but one cannot help but feel somewhat suspicious of their optimism" (*RR*, viii-ix). As we have already seen, de Man claims that his own approach of "true mourning" best accounts for the "materiality of actual history" because it attends to "*historical* modes of language power" (*RR*,

262)—the tropological forms of disjunction and displacement. For de Man, "history" designates the passing of time or temporality, while literary history or historiography is the discourse that attempts to monumentalize or at least unify it. In that context, the word "historical," Hartman notes, "is but a word for 'mortal,' or that which threatens lasting monument or totalizing mind."[34] De Man's resistance to traditional historiography is compounded by what I have called his resistance to the degenerative process of temporality: he momentarily removes himself from both elements by focusing on the preexisting linguistic *condition* for our portrayal of history or the figural vacillations of a text. This is why he emphasizes—especially with respect to irony and allegory—the spontaneous and simultaneous, what he calls "synchronic juxtaposition": irony, he observes, "appears in an instantaneous process that takes place . . . in one single moment"; and "the fundamental structure of allegory," furthermore, appears "in the tendency of the language toward narrative, the spreading out along the axis of an imaginary time in order to give duration to what is, in fact, simultaneous within the subject."[35]

De Man's emphasis on the synchronic has provoked attacks by several critics who in many ways are initially sympathetic with his approach, including Michael Ryan, Gayatri Spivak, Frank Lentricchia, Suzanne Gearheart, and Andrew Parker. Lentricchia, Ryan, and Spivak have criticized de Man's work from a Marxist perspective, and Lentricchia, in *After the New Criticism*, has been the most stringent. Gearheart, like all these commentators, compares de Man unfavorably with Derrida, objecting that de Man consistently privileges textual literariness over historical analysis. Parker, in turn, rejects de Man's view of history in favor of Derrida's, because "rather than granting to history a value (whether positive or negative, 'true' or 'false') of 'its' own, Derrida would twice inscribe the term in a way that privileges neither presence nor absence but posits both."[36] More recently, however, these and other critics have revaluated de Man's position in order to suggest that perhaps it can be shifted or revised for historical or political purposes. In *Criticism and Social Change* (1983), for instance, while still regarding de Man as something of an antagonist, Lentricchia salvages aspects of de Man's rhetorical approach that can be usefully combined with the political commitments of Kenneth

Burke.[37] For their part, Miller and Derrida have vigorously defended de Man's views by arguing that they have always been politically engaged and continue to be socially relevant.[38]

Rather than entering this discussion by defending de Man or comparing him with still another of his contemporaries, I would like instead to consider a crucial aspect of de Man's discussion of historiography—his remarks on the "genetic pattern" of historical writing. That discussion is extremely provocative, because even when he appears to be the most obviously opposed to the way historical texts portray the temporal process, de Man's own arguments rely on a similar pattern. In a sense this is the resurgence—or *in*surgence—of history, and I think it suggests another way of opening out de Man's approach to historical and political contexts.

De Man argues that all historical texts depend on a basic genetic pattern, in which narrative movement is conceived in terms of "teleological intent," whereby the events in the narrative "all spring from a common source and converge toward a common end" (*AR*, 81–83). That convergence is insured by a continuous sequential linkage from beginning to end, in which the events follow a cause-and-effect logic that is modeled—often subtly or obliquely—in terms of genetic filiation. In the clearest manifestation of this paradigm, the historical narrative "resembles a parental structure in which the past is like an ancestor begetting, in a moment of unmediated presence, a future capable of repeating in its turn the same generative process" (*BI*, 164). De Man's general strategy for dismantling this genetic pattern is to find where this reproductive process miscarries, where the tropological level of the historical story disrupts its generational continuity.

Since de Man calls this tactic a "genetic 'deconstruction'" (*AR*, 83), a troubling ambiguity arises in his choice of phrase: Does this deconstruction merely *focus on* the genetic pattern, or might it not also *participate* in its design? This is an important question because it applies not only to de Man's deconstruction of historical texts in particular, but also to his rhetorical analyses as a whole. As we have already seen, de Man persistently locates the synchronic structure of a text that can account for its narrative rhythms of formal (or thematic) consolidation and dissolution. That structure is usually a trope or system of tropes that produces the effects of fluctuation and duration. This description confronts a significant problem, however, since de Man must find a way to explain exactly how these two textual aspects are connected—a connection that turns out, in the end, to resist his deconstructive procedure. De Man most frequently describes that connection—from his earliest essays in *Blindness and Insight* to the more recent ones in *The Rhetoric of Romanticism*—as a causal relation expressed by the metaphors of "generation" and "engendering." To cite only two examples: In "The Rhetoric of Temporality" (1969), de Man says that in Schlegel's work the structure of "irony engenders a temporal sequence of acts of consciousness which is endless" (*BI*, 220). Later, when considering in *Allegories of Reading* (1979) the problem of referentiality, he concludes: "the notions of audience and of narrator that are part of any narrative are only the misleading figuration of a linguistic structure. And just as the indeterminacy of reference generates the illusion of a subject, a narrator, and a reader, it also generates the metaphor of temporality" (*AR*, 162).[39]

The term "generation" captures extremely well the nature of de Man's double bind, because it suggests both the mechanical operation he invokes by characterizing texts as machines, as well as the reproductive function of a genetic process. "Engendering," however, makes the procreative connection all the more emphatic. De Man is aware of his strategic difficulty, because in one instance he calls "engendering" and other such connective terms "aberrant verbal metaphor[s]" (*RR*, 262). But that does not mitigate the fact that a generative linkage insinuates itself at precisely the juncture in de Man's procedure where he is attempting to undo genetic or historicist operations. Still, even if de Man's analyses do in fact exhibit a genetic pattern, that pattern turns out to be substantially different from the usual formulation he criticizes: now, since the "origin" of the narrative is itself multiply constituted and tropological, the resulting sequence is provisional, both in terms of continuity and final end. Rather than simply concluding, therefore, that the genetic paradox in de Man's arguments makes them unreadable, I want to suggest that it can reopen the question of historical writing. In other words, instead of wrestling with de Man, I want to wrest this mutated genetic pattern from his work in order to use it for historical, cultural, and political analyses—but without, in the meantime, arresting the momentum of his rhetorical approach.

Perhaps the best way to characterize this move is as a process of *rewriting* on the analogy of a generic transformation from an epic, elevated mode to a more prosaic, historical one. This approach is similar to Derrida's tactic of rewriting philosophy in the mode of satire or letterwriting, or his secular revision of apocalyptic theology. (Another similar example comes from the eighteenth century, when writers resituated the genres of epic and tragedy within historiographical, domestic, and other lower generic modes.) In this case I want to propose a reconfiguration—or, in rhetorical terms, a refi*gura*tion—of de Man's tendency for near-epic treatment of the process of textual signification, in which we witness the intense struggle of grand dualities such as Truth and Error, Blindness and Insight, Knowledge and Forgetfulness, Life and Death. We would rewrite this scenario by making these epic protagonists more or less equal players (depending on the context or the purpose at hand) with other (prosaic) agents such as historical situation, political environ, institutional practice, and cultural function. This procedure would be analogous to the one de Man finds in Baudelaire's prose revisions of the poems in *Les Fleurs du mal*: "they bring out the prosaic element that shaped the poems in the first place."[40]

Toward the end of his career, de Man had of course already started in the direction of explicitly analyzing ideological and political issues, but he made this move despite considerable reluctance. In an interview with Stefano Rosso in 1983, de Man explained that, although politics had always been "uppermost" in his mind, he had first set himself the task of gaining "control over technical problems of language" (*RT*, 121). Only after achieving that did he feel ready to consider political issues "a little more openly," and he identifies that turning point with his study of Rousseau. His explorations of social and political contexts include his essay on the sublime in Hegel, his discussion in "The Resistance to Theory," and the seminar he taught at the School of Criticism and Theory in 1982 entitled "Rhetoric, Aesthetics, Ideology." Even so, he remained hesitant, because in several of his lectures during this period de Man announced his intent to conduct a substantial study of Marx's work—a study that never materialized, at least not to the extent that he felt ready to present it publicly. De Man explains in his interview with Rosso, in fact, that he made those premature announcements in order to overcome his reluctance: "the fact that I keep announcing that I am going to do something about it is only to force myself to do so, because if I keep saying I'm going do this and I don't do it, I end up looking very foolish. So I have to force myself a little to do this" (RT, 121). In the end, however, hesitation won out.

It is possible, of course, that this lingering reluctance was part of de Man's reaction to the catastrophic consequences of his earlier espousal, when he was in Belgium during the 1940s, of anti-Semitic and pro-German views. The extermination of Belgian Jews, aided in part by the kind of arguments offered by de Man in *Le Soir* and other Belgian newspapers, must have haunted his memory. It may be, then, that the prospect of *any* kind of explicit political stance in his later work remained persistently unnerving—and could explain his emphasis on the unreliability of all ideological constructs. Given the extent of de Man's critical influence and the prominence of deconstruction in the academy, the problem of de Man's past political affiliations will no doubt form a crucial part of the dominating interest now in the "politics of language"—in this case, the possible political implications of de Man's deconstructive theory, if not of deconstruction in general. At this point, however—when the full extent of de Man's contribution to *Le Soir* and other newspapers remains unclear, and when we have yet to evaluate in detail both his articles and murky aspects of his biography—it seems too early either to assess carefully de Man's motives and actions during his years in Belgium, or to make thoroughgoing conclusions about the relation of his journalistic essays to his later theoretical work.[41] So far, the general tendency has been to claim too much based on too little, both in attacking and defending de Man's person or career. Too many, in fact, have already denounced any kind of deconstructive approach by taking the news of de Man's dismaying past as confirming evidence that something deplorable has indeed resided beneath the surface of deconstruction's implacable rigor or putative "nihilism."[42] Summary pronouncements of this kind, however, besides being simplistic, must mistakenly assume that deconstruction has some necessary and *inherent* social agenda or political ideology, when, on the contrary, it has been adopted and employed by critics with extremely different political commitments—compare, for instance,

Stanley Fish's self-avowed conservatism with Michael Ryan's or Gayatri Spivak's Marxism.

It would be equally myopic to reduce de Man's particular version of deconstruction—from either a hostile or sympathetic point of view—to a theoretical position that, on the one hand, either harbored clandestine elements of his "collaborationist" past, or, on the other, attempted to dismantle or eradicate them altogether. We must no doubt contend with the troubling details of de Man's psychobiography, which may, in the end, help us understand the shape and substance of his career. De Man's deconstruction of the pattern of genetic history, for example, is an implicit critique of the Nazi (or collaborationist) goal of forging a totalized, purified national identity, since that program depends in part on forming a seamless and organic historical account of national (or racial) origins and development. These kinds of connections may often be suggestive, but we should note that de Man consistently focuses on *all* versions of ideology as "precisely the confusion of linguistic with natural reality" (*RT*, 11). In some cases, that generalized strategy may have camouflaged the specific historical conditions for de Man's preoccupation with such issues. But it also suggests that, despite those troubling conditions for his analyses— indeed, *because* of them—his approach can and should be modified and extended. In other words, without overlooking the importance and culpability of de Man's past, we can draw on the usefulness of his rhetorical strategies on their own terms, with an eye toward "rewriting" them for more desirable historical or political purposes. Otherwise we lose far too much of his powerful critical acuity.

Revising de Man's rhetorical strategy in the way I have generally proposed can potentially move us past his pronounced hesitation at the prospect of historical and political analysis in several ways. One possibility is to take Miller's suggestion to examine the figures of speech and rhetorical moves that characterize historiographical descriptions of the relation between cultural texts and material contexts. This could help discriminate among the various advantages and disadvantages of different historical terminologies—not with the ambition of forming some kind of systematic taxonomy, but in the attempt to trace historical similarities and differences for practical, comparative purposes.

A second possibility I would like to discuss in more detail is to reconsider the function of tropes in terms of mutual historical influence, regarding them as equally formed by social change as they are formative of texts' social impact.[43] In his analysis of John Locke's *An Essay concerning Human Understanding*, de Man argues that, despite Locke's attempt to restrict the deleterious potential of metaphor, his own philosophical project for reliable linguistic meaning and referentiality is not only contaminated, but fundamentally constituted by elusive tropological exchanges. De Man applies this point especially to Locke's characterization of true knowledge in terms of seeing and light. For the most part, Locke's work is for de Man only one more exemplary instance of the recurrent linguistic dilemma in philosophy from the Enlightenment to the twentieth century. But that global perspective can be shifted by pressing harder on his remark that "one has to pretend to read [Locke] ahistorically, the first and necessary condition if there is to be any expectation of ever arriving at a somewhat reliable history."[44] There would no doubt be many ways to pursue the historical context of the tropological pattern in Locke's work; one suggestive possibility is to examine how Locke's metaphor of seeing functions in his extended treatise on pedagogy, *Some Thoughts concerning Education* (1693), a work that attempts to apply the theory in the *Essay* to the more "prosaic" context of forming a sound moral foundation for Britain's newly emerging middle-class society.

In the *Education*, seeing is the central metaphor for the tutor's unobserved observation of the pupil—a process that must then be periodically supplemented by intervening in the child's behavior in order to correct errors and produce, in the end, an ethically sound adult citizen. That process is repeatedly expressed by the tropes of horticulture, medicine, and theater: the tutor is thereby the watchful gardener tending to the pupil's growth, the attentive physician noting symptoms and prescribing cures, or the stage director watching his actor/pupil rehearse his role and prompting him accordingly. In all of this, Locke must constantly modify and adjust the claims of his arguments, since this tropological structure—which must mediate between theory and practice, social norms and the individual subject—introduces considerable slippage in the proposed project of successful education. To take only one instance, Locke must repeatedly confront the problem that, despite his insistence on the need for the educational process to be "natural," that same "nature" is the very source of the inevitable moral "weeds" that emerge to threaten a student's correct development.[45] As a result, Locke's account must constantly negotiate among potentially disruptive extremes, taking on an increasingly narrative pattern that reminds one of de Man's remark that "from the recognition of language as trope, one is led to the telling of a tale" (EM, 21)—though here that recognition and telling goes on surreptitiously and in concrete social terms.

The social and political pressures partially responsible for Locke's particular construal of education are one important context for this tropological structure, but for the moment I will only mention two of its important effects. The first is that Locke's metaphorical paradigm of observation, intervention, and resolution served as an impetus for writers experimenting with prose in the eighteenth century with the goal of providing their readers with a social education—including Addison, Steele, Mandeville, Defoe, Fielding, and others. Locke's educational treatise, in fact, was read at least as widely as his *Essay*, establishing an educational agenda as well as a narratological paradigm, for example, for novels such as *Robinson Crusoe* and *Tom Jones*. Locke's fluid modulation between observation and alteration provided an authoritative analogue for one of the hallmarks of the eighteenth-century novel: its entangled emphasis on "true" or "natural" sequences of events as well as on the contrived or fictional quality of their composition—all in service of an exemplary socialization of not only the protagonist, but also the reader. A second effect of Locke's pedagogical theory was the implementation of his proposal to the London Board of Trade in 1697 that Britain be spared the inconvenience and danger of the indolence of poor children and adolescents by putting them to work in large, factorylike establishments in which they could learn a particular trade. Though this plan altered the genteel demeanor of Locke's original theory, it retained the basic metaphorical structure: the children worked at their crafts while being monitored by a few supervisors, who interrupted on occasion to correct their mistakes and, in the end, evaluated their readiness to leave as fully skilled apprentices. This plan served as an important impetus to the incipient charity school movement and to Britain's general concern for managing its restless lower classes.[46]

This is one example of how de Man's rhetorical analyses, couched in broad linguistic or philosophical terms, can be given useful historical and political specificity without relying on simplistic genetic relations between texts and contexts. Furthermore, it suggests how the shifting indeterminacy of tropological structures, while being philosophically suspect, can provide a kind of practical torsion or movement that can be put to work—in the largest sense of that word—in helping maintain social organization and institutions. The pattern I have described has remarkable similarities with Jeremy Bentham's Panopticon, especially in terms of the way Michel Foucault has described it; but that pattern should also indicate that using de Man's more sophisticated concept of rhetorical structure can usefully modify and extend Foucault's approach to the composition of social discourse and its role in empowering public institutions. Perhaps most important, whatever historical approach we may choose, we need to work provisionally, proceeding with both the rhetoric of history and the history of rhetoric in mind. We should always be ready to pause, when it seems necessary, over the rhetorical difficulties that no doubt will arise in the course of historical analysis; and we should in turn be prepared to historize—to contextualize, position, make "prosaic"—such rhetorical moments, so as not to render them monumental or complete discursive roadblocks.

In conclusion, besides revising de Man's rhetorical approach, we might also briefly contemplate the contemporary context of his work, since that context further discourages any inclination to characterize de Man's theoretical arguments only in terms of his personal history. We should not overlook the fact that de Man's suspicion of language has strong resonances with what could be called a Western subculture of suspicion. Have we not witnessed, both in western Europe and in the United States, an increasingly defensive cultural posture promulgated by an increasingly complicated entanglement of technology, commerce, the media, and political institutions? Are we not in the age of *dis*information, which, like *de*construction, both informs and deforms at the same time? During at least the last twenty-five years, the business of packaging, merchandising, and image-making has enormously accelerated the pace of trying to persuade consumers to buy, borrow, or subscribe, and this has largely taken place by means of increasingly sophisticated forms of communicative appeal, especially in the electronic media. American politics, moreover, has been all the more ready to engage in this late-capitalist phenomenon of packaging and merchandising, whether it be by voter canvassing, demographic surveys of special interests, press agents, or public relations consultants—all for the purpose of "selling" candidates or political programs. The population's general response to American commerce and especially politics, on both an individual and an institutional basis, has been markedly defensive, even if that defensiveness is usually taken for granted as the commonsensical, necessary attitude in a capitalist, democratic society. As consumers or political constituents, we must constantly scrutinize claims, search for implicit statements, pause at omissions, look for the bottom line. We are also a culture of institutionalized wariness, in which investigations are almost routine—whether they come in the form of Senate hearings, journalistic investigative reporting, private investigation, consumer advocate publications, or biographical exposés. This general pattern of interpretive cautiousness, moreover, can easily be aggravated into distrust, if not cynicism, in the face of new and improved devices for selling commodities, or the most recent revelation of political scandal or governmental corruption.

In the context of this cultural wariness, de Man's doubtful and ironic study of language is only too appropriate. To be sure, his own strategies are far more sophisticated and rigorous than those of Senate subcommittees or reporters, and deconstruction will probably remain a specialized and technical vocabulary, although some of its terminology has filtered down to publications such as *Time* magazine, the *Village Voice*, and the *Washington Post* (the last two, of course, well known for inveterate suspiciousness). It should also be pointed out that deconstruction has by no means remained a simple antidote to the machinations of American commerce, since the business of academic publishing has made "deconstruction" and "post-structuralism"—and in particular the work of de Man and Derrida—perhaps the most successfully marketed and widely disseminated critical "movement" in American letters. One result is that deconstruction has successfully endured something close to what William James calls the "classic stages of a theory's career": "First," says James, "a new theory is attacked as absurd; then it is admitted to be true, but obvious and insignificant; finally it is seen to be so important that its adversaries claim that they themselves discovered it."[47] Certainly deconstruction has already passed through the first two stages, and although few conservative critics now go so far as to claim it as their own, deconstruction has nonetheless become a crucial cautionary perspective that has modified their usual arguments. The recent turn of events concerning de Man's past has prompted some to announce it as the last nail in the deconstructive coffin. But if deconstruction is "dead" in any real sense, it is as a dead *metaphor*, because it has become profoundly interwoven with our current notions of authorial intent, textual structure, and rhetorical effect—so much so that we hardly pause when employing, sometimes piecemeal, its vocabulary of difference, discontinuity, or indeterminacy. That is an important reason why the academy has been so anxious at the news of de Man's "collaborationist" affiliations. It is also why, it seems to me, merely brushing aside de Man's work in hostile reaction to his political past is extremely risky at best, because it would reject the ostensible corpus of his work without examining the ways in which it has already been assimilated in our theoretical and critical practice. Ours is now the difficult task of negotiating between two trajectories: a painful revaluation of the relationship between Paul de Man's life and his work, and an assessment of the importance of his rhetorical approach and how best to use it for our present purposes. That task, in its entirety, will no doubt demand of us considerable effort, perspicuity, and persistence.

NOTES

1. Paul de Man, *Allegories of Reading: Figural Language in Rousseau, Nietzsche, Rilke, and Proust* (New Haven: Yale University Press, 1979), 150; hereafter cited in text as *AR*.
2. Shoshana Felman, "Postal Survival, or the Question of the Navel," *Yale French Studies* 69 (1985): 54.
3. Søren Kierkegaard, "For Orientation," in *The Concept of Irony*,

trans. Lee M. Capel (New York: Harper & Row, 1966), p. 274. Geoffrey Hartman, in *Criticism in the Wilderness* (New Haven: Yale University Press, 1980), pp. 278–79, cogently summarizes this distinction: "the doubting subject constantly seeks to penetrate an object that eludes him, while with irony the subject is always seeking to get free of an object that never acquires reality for him."

4. Paul de Man, *The Rhetoric of Romanticism* (New York: Columbia University Press, 1984), p. 242; hereafter cited in text as *RR*.

5. Barbara Johnson, "Rigorous Unreliability," *Critical Inquiry* 11 (1984): 278–85; rpt. in her *A World of Difference* (Baltimore: Johns Hopkins University Press, 1987), pp. 17–24.

6. See William H. Pritchard, "The Hermeneutical Mafia or, After Strange Gods at Yale," *Hudson Review* 28 (1975–76): 601n2, who calls de Man "the sublest and best writer" of the heretical critics at Yale; and Frank Lentricchia, *After the New Criticism* (Chicago: University of Chicago Press, 1980), p. 283.

7. Jacques Derrida notes this in his *Memoires for Paul de Man*, trans. Cecile Lindsay, Jonathan Culler, and Eduardo Cadava (New York: Columbia University Press, 1986), p. 65; hereafter cited in text as *M*.

8. Geoffrey Hartman, *Saving the Text: Literature/Derrida/Philosophy* (Baltimore: Johns Hopkins University Press, 1981), p. xxi; see also p. 121.

9. See, respectively, Geoffrey Hartman, "Preface," in Harold Bloom et al., *Deconstruction and Criticism* (New York: Continuum, 1979), p. ix; and Robert Moynihan's interview with Bloom in *Diacritics* 13: 3 (1983): 68.

10. See Nathan A. Scott, Jr., "The New *Trahison des Clercs*: Reflections on the Present Crisis in Humanistic Studies," *Virginia Quarterly Review* 62 (1986): 402–21; and John Ellis, "What Does Deconstruction Contribute to Theory of Criticism?," *New Literary History* 19 (1988): 259–79.

11. M. H. Abrams, "A Reply," in *High Romantic Argument: Essays for M. H. Abrams*, ed. Lawrence Lipking (Ithaca: Cornell University Press, 1981), pp. 167, 174. For Abrams's analyses of deconstruction, see, e.g., his "How to Do Things with Texts," *Partisan Review* 46 (1979): 566–88; and "The Deconstructive Angel," *Critical Inquiry* 3 (1977): 425–38.

12. See Gerald Graff, *Professing Literature: An Institutional History* (Chicago: University of Chicago Press, 1987), for a lucid account of the problematic effects of academic specialization. Howard Felperin, in *Beyond Deconstruction: The Uses and Abuses of Literary Theory*

(Oxford: Clarendon, 1985), pp. 104–46, provides an interesting but somewhat overdrawn discussion of deconstruction's "anxiety" concerning its incorporation into the academy.

13. For mention of de Man's forthcoming books, see Tom Keenan, "Bibliography of Texts by Paul de Man," *Yale French Studies* 69 (1985): 322; rpt. in Paul de Man, *The Resistance to Theory* (Minneapolis: University of Minnesota Press, 1986), pp. 127; hereafter cited in text as *RT*. For other bibliographies of de Man's work, see Richard A. Barney, "Deconstructive Criticism: A Selected Bibliography," supplement to *SCE Reports* 8 (Fall 1980): 16–20; Jonathan Culler, *On Deconstruction* (Ithaca: Cornell University Press, 1982), pp. 284–85; *Rhetoric and Form: Deconstruction at Yale*, ed. Robert Con Davis and Ronald Schleifer (Norman: University of Oklahoma Press, 1985), pp. 242–46; and *The Yale Critics: Deconstruction in America*, ed. Jonathan Arac, Wlad Godzich, and Wallace Martin (Minneapolis: University of Minnesota Press, 1983), pp. 207–9.

14. *Yale French Studies: The Lesson of Paul de Man*, No. 69 (1985).

15. E. S. Burt, "Developments in Character: Reading and Interpretation in 'The Children's Punishment' and 'The Broken Comb,'" *Yale French Studies* 69 (1985): 192n1.

16. J. Hillis Miller, "Impossible Metaphor: Stevens's 'The Red Fern' as Example," *Yale French Studies* 69 (1985): 151; hereafter cited in text as IM.

17. J. Hillis Miller, "The Triumph of Theory, the Resistance to Reading, and the Question of the Material Base," *PMLA* 102 (1987): 283.

18. In *The Ethics of Reading: Kant, de Man, Eliot, Trollope, James, and Benjamin* (New York: Columbia University Press, 1987), Miller reiterates his concern for "clearheaded reflection on what really happens in an act of reading" (pp. 3–4). He concludes further that "deconstruction is nothing more or less than good reading as such" (p. 10), but given his subsequent discussion of Kant's concept of "the law as such," Miller's claim again seems dubious. If, as he persuasively argues, the idealized standard of the law as such is finally unattainable, then certainly reading as such is equally fated. Though he implies in places that he is aware of this difficulty, Miller sticks to his initial characterization of the deconstructive reading process.

19. Paul de Man, *Blindness and Insight: Essays in the Rhetoric of Contemporary Criticism*, 2nd ed. (Minnesota: University of Minnesota Press, 1983), p. 107; hereafter cited in text as *BI*.

20. See de Man's comments in " 'Conclusions': Walter Benjamin's 'The Task of the Translator,'" *Yale French Studies* 69 (1985): 39; rpt. in *The Resistance to Theory*, pp. 86–87.

21. See, e.g., Jacques Derrida, "The Ends of Man," in *Margins of Philosophy*, trans. Alan Bass (Chicago: University of Chicago Press, 1982), pp. 109–36; the special issue of *Diacritics* 14: 3 (1984) entitled *Nuclear Criticism*; Jacques Derrida, "Of an Apocalyptic Tone Recently Adopted in Philosophy," *Oxford Literary Review* 6: 2 (1984): 3–37; and J. H. Plumb, *The Death of the Past* (Boston: Houghton Mifflin, 1969).

22. For one of the first discussions of de Man's relationship to existentialist philosophy, see Frank Lentricchia, *After the New Criticism*, pp. 284–98. Allan Stoekl, in "De Man and the Dialectics of Being," *Diacritics* 15: 3 (1985): 36–45, also discusses de Man's views on existentialism, though he disagrees with Lentricchia that de Man practiced a version of existentialist criticism early in his career.

23. Felman, "Postal Survival," p. 54.

24. See de Man, " 'Conclusions,' " p. 40 (in *The Resistance to Theory*, p. 88). For other instances of this kind of self-resistance, see his preface to *Allegories of Reading*, p. ix, and the preface to *The Rhetoric of Romanticism*, pp. viii-ix.

25. See, respectively, Geoffrey Hartman, "In Memoriam," *Yale French Studies* 69 (1985): 6; and Derrida, *Memoires*, p. 62.

26. See Richard Rorty, "Philosophy without Principles," *Critical Inquiry* 11 (1985): 462.

27. Rorty mentions de Man in "Philosophy without Principles," pp. 460, 464n4, and in his *Consequences of Pragmatism (Essays: 1972–1980)* (Minneapolis: University of Minnesota Press, 1982), p. 139; hereafter cited in text as *CP*. I have especially in mind Rorty's comments on de Man during his talks and courses at the University of Virginia.

28. Berel Lang, "Postmodernism in Philosophy: Nostalgia for the Future, Waiting for the Past," *New Literary History* 18 (1986): 213.

29. Richard Rorty, "Deconstruction and Circumvention," *Critical Inquiry* 11 (1984): 20–21; hereafter cited in text as DC.

30. See Felperin, *Beyond Deconstruction*, p. 143, who confirms this by concluding that "de Man is certainly no 'weak textualist.'"

31. See Jonathan Arac, *Critical Genealogies: Historical Situations for Postmodern Literary Studies* (New York: Columbia University Press, 1987), pp. 299–305; and Christopher Norris, "Deconstruction Against Itself: Derrida and Nietzsche," *Diacritics* 16: 4 (1986): 61–69.

32. See in particular Rorty's discussion of moral issues in *Consequences of Pragmatism*, pp. 158, 171–75, 203–8.

33. Most recently, in "Private Irony and Liberal Hope," chapter 4 of his forthcoming book *Contingency, Irony, and Solidarity* (Cam-

bridge: Cambridge University Press), Rorty attempts to resolve the difficulty I have described by sharply distinguishing between "private" and "public" endeavors. In these terms, engaging in metaphysical "wrestling" for personal or private purposes is entirely appropriate, even when it takes the "public" form of print (in commenting on this point, Rorty has suggested as an example Derrida's ruminations in *The Post Card*). But when larger public and political issues are at stake, says Rorty, practical conversation is the better choice. In making this distinction, Rorty is consistent with remarks he has made elsewhere concerning Habermas, Lyotard, Adorno, and others. Now, however, he will no doubt have to contend with the problem of whether a separation of the private and public spheres can be consistently maintained.

34. Hartman, *Criticism in the Wilderness*, p. 110.

35. De Man, *Blindness and Insight*, pp. 163, 225. See also his discussion of modernity and history: during the "steady fluctuation of an entity away from and toward its own mode of being," "the sequential, diachronic structure of the process stems from the nature of literary language as an entity, not as an event" (p. 163).

36. Andrew Parker, " 'Taking Sides' (On History): Derrida Re-Marx," *Diacritics* 11: 3 (1981): 69. For these other views, see Lentricchia, *After the New Criticism*, pp. 282–317, and Suzanne Gearheart, "Philosophy *Before* Literature: Deconstruction, Historicity, and the Work of Paul de Man," *Diacritics* 13: 4 (1983): 63–81; Michael Ryan, in *Marxism and Deconstruction* (Baltimore: Johns Hopkins University Press, 1982), pp. 24, 35–42, and Gayatri Chakravorty Spivak, in "Sex and History in *The Prelude* (1805): Books Nine to Thirteen," *Texas Studies in Literature and Language* 23 (1981): 357, have made their criticism more general by focusing on the Yale Critics as a whole. See also my discussion of the Marxist response to de Man in "Uncanny Criticism in the United States," in *Tracing Literary Theory*, ed. Joseph Natoli (Urbana: University of Illinois Press, 1987), pp. 198–204.

37. See Frank Lentricchia, *Criticism and Social Change* (Chicago: University of Chicago Press, 1983), esp. pp. 64–65, 72–75, 81, 115–17, 159–60. As another example, Michael Ryan, in "The Marxism Deconstruction Debate," *Critical Exchange* 14 (1983): 59–68, concludes that de Man's analyses are in fact useful for a critique of bourgeois liberalism.

38. See, e.g., Miller, "The Triumph of Theory," p. 284, and Derrida, *Memoires*, pp. 21, 68, 142–45.

39. For other of the many instances when de Man employs the language

of generation and engendering, see *Blindness and Insight*, pp. 218, 226; *Allegories of Reading*, pp. 131, 205, 240, 272, 294–95; and *The Rhetoric of Romanticism*, pp. 75, 96, 107, 109, 110, 114, 117, 120, 247, 262.

40. Paul de Man, "Hegel on the Sublime," in *Displacement: Derrida and After*, ed. Mark Krupnick (Bloomington: Indiana University Press, 1983), p. 153.

41. De Man's contribution of at least 92 articles to *Le Soir* was first made public in "Yale Scholar Wrote for Pro-Nazi Newspaper," *New York Times*, 1 Dec. 1987, sect. B, pp. 1, 6 (this piece contains several inaccuracies, which include reporting the date of de Man's death as December 1984, and citing him as the "originator" of deconstruction). The most useful pieces to appear since then include: Jon Wiener, "Deconstructing de Man," *The Nation*, 9 Jan. 1988, pp. 22–24; Christopher Norris, "Paul de Man's Past," *London Review of Books*, 4 Feb. 1988, pp. 7–11; Geoffrey Hartman, "Paul de Man, Facism, and Deconstruction: Blindness and Insight," *The New Republic*, 7 March 1988, pp. 26–31; and Jacques Derrida, "Like the Sound of the Sea Deep within a Shell: Paul de Man's War," *Critical Inquiry* 14 (1988): 590–652. These writers have provided considerably more details, but the evidence remains substantially incomplete, making any steadfast conclusions seem precarious at best. Wiener reports, for instance, that researchers in Belgium are still tracking down other essays de Man may have written both earlier and later than the ones already discovered (written from February 1941 to October 1942). According to Wiener, it remains unclear whether de Man knew about the destruction of Jews while he was writing these pieces, and the last article he wrote may be a clue to that puzzle (pp. 23–24). Hartman, on the other hand, agreeing with historians such as Raoul Hilberg, concludes that by the fall of 1942 "all but the deliberately ignorant" would have known about the fatal turn in Jewish persecution (p. 26). This particular issue may turn out to be an unresolvable detail in de Man's biography, but it does suggest that, despite the acute perceptions already offered by Hartman, Derrida, and others, we have a good way to go before a clear trajectory of de Man's career can be charted. Even Derrida, who has collected considerable information about de Man's years in Belgium, and who devotes 62 pages to strenuously defending him, acknowledges having access to only 29 of the articles that de Man wrote (p. 598). Two new books, Paul de Man, *Wartime Journalism, 1940–42*, and *Responses: On Paul de Man's Wartime Journalism*, both ed. Werner Hamacher, Neil Hertz, and Tom Keenan (Lincoln: University of

Nebraska Press, forthcoming), include several of de Man's Flemish articles in translation as well as commentaries by several critics and should be a crucial first step in attempting to assess de Man's early career in careful, thoroughgoing fashion.

42. David Lehman, in "Deconstructing de Man's Life," *Newsweek*, 15 Feb. 1988, pp. 63–65, and in "The (de) Man Who Put the Con in Deconstruction," *Los Angeles Times Book Review*, 13 March 1988, p. 15, poses a glaring example of this reductive impulse; but so far, David H. Hirsch, in "Paul de Man and the Politics of Deconstruction," *Sewanee Review* 96 (1988): 330–38, has been the most flagrantly extreme. Walter Kendrick's account, in "De Man That Got Away," *Village Voice Literary Supplement*, April 1988, pp. 6–8, is more balanced, though in the end he charges de Man with pretentiousness and professional opportunism.

43. Peter De Bolla, in "Disfiguring History," *Diacritics* 16: 4 (1986): 56, makes some interesting suggestions along these lines in the context of Hayden White's work.

44. Paul de Man, "The Epistemology of Metaphor," in *On Metaphor*, ed. Sheldon Sacks (Chicago: University of Chicago Press, 1978), p. 14; hereafter cited in text as EM.

45. For a few of the places where Locke portrays education in terms of these three metaphors, see *Some Thoughts concerning Education*, in *The Educational Writings of John Locke*, ed. James L. Axtell (Cambridge: Cambridge University Press, 1968), pp. 139, 160, 171, 184 (gardening); 182–85, 221, 232–33, 246, 319 (medicine); 207 (drama).

46. For Locke's proposal to the London Board of Trade, see H. R. Fox Bourne, *The Life of John Locke* (New York: Harper, 1876), II, 377–91; and for a useful account of the charity school movement, see Mary G. Jones, *The Charity School Movement: A Study of Eighteenth-Century Puritanism in Action* (Cambridge: Cambridge University Press, 1938).

47. William James, *"Pragmatism" and "The Meaning of Truth,"* ed. Fredson Bowers and Ignas K. Skrupskelis (Cambridge: Harvard University Press, 1978), p. 95.

WILLIAM A. JOHNSEN

Myth, Ritual, and Literature after Girard

The nineteenth-century dream of the comparative method, so spectacularly successful in natural science, economics, and linguistics, has remained for literary intellectuals tauntingly unfulfilled, backing up into provocative but unstable analogies between comparative structural analyses of myth, ritual, and literature. The chronological derivation of myth from ritual, or ritual from myth, and literature from both, in the early part of this century, especially by the Cambridge Ritualists (Fraser, Harrison, Murray, Cornford[1]), and in Freud's anthropological speculations, was prudently reduced to logical derivation by the 1950s. Lévi-Strauss had chosen synchronic linguistics, which put aside the question of language's origin, as the model for structural anthropology. Neumann borrowed "sequence-dating" from Flinders Petrie to rule anachronism out of depth psychology's parallel development of individual and cultural consciousness. Universally recurring archetypes became, for Northrop Frye, the metahistorical building blocks for literature as a whole. What remained as the transcultural authority for these universally recurring archetypes, sequences, and structures was, in Edward Said's oppositional term for structuralism, the "totalitarianism of mind."[2] Homologies followed from the common structuring principles of the human imagination of every time and place. Structure, as the key to all explanation, could not itself be further explained.

René Girard has consciously positioned himself to follow through on the consequences of comparison. Beginning in the domain of myth, ritual, and literature, this means nothing less than to make good on the dream of a hypothesis that ultimately accounts for the generation of all cultural forms. One future for the systematic study of literature made possible by Girard becomes the comprehending of the relation of the modern to myth, ritual, and literature as a whole. This essay will argue "after Girard" in two related ways: "according to" his hypothesis, as well as estimating what "follows" from its explanatory power. I leave the contentious sense of "getting after" Girard to those who are captured by the contemporary myth that being critical in the human sciences means discarding without further consideration any hypothesis that claims by comparison to be superior to others.

Mensonge romantique et vérité romanesque (1961), translated as *Deceit, Desire, and the Novel* (1965),[3] Girard's first book, is founded on the kind of historical threshold that is everywhere in his work. Man once acknowledged his own incompleteness in deferring to the superior beings of the gods, kings, or nobility. Imitation was to properly follow their example, with no thought of equality. When the Enlightenment rationalized divinity for man's sake, there was no further excusing any deficiency of human autonomy. Yet fictional texts show this promise unfulfilled, to each alone; to mask this private shame, all pretend to possess the sufficiency that each lacks. Each must copy the apparent originality of others, without giving himself away as a rank imitator. Such imitation among "equals" can only lead to rivalry, with the disciple reaching for whatever object the model has indicated as desirable, as the apparent source of his autonomy. In early stages, the model can deny any coquetry, and the disciple can deny any rivalry; but in later stages of "deviated transcendency" the disciple will find divinity not in objects themselves, but only in those who reject him. Modern desire is metaphysical, a fight over increasingly elusive and intangible goals. Sadism and narcissism become the decisively modern masks of autonomy, the expression of being desired while wanting (lacking) nothing, rejecting all.

Such a profound revolution in the way desire is understood could not but evolve as well a theory of consciousness and the unconscious, instincts and their repression. Furthermore, it leads to a radical revision, within the human sciences, of theories of prohibition, then ritual, then myth, and finally culture itself, the process of hominization. If desire depends on a model for instruction, then the repression and prohibition of desires cannot be the restraining of instinctual drives, or the tabooing of instinctually indicated desirables. If desire is imitative, then prohibition and tabooing must be a restraint of imitation itself—in particular, the mimesis of appropriation, but more generally, of all intersubjectivity. Religious ritual can no longer be (for believers and skeptics alike) the "symbolic" or imaginary exorcizing of spiritual or instinctual agencies, a primitive form of metaphoric inoculation against real micro- and macrobic invasion. Instead, it becomes an effective if misunderstood restructuring of imitation as a potentially catastrophic behavior.

Girard's method is appropriately comparative, appropriately initiated in nineteenth-century material, but distinctive in the seriousness that he allows literary as intellectual (ultimately, scientific) labor. Girard first develops this mimetic hypothesis on the authority of his comparison of nineteenth-century European fiction, which proposes two rival traditions for the novel: the *romantic*, which reflects, without comprehending, the mediation of desire, and the *romanesque* (novelistic), which reveals it. The romanesque work of Stendhal, Proust, and Dostoyevsky learns, first in others, finally in itself, the pretensions of romantic (autonomous) desire.

How does *La Violence et le sacré* (1972), *Violence and the Sacred* (1977),[4] make good on the scientific potential of the novelistic tradition? First, by suggesting violence as an intra- and transcultural constant that enables comparison of all cultural forms. Nothing more closely resembles a violent man than another, from within or without the culture, and nothing better consolidates this resemblance than their mutual conflict. But if we learn, following Girard, to associate violence with the erasing of differences, what do we do with our modern enlightened presupposition that differences, not similarities, breed conflict? Girard turns this presupposition of peaceful equality back on itself: What powerful modern institution could cultivate a presupposition so different from the primitive horror of the Same? The discrepancy between primitive and modern ideas about difference leads to a significant distinction between primitive and modern culture, based on their ratios of preventive to curative procedures for expelling violence from the community. After some extremely suggestive paragraphs on the superior efficacy of the judicial system for incarnating divine vengeance, before which all are equal, he turns to the primitive world of preventive procedures. The return to modern ritual and myth occurs, up to this point in Girard's writing, mostly in the margins of something else, especially his readings of Freud.[5] Our itinerary here will be to summarize Girard's hypothesis for cultural mimesis, as the key to primitive myth and ritual. Next we will observe his unique sense of the role of literature for *desymbolizing* myth and ritual (especially novelistic fiction, Greek and Elizabethan drama, and the tradition he names *l'écriture judéo-chrétienne*). As we proceed, we will relate Girard's theory to those of others, especially Claude Lévi-Strauss, Walter Burkert, Jean-Pierre Vernant, and Northrop Frye. Finally, we will consider the potential future of Girard's theory ("after Girard") for the myths and rituals of modern culture, especially in coordination with Edward Said on literary representations of the myths and rituals of imperialism.[6]

If violence travels so well, what keeps it from spreading like a contagion, enveloping and breaking down a whole community? Sometimes nothing works (any longer), as in the case of the Kaingang tribe in Brazil; their transplantation, which has deprived them of their hereditary enemy (everyone else), has left them to an internal bloodfeuding certain to wipe them out in a generation. Put another way, a community, hominization itself, is sustainable only in the presence of some working solution to the contagion of spontaneous violence. All societies that have survived, or that have survived long enough to have entered history, must have had some answer of varying effectiveness. If violence is a constant, what permissible variables effectively contain it? Prohibition and ritual. If one reverses the proliferation of modern theories of psychic complexes, agencies, and archetypes (which resemble all too closely the primitive myths of the gods as sufficient cause) in favor of the mimetic hypothesis, prohibition and ritual can be seen as the restraint of imitation itself. In particular, the restrained mimesis is that of appropriation: father, then son, reaching for the same object made irresistible by the indication of each other's rivalry. Primitive prohibition also taboos all other indications of doubling as signs of incipient violence: mirrors, representations, twins. If Girard is a more economical psychologist than Freud, he is a more down-to-earth anthropologist than Lévi-Strauss. Primitive rituals do not put twins to death as organizational misfits, scandalous signs of two applying for the structural position reserved for one. Adults' reasons for putting children to death are abominably mistaken, but hardly philosophical. For Girard, primitives are not to be understood as proto-structuralist intellectuals; behind the issue of structuralism there is always the more crucial issue of a social order threatened by, yet generated from, violence misunderstood as a divinity.[7]

If taboos prohibit imitation, ritual legislates its effects. Ritual functions by imitating the progress of spontaneous violence. Because it is eminently imitable, violence spreads easily, uninterrupted until it has exhausted itself with the peace that follows the satisfaction of violence by imitating its finale of all against (the last) one. In spontaneous violence, each is the other's enemy; as it ends, one is the enemy of all. Ritual legislates this process: the ritual victim substitutes for each one's enemy. Because violence erases differences, one can stand as the enemy of all, their monstrous double. The double valence of the *pharmakos*, defiled as monstrous yet holy in his office, is *sacer*, sacred. Girard's mimetic hypothesis comprehends those discussions of symbolic action that terminate themselves in the circular answers of ambivalence, human duplexity, and undecidability as the last word.

Freud saw the father, as Hubert and Mauss saw ritual, as at once a potent source and unexplainable explanation of contradictory commands: "I am your progenitor; I am your enemy." Girard analyzes the Freudian father within the context of Freud's theoretical attempt to reconcile a mimetic with an instinctual model of desire (*Violence and the Sacred*, Ch. 7). In the chapter of *Massenpsychologie und Ich-Analyse* (1921) on identification, Freud identifies the father as the child's primary model, whose place he would take everywhere (*an allen seinen Stellen treten*).[8] In the child's mental life, identification with the father (mimetic) and a cathexis toward the mother (instinctual) develop side by side, until he sees the father in the way of the mother. His way blocked to the object by the father, who had helped to identify it as desirable, his identification now (*jetzt*) takes on a hostile coloring: the son would take that place (*zu ersetzen*) as well (*auch*). Girard brilliantly queries the offhandedness of *auch*: Does this mean that the child warily observed, up until now, the incest taboo meant to prohibit conflict? How can we account for this special category of the mother in the child's mental life, among the "everywheres" of the father, otherwise sufficiently comprehensible through the father's mediation of the son's desire?

Girard follows Freud's discussion of the Oedipus complex to *Das Ich und das Es* (1923), where a primary desire for the mother, originating in the son, now preempts the *nebeneinander* development of the father's mediation.[9] Thus Freud has chosen an instinctual theory of desire over a mimetic theory. Furthermore, because the father no longer prepares the way he will later block, he (and/or patriarchal culture in general) is absolved of any responsibility for scandalously drawing the unsuspecting child into rivalry. He is absolved as well of responsibility for his own "ambivalence"; the instincts now serve the god-function, determining the fate of every modern Oedipus. Although it deserves fuller treatment elsewhere, a coordination of feminist theory with Girard might begin here, by considering Freud's profoundly influential decision to blame the instincts (that is, the body, nature itself) for the regrettable ambivalence of the father for the child, and how that is the same as blaming women.[10] Such a beginning in a critique of Freudian myth could follow out Girard's provocative (but essayistic) suggestion for primitive culture, that the negative symbolization in myth and ritual of menstrual blood responds to "some half-repressed desire to place the blame for all forms of violence on women" (*Violence and the Sacred*, p. 36).

To sketch out this future, let us follow Girard's reading over Freud's shoulder, to pay yet closer attention to Freud's development of his theory. In the *Massenpsychologie*, father-identification is at first healthy, competitive, an intimate, active sparring that prepares the son to assume in due time his manly prerogatives (*Dies Verhalten hat nichts mit einer passiven oder femininum Einstellung zum Vater (und zum Manne Überhaupt) zu tun, es ist viehlmehr exquisit männlich*). Once the father is seen as blocking the path to the mother, however—or once the mother refuses the "advances" of the son in the name of some absent adult male, who may or may not exist—father-identification becomes identical with the wish (*wird identisch mit dem Wunsch*) to *take* (*zu ersetzen*), not to assume or inherit eventually, the father's place. We see that the language of father-identification now clearly voices violent rivalry, the son wishing to contest the Father-in-the-way, head on, for the *same* place.

In the chapter of *Das Ich und das Es* on the "Über-Ich," Freud refers to his earlier discussion in *Massenpsychologie*. Although he repeats the phrase about father-identification taking on a hostile coloring, he no longer finds it identical to a previous father-identification now recklessly (that is, threateningly) exercised in a forbidden place. Rather, the intensification of sexual desire for the mother precedes the recognition of the father as an obstacle (*ein Hindernis*; p. 37) Father-identification changes into a violent rivalry that had not before existed, "a wish to get rid of his father in order to take his place with his mother" (*wendet sich zum Wunsch, den Vater zu beseitigen, um ihn bei der Mutter zu ersetzen*). The universal logic behind the universal prohibition of incest identifies women of every human society as the source of violence to be legislated, isolated. Like violence, they are sacred (*Violence and the Sacred*, pp. 219-20). When we trace the customary history of the development of sacrificial substitution, given its most popular form by Robert Graves,[11] back toward its origins (totemic animal substitutes for *pharmakos*, who substitutes for *tyrannos*, who was once sacrificed for the queen), we must think past the premature termination of this sequence of substitutions in the cultic figure of the *magna mater*. Her sacred ambivalence, definitively mapped in Neumann's work,[12] derives, like the king's, from a prior role as a sacrificial victim.

At this point we must bring ourselves back from the interminable deconstruction of other theories which, as Said suggests,[13] easily confuses the power to critique cultural mythology with the ability to contest its influence with an alternative. Girard is reading Freudian theory to recover the mimetic hypothesis, which would place violent rivalry within the domain of cultural, not natural propagation, within the domain of pedagogy, not instinct, and for social reciprocity, not for repression.

How, then, does Girard's mimetic reading of father-identification differ? First, the child who follows the familial and cultural indications of the father as a proper model is the last to learn that imitation is rivalry—that father-identification is appropriative, patricidal. Forbidden "this" place, he can only assume that the father's ambivalence, his mercurial change of attitude, is a rejection justified by the son's failure; and he can only conclude that such failure has been measured before an especially desirable object. Violence will thereafter indicate the desirable, an obstacle (*ein Hindernis*) the surest sign of an opportunity to retrieve the full being denied him. Subsequent identifications will take on the coloring of the ambivalent father-identification.

The consequences of such a reading open up a future for the practice of psychoanalysis apart from myth and ritual, and the possibility of situating this practice in a diachronic plan.[14] By recognizing the compelling yet arbitrary nature of the distinction between those places where imitation is required or prohibited, treatment can avoid the parallel fetishism of adjustment and perversion. It can comprehend at once the function of prohibition, and the perspicacity of those unfortunate analysands who cannot blind themselves to its arbitrary nature (*Violence and the Sacred*, p. 172).

The ambivalence of the father as the primary model and obstacle who influences all subsequent identifications can only occur, Girard insists, in a patriarchal culture where the father's role is weakened but not yet effaced (*Violence and the Sacred*, p. 188). Freud tried to generate the incest taboo historically by arguing, in *Totem and Taboo*, that in Darwin's horde the king is father of all and is killed by his "sons" in sexual jealousy over "his" women. In remorse for this killing, or in "delayed obedience," the men prohibit themselves incest and commit themselves to exogamy. Following the mimeticization of Freud's psychology, Girard depaternalizes Freud's anthropological theory as well. Prohibition prevents rivalry: for the single murder of a single father, Girard substitutes rite as the mimesis of spontaneous violence, saving Freud's essential insight of collective violence as the origin of totem and taboo. Thus the mimetic hypothesis explains the ambivalence of the sacred as well as the father (or mother). Ritual prepares a sacrificeable victim by making him violate every taboo, by making him everyone's rival. Before such a rival all are united. He is the savior as well as the scourge because he is signed with the sacred, with the beneficial resources of sacrifice itself. Such awe can easily transform the enemy after his sacrifice, into the progenitor who allows his own sacrifice, who makes laws, who establishes prohibitions against his (former) misbehavior and even requires sacrifice to keep the peace he alone provides.

Walter Burkert's *Homo Necans*, which appeared in the same year as *Violence and the Sacred*, is a prodigious garnering of the literature of myth and ritual, under a hypothesis in many ways akin to Girard's reading Freud.[15] Like Girard, Burkert is interested in relating classical studies to anthropology and psychology. He suggests the origin of the gods in the prohibition of some prior act of collective violence, but he derives prohibition from the *psychologisme* of Paleolithic hunters who regret the killing of the animal they have hunted, because they belatedly identify with their victim. In reaction, they set this animal off limits; eventually this difference becomes sacred. The weak link is the dynamic that Burkert shares with Freud in *Totem and Taboo*; guilt, or remorse for murder, energizes a universal system of prohibitions. How could one moment of remorse (putting aside for now the problem of where that moment of remorse comes from) maintain its influence throughout human culture? The mimetic hypothesis has a superior scientific value that can be exampled in the hunt, but it can function equally well for an agricultural society. A being who draws back from claiming an object, for the sake of another or in fear of another's desire, has acknowledged and limited the dangerous power of the mimesis of appropriation. Hunters circling their prey reinforce mimetically each other's reluctance to lay the first hand (which could provoke a second), to get too close to being on the other side with the victim. Prohibition and ritual legislate this prudence into protocols that insure peace by making certain no one else gets mixed up with the victim's sacred difference.[16]

By showing the persistent influence of archaic ritual violence on the cultural forms of democratic Athens, Louis Gernet provided the historical scholarship required to evaluate the speculative profusion of the Cambridge Ritualists, who saw ritual sacrifice behind every king, every tragedy. Jean Pierre Vernant, Pierre Vidal-Naquet, and Marcel Detienne have followed out Gernet by structuralizing the observation of misrule becoming rule in ritual (as in literature) as a regulation of man's ambiguous nature: Oedipus as Everyman, *homo duplex, tyrannos-pharmakos*.[17]

To the persistent observation that Oedipus plays all the roles, father-brother, son-lover, savior-scourge, Vernant brings the structuralist hypothesis of binary opposition composing all symbolic forms. To play everyone is nevertheless to play by the iron rules of structuration: the king must ultimately suffer reversal to the opposite pole of anathema. But what is the answer to binary opposition itself as a hypothesis? Mind? How can this *tyrannos* serve as both tyrant and king; how can this *pharmakos* be the cure and the scourge of the city?[18] Girard's rethinking of structuralism, in its early stages, parallels deconstructive thinking. Such orders can never be neutral, philosophical. Oppositions are privileged, interested, worldly; they make a difference for someone's sake.

Who benefits from each role that Oedipus plays? The proper opposition to watch is not that of scourge versus savior, but the opposition of each to the city, the one posed against all, which Girard insists is the primary sign of sacrificial reconciliation, the origin of all symbolic representation, of symbolicity itself.[19] To see the play of the *pharmakos* as undecidable is, in one sense, true. (Here Girard follows Derrida.) The identification of the victim is truly arbitrary—s/he is no more guilty of contagious violence than is anyone else. Yet to terminate analysis in ambiguity is to play along with the purification that tragedy comes to, to ignore the final decision (*de-cidere*) that always occurs at the moment purgation requires: the perepeteia of the hero.

In Girard's reading, Sophocles intolerably delays this expected moment of decisiveness as Oedipus tries to dodge his "fate." Girard's attention to such delays and reservations marks off his reading from those of Freud, Burkert, Vernant, the archetypalists, and Frye. What interests mythographers like Lévi-Strauss (or Robert Graves, for that matter) in *Oedipus Tyrannos* is a unidirectional, irresistible homology to another myth, leading as soon as possible to the myth of myth.[20] The myth, whether Classical or Freudian, never expresses any doubt about Oedipus's guilt. Audiences, whether in Athens or New York, consolidate themselves in impatient opposition to Oedipus's obstinate resistance to admitting what they already know.

But Girard suggests that certain literary works, especially in times of social crisis (modern fiction, Greek and Elizabethan tragedy, *l'écriture judéo-chrétienne*), desymbolize the myths that corroborate violent rituals of social cohesion. Sophocles goes part way, according to Girard, in calling the certitude of Oedipus's guilt into question. To follow out Sophocles, we must delay our accusation of *hamartia* against an Oedipus who is the only intellect, temper, or unconscious out of control. Girard would have us see that Creon, Tiresias, and even Jocasta give way to anger in their turn. Each becomes a mimetic rival to the other as each accuses the other of the same crimes, for the sake of the city's institutions. Sophocles rejoins the reciprocity between antagonists that myth decides. The play itself contains, as many have argued, uncertain evidence for Oedipus's guilt. The account of one or many murderers of Laios is never verified, nor is the context of that account, whether it was given before or after the Herdsman found Oedipus as king.[21] Even if the play more or less acquiesces to the myth's account of Oedipus's guilt, audiences, following Aristotle, agree rather on the all-too-human sin of pride, and the causal link of either sin to plague is never verified by the play's conclusion. Vernant concludes as well that Sophocles locates an unstructurable ambiguity between Oedipus as Everyman and the social positions that would name him. But Girard takes Vernant's discussion beyond ambiguity, arguing that Vernant's own observation of Oedipus as scapegoat (*bouc émissaire*) as well as *pharmakos* critically identifies the structuring principle of the myth that Sophocles discovers: "The traces of religious anathema unearthed in tragedy should be regarded not as anachronistic survivals from a primitive past but as being in the nature of an archaeological find" (*Violence and the Sacred*, p. 84).

Violence and the Sacred openly acknowledges the priority of Gernet, Vernant, Benveniste, and Derrida. In each case Girard attempts a comprehension of their work. The mimetic hypothesis accounts for the ambiguity of the sacred in ritual (Gernet, Vernant) and in language (Benveniste, Derrida), but also for its partial demythologization in Sophocles.

If Girard is a brilliant reader of others, he is also particularly gifted in finding answers for the most stubborn misreadings of his own work. *Violence and the Sacred* first encountered an anti-referential prejudice that prohibited any belief that myth (or, more generally, religion) could refer to anything outside itself, and a pseudo-scientific skepticism that knew all truth claims are now obsolete. Almost immediately Girard began to answer with the medieval "texts of persecution," documents composed of the same stereotypes as the myths he analyzes in *Violence and the Sacred*.[22] Furthermore, he insists that his reading of mythology and primitive religion, which scandalizes contemporary notions of textuality, is the method of reading that everyone uses for these medieval texts, which describe how Jews poisoned wells, caused stillbirths, and cast evil eyes until all problems were cured by their elimination. Girard defies any reader to argue with this modern consensus which shows the contemporary literary intellectual's version of textual practice as an anachronism. Who would deny (1) that there are real persecutions behind such texts, even when independent corroboration is impossible; (2) that the intention of the authors of persecution, to find the single cause, is knowable; (3) that we can, with certainty, replace the persecutors' interpretation, which we know, with our own (the victims are not guilty, and their persecutors know not what they do), with an interpretation that is theoretically and morally superior?

As in the case of Lévi-Strauss, Burkert, Mary Douglas, or, more generally, the fields of psychology, anthropology, and biblical scholarship, to ask who is the more competent specialist is to foreclose all futures for the disciplines except departmental snobbery.[23] The only course, even in those cases where Girard seems to have read lightly (or not at all), is to follow the theory that comprehends all this work, even if it comes from one who has earned no credits in the field or the clinic, but who puts "the literature" to best use.

The most influential modern theorist for the relation of myth and ritual to literature has been Northrop Frye. In one of the most famous sentences of *Anatomy of Criticism* (1957),[24] Frye argued that literary structure derives logically, if not chronologically, from myth and ritual. This strategic retreat from the contested question of generative origins consolidated Cornford on comedy, Aristotle on tragedy, Jung and Neumann on romance, and the best local authority on the pertinence of myth, ritual, and the primitive for modern writing.

Frye has been outmoded by the journalists of critical theory because of the questions he strategically, but only momentarily, set aside: in particular, the question of why literary structure resembles the structure of myth and ritual. Such questions have occupied both Frye and Girard for more than twenty years. Such mythical lustrations as Lentricchia's *After the New Criticism* (1980),[25] which washes its hands of Frye after 1970, are necessarily ignorant of Frye's later work.

Frye's anatomy presents the constituting literary structure as the story of a dying and resurrecting god, whose motive is to resolve the loss of identity between the human and natural world. Frye correlates the recurring narrative myths of comedy, romance, tragedy, and irony into a monomyth, the story of one being who rises, sets, and returns like the sun: the spirit of comedy for the regeneration of society is reborn in a young man of mysterious birth, the knight of romance, who becomes the king of tragedy, who becomes the *pharmakos* of irony whose *sparagmos* feeds a new comedy.

Why does literature follow myth and ritual, according to Frye? Because it wants to. That is, the motive for literature is to articulate the desirable already comprehended most clearly in myth and ritual, which are the structural building-blocks of the imagination. Myth narrates the adventures of beings empowered to do whatever they want. The "Theory of Modes" sees a descent in literary history from the classical to the modern period, in the hero's power of action, and a descent in narrative myths from the most powerful heroic actions to the least, ending in modern literature's preference for ironic myth and mode.

But why is literature as a whole headed in the opposite direction from the desirable? Frye describes this progress as displacement: accommodating the dream of literature to the pressure of the reality principle at any given historical moment. This gap between myth and mode, the relation between myth and history, and the corresponding underdetermination of the relation of secular to sacred scripture is still a pressing issue in Frye's work.[26] Yet a term like "displacement" suggests that Frye begins by seeing literature measured against the norm of myth and ritual. Frye's earliest attempt to reconcile the historical descent of modes with the cyclical return of myth was to suggest that the modern interest in the ironic victim, in primitive cult and ritual, signifies the *sparagmos* of myth, a successful sacrifice, which sacramentally fortifies the emerging spirit of a new comic society.

What would a mimetic reading of Frye look like? Like Girard, Frye defines desire interdividually, in the sense that he defers plotting the intentions and desires of single authors whose only wish is to make a work, until such work accumulates in the archetypal phase, where collectively recurrent desires and their prohibition articulate a dream of identification, all the world absorbed by one desiring human form. That is, human desires become legible as the drives that cultural prohibitions imperfectly restrain. Frye's theory of identification in *Anatomy of Criticism*, the "motive for metaphor" in *The Educated Imagination* (1964),[27] follows Freud: to identify is to absorb. In the *Massenpsychologie*, the ambivalence of father-identification, from which all future forms of identification take their coloring, behaves like a derivative of the oral phase, "*in welcher man sich das begehrte und geschätzte Objekt durch Essen einverleibte und es dabei als solches vernichtete. Der Kannibale bleibt bekanntlich auf diesem Standpunkt stehen; er hat seine Feinde zum Fressen lieb, und er frisst nur die, die er lieb hat*" (67) ("in which the object that we long for and prize is assimilated by eating and is in that way annihilated as such. The cannibal, as we know, has remained at this standpoint; he has a devouring affection for his enemies and only devours people of whom he is fond" [37]). Such a desire for identification/absorption is, in the language of *Deceit, Desire, and the Novel*, "ontological sickness," an attempt to appropriate for one's own depleted resources the greater being of the other.[28]

As we have seen, the mimetic hypothesis absolves the disciple of any instinctive, violent urge to appropriate, referring such accusations back to their mediators. If desire is mediated, if prohibitions control the consequences of mimesis, then archetypes can be understood as "articulating" the desires that cultural prohibitions project onto the disciples. The progressive displacement of desire in Frye's "Theory of Modes," read mimetically, becomes, adapting Raymond Williams's phrase, "the long devolution," literature's progressive desymbolization of *mythic* desires, projected by prohibition and ritual as instinctive, as originating in nature, in the child. This devolution culminates in the modern period. The modern interest in myth and ritual is not a historical residue, not a return, but an archaeological dis-covery of the roots of all human societies in violent sacrifice.

Frye identifies literary structure with the *pharmakos* (which Derrida quotes approvingly[29]) and, like Vernant, uses "scapegoat" as a synonym. Girard uses *pharmakos* and scapegoat, respectively, to distinguish between the reflection and revelation of victimization. When we see that Jews and witches are scapegoats, we see the dynamic invisible to the persecutor-author, the dynamic that structures the text. A text that talks openly about victimization has a scapegoat theme, whose structure, then, is post-sacrificial.

For Girard "scapegoat" is a term in the West's development of the precious critical vocabulary of social relations, generated by the comparative studies of cultures, religions, and languages. But comparison must not prematurely terminate itself by regarding all cultures as equally ethnocentric, racist, sexist. Such collective, comparative labor, on such an unprecedented scale, suggests an anthropological or even logological motive of our culture. We have improved our comprehension of all cultural languages by minimizing our own; when positive rules of kinship (which cross-cousin one should marry) desymbolize, we are left with only the minimal prohibitions necessary to forestall violent rivalry.

Girard pursues the consequences of comparative religion in the nineteenth century beyond the premature termination in collecting homologies between the Bible and other stories of dying and resurrecting gods. He goes on to ask, "What makes such comparisons possible?" His answer is: "Judeo-Christian writing," which emphasizes the innocence of the persecuted: Joseph in Egypt is not guilty of desiring to replace his "father" everywhere. The capacity to see those who are sacrificed as marked with the sign of the perfectly innocent victim makes possible the fundamental distinction between reflection and revelation of scapegoating.

Frye's positing of myth as the structural paradigm for literature, and his commitment to expel all value judgment as comparative class determination, proposes the equivocal position of regarding any hero's *sparagmos* as good as any other, only arbitrarily authorized by a dominant interest. Dionysus would do just as well. A mimetic rereading of Frye's heroic categories would be less resigned to Zeus's criminal sexual practice as the articulation of the desirable. Zeus's desire is transgressive, mythologically attracted to obstacles, prohibitions, taboos. All such "heroic" crimes are signs of the sacrificial origin of the divinity in a plague of rivalry resolved by his expulsion.

If one theorizes the historical preference for Judeo-Christian writing over other local myths in Western literature as something more than class privilege, "the long devolution" (the mimetic reading of the "Theory of Modes") is the contest of violence and nonviolence, the two logoi of Satan and the Paraclete, the accuser and the advocate, respectively, of the persecuted (*The Scapegoat*, Chs. 14, 15). Following Frye according to Girard recovers the prematurely "outmoded" future of "literature as a whole," in relation to myth and ritual, as the revelation of violence from an emerging post-sacrificial comprehension.

For Frye, the scapegoat structure in modern literature is the victory of the obstacle or reality principle over the solar hero of romance, who bears the dream of literature. A mimetic reading of mode suggests that modern literature finalizes Western literature's *thematization* of the scapegoat mechanism. The sacred power of queens as well as kings was inherently unstable, was earned through victimization; they are victimized again when anything goes wrong because they are the sole cause of violence and/or peace. The secularization of violent myth and ritual sustains, over time, the dissolution of violent difference between the turbulent audience and its heroes. An ironic hero who proves his power is less than ours is, in effect, our victim. The vertiginous rise and fall of leadership in modern societies replays this devolution in a matter of years. The parallel desymbolization of social and literary forms forces us to consider that the crowd dynamic, not some reality principle or unique character flaw, is responsible for social crisis.

Let us conclude our following of Girard's theory by seconding the credit he gives to literature's "quasi-theoretical potential,"[30] by considering two writers who consciously project work before and after the post-sacrificial revelation of violence. Shakespeare, in *King Lear*, deals with those who, because they do violence in the name of peace before scriptural revelation, cannot know what they do. Orwell, in *Nineteen Eighty-Four*, examines those of an anthropological post-critical age who know exactly what they are doing. (These are but two texts for Girard's future that have been temporarily deferred by his fifteen-year centering on the Bible. If Girard never writes separately on *Nineteen Eighty-Four*, his comments on the modern totalitarian state in *Job* remain extremely useful; and the amount and quality of his work on Shakespeare make it certain that he will turn eventually to *King Lear*.)

Frye refers repeatedly to a Shakespeare who returns to myth and ritual as the bedrock of drama. For Girard, Shakespeare is equally important in a mimetic tradition: as an imitator not of universal forms, literary genres, or nature, but of the social play of imitation itself. Shakespeare's reading of conflictive mimesis is not a structuring of the play by archetypes, but a revelation of how stereotypes of persecution control the machinations of the characters.

Even in England's prehistory, desire is already modernized, metaphysical: to mimetically contend for the father's blessing is to fight over nothing, for nothing comes of nothing. After a somewhat perfunctory description of real estate ("plenteous rivers, and wide-skirted meads"; I, i, 65), *King Lear* nowhere pays any further attention to whatever wealth, privileges, and pleasures follow from taking the father's place everywhere.

The play begins in apparently arbitrary donations and rescensions of paternal blessing which only the mimetic hypothesis can clarify. Gloucester equalizes Edmund to Edgar, but mocks his getting, and talks offhandedly about sending him off again. Yet when Gloucester looks to Lear, he doesn't know what he is doing. Too late will he know that, when he had eyes, he could not see.

To be more precise, Gloucester and Kent don't know why Lear has made a contest to decide what everyone already knows. If Gloucester and Kent know that Lear prefers Albany to Cornwall, Cordelia before her "stepsisters," it can only mean that Lear has performed such "decisions" before. Why is it necessary to go through all this again?

Lear requires this repetition because previous instances have been somehow unsatisfactory. Why hasn't Lear ever gotten what he wants, and why does this failure happen again and again? Girard explains the obsessive failures of metaphysical desire as having nothing to do with desiring defeat. A disciple drawn to insuperable obstacles is still interested in victory, but the only meaningful victory will be over the kind of obstacle that has defeated him previously.

Lear first asks Goneril which daughter loves him best. Goneril was once Lear's only daughter, in a time when such questions were inconceivable; but subsequent paternal blessings have been divided, first in half, then in thirds. Cordelia alone has never suffered this critical diminution of being. Goneril says (as she always has, with progressively diminishing returns) that she loves him best—she presents no obstacle to his desire. His dissatisfaction, signaled by his public reservation of a more ample third for another daughter, can only scandalize her anew. Regan is a more violent contestant that Goneril. She forcibly removes all rivals to Lear's desire: she is enemy to her sister, as well as to all other "joys." Yet Regan's claim of superior difference is likewise annulled.

Why is Cordelia loved best by all? The temptation (to which Kent, and audiences at large, usually succumb) is to take Cordelia's side against all these *other* snobs and hypocrites. But how could such a daughter ever have become the favorite of such a father? The most lucid response is the simplest: this ritual only repeats, in an exacerbated form, what has always happened. The father is unsatisfied by those daughters who love him without reserve, and he is drawn rather to that daughter who does as he does, reserving a portion of her love to some rival.

It is to such rivals for Cordelia that Lear now turns, first by vanquishing Kent's paternal intercession for Cordelia, then by intervening between the competition of France and Burgundy. Burgundy, who would be the establishment suitor of Frye's comic archetype, obeys Lear's prohibition. Burgundy, like Cornwall and Albany, is vanquished as a rival for the daughter's love. But when Lear urges France, the comic suitor, away from loving where he hates, France, like Cordelia, opposes Lear's desire:

> Fairest Cordelia, that art most rich being poor,
> Most choice forsaken, and most loved despised,
> Thee and thy virtues here I seize upon.
> Be it lawful I take up what's cast away.
> Gods, gods! 'Tis strange that from their cold'st neglect
> My love should kindle to inflamed respect (I, i, 250-55)

"Most" modifies both "choice" and "forsaken," "loved" and "despised." That any action could make the one most worthless, most precious, is incomprehensible to France. Therefore he attributes such magic to the gods, not to Lear. The Father's imperious obstacle inflames France's re-gard, re-spect. Paternal violence indicates the desirable. The prohibition against rivalry makes desire transgressive. Violence is the Father of all.

Gloucester blames the "machinations" of Edgar's rivalry on the gods as well, but it is Edmund, and not a messenger from the oracle at Delphi, who tells him his son would replace him everywhere. The quasi-theoretical power of *King Lear* is remarkable. Here are Frye's archetypes of tragic and comic action within the dynamic of a single stereotype of persecution—tragic from the point of view of the victim, comic to the society that profits by his expulsion. The symmetry of such a dynamic does not reflect the untranscendable structure of Mind. Symmetry is the consequence of the mimetic rivalry of age and youth for elusive goals. Edmund consciously mimics the stereotype of Gloucester's anticipation of the other's violence, youth's comic agenda of replacing the aged everywhere.

It should be clear by now that to decide who gets the blame, to expel all the bastards, demonstrates the futility of all violent mythologies. All are guilty, yet none does offend. All (even Edmund) are applying preventive measures to forestall the violence they suspect in others; all are one with Lear's intent that "future strife be prevented now." Goneril ungratefully plots against her father immediately after receiving his "blessing," because she is certain Lear's riotous knights provoke her, grow dangerous in prompting a sign of ingratitude that would require Lear's redress. Goneril and Regan already suspect that their mercurial father (like other retiring father figures in Shakespeare's plays) could arbitrarily take back what he has given. When Oswald faithfully breeds an occasion of insult to Lear (to justify the preventive measures Goneril knows she must take), one of Lear's knights sees this insult as only the latest in a series.

> KNIGHT: My lord, I know not what the matter is; but to my judgement your Highness is not entertained with that ceremonious affection as you were wont. There's a great abatement of kindness appears as well in the general dependents as in the Duke himself also and your daughter.
>
> . . . .
>
> LEAR: Thou but rememb'rest me of mine own conception. I have perceived a most faint neglect of late, which I have rather blamed as mine own jealous curiosity than as a very pretense and purpose of unkindness. (I, iv, 55-67)

Jealous curiosity fathers rivalry everywhere. Albany insulting Lear is an especially incredible accusation. We are shown nothing in the play to suggest that he would ever insult the king, or even rival Cornwall (another rumor). If Cornwall is well known to be "fiery," sufficiently susceptible to retributive violence, we must remember our first glimpse of these fraternal rivals, when Albany and Cornwall act in unison to restrain Lear's violence against Kent: "Dear sir, forbear!" (I, i, 162). Violent reciprocity, once initiated, is a runaway mechanism whose cause is mythical, a plague for which everyone blames everyone else.

King Lear blames women; *King Lear* exonerates all the accused. The difference between the father and the play, the proper name and the title, is the difference, *a real difference*, between reflecting and revealing the scapegoat mechanism. The voices of the fathers begin in coarse play on the place of Edmund's unlawful getting; Lear immediately associates Cordelia's independence to the barbarous, anthrophagous Scythians. The alacrity with which Lear curses each of his daughters in turn a beast, monster, rhymes with the servant who sums this fear of contagion: "If she live long,/ And in the end meet the old course of death,/Women will all turn monsters" (III, vii, 100-102). Women are monstrous doubles, pretenders to autonomy. They are contaminated by the sacred, which is to be plagued by all that threatens social order.

> O, how this mother swells up toward my heart!
> Hysterica passio, down, thou climbing sorrow;
> Thy element's below. Where is this daughter? (II, iv, 54-56)

"Hysterica passio" connects "mother" to "daughter"; their element—like madness, misrule, lechery—is properly below, what violent rivalry leads Regan to name, perhaps by synecdoche, but perhaps not, "the forfended place" (V, i, 11). Prohibition fathers transgressive desires, fetishized desirables. The sacred is behind the play's mercurial veneration and fear of women, and violence is behind the sacred. Lear's madness is his raving fear of being contaminated by the infernal regions of the feminine: "There's hell, there's darkness, there is the sulpherous pit; burning, scalding, stench, consumption" (IV, vi, 127-28).[31]

That future strife may be prevented now, sister contends with sister, brother and brother-in-law with brother, father with son, godson, daughter, bastards all. But the decisive blow can never be struck, and such "plays" of violence can only end for those who renounce their own stereotypes of persecution in humility before the abominable spectacle of breakaway violence.

> The weight of this sad time we must obey,
> Speak what we feel, not what we ought to say.
> The oldest hath born most: we that are young
> Shall never see so much, nor live so long. (V, iii, 324-27)

Whether we follow the folio reading or the quarto, the speaker is a son, godson (Edgar), or son-in-law (Albany) who "ought to" stick up for his own side, youth, the spirit of comedy. Instead, in all humility, this choral voice defers to age. This same humble deference characterizes Lear and Cordelia's reconciliation to each other. Captured by their rivals, they renounce divine autonomy, prestige, all that violence promises for all the father's places. It is sufficient to be father of this daughter, daughter of this father.

But that is not all. When Shakespeare frustrates a narrative expectation uncertainly placed in Holinshed between pagan myth and English dynastic history to rob Lear of Cordelia in the end, he reveals the "things hidden since the foundation of the world." The play enacts the last possible occasion when all could still unilaterally renounce these scandalous repetitions of mimetic entanglements for peace. Because they live before Judeo-Christian revelation, they cannot know the day and the hour. It is futile to prosecute any sides, to contest comic myth and tragic myth against each other. *King Lear* forgives all those who know not what they do.

But what of us, the beneficiaries of the precious critical terminology of a fundamental anthropology, interdividual psychology, and the Judeo-Christian scriptures? What forgiveness for those who have eyes yet cannot see?

Let us re-gard, re-spect a text that we, as literary intellectuals, have twice modernized (after its publication in 1949, and after its resuscitation in 1984), each time putting it behind us with the same complacency with which Lentricchia outmodes New Criticism and Northrop Frye: Orwell's *Nineteen Eighty-Four*. Furthermore, let us test the future of Girard's theory this time against Edward Said, a self-confessed opponent of "religious criticism" (although secular criticism, Said's alternative, is opposed solely to the title of Girard's work).[32]

The critic's job, according to Said, is not to serve wall-to-wall discourses that absorb any individual, resisting voice. Criticism must limit theory (rather than spreading it) by localizing, circumscribing its itinerary from one site to another. A sanative interest in delimiting theory, however, faces its own challenge of premature limitation. Said unpersuasively restricts the travel of his reading of Orientalism to other archival formations, and he resigns himself philosophically, despite the example of his own passionate resistance, to culture as an exclusionary mechanism.[33]

Both Said and Girard agree on the cultural strength that the West derives from its anthropological interests, but Said has a more ominous vision of what these "interests" are. Balfour, he reminds us, defended England's imperium in Egypt, a culture with an admittedly greater cultural pedigree, because it was Europe alone that could make such a comparison (*Orientalism*, p. 32). Yet what makes the work of Girard and Said compatible is their belief in the critical power of individual texts to reveal, as well as reflect, cultural mythology. For Girard, this critical position (Said's term is "strategic location") is achieved by the power of theory to be more scientific, more reductive than the dominant discourse; for Said, criticism *places* the worldliness of a dominant theory, influential texts, showing by inference where theory does not or cannot extend.

Now we may turn to two related considerations: the worldliness of theory and text in Orwell's novel *Nineteen Eighty-Four* and the worldliness of the novel as theory, as text, from 1949. This second consideration can be subdivided into three related categories: (1) the historical moment of the novel's composition—in general, the work of cultural historians, British studies specialists, Bernard Crick, as well as the personal reminiscences of family and friends; (2) the predictive value of the novel, over thirty-five years, for the year 1984 which made "Orwellian" a parody of the signifying power of symbolic language; (3) most interestingly, the imagined world of its own composition. *Nineteen Eighty-Four* is attributed to an anonymous, post-1984 scholiast who looks back complacently on 1984 as we do now, with no sense of limits on its knowledge of Winston's limits.

What is the place of a scapegoat hypothesis in a worldly text like *Nineteen Eighty-Four*? Winston, as the last man in a venerable European tradition, maintains the historical animus against Jews, women, and Orientals, but Oceania has suppressed the modern critical vocabulary of anti-Semitism, sexism, and racism. Propaganda efficiently applies some hidden theoretical model for violent unanimity, transferring enmity the way the "capitalists" transferred luggage and laundry onto someone else's back. The two-minute hate, which provokes Winston's diary, conforms to Girard's analysis of the scapegoat mechanism: (1) the characteristic preparation which qualifies a sacrificial victim; (2) the moment of oscillation, the crisis of difference, when violence apparently ranges at will, to choose its victims; (3) the technique of transference; (4) the order of polarization, where everyone is united in opposition to a single victim responsible for all their troubles; (5) and finally, the sacred peace attributed to the divinity that follows the successful resolution of the sacrificial crisis.

The narrator places us so that we can see what Winston ought to see, a classic demonstration of scapegoating. (1) Sacrificial victims chosen outside the group to be unified must be rehabilitated, incorporated so that they can stand for the whole community; victims from inside must be estranged, to separate them from potential allies who might enter the conflict on their behalf. The double valence of familiar and stranger essential to the proper victim is well satisfied by Goldstein's qualifications: betrayer, parodist of Newspeak, Jew. (2) The moment of oscillation is when the ritual re-enacts the crisis of degree, the moment when the whole community could fall into a violent, interminable conflict, into a loss of difference, because everyone has become everyone else's enemy. Not only does the contest of violent hatred oscillate back and forth between Big Brother and Goldstein (like the contest of violent mastery between Oedipus and Creon, or Bacchus and Pentheus), but Goldstein is also surcharged with the image of non-differentiation: he bleats like a sheep (a classic sacrificial animal), he stands for the faceless Asiatic hordes. (3) Violent antagonism is channeled, transferred to Goldstein; everyone hates the same man, the Enemy of the People. Thus (4) the community is united in polar opposition to their single common enemy, who is responsible for all crimes, all treacheries. Finally (5), there is the theophanic moment, when the god for whom the sacrifice is performed appears, to give his blessing. The sandy-haired woman sitting by Winston who offers her savior, Big Brother, a prayer is essential for blocking recognition of the real mechanism. The transcendent god is the misrepresentation of human violence successfully transferred, channeled to a single victim, which produces peace for everyone else.

Winston makes an important observation that could lead to a full critical understanding of the scapegoat mechanism: the arbitrariness of the victim. Winston sees that the collective animus against Goldstein is charged like an electric current, polarized, abstract, capable of being directed at Big Brother or Julia as well as at Goldstein. Characteristically, this observation doesn't make it into his diary, his text, but it is clearly there as already understood by us.

Why? It will take the rest of this essay to give an answer, but perhaps you are already anticipating that I will finally succumb to a theoretical snobbism attributed to all non-Girardian critics who minimize the quasi-theoretical potential of literary texts. You may suspect that I will show up Winston and/or Orwell before (me and) Girard, the way Culler reads Flaubert as a hesitating anticipation of what we already know.

The first answer is that we are all already accused of being theoretical snobs by Orwell himself. The text is structured so that reader and narrator are assumed to know full well what Winston at best suspects. This would remain true to Orwell's text even if, or when, we do exceed Orwell's understanding of totalitarianism. As I hope to show, it is not the possession of superior theoretical knowledge alone that characterizes the strategic location of the reader of *Nineteen Eighty-Four* in whatever after-year. Rather, it is the scandal of such knowledge coexisting hypocritically (in the most literal sense) with violent mechanisms of social cohesion no longer misunderstood as divine.

If our interest is in the worldliness of text and theory, then surely the place to begin is with the Oceanic ambitions for the Eleventh Edition of the Newspeak Dictionary: " 'The Eleventh Edition is the definitive edition,' he said. 'We're getting the language into its final shape—the shape it's going to have when nobody speaks anything else. When we're finished with it, people like you will have to learn it all over again. You think, I dare say, that our chief job is inventing new words. But not a bit of it. We're destroying words—scores of them, hundreds of them, every day. We're cutting the language to the bone. The Eleventh Edition won't contain a single word that will become obsolete before the year 2050.' "[34] The theoretical potential of *Nineteen Eighty-Four* is strikingly different from the postmodernism of new criticisms and new novels, in covert ideological harmony with the modernization of underdeveloped labor and nations. Modernization is only apparently the production of new forms; "ungood" is a linguistic device for setting aside the history in language that might resist a purification to perfect instrumentality.

> "It's a beautiful thing, the destruction of words. Of course the great wastage is in the verbs and adjectives, but there are hundreds of nouns that can be got rid of as well. It isn't only the synonyms; there are also the antonyms. After all, what justification is there for a word which is simply the opposite of some other word? A word contains its opposite in itself. Take 'good,' for instance. If you have a word like 'good,' what sense is there in having a whole string of vague useless words like 'excellent' and 'splendid' and all the rest of them? 'Plusgood' covers the meaning, or 'doubleplusgood' if you want something stronger still. Of course we use those forms already, but in the final version of Newspeak there'll be nothing else. In the end the whole notion of goodness and badness will be covered by only six words—in reality, only one word. Don't you see the beauty of that, Winston? It was B.B.'s idea originally, of course," he added as an afterthought. [45-46]

What does our attention to the worldliness of Orwell's text, and the worldliness of our privileged, strategic location of superior theory in relation to the year 1984, require us to see in the world projected by the Eleventh Edition? A structuralist model of language, of course, a system of pure differences with no positive terms; but also a deconstruction of these oppositions as interested, anything but pure. Finally, the polarization of good/ungood as a violent structuration, the linguistic parallel to the scapegoat mechanism. From a Girardian perspective, the oppositions that structuralists are so fond of collecting (and that post-structuralists are so fond of deconstructing) occur because there are ultimately only two sides to any violent resolution. We see not how language works by "itself" (we are not fooled by Syme's theory) but how it is to *be* worked, for ideological purposes, in the future. Structural oppositions that dissolve the referential power of symbolic thought are themselves deconstructed, to disable the language and the literature of the past that it renders obsolete.

This is the key to the work that Smith, as a literary intellectual, is asked to do with the public record, the social text. It is not simply (as Winston seems to think) the legitimation of the Party's day-to-day interests, but involves the transformation of daily life into a system of pure oppositions with no positive terms—a network of pure intertextuality that renders the material reality of any opposition to the State obsolete, ungood, vaporized. We know, even better than Winston, how unworldly his manuscript evidence of Party misrepresentation is, against the Party's textual power, or even against O'Brien's offhand claim of authorship of *The Theory and Practice of Oligarchical Collectivism*.

How, then, is Winston's diary contained in the worldliness of *Nineteen Eighty-Four*? What happens to the potential value of what Winston has seen, for the necessary inventory of Oceania's traces on him? *Nineteen Eighty-Four* in fact begins with Winston coming home for lunch after the Two-Minute Hate, to begin his diary: "For whom, it suddenly occurred to him to wonder, was he writing this diary? For the future, for the unborn. His mind hovered for a moment round the doubtful date on the page, and then fetched up with a bump against the Newspeak word *doublethink*. For the first time the magnitude of what he had undertaken came home to him. How could you communicate with the future? It was of its nature impossible. Either the future would resemble the present, in which case it would not listen to him, or it would be different from it, and his predicament would be meaningless" (7). We see how well, in Winston's *rezeptiontheorie*, the structures of opposition embedded in social and linguistic forms erase the future, *by nature*, in advance.

Such structures dog Winston's view of Julia as well, as he desires and hates her by turns. When she sends him something to read, he already knows she belongs to one of two oppositions, the Party or the Brotherhood. She becomes the sign of Winston's remedial education in Room 101, where he learns to transfer the violence that threatens him: "Do it to Julia!"

How can we estimate what has happened to the potential for "critical elaboration" in Winston's recognition of the arbitrary sign of the victim, his knowledge that violence could have chosen another? Two aspects of Girard's theory will help us read the cultural order of Oceania. (1) Girard disagrees with Frazer and the Cambridge Ritualists, by insisting that primitives are not hypocrites. The social link missing from the victim, which allows collective violence against it to remain unanswered, is not a conscious criterion for choice. The scapegoat is not seen as sacred because he is victimizable, but victimizable because he is seen as sacred. (2) Girard's mimetic model makes unnecessary Freudianism's proliferation of psychic agencies, especially an unconscious produced and repressed by a fleeting recognition of incestuous desires. *Doublethink*, directed toward the recognition of violence's arbitrary signification of The Enemy of the People, unites all Oceania in a post-Frazerian *hypocritical* practice of sacrifice. Furthermore, each shares a post-Freudian unconscious produced not by a fleeting recognition of incestuous desires, but by doublethinking the arbitrary transfer of violence and then doublethinking itself, the trace of the trace. Doublethink becomes the primary psychic agency, solid enough for Winston's mind to bump into, in the passage above.

We watch Winston fail to understand the founding of the symbolic in unanimous violence, which allows only two sides to any question, in the clothes philosophy of Oceania. Forced to wear uniforms, Winston and Julia politicize taking them off. Winston dreams of Julia's gesture of throwing her clothes aside, which seems to "annihilate a whole culture, a whole system of thought, as though Big Brother and the Party and the Thought Police could all be swept into nothingness by a single splendid movement of the arm" (29). Similarly, Winston dutifully asks his prole-informant if the capitalists wore tophats. The yes-or-no answer Winston's question allows cannot compare with what the prole offers him when he mentions that tophats could be hired for the occasion. We can see how radically this shifts the ground of understanding power, from the acquisition of property whose signified value is accepted, constant, natural, to the regulated envy and obsolescence of arbitrated symbols of (violently, mimetically contested) being.[35]

It is hard not to sense Orwell's justifiable pride in the acuteness of his own down-and-out fieldwork during the 1930s.

Although Winston's diary becomes more worldly, more interested in both circumstantial detail and theory, it never overcomes the influence of O'Brien, seen in the first chapter:

> Momentarily he caught O'Brien's eye. O'Brien had stood up. He had taken off his spectacles and was in the act of resetting them on his nose with his characteristic gesture. But there was a fraction of a second when their eyes met, and for as long as it took to happen Winston knew—yes, he *knew!*—that O'Brien was thinking the same thing as himself. An unmistakable message had passed. It was as though their two minds had opened and the thoughts were flowing from one into the other through their eyes. "I am with you," O'Brien seemed to say to him. "I know precisely what you are feeling. I know all about your contempt, your hatred, your disgust. But don't worry. I am on your side!" And then the flash of intelligence was gone, and O'Brien's face was as inscrutable as everyone else's. [13]

Winston never followed out the consequences of his critical consciousness of the scapegoat mechanism in the Two-Minute Hate, even to the point of entering it in the diary, because O'Brien understands, always already, precisely what he feels, thinking exactly what Winston thinks. The diary remains only interpersonal communication written, finally, for O'Brien, not analysis of the social text for some future. Like Winston's reductive formula for dismissing the future of his diary, the opposition of history and writing misplaces the real option of usable political analysis. Winston's "knowledge" of O'Brien is as dangerously totalized as the screen version of Goldstein.

But if O'Brien is Winston's future reader, so is the narrator of *Nineteen Eighty-Four*—and, following the narrator, so are we. If Winston is victimized by O'Brien's gaze of comprehension, how are we to place the understanding that we have been assumed by Orwell to share with the narrator, as we look back to 1984? Where did this narrator's knowledge of Winston's thought come from, and what is the context, the world of our own critical understanding?

We seem unable or unwilling to protect theory from modernization. The rise and fall of critical fame is *fama*; the model behind the turbulence of the institution of criticism is the *turba*, which also requires a Girardian reading. It would be hypocritical—*hypocriticism*, in fact—to blind ourselves to the cyclothymia of the critical languages of anti-Semitism/orientalism, racism, and sexism, before the perdurable violence they comprehend. The cultural strength of critical theory for the future is now decided by the mechanism of news: not just advertising, whose model is mimetic desire, but the turbulence and the modernizing of public attention itself.

NOTES

1. See James George Frazer, *The Golden Bough* (London: Macmillan, 1911–15), 12 vols. Most pertinent to this discussion is *The Scapegoat* (1913). For Jane Harrison, see *Prolegomena to the Study of Greek Religion* (London: Cambridge University Press, 1927). The second edition contains essays by Gilbert Murray and F. M. Cornford.

2. Edward Said, "The Totalitarianism of Mind," *Kenyon Review* 29 (March 1967): 256–68.

3. René Girard, *Mensonge romantique et vérité romanesque* (Paris: Bernard Grasset, 1961); *Deceit, Desire, and the Novel* (Baltimore: Johns Hopkins University Press, 1965).

4. René Girard, *La Violence et le sacré* (Paris: Bernard Grasset, 1972); *Violence and the Sacred* (Baltimore: Johns Hopkins University Press, 1977).

5. See René Girard, "Interdividual Psychology," *Things Hidden since the Foundation of the World* (Stanford: Stanford University Press, 1987), pp. 283–431, but also *Job: The Victim of His People* (Stanford: Stanford University Press, 1988), 111–23.

6. This essay takes the position that one must follow the most comprehensive theory of the relation between myth, ritual, and literature. For an alternative approach that maps all mythographers without choosing between them, see William G. Doty, *Mythography* (University: University of Alabama Press, 1986). The choice being argued in this essay isn't who (not) to read, but how to read them all. One ought to read *everything* by Freud, Gernet, Lévi-Strauss, Frye, Vernant, and Burkert *again*, from a mimetic hypothesis.

7. For Girard on Lévi-Strauss, see especially *Violence and the Sacred*, Ch. 9. Pages 328–32 of *La Violence et le sacré* were cut from what is now the first paragraph on p. 240 of *Violence and the Sacred*. See

also Chs. 8 and 9 in *To Double Business Bound* (Baltimore: Johns Hopkins University Press, 1978).

8. Sigmund Freud, *Massenpsychologie und Ich-Analyse* (Leipzig: Internationaler Psychoanalytischer Verlag, 1921); *The Standard Edition of the Complete Psychological Works of Sigmund Freud*, trans. James Strachey (London: Hogarth Press, 1961), 19:66.

9. Sigmund Freud, *Das Ich und das Es* (Leipzig: Internationaler Psychoanalytischer Verlag, 1923); *The Standard Edition of the Complete Psychological Works of Sigmund Freud*, trans. James Strachey (London: Hogarth Press, 1955), Vol. 18.

10. Sarah Kofman, "The Narcissistic Woman: Freud and Girard," *Diacritics* 10 (September 1980): 36–45; Toril Moi, "The Missing Mother: The Oedipal Rivalries of René Girard," *Diacritics* 12 (Summer 1982): 21–31; Mary Jacobus, "Is There a Woman in This Text?," *New Literary History* 14 (Autumn 1982): 117–41. The reading of Girard in these essays is sacrificial: Girard is blamed for excluding women. Like Freud, he resents their self-sufficiency. Further, Kofman argues that Girard fears the female genitalia, which he will only refer to in Freud's German. Can the patriarchy be undone by a few women clad in trenchcoats, lurking in the bushes by Lake Lagunita? A real dialogue between Girardian and feminist theory might take up the following issues: (1) Girard's theory comprehends the patriarchal dynamics that exlude (sacralize) women; (2) the mimetic theory denies patriarchal and matriarchal "essentialism," the autonomy of narcissism as well as coquetry; (3) Girard's commitment to the quasi-theoretical potential of literary texts might challenge the emerging orthodoxy of diagnosing as masochistic Virginia Woolf's unilateral renunciation of masculine competition, anger, violence. *A Room of One's Own* (1929) insists that masculine violence is mimetic, metaphysical, contagious. Men dominate the world by crediting themselves with twice the being of women. Resentment alternates with veneration (cyclothymia), which can provoke women's writing into doubling male competitive "hysteria," blocking the possibility of seeing things nonviolently, in themselves. See Adrienne Rich, "When We Dead Awaken: Writing as Revision," in *On Lies, Secrets, and Silence: Selected Prose, 1966–78* (New York: Norton, 1979); Elaine Showalter, *A Literature of Their Own: British Women Novelists from Brontë to Lessing* (Princeton: Princeton University Press, 1977); Jane Marcus, "Art and Anger," *Feminist Studies* 4 (1978): 66–99. Despite playing an important part in the renaissance of Woolf studies, these essays add themselves to the depressing tradition of diagnosticians who know better than Woolf herself the

cause and cure of her illness. Perhaps we could finally try out Woolf's own hypothesis: that being angry was like being mad.

11. Robert Graves, *Greek Myths* (Harmondsworth: Penguin Books, 1972).

12. See especially Erich Neumann, *The Origins and History of Consciousness* (Princeton: Princeton University Press, 1970) and *The Great Mother* (Princeton: Princeton University Press, 1972). Neumann explains the sacred ambivalence of the feminine as "dynamic reversal," the point when a "good" feminine archetype mercurially turns against consciousness.

13. Edward Said, *The World, the Text, and the Critic* (Cambridge: Harvard University Press, 1983), esp. Ch. 8.

14. Jean Michel Ourghourlian, *Un Mime nommé desir* (Paris: Bernard Grasset, 1982).

15. Walter Burkert, *Homo Necans* (Berkeley: University of California Press, 1983); also see *Structure and History in Greek Mythology and Ritual* (Berkeley: University of California Press, 1979); *Greek Religion* (Cambridge: Harvard University Press, 1985).

16. See the papers from a 1983 conference in which both Girard and Burkert participated, in *Violent Origins*, ed. Robert G. Hamerton-Kelly (Stanford: Stanford University Press, 1987). For the first mimetic reading of Burkert's hunting hypothesis, see Andrew McKenna, "Introduction," *René Girard and Biblical Studies, Semeia 33* (Decatur, Ga.: Scholars Press, 1985), pp. 5–6.

17. Louis Gernet, *The Anthropology of Ancient Greece*, trans. John Hamilton, S.J., and Blaine Nagy (Baltimore: Johns Hopkins University Press, 1981); Jean Pierre Vernant et Pierre Vidal-Naquet, *Myth et tragédie en Grèce ancienne* (Paris: François Maspero, 1972); *Myth et tragédie en Grèce ancienne, T.II* (Paris: Éditions La Découverte, 1986); Detienne et Vernant, *Les Ruses de l'intelligence* (Paris: Flammarion, 1974).

18. See Vernant, "Ambiguité et renversement," In *Myth et tragédie*, pp. 101–31.

19. Girard, *Violence and the Sacred*, pp. 234–36; *Things Hidden since the Foundation of the World*, pp. 99–104.

20. Claude Lévi-Strauss, *Structural Anthropology*, trans. Claire Jacobson and Brooks Grundfest Schoepf (New York: Basic Books, 1963), pp. 206–31.

21. Sandor Goodhart, "Leskas Ephaske: Oedipus and Laius' Many Murderers," *Diacritics* 8:1 (Spring 1978): 55–71.

22. "Discussion avec René Girard," *Esprit* 429 (Novembre 1973): 528–63; "Interview," *Diacritics* 8:1 (Spring 1978): 31–54: Girard, *Things*

Hidden since the Foundations of the World, pp. 126–38; René Girard, *Le Bouc émissaire* (Paris: Grasset, 1982); trans. Yvonne Freccero as *The Scapegoat* (Baltimore: Johns Hopkins University Press, 1986).

23. See *L'Enfer des choses: René Girard et la logique de l'economie*, ed. Paul Dumouchel et Jean Pierre Dupuy (Paris: Grasset, 1982); *René Girard et le probleme du Mal*, ed. Michel Deguy et Jean-Pierre Dupuy (Paris: Grasset, 1982); *Disorder and Order: Proceedings of the Stanford International Symposium* (Sept. 14–16, 1981), ed. Paisley Livingston, in *Stanford Literature Studies* 1 (1984); *Violence et vérité: autour de René Girard*, ed. Paul Dumouchel (Paris: Grasset, 1985); *Violence and Truth, On the Work of René Girard*, ed. Paul Dumouchel (Stanford: Stanford University Press, 1988); for a full bibliography of primary and secondary sources, see *Stanford French Review* 10:1–3 (1986).

24. Northrop Frye, *Anatomy of Criticism* (Princeton: Princeton University Press, 1957).

25. Frank Lentricchia, *After the New Criticism* (Chicago: University of Chicago Press, 1980), pp. 3–26. For a more complex assessment of Frye, see *Centre and Labyrinth: Essays in Honour of Northrop Frye*, ed. Eleanor Cook, Chaviva Hošek, Jay Macpherson, Particia Parker, and Julian Patrick (Toronto: University of Toronto Press, 1983), especially the essay by Paul Ricoeur.

26. Northrop Frye, *The Secular Scripture* (Cambridge: Harvard University Press, 1976): *The Great Code* (New York: Harcourt Brace Jovanovich, 1982).

27. Northrop Frye, *The Educated Imagination* (Bloomington: Indiana University Press, 1964).

28. See my essay, "The Sparagmos of Myth Is the Naked Lunch of Mode: Modern Literature as the Age of Frye and Borges," *boundary 2* 8 (Fall 1980): 297–311.

29. Jacques Derrida, *Dissemination*, trans. Barbara Johnson (Chicago: University of Chicago Press, 1981), p. 132.

30. Girard, "Introduction" to *To Double Business Bound*, pp. vii–xvi. See also "Lévi-Strauss, Frye, Derrida and Shakespearean Criticism," *Diacritics* 3 (Fall 1973): 34–38; "Myth and Ritual in Shakespeare: *A Midsummer Night's Dream*," in *Textual Strategies: Perspectives in Post-Structural Criticism*, ed. Josué V. Harari (Ithaca: Cornell University Press, 1979), pp. 189–212; "To Entrap the Wisest": A Reading of *The Merchant of Venice*," in *Literature and Society*, ed. Edward Said (Baltimore: Johns Hopkins University Press, 1980), pp. 100–119; "Comedies of Errors: Plautus-Shakespeare-Molière," in *American Criticism in the Post-Structuralist Age*, ed. Ira Konigsberg

(Ann Arbor: University of Michigan Press, 1981), pp. 68–96; "Hamlet's Dull Revenge," *Stanford Literature Review* 1 (Fall 1984): 159–200.

31. I have found the following essays useful: Esther Fischer-Homberger, "Hysterie und Misogynie—ein Aspekt der Hysteriegeschichte," *Gesnerus* 26: 1–2 (1969): 117–27; Madelon Gohlke, " 'I wooed thee with my sword': Shakespeare's Tragic Paradigms," in *Representing Shakespeare: New Psychoanalytic Essays,* ed. Murray M. Schwartz and Coppélia Kahn (Baltimore: Johns Hopkins University Press, 1980), pp. 170–87; Coppélia Kahn, "Excavating 'Those Dim Minoan Regions': Maternal Subtexts in Patriarchal Literature," *Diacritics* 12 (1982): 32–41. See also Lawrence R. Schehr, "King Lear: Monstrous Mimesis," *SubStance* 11:3 (1982): 51-63; Michael Hinchliffe, "The Error of King Lear," *Actes du Centre Aixois de Recherches Anglaises* (Aix: Université de Provence, 1980).

32. Said, *The World, the Text, and the Critic,* pp. 290–92.

33. Edward Said, *Orientalism* (New York: Pantheon, 1978), pp. 23, 45; and *Blaming the Victim,* ed. Edward Said and Christopher Hutchins (London: Verso Books, 1988), p. 178.

34. George Orwell, *Nineteen Eighty-Four* (New York: New American Library, 1982), pp. 45–46.

35. See especially Dumouchel and Dupuy, *L'Enfer des choses.*

RELATIONS:
TRANSDISCIPLINARY

EDWARD DAVENPORT

The Scientific Spirit

> Ironically enough, objectivity is closely bound up with the
> *social aspect of scientific method*, with . . . the *friendly-*
> *hostile co-operation of many scientists.*
> —Karl Popper

> A particular set of shared values interacts with the
> particular experiences shared by a community of specialists
> to ensure that most . . . will ultimately find one set of
> arguments rather than another decisive.
> —Thomas Kuhn

Which Scientific Spirit?

The trouble with the scientific spirit is that there are so many of them. Thus, when we ask whether literary criticism can be conducted in a scientific spirit, it is important to determine which spirit of science is under our lens. Andrew Field, justifying his artistic approach to literary biography in his life of Vladimir Nabokov, takes as his critical credo an anti-scientific blast from H. L. Mencken:

> The assumption that it may be scientific is the worst curse that lies upon criticism. It is responsible for all the dull, blowsy, "definitive" stuff that literary pedagogues write, and it is responsible, too, for the heavy posturing that so often goes on among critics less learned. Both groups proceed upon the theory that there are exact facts to be ascertained, and that it is their business to ascertain and proclaim them. That theory is nonsense. There is, in truth, no such thing as

an exact fact in the whole realm of the beautiful arts. . . . The critic survives, when he survives at all, mainly as artist. His judgments, in the long run, become archaic, and may be disregarded. But if, in stating them, he has incidentally produced a work of art on his own account, then he is read long after they are rejected, and it may be plausibly argued that he has contributed something to the glory of letters.[1]

The literary scientists so effectively skewered by Mencken have a number of specific qualities: they view science mainly as the gathering of exact facts; they see the compilation of such facts as resulting in definitive knowledge; and they write badly because they reject any artistic element in criticism. It does not take an excess of sympathetic counterreading to imagine literary scientists rather different from this. The notion of science as fact-gathering is certainly a venerable one, going back beyond Bacon to Aristotle, but it was hardly the reigning theory of science by Mencken's time, and it was not the theory of science which motivated such would-be literary scientists as Hippolyte Taine or I. A. Richards. To quote Thomas Kuhn: "Though this sort of fact-collecting has been essential to the origin of many significant sciences, anyone who examines, for example, Pliny's encyclopedic writings or the Baconian natural histories of the seventeenth century will discover that it produces a morass. . . . No natural history can be interpreted in the absence of at least some implicit body of intertwined theoretical and methodological belief that permits selection, evaluation, and criticism."[2]

By the time Mencken wrote, the notion of definitive or final truth in science had also been definitively undermined by Einstein's revolution in physical theory, although this tottering of scientific certainty was, perhaps, not so well understood by literary researchers or others outside physics. Finally, the claim that the classics of criticism survive only as art works—not as structures of knowledge—is belied by the intensity with which the literary conjectures of Plato and Aristotle, Kant, Coleridge, and Schleiermacher are still debated.

Even in their artistic aspect, critical works have to do with facts and truth. Gerald Graff made that point about art in general in *Poetic Statement and Critical Dogma*.[3] E. D. Hirsch has made the point that, when we speak of knowledge and truth claims in the arts, we are not speaking of a special artistic way of knowing separate from the spirit of natural science.[4]

Criticism, like philosophy, perhaps survives as a kind of hybrid of science and art, but the idea that facts—even "exact facts"—never matter in literature and criticism, cannot stand. It is true that Nabokov himself, in his novel about literary biography (*The Real Life of Sebastian Knight*), warns us that literary facts are elusive: "Beware of the most honest broker. Remember that what you are told is really threefold: shaped by the teller, reshaped by the listener, concealed from both by the dead man of the tale."[5]

But that novel also contains a virulent attack on the slipshod literary biographer Goodman and his carelessness with facts. At one point, Nabokov's narrator reminds himself that he cannot reject everything Goodman says just because Goodman is so irresponsible about accuracy: "I want to be scientifically precise. I should hate being balked of the tiniest particle of truth only because at a certain point of my search I was blindly enraged by a trashy concoction."[6]

Modern literary criticism has been haunted by the scientific spirit—in fact, by several divergent shades of science—from its very beginnings in Spinoza's book on the scientific approach to interpreting scripture.[7] To understand what literary criticism has been, and (even more) to understand what it can be, depends in part on a clearer articulation of the various styles of scientific practice underlying the methods of investigation and argument that critics use.

We could start with the popular distinction according to which science is opposed to literature and life: "Science is crude, life is subtle, and it is for the correction of this disparity that literature matters to us."[8] So writes Roland Barthes, and he elaborates the distinction according to two views of knowledge—as statement and as action:

> According to scientific discourse—or a certain discourse of science—knowledge is statement; in writing, it is an act of stating. The statement, the usual object of linguistics, is given as the product of the subject's absence. The act of stating, by exposing the subject's place and energy, even his deficiency (which is not his absence), focuses on the very reality of language, acknowledging that language is an immense halo of implications, of effects, of echoes, of turns, returns,

and degrees. . . . Words are no longer conceived illusively as simple instruments; they are cast as projections, explosions, vibrations, devices, flavors. Writing makes knowledge festive.[9]

For Barthes, the student of literature is both a scientist and a writer, caught between two uses of language, two views of knowledge, in attempting to know literature. Thus Barthes writes with mock modesty: "And though it is true that I long wished to inscribe my work within the field of science—literary, lexicological, and sociological—I must admit that I have produced only essays, an ambiguous genre in which analysis vies with writing."[10]

Moreover, the student of literature is not alone in this ambiguous position of having to combine scientific analysis with respect for the "immense halo" of language. Students of human culture generally (social scientists and humanists) have found their analyses subject to this ungainly constraint. Marxist science, one of the most influential varieties of scientific spirit today, has undergone severe reconceptualization in recent years. Jürgen Habermas, a foremost theoretician of neo-Marxism, tells us that the Marxist spirit of science must be viewed no longer as a positivist but as a dialogical spirit.

Habermas reminds us that science seeks not just data, but meanings—the Barthesian "immense halo" of meanings that surround human thought, intentions, and behavior, and that must somehow be taken account of when seeking knowledge of humans.[11] His solution is to substitute psychoanalysis for physics as the model for Marxist science. One must give up the anonymity (exchangeability) of the observing subject, and thus give up the reproducibility of the observation, in exchange for "a participatory relation of the understanding subject to the subject confronting him."[12]

And if the psychological or sociological observer is no longer to be taken as exchangeable, how much less so the literary observer (reader). And how much less, then, can we expect the simple reproducibility of the literary observation—a conclusion extensively amplified in the contemporary reader-response theory of Holland, Bleich, and others.[13]

Yet Habermas clings to the difficult gesture of attempting to balance science viewed as factual statement with science viewed as action: "To be sure (as the example of the ground rules for the psychoanalytic dialogue shows) this makes disciplinary constraints more necessary than ever. The fashionable demand for a kind of 'action research,' that is to combine political enlightenment with research, overlooks that the uncontrolled modification of the field is incompatible with the simultaneous gathering of data in that field, a condition which is also valid for the social sciences."[14] In other words, it is still possible and desirable not to precook the facts, even if all facts are theory laden.

To be historically accurate, the Marxist spirit(s) of science always were distinct from (other) positivist spirits of science, since the Marxist science of literature (for example) did not merely seek to causally connect literature to the social and physical world (as Hippolyte Taine did) but sought causal connections to the social and physical world *as understood in the axioms of Marxism*. In a Marxist critique, the social and physical world will be presented in the vocabulary developed for this purpose by Marx, rather than, for example, in the vocabulary of Malthus or Darwin. This can be illustrated by a passage from Georg Lukacs's essay, "Franz Kafka or Thomas Mann?":

> The diabolical character of the world of modern capitalism, and man's impotence in the face of it, is the real subject-matter of Kafka's writing. His simplicity and sincerity are, of course, the product of complex and contradictory forces. Let us consider only one aspect. Kafka wrote at a time when capitalist society, the object of his *angst*, was still far from the high mark of its historical development. What he described and "demonized" was not the truly demonic world of Fascism, but the world of the Hapsburg Monarchy. *Angst*, haunting and indefinable, is perfectly reflected in this vague, ahistorical, time-less world, steeped in the atmosphere of Prague. Kafka profited from his historical position in two ways. On the one hand, his narrative detail gains from being rooted in the Austrian society of that period. On the other hand, the essential unreality of human existence, which it is his aim to convey, can be related to a corresponding sense of unreality and foreboding in the society he knew. The identification with the *condition humaine* is far more convincing than in later visions of a diabolical, *angst*-inspiring world, where so much has to be eliminated or obscured by formal experimentation to achieve the desired ahistorical, timeless image of the human condition. But this, though the reason for the astonishing impact and lasting power of Kafka's work, cannot disguise its basically allegorical character. The

wonderfully suggestive descriptive detail points to a transcendent reality, to the anticipated reality—stylized into timelessness—of fully developed imperialism.[15]

Lukacs's vocabulary—"capitalism," "contradictory forces," "historical development," "ahistorical," "rooted in society," "imperialism"—is characteristic and reveals the metaphysical framework (for Lukacs, no doubt, an "objective framework") in which Lukacs writes his "natural history" of literature. For Lukacs, the scientific outlook itself, especially as it affected literature, has to be explained in terms of the Marxist interpretation of society. Lukacs elsewhere equates the late nineteenth century scientific spirit with intellectual alienation, thus not only explaining it, but also distancing Marxist science from the rest of science, since Marxist science ought to be in a position to understand and transcend such alienation.[16]

The social axioms of Marxist literary science (be they true or false) provide a valuable framework for developing causal explanations, as the Lukacs passages should illustrate. The social world must, of necessity, be interpreted fairly fully before one can possibly begin to develop any causal links between literature and society. That the Marxist literary scientist has had a full interpretation of the social world at hand is perhaps the reason why Marxist causal explanations of literature have survived and flourished so much longer than other positivist causal explanations.

These days causal explanations of literature are often referred to as positivist, or "naively positivist"; but here, too, a more accurate differentiation of scientific spirits could be helpful. Strictly speaking, positivists did not seek causal explanations, since positivists considered the notion of cause to be too metaphysical to be scientific. So someone like Taine, who sought causal explanations for literature, ought not to be considered a positivist (as indeed René Wellek says, though perhaps more with an eye to Taine being a much better literary critic than Wellek thinks positivists have any right to be).[17]

The question whether causal explanations can be considered scientific still surfaces occasionally. A recent (1984) Soviet text on philosophy of science, *Alternatives to Positivism*, by Igor Naletov, surveys contemporary philosophers of science, including Popper, Kuhn, Lakatos, Feyerabend, Agassi, and Rorty, in order to fit them into the Soviet Marxist scientific framework. While Naletov examines in detail the ways these philosophers offer "alternatives to positivism," in the end none escapes far enough from positivism to suit him. A crucial distinction is the question of causality. Naletov writes: "Throughout its entire history positivism has been denouncing, in one or another form and more or less resolutely, the principle of causality as typically metaphysical. Significantly, Machism and logical positivism rejected this principle and the meaningfulness of the categories 'cause' and 'effect' on the grounds that they could not be tested empirically, i.e. verified or confirmed."[18]

Naletov says that post-positivist philosophers of science like Popper are almost as bad because they hold "cause" to be conjectural and not objective. For Naletov, it is important not only that causes and effects themselves be objective, but also that the causal relation be objective "independent of consciousness." Otherwise Marxist axioms about causal relations in the social world would have to be seen as conjectural, which is not yet a possibility for Soviet Marxism.

Naletov reminds us of something often forgotten today, that positivism per se was more interested in observing and describing than in making causal conjectures. This is why something like literary structuralism is much more "positivist" than Taine's causal explanations. Both the structural linguistics of Saussure and Russian formalism, which stand behind the structuralism of Lévi-Strauss, were of positivist origin. Interestingly, Victor Erlich, in his book *Russian Formalism*, speaks of two strands of literary positivism: the evolutionary-determinist-causal positivism of Taine, and the structural-descriptive positivism of formalists like Eichenbaum. Erlich says that, in the heyday of Taine and the "genetic method," the structural approach to literature was made impossible. Later, however, the Russian formalists were also positivists (in the more precise sense): "Avowed champions of 'neo-positivism,' they sought to steer clear of 'philosophical preconceptions' as to the nature of artistic creation; they had little use for speculations about Beauty and the Absolute. Formalist esthetics was descriptive rather than metaphysical."[19]

One sees the same descriptive urge in modern structuralism, and indeed in Foucault's archeology, in semiotics, and to some extent in deconstruction's occasional obsession with tracking binary oppositions. Jonathan Culler discusses this descriptive notion of science in *Structural Poetics* and points out that, for Hjelmslev, all the humanistic disciplines should adopt such a descriptive and structural approach in order to become scientific.[20]

This powerful undercurrent of positivism in contemporary theory is usually missed because of the hostility of many of these theorists to science and often to rationality. The importance of this positivist undercurrent should not be minimized.[21] Derrida, it is true, begins his work with a critique of some of the positivist elements of structuralism, and he criticizes Althusser's attempt to create a Marxist-structuralist science.[22] Indeed, the anti-scientific attitude in both Derrida and the late Barthes must be seen as specifically directed against the failures of the inadequately conceived scientific ventures of structuralism and semiotics, rather than against all forms of the scientific spirit in criticism.

Yet Derrida's program of rooting out what he calls metaphysics is a positivist program and conceives of metaphysics, much as the positivists did, as blind prejudice. Derrida's work lacks the crucial differentiation between a dogmatic and a conjectural metaphysics. Derrida also does not improve on the blind descriptiveness of structuralism in that he has no more concept of the scientific problem than the structuralists had. He shows that the attempt to fix meaning leads to an infinite regress, but this is true only when meaning is sought in some blindly comprehensive descriptive sense. When we seek the meaning of a word in connection with solving a specific problem, the difficulties diminish.

In this regard, the program of Popper and Agassi to recognize the place of metaphysics in scientific inquiry, and to study metaphysics scientifically, looking to find ways to test metaphysics, is much more post-positivist than Derrida or Foucault. In *Towards a Rational Philosophical Anthropology* Agassi gives an example of the necessity and possibility of treating metaphysics scientifically, an example that cuts across the fields of biology, anthropology, and linguistics:

> Sometimes one and the same scientific problem is attacked with the aid of different metaphysical ideas, borrowed from different fields; this leads to amusing contrasts. Darwin's theory of plasticity has led thinkers in the neo-Darwinian era to suggest that those species

of animals which are equipped with fewer innate release mechanisms (I.R.M.) have higher adaptive abilities, and so are better fitted for survival. This is counter-intuitive, since it means that species of animals which at birth need more intense and prolonged nursing survive better than species of animals which are born with their mature capacities available at once. Such species, we are told, are not very pliable and so they are slow to adapt and hence poor at surviving in changing conditions. They need long periods of mutation to make any adaptive progress. So much for one approach. On the basis of logic and information theory and the like, Noam Chomsky developed a different approach. He has arrived at the opposite view of man as born with a tremendous and most complex innate system, indeed with a whole linguistic capacity. So man's linguistic capacity is a crucial substitute for his lack of I.R.M.s, and becomes, for Chomsky, something at least partially like an I.R.M. itself. I do not wish to argue the pros and cons of these two views. They seem to clash, and they are obviously both too elusive to be put to empirical tests and crucial experiments. They are thus unscientific, yet they embrace scientific views: in short, they are metaphysical. It is hard to see what we can do with them—except, of course, put them to work against each other. Kant would have been delighted, then, as he thought the only role a metaphysics can play is to combat another metaphysics, resulting in a stand-off. Yet, this view of the barrenness of metaphysics, he admitted, did not quench his passionate interest in the subject. Today we more easily ignore both the injunction against metaphysics and the passion for metaphysics, and merely ask a question—one possibly rich with metaphysical implications, but nevertheless empirical: is man equipped with few innate release mechanisms or with many? How do I.R.M.s affect an animal's capacity for survival?[23]

Although this discussion may seem far afield from literary theory, it is richly relevant. If, as Agassi says, the biological and linguistic views he discusses are "too elusive to be put to empirical tests and crucial experiments," how much more is this the case with the views of literary theorists and critics. This is the prima facie case for dismissing the scientific spirit in criticism. Yet we cannot afford so easily to abdicate the attempt to test.

As Agassi argues, one cannot simply disentangle metaphysical debates from scientific inquiry. Investigation conducted in the scientific spirit is a constant dialectic between the metaphysical views that provide frameworks and articulate the goals of inquiry, and the attempt to find testable versions of the problems raised by the clash of such metaphysical views. How much can we do in the way of developing the empirical side of literary theory? That is still a wide-open question.[24]

Paul Ricoeur reminds us that the idea of testing metaphysics would do much to liberate Marxist literary science, which defines its metaphysics as "objective social reality," from dogmatically defending its metaphysical axioms about society. The axioms of twentieth-century Marxist science must be criticized from the perspective of one of their own scientific offspring—Mannheim's sociology of knowledge. Ricoeur quotes Mannheim: "What is needed is a continual readiness to recognize that every point of view is particular to a certain definite situation, and to find out through analysis of what this particularity consists. A clear and explicit avowal of the implicit metaphysical presuppositions which underlie and make possible empirical knowledge will do more for the clarification and advancement of research than a verbal denial of the existence of these presuppositions accompanied by their surreptitious admission through the back door."[25]

Looking for the particular social context for contemporary Marxist doctrine, Ricoeur writes:

> Just as religion is accused of having justified the power of the dominant class, so too Marxism functions as a system of justification for the power of the party as the *avant-garde* of the working class, and for the power of the ruling group within the party. This justificatory function with respect to the power of a dominant group explains why the sclerosis of Marxism provides the most striking example of ideology in modern times. . . . These severe remarks do not imply that Marxism is false. Quite the contrary, they imply that the critical function of Marxism can be liberated and manifested only if the use of Marx's work is completely dissociated from the exercise of power and authority and from judgments of orthodoxy; only if his analyses are submitted to the test of a direct application to the modern economy, as they were by Marx to the economy of the mid-nineteenth century; only if Marxism becomes one working tool among others.[26]

Ricoeur's argument that Marxism can only remain scientific if it is testable—falsifiable—is an explicit echo here of the key term of Karl Popper's scientific methodology. Since Ricoeur is well known as an exponent of the hermeneutic school of interpretation, it might seem paradoxical for him to insist on Popper's scientific standards. Hermeneutics, along with the more "postmodern" schools of literary theory, is often cited as a theory of interpretation which has rendered the whole notion of testability problematic.

Indeed, neither Ricoeur nor Popper denies that testing is problematic, especially in the cultural sciences. But Ricoeur follows both Barthes and Habermas in seeing scientific analysis and testing as one pole in the process of inquiry, a necessary balance to the more intuitive appreciation for the "halo" of meanings. Ricoeur applies this concept of testing not only to Marxist and other social science, but also to the process of literary interpretation. E. D. Hirsch, in *Validity in Interpretation*, had criticized the circularity of hermeneutic literary theory and had backed up his criticism with a somewhat overly positivist interpretation of Popper.[27]

Ricoeur responds by saying that the hermeneutical circle is not a vicious circle. He, too, is a Popperian: "To the procedures of validation also belong procedures of invalidation similar to the criteria of falsifiability emphasized by Karl Popper in his *Logic of Scientific Discovery*. The role of falsification is played here by the conflict between competing interpretations."[28] Ricoeur thus accepts in principle the necessity of testing, as advocated by Hirsch. Though Ricoeur sees his view as analogous to Popper's, he clearly does not see it as the same spirit that possessed positivistic science.[29]

To a large extent the materials for beginning to discuss how to test various sociological models of literature—like those of the Marxists—already exist, as Jeffrey Sammons shows in his comprehensive and critical survey of the whole field, *Literary Sociology and Practical Criticism*. However, there are enormous problems in getting the speculative and empirical sides of the field into contact. To quote Sammons:

> In the first place, either literary critics are going to have to make an effort to master the neo-Hegelian pidgin in which German, some French, and increasingly, English-language contributions to this subject are written, or scholars pursuing sociological criticism must be encouraged to express themselves in some language spoken by human beings. I have a personal preference for the latter solution— that it can be done has been demonstrated by the Marxist George Thompson—but I think it is the less likely one, especially as Germans

and German traditions are centrally involved; therefore both sympathetic and critical translators are needed. In English, Fredric Jameson has made a beginning, but it would be good to have similar studies from observers less afflicted with true faith.[30]

The Politics of Science: Popper or Kuhn?

If we want to rise above the trees for a moment, to get an overview of the whole forest of contemporary versions of science on offer, it is possible to make a rough division according to the names of Karl Popper or Thomas Kuhn—that is, according to whether emphasis is laid on science as an institution for perpetuating criticism and testing of established scientific opinion, or whether emphasis is laid on science as a closed community following rigid and often unspoken (tacit) rules of procedure that generally remain untouched by criticism and testing.

There is no longer any question of choosing decisively between Popper and Kuhn, such as there might have been, for example, during the famous debate at the 1965 Colloquium in the Philosophy of Science, held just three years after the publication of important books by both.[31] That debate collected not only Popper and Kuhn, but also Feyerabend, Lakatos, Toulmin, and others to discuss the question of Popper's "revolutionary" or "critical science" versus Kuhn's "normal science."

At that time, Imre Lakatos, a colleague and student of Popper, was able to say, "In Kuhn's view scientific revolution is irrational, a matter for mob psychology."[32] But even in that important paper ("The Methodology of Scientific Research Programs") Lakatos was already explicitly offering a partial compromise between Popper and Kuhn. Although stating that he viewed science through "Popperian spectacles" (an echo of Kuhn), Lakatos made a strategic Kuhnian concession when he wrote: "In my conception criticism does not—and must not—kill as fast as Popper imagined. *Purely negative, destructive criticism, like 'refutation' or demonstration of an inconsistency, does not eliminate a programme. Criticism of a programme is a long and often frustrating process and one must treat budding programmes leniently.*"[33]

This is a partial concession to Kuhn's view that the critical tradition described by Popper, "the tradition of claims, counter-claims and debates over fundamentals," characterizes philosophy and the social sciences but not science. As Kuhn said in this debate: "In a sense, to turn Sir Karl's view on its head, it is precisely the abandonment of critical discourse that marks the transition to a science. Once a field has made that transition, critical discourse recurs only at moments of crisis when the bases of the field are again in jeopardy."[34]

Kuhn deemphasizes criticism because he sees science as a close-knit community of experts with similar socialization: "Because he there joins men who learned the bases of their field from the same concrete models, his subsequent practice will seldom evoke overt disagreement over fundamentals. Men whose research is based on shared paradigms are committed to the same rules and standards for scientific practice. That commitment and the apparent consensus it produces are prerequisites for normal science, i.e., for the genesis and continuation of a particular research tradition."[35] People outside the community have not shared this socialization and so might disagree with the goals, problem choice, methods, or standards of the experts, but their disagreement is largely irrelevant. Kuhn holds that for the most part "the members of a given scientific community provide the only audience and the only judges of that community's work."[36]

It was for assertions such as this that Kuhn was criticized in this debate, both by Popper and by Paul Feyerabend, for being too conservative and for providing a bad model for science. Popper replied: "The 'normal' scientist, as described by Kuhn, has been badly taught. He has learned a technique which can be applied without asking for the reason why (especially in quantum mechanics). As a consequence, he has become what may be called an *applied scientist*, in contradistinction to what I should call a *pure scientist*."[37]

Feyerabend recounted an experience that has, in succeeding years, been recapitulated in nearly every corner of the humanities and social sciences: "More than one social scientist has pointed out to me that now at last he had learned how to turn his field into a 'science'—by which of course he meant that he had learned how to *improve* it. The recipe, according to these people, is to restrict criticism, to reduce the number of comprehensive theories to one, and to create a normal science that has this one theory as its paradigm. Students must be prevented from speculating along different lines and the more restless colleagues must be made to conform and 'to do serious work.' *Is this what Kuhn wants to achieve?*"[38]

Feyerabend, for his part, wants a more hedonistic science where "anything goes," and where choice between theories can become "a matter of taste" (a phrase partly qualified by his saying that even taste can be argued about). Feyerabend takes this line, as he explains, partly for reasons of philosophy of life and partly for reasons of scientific progress. He disagrees with Kuhn's assessment that scientific progress is dependent on consensus, asserting instead that "progress can be brought about only by the active interaction of different theories."[39] How Feyerabend thinks that progress comes about, given his acceptance and even stronger interpretation of Kuhn's idea of the incommensurability of competing theories, is left unclear.

For Kuhn, by contrast, the simultaneous competition of different theories belongs only to the pre-scientific or pre-paradigmatic stage of inquiry; thereafter, theories or paradigms must succeed one another in serial fashion. And even then, as Kuhn argues in his book on Max Planck, the very inventor of the new paradigm will often resist recognizing and acknowledging what he has done, preferring at first to believe he has not changed the paradigm, and later to believe that he always held the new paradigm. The reasons Kuhn gives for this are psychological; he compares entering a new paradigm to entering a foreign culture: "Entry into another culture does not simply expand one's previous form of life, open new possibilities within it. Rather, it opens new possibilities at the expense of old ones, exposing the foundations of a previous life as contingent and threatening the integrity of the life one had lived before. Ultimately the experience can be liberating, but it is always threatening."[40]

Though Kuhn describes a recognizable phenomenon, one wonders whether all scientists and all inquirers need to be so rigid. Kuhn seems to assume that such rigidity is both psychologically necessary and beneficial to the practice of normal science. But there are fields of inquiry where one simply must be more resilient in the face of culture shock. These fields Kuhn seems to relegate to the permanently unscientific.

Literary criticism, a field where the simultaneous competition of theories is endemic, is a model of Kuhn's pre-paradigmatic state, and perhaps also a model of the hedonistic science Feyerabend envisages. Is this hubbub of voices a blessing or a curse? Even before Kuhn proposed his paradigmatic model of science, literary theorists such as I. A. Richards and Northrop Frye had lamented "the chaos of critical theories"[41] and had proposed one or another scientific approach as a way of reducing the controversy in the field. By contrast, many contemporary theorists tend toward Feyerabend's approach, saying that progress requires diversity more than discipline. An example is Joseph Natoli's celebration, using the language of Bakhtin and Serres, of a "theory carnival": "Theory's quest is to hear the unheard voice of literature, to go beyond meaning that is heard only within and through a prevailing chronotope. . . . Literary theory is part of a multiple discourse in which, according to Michel Serres, 'polymorphism remains irreducible,' a multiple discourse in the world and for the world, a discourse whose polymorphism subsumes all monologic voices. Not only discourse is irreducibly polymorphic; we—as readers and interpreters—are also 'constituted in polyphony.' "[42]

Such an approach might seem considerably more achievable than the monologic constraint attempted by Richards and Frye: it would seem to require a simple acceptance of the existing "chaos of critical theories." But for the proponents of "polyphonous" theory, the threat of censorship or exclusion by the institutions of literary theory is always real and requires vigilance. Attempts to speak "in the scientific spirit" tend to be met with the suspicion that an attempt is being made to limit discussion (not an unjustifiable suspicion, either in Kuhnian terms or speaking historically). Whether the scientific spirit can coexist with a more liberal politics of inquiry than Kuhn suggests will be discussed shortly.

Since the 1965 Popper/Kuhn debate, the positions associated with the names of Popper and Kuhn have diversified and cross-pollinated to a considerable degree. Some of the most important interpreters of Popper (e.g., Agassi) and of Kuhn (e.g., Rorty) hold positions which are hardly orthodox to Popper or Kuhn. Yet the names of Popper and Kuhn still serve handily to mark out two major emphases among our current views of science—the emphasis on conjectures and testing (Popper), versus the emphasis on science as a social institution in which both conjectures and testing are minimized.

As we have seen, literary theorists as diverse as Barthes and Graff, Hirsch and Ricoeur, are in agreement that literary criticism needs a critical-scientific-testing aspect. This is where the name of Popper is most often invoked, especially because Popper and Agassi have widened the concept of testing so that it can be applied to cultural and metaphysical inquiries, playing an important (but no longer deterministic) role in helping evaluate conjectures. Taking up the question whether metaphysical questions can be discussed "rationally and critically" (a question raised, as noted above, by Kuhn's notion of the incommensurability of such theories), Popper writes:

> My solution is this: if a philosophical theory were no more than an isolated assertion about the world, flung at us with an implied "take it or leave it" and without a hint of any connection with anything else, then it would indeed be beyond discussion. But the same might be said of an empirical theory also. Should anybody present us with Newton's equations, or even with his arguments, without explaining to us first what the problems were which his theory was meant to solve, then we should not be able to discuss its truth rationally— no more than the truth of the *Book of Revelation*. Without any knowledge of the results of Galileo and Kepler, or the problems that were resolved by these results, and of Newton's problem of explaining Galileo's and Kepler's solutions by a unified theory, we should find Newton's theory just as much beyond discussion as any metaphysical theory. In other words, every *rational* theory, no matter whether scientific or philosophical, is rational is so far as it tries to *solve certain problems*. A theory is comprehensible and reasonable only in its relation to a given *problem situation*, and it can be rationally discussed only by discussing this relation. Now if we look upon a theory as a proposed solution to a set of problems, then the theory immediately lends itself to critical discussion—even if it is non-empirical and irrefutable. For we can now ask questions such as: Does it solve the problem? Does it solve it better than other theories? Has it perhaps merely shifted the problem? Is the solution

simple? Is it fruitful? Does it perhaps contradict other philosophical theories needed for solving other problems? Questions of this kind show that a critical discussion even of irrefutable theories may well be possible.[43]

This is an example of Popper's definitive break with positivism, with its refusal to deal with metaphysical questions, and concomitant narrowing of the social sciences and humanities. Popper again opens the possibility of rationally discussing all kinds of value-laden questions in the "cultural sciences" without prejudging how scientifically they can be answered. Given that Popper, rather than Kuhn, has addressed the problem of the scientific spirit in the humanities, one might expect that Popper's work had more influence than Kuhn's on literary theory. At present, however, the opposite is true. The explanation has almost entirely to do with Popper's and Kuhn's contrasting views of the institutions that conduct scientific and humanistic inquiry.

Kuhn's work speaks more directly to humanists' widely shared perception that the institutions of inquiry themselves are highly political—a perception central to feminist criticism and increasingly characteristic of self-styled "postmodern" theory. This suspicion that science is political, with its roots in Marx and Nietzsche, was formulated more fully in Mannheim's sociology of knowledge. The sociological approach to science was developed by Ludwik Fleck, Michael Polanyi, and Robert Merton.[44] Kuhn, as the inheritor and popularizer of this tradition, has been the first to make the social and political nature of science a widely understood (or at least widely acceptable) notion. He places a list of questions for further research at the end of his 1969 "Postscript" to *Structure*, which catches widely shared concerns: "How does one elect and how is one elected to a community, scientific or not? What is the process and what are the stages of socialization of the group? What does the group collectively see as its goals; what deviations, individual or collective, will it tolerate; and how does it control the impermissible aberration?"[45]

Such questions are at the heart of a book like Sandra Harding's *The Science Question in Feminism*, which is why Harding can divide thinking about science into pre-Kuhnian and post-Kuhnian. Harding says *The Structure of Scientific Revolutions* "is the single work that has done the most to cast doubt on purely intellectual histories [of science]."[46] She proceeds to carry Kuhn's ideas to a length she is well aware he would disagree with. One of the theses of her book is that traditional science is so permeated with sexist assumptions that a totally new, genderless science must be imagined and created: ". . . as Kuhn pointed out, paradigmatic theories in particular areas of inquiry eventually wear out as fruitful guides to research. Shouldn't this also be true for science as a whole?"[47]

Harding set herself the problem of rescuing science from its misogynistic and patriarchal history. She easily explodes the myth (perhaps no longer widely believed) that science is purely objective and value free, showing sexist bias not only in its institutions, but also in the basic concepts with which it cuts up and shapes the reality it hopes to observe and explain. Although Kuhn and the post-Kuhnians are also guilty of "the usual array of androcentric gaps and distortions," Harding finds Kuhn's work "paradigmatic" because "Kuhn showed that activities once regarded as irrelevant or even detrimental to the growth of scientific knowledge were, on the contrary, an integral part of the processes through which hypotheses are developed and legitimated."[48]

Among these no longer irrelevant activities is the use of sexist metaphor in scientific theory, which Harding discusses at some length:

> If we are to believe that mechanistic metaphors were a fundamental component of the explanations the new science provided, why should we believe that the gender metaphors were not? A consistent analysis would lead to the conclusion that understanding nature as a woman indifferent to or even welcoming rape was equally fundamental to the interpretations of these new conceptions of nature and inquiry. Presumably these metaphors, too, had fruitful pragmatic, methodological, and metaphysical consequences for science. In that case, why is it not as illuminating and honest to refer to Newton's laws as "Newton's rape manual" as it is to call them "Newton's mechanics"?[49]

Harding does not see her suggestion as merely provocative. She believes modern science has been responsible for something like the rape of the status of women: "Why should we regard the emergence of modern science as a great advance for humanity when it was achieved only at the cost of a deterioration in social status for half of humanity?"[50] She does not try to argue or even to illustrate this more general claim, that the political and social condition of women has actually deteriorated over the past three hundred years as a result of science. This is too bad, since the claim is so counter-intuitive and cries out for explanation. Perhaps her lack of discussion of how this claim has been or could be tested comes from her general disdain for the Popperian or critical side of science.

Harding is quite right to say that Popper, for all his praise of searching criticism, is hostile to what he calls "the skeptical attack upon science launched by the sociology of knowledge."[51] Popper argues that, so long as there is no outside political interference, the institutions of science can be relied upon to be self-correcting, so that individual biases will not matter. The internal and tacit politics of science and academe, traditionally ignored with harsh consequences for women and other excluded groups, are minimized by Popper as well. As we shall see, however, a Popperian approach to the politics of science has been developed by others.

Scientific institutions are not as self-correcting as Popper hopes. Yet, even so, the critical perspective is ignored at post-modernism's peril. In Harding's case, one danger is that the more secure parts of her argument will not be taken seriously because of rhetorical excesses. Another danger is that the reader has no specific notion of how the undoubted sexism in scientific society is supposed to have been worse than the undoubted sexism in pre-scientific society. Such specific knowledge will undoubtedly be necessary for the new feminist paradigm of science Harding wishes to launch.

Harding doesn't really need Kuhn to make her claim that science doesn't work quite the way Popper says it does; it is enough for her to show that science is still highly sexist in its operation and its concepts. But using Kuhn strengthens her case, because Kuhn argues that even on questions of pure knowledge (rather than areas such as the hiring of women, or other overtly political areas) the institution of self-criticism in science is generally secondary to the normal scientist's faith in his (usually his) paradigm. If Kuhn is correct, so left-wing Kuhnians argue (Kuhn interprets himself more conservatively), then science's pretensions to progress through rational criticism are hollow.

Harding dismisses Popper's vision of scientific self-reform through criticism as "not even the view of most major scientists." Yet Harding advocates criticism of the paradigm of science itself (as Popper does, in principle) rather than merely solving problems within the paradigm (as Kuhn does). Here we see a paradox. Kuhn, because he is taken to undermine the rationality of science, is often cited by those who wish to change the politics of science; yet Kuhn thinks that, because the rationality of science is so limited, the status quo is the best politics of science we can get. By contrast, Popper, who says he trusts both the politics and the rationality of science, nevertheless prescribes the kind of open criticism of the foundations of science for which radicals are looking.

An analogy to Harding's kind of argument can be found in literary studies. Edward Said's *Orientalism* is a good example of a book that sees the institutions of inquiry as political through and through. At times Said argues, in Kuhnian fashion, that the Orientalist perspective is a paradigm that has been all but inescapable for Western scholars; at other times Said argues, in more Popperian fashion, that the more critical-minded scholars have always been able to liberate themselves from this prejudiced and politically motivated perspective.[52]

Kuhn's approach has been elaborated by Richard Rorty, who argues that not only science but also all the other disciplines are functioning about as well as can be expected, and that we should refrain from trying to improve them—or at least we should cease trying to make them "more scientific." Of literary studies Rorty says: "The reason 'literary criticism' is 'unscientific' is just that whenever anybody tries to work up such a vocabulary he makes a fool of himself. . . . By 'literature,' then, I shall mean the areas of culture which, quite self-consciously, forgo agreement on an encompassing critical vocabulary, and thus forgo argumentation."[53]

Rorty hopes to convince us to forgo argumentation in philosophy and literary criticism, and to substitute what he calls "conversation." He errs, I believe, in assuming that argumentation can only be carried on within a positivist framework where "vocabularies" are "agreed upon." And his resistance to argumentation in metaphysical and moral areas only apparently, I think, spares us strife. In actuality it leads, as I have argued, to a dangerous political complacency.[54]

What is needed in the politics of inquiry, it seems to me, is an approach that is less trusting of the institutions of inquiry than Popper's approach, yet less skeptical about improvement of the status quo than Kuhn's approach. Both Feyerabend and Agassi have tried to formulate a politics of science in a reformist vein. Feyerabend's "hedonistic" and anarchistic politics of science has been referred to above. Agassi has recently explained the appeal of Feyerabend's writings, despite their obvious exaggeration, as due to the justness of Feyerabend's complaint that "science exhibits intolerance which reaches levels which should be a cause for concern."[55] It seems that Feyerabend's writings are almost the sum of the existing literature on the politics of science. There is no other literature, Agassi argues, because most people (including scientists) think there should be no politics of science, and they conclude (perhaps wishfully) that there are none.

Agassi lists among the political aspects of science "the political power of journal editors and conference organizers, its use and abuse, the political control of access of scientists to mass media, legislators and more."[56] He argues that these and attendant questions have hardly been studied yet. Up to this point Agassi seems to be echoing Kuhn, except that he calls "politics" what Kuhn calls "sociology." This is perhaps no minor difference, since it stems from Kuhn's positivistic preference for describing science and not prescribing to it (a preference also central to Rorty) versus Agassi's willingness to censure existing scientific institutions severely. The difference increases with Agassi's main prescription to science, which is that the politics of science can be reformed to be more democratic, and that this requires that we first acknowledge and study the existing politics of science and set an agenda for changing them rationally and democratically.

This appeal can be generalized to the politics of inquiry in other disciplines, including literary studies. Both in literature and in science I suspect that Agassi's call for democratization will be met with far more hostility than Feyerabend's call for anarchy or Kuhn's complacency about the status quo. Kuhn's views lead to a strengthening of existing establishments, while Feyerabend's views are not presented so as to be taken seriously. In contrast, Agassi's democratization is a practicable program, the dangerous flaws and dangerous appeal of which can be seen immediately.

Whether we can improve on current notions of democratizing inquiry is less clear.

We have seen feeble attempts at democratization of the Modern Language Association, with mixed results. I somehow doubt that further such attempts have much popular appeal among the literati of either left or right. (Who gets excited about the cumbersome MLA election process?) It seems likely that the idea of democratizing inquiry could be improved, if it were explored more seriously than it has been. But, for the moment, the politics of inquiry are pretty much articulated by Kuhnians of either the right or the left.

Testing Literary Conjectures: Science or Rhetoric?

Any theory or conjecture in literary criticism can easily be immunized against criticism.[57] Moreover, as long as we regard literary inquiry as "merely rhetorical," we have no motivation *not* to immunize our theories. As I argued in regard to feminist science theory, however, even the most radical postmodern theories have a need for a critical component, to learn which of various possible radical conjectures is better. They have a need for learning and so a motivation not to immunize their theories against criticism and testing. As Imre Lakatos put it, "Intellectual honesty does not consist in trying to entrench, or establish one's position by proving (or probabilifying) it—intellectual honesty consists rather in specifying precisely the conditions under which one is willing to give up one's position."[58]

This kind of intellectual honesty is self-imposed, rather than imposed by the data. One might say that it substitutes a call for "fair play" for the old rigid rules of positivist method. But if this is the case, it is fair to ask whether we should go on using the language of science at all. Why should we continue to speak of the scientific spirit when we have the option of switching to some more rhetorical or literary language, as advocated by Rorty, Fish, and others? If I may hazard a testable prediction, what is likely to happen is that literary critics will work both options, and this is as it should be. What remains to be seen, however, is whether those pursuing these divergent programs of research will continue to try to learn from one another (working beyond paradigms, in Popperian fashion), or whether they will accept the insularity and incommensurability of discourse that a Kuhnian map of inquiry predicts.[59]

A case in point is a new book, *The Rhetoric of the Human Sciences*, which brings together arguments from many social scientists and humanists for regarding inquiry in their fields as primarily rhetorical, not scientific.[60] As the editor, John Nelson, says in the final essay, "Rhetoric—rather than logic or some equivalent—should form the grounds of postmodern epistemology. . . . Rhetoric of inquiry neither wants nor needs to banish logic of inquiry; instead the challenge is to pluralize it. . . . We will remember that, even within a single science, the logics must remain plural as long as the discipline avoids monism and dogmatism."[61]

Nelson thus sees no either/or choice between testing and rhetorical analysis. He does, however (along with many other contributors), take too much for granted that a "scientific" approach to inquiry can only be a positivistic one, and this limits his appreciation of the scientific side of the dialectic. Still, his proposals for a "poetics" and a "tropics" of inquiry raise in a more general way the sort of issues that Harding raised for feminist theory of science: "Poetics of inquiry confine themselves to comprehending how specific figures of research arise, reproduce, and decline. Tropics of inquiry address overt or patent characters (economic man), images (equilibrium), models (free markets), statistics (significance tests), and other figures of research. Poetics of inquiry assess covert assumptions and latent figures to discern how they contribute to forming the particularly ready, apparent tropes that configure reasoning and communication."[62]

Nelson and his contributors thus seek to deflate the scientific pretensions of many of the human sciences by exposing the role that rhetoric plays in them. Yet Nelson seems amenable to treating conventions of inquiry as something more than "mere" conventions—possibly as the "conjectures about the best standards of inquiry" which I mentioned above. He writes: "Rhetorical reflection . . . treats conventions less as polar opposites of anything natural or inevitable than as diverse practical conceptions of how to relate to whatever might prove enduring in human experience."[63]

The rhetorical perspective outlined in Nelson's book seems to me an inevitable part of the context in which we must now view the theory of inquiry. Yet Nelson and his contributors are far less willing to go as far as Rorty in speaking of humanistic inquiry as mere conversation or story-telling. What Nelson calls "tropics of inquiry" (for example) will require a great deal of empirical research, and its theses about conceptual evolution will need to be tested. Some of contributors to Nelson's volume preserve the concepts of test, mistake and learning; others do not.

Two who do preserve those concepts are Charles Bazerman and Jean Bethke Elshtain. Bazerman writes a chapter called "Codifying the Social Scientific Style: The APA Publication Manual as a Behaviorist Rhetoric." In it he shows how the current style of much social science evolved in interaction with the rhetorical guidelines of the gradually evolving APA manual. Although Bazerman argues that scientific language is built on rhetorical assumptions and that, as these assumptions are challenged and altered, so is scientific language altered over time, he does not reach relativistic conclusions. He points out that specific rhetorical styles are more appropriate for one purpose than for another: "As anyone who has worked with [the APA Publication Manual] can attest, it is very convenient for listing and summarizing a series of related findings, but it is awkward for extensive quotation, and even more awkward for contrasting several texts in detail. The format is not designed for the close consideration of competing ideas and subtle formulations."[64] Thus we can identify mistaken rhetorical choices relative to goals we may wish to achieve— and those goals, too, can be evaluated and debated.

Jean Bethke Elshtain, in her chapter on feminist political rhetoric, takes up the problem of retaining a critical component in an overtly political field. Women's studies, she says, is a field with a diversity of perspectives: "The rhetoric of feminist politics, however, shares with ideologies in general a 'will to truth' that quashes ambiguity and squeezes out diversity. . . . Feminist political rhetoricians have problematized received categories and understandings. This essay aims at a similar defamiliarization with reference to their own, by now familiar, constructions."[65]

Elshtain gives an example of the way feminist inquiry can become immunized against learning by the very momentum of its chosen narrative strategy:

Hardening of the categories is unavoidable. For example: Juliet Mitchell, in her bold *Psychoanalysis and Feminism*, declared the Law of the Father (patriarchy) to be "culture itself," with women universally subject to, and subjugated by, this law even into the interstices of "the Unconscious." Mitchell not only presumes that she can advance law-like claims about *every* culture without describing in detail *any* culture; she is compelled by the force of her narrative to *interpret* all points of contact between men and women, no matter what they may appear to be and no matter how the subjects themselves may understand these matters, as instances of the working out of "the universal culture" of female subordination.[66]

Asking "how the subjects themselves understand these matters" is, of course, not a compelling test, since there are many cases where we would say people do not really understand what is happening to them. Yet this test does not lose all force just because it is not compelling. A scientific inquiry must be open to the possibility, at least, that the subjects may know more than their observers. The fact that Mitchell's rhetoric totally overrides such a test makes Mitchell's rhetoric look dogmatic and ideological.

If learning is our aim, we need not choose between rhetoric and science. Tests in scientific inquiry today are seen to have a partly rhetorical form; they are arguments, rather than proofs. But they can help us learn, by exposing weak points in our theories and thus articulating unsolved problems, and by marking off areas of uncertainty. Tests can help us see what might or ought to interest us in theories different from ours (a bridge across incommensurability).

An example parallel to Elshtain's in literary studies is the perennial question of whether a text means what its author says it meant. The answer is certainly "Not necessarily," yet the author's recollected intentions are a test that we ignore at our peril. How much weight to give them depends on other factors: there is no hard-and-fast rule that can settle debates between interpreters.

In the case of Tolstoy's *Anna Karenina*, for instance, we may wonder what is the meaning of all the talk about love, all the descriptions of people falling in love, suffering from love, exulting in love, and so on. When Vronsky declares his love for Anna, in a snowstorm, at a stop during a train journey, Tolstoy writes: "At that moment the wind, as if it had mastered all obstacles, scattered the snow from the carriage roofs, and set a loose sheet of iron clattering; and in front the deep whistle of the engine howled mournfully and dismally. The awfulness of the storm appeared still more beautiful to her now. He had said just what her soul desired but her reason dreaded."[67]

All of Tolstoy's famed objectivity of presentation doesn't disguise for a moment what Tolstoy himself also tells us—that he had the strongest moral reservations about this business of falling in love. Yet a great deal has been said about the story having escaped its author, and its having taken on a meaning he didn't intend, and ultimately Tolstoy himself believed this.[68] Moreover, with this novel, as with so many others (one thinks of Dickens), it is easy to feel that the work achieved greatness only because it did escape and transcend the author's conscious intentions.

What then? Are we left in an interpretive chaos, free to interpret the novel in any way we see fit? On the contrary: we are free neither to ignore the author's expressed and apparent intent, nor to ignore the evidence for reading the novel another way. Stanley Fish argues that this relative stability of meaning is due not to any stability in the text, but only to stability in the reading community's interpretive conventions.[69] Maybe so. We do use standards of some kind to read by. Maybe they are community conventions; maybe they can be articulated; maybe they can even be criticized and improved. The important thing for intellectual honesty is that literary scholars give some thought not only to what standards of evidence support their readings, but what standards of evidence they would take as tending to falsify their readings.

Such thinking about tests can sometimes lead us to more precise tests. If, as Lakatos suggests, we try to specify what would make us give up the position we hold, this leads us (or others) to look for that evidence. If such evidence is found, we are free to reassess whether it is compelling. We are not automatically refuted, but neither need the situation be one of total anarchy. The negotiation of acceptable standards for evidence is part of the scientific process. Whether we call such negotiation science or rhetoric probably doesn't matter. What is important is that we don't treat it as "mere" science (a deterministic or algoristic procedure) or "mere" rhetoric (a process from which the concept of "mistakes" is banished). Whether testing literary conjectures remains scientific or becomes "merely" rhetorical depends on the spirit of our inquiry: on whether we have set out to learn, or merely to persuade.

NOTES

1. Andrew Field, *Nabokov: His Life in Art* (Boston: Little, Brown, 1967), p. 8.
2. Thomas Kuhn, *The Structure of Scientific Revolutions* (Chicago: University of Chicago Press, 1962, 1970), pp. 16–17.
3. Gerald Graff, *Poetic Statement and Critical Dogma* (Chicago: University of Chicago Press, 1970, 1980), p. xiv.
4. E. D. Hirsch, Jr., "Value and Knowledge in the Humanities," in *In Search of Literary Theory*, ed. Morton Bloomfield (Ithaca: Cornell University Press, 1972), pp. 61–62. For further discussion of the unnecessary polarizations of art/science, theory/science, see my "Why Theorize about Literature?" in *What Is Literature?*, ed. Paul Hernadi, (Bloomington: Indiana University Press, 1978), pp. 35–46, as well as my "Literature as Thought Experiment," in *Philosophy of the Social Sciences* 13:3 (September 1983): 279–306.
5. Vladimir Nabokov, *The Real Life of Sebastian Knight* (New York: New Directions, 1959), p. 52.
6. Ibid., p. 65.
7. Benedict de Spinoza, *A Theologico-Political Treatise* (New York: Dover, 1951). Spinoza holds that the methods for interpreting scripture are the same as methods for interpreting nature (p. 99), and he sets forth in great detail how his scientific method of interpretation will differ from traditional methods of reading.
8. Roland Barthes, "Inaugural Lecture, Collège de France," in *A Barthes Reader*, ed. Susan Sontag (New York: Hill and Wang, 1982), p. 463.
9. Ibid., p. 464.
10. Ibid., p. 457.
11. Jürgen Habermas, *Theory and Practice* (Boston: Beacon Press, 1973), p. 10.
12. Ibid., p. 10.
13. Norman Holland, *5 Readers Reading* (New Haven: Yale University Press, 1975); David Bleich, *Subjective Criticism* (Baltimore: Johns Hopkins University Press, 1978).
14. Habermas, *Theory and Practice*, pp. 10–11.
15. Georg Lukacs, "Franz Kafka or Thomas Mann?" in *Marxists on Literature*, ed. David Craig (Harmondsworth: Penguin, 1975), pp. 380–81.

16. Georg Lukacs, "Tolstoy and the Development of Realism," ibid., p. 284.

17. René Wellek, *A History of Modern Criticism: 1750–1950, Volume 4: The Later Nineteenth Century* (Cambridge: Cambridge University Press, 1983), p. 35.

18. Igor Naletov, *Alternatives to Positivism* (Moscow: Progress Publishers, 1984), p. 307.

19. Victor Erlich, *Russian Formalism: History, Doctrine,* 3rd ed. (New Haven: Yale University Press, 1981), p. 171.

20. Jonathan Culler, *Structuralist Poetics* (Ithaca: Cornell University Press, 1975), p. 7.

21. For further discussion of the troubled history and reputation of positivism(s), see my "The Devils of Positivism," in *Literature and Science: Theory and Practice,* ed. Stuart Peterfreund (Boston: Northeastern University Press, forthcoming). For the classic article against positivism in literary study, see René Wellek, "The Revolt against Positivism in Recent European Literary Scholarship," in his *Concepts of Criticism* (New Haven: Yale University Press, 1963), pp. 256–81.

22. Christopher Norris, *Deconstruction: Theory and Practice* (New York: Methuen, 1982), pp. 51, 84.

23. Joseph Agassi, *Towards a Rational Philosophical Anthropology* (The Hague: Martinus Nijhoff, 1977), pp. 25–26. See also *Science in Flux* (Boston: D. Reidel, 1975), pp. 208–39.

24. For further discussion of testing the metaphysical views in criticism, see my "Scientific Method as Literary Criticism," *Et cetera* 42:4 (Winter 1985): 331–50, as well as my "Pursuing Truth in Criticism," *Publications of the Society for Literature and Science* 2:2 (March 1987): 1–5.

25. Karl Mannheim, *Ideology and Utopia* (London: Routledge and Kegan Paul, 1936), p. 80.

26. Paul Ricoeur, *Hermeneutics and the Human Sciences* (Cambridge: Cambridge University Press, 1981), p. 236.

27. Ibid., p. 25.

28. Ibid., pp. 212–13.

29. For further discussion of a Popperian approach to the conflict of interpretations, see my "Updating Wilhelm Dilthey: Values and Objectivity in Literary Criticism," *Mosaic* 14:4 (Fall 1981): 89–105.

30. Jeffrey Sammons, *Literary Sociology and Practical Criticism: An Inquiry* (Bloomington: Indiana University Press, 1977), pp. 157–58.

31. The books just published were: Thomas Kuhn, *The Structure of Scientific Revolutions,* and Karl Popper, *Conjectures and Refutations*

(New York: Basic Books, 1962). The debate was collected in *Criticism and the Growth of Knowledge*, ed. Imre Lakatos and Alan Musgrave (Cambridge: Cambridge University Press, 1970).

32. Imre Lakatos, "The Methodology of Scientific Research Programs," in *Criticism and the Growth of Knowledge*, p. 178.

33. Ibid., p. 179.

34. Thomas Kuhn, "Logic of Discovery or Psychology of Research?" ibid., pp. 6–7.

35. Thomas Kuhn, *The Structure of Scientific Revolutions*, p. 11.

36. Ibid., p. 209.

37. Karl Popper, "Normal Science and Its Dangers," in *Criticism and the Growth of Knowledge*, p. 53.

38. Paul Feyerabend, "Consolations for the Specialist" ibid., p. 198.

39. Ibid., p. 203.

40. Thomas Kuhn, *Black Body Theory and the Quantum Discontinuity: 1894–1912* (Chicago: University of Chicago Press, 1978), p. 368.

41. I. A. Richards, *Principles of Literary Criticism* (New York: Harcourt, Brace and World, 1925), p. 5.

42. Joseph Natoli, "Tracing a Beginning through Past Theory Voices," in *Tracing Literary Theory*, ed. Joseph Natoli (Urbana: University of Illinois Press, 1987), pp. 22–23.

43. Karl Popper, "Metaphysics and Criticizability," in *Popper: Selections*, ed. David Miller (Princeton: Princeton University Press, 1985), pp. 216–17.

44. Ludwik Fleck, *Genesis and Development of a Scientific Fact* (Basel, 1935); Michael Polanyi, *Personal Knowledge* (Chicago: University of Chicago Press, 1958); Robert Merton, *The Sociology of Science: Theoretical and Empirical Investigations* (Chicago: University of Chicago Press, 1973).

45. Kuhn, *Structure*, p. 209.

46. Sandra Harding, *The Science Question in Feminism* (Ithaca: Cornell University Press, 1986), p. 203.

47. Ibid., p. 43.

48. Ibid., p. 199.

49. Ibid., p. 113.

50. Ibid., p. 125.

51. Miller, ed., *Popper: Selections*, pp. 373, 375.

52. Edward Said, *Orientalism* (New York: Random House, 1978), pp. 3, 326.

53. Richard Rorty, *The Consequences of Pragmatism* (Minneapolis: University of Minnesota Press, 1982), p. 142.

54. See my "The New Politics of Knowledge: Rorty's Pragmatism and

the Rhetoric of the Human Sciences," in *Philosophy of the Social Sciences* 17:3 (September 1987): 377–94.

55. Joseph Agassi, "The Politics of Science," *Journal of Applied Philosophy* 3:1 (1986): 35–48.

56. Ibid., p. 47.

57. For discussion of the immunization of theories against criticism and testing, see Miller, ed., *Popper: Selections*, pp. 125ff.

58. Lakatos, "The Methodology of Scientific Research Programs," p. 92.

59. The literature in the anti-critical vein is already vast. See some of the following: Gillian Beer, *Darwin's Plots* (London: Routledge & Kegan Paul, 1983); Jacques Derrida, *Dissemination* (Chicago: University of Chicago Press, 1981); Jean-François Lyotard, *The Postmodern Condition: A Report on Knowledge* (Minneapolis: University of Minnesota Press, 1984); Michel Serres, *Hermes: Literature, Science, Philosophy* (Baltimore: Johns Hopkins University Press, 1982). See also my discussion of Beer in my "Fiction Science," *Philosophy of the Social Sciences* 17:4 (December 1987): 579–84.

60. John Nelson, Allan Megill, and Donald McClosky, eds., *The Rhetoric of the Human Sciences: Language and Argument in Scholarship and Public Affairs* (Madison: University of Wisconsin Press, 1987).

61. Ibid., pp. 415–16.

62. Ibid., p. 417.

63. Ibid., p. 422.

64. Ibid., p. 141.

65. Ibid., pp. 322–23.

66. Ibid., p. 328.

67. Leo Tolstoy, *Anna Karenina* (New York: W. W. Norton, 1970), p. 94.

68. See Boris Eikhenbaum, "The Puzzle of the Epigraph," ibid., pp. 819–20; see also D. S. Mirsky, "Tolstoy," ibid., pp. 769–75.

69. Stanley Fish, *Is There a Text in This Class?: The Authority of Interpretive Communities* (Cambridge: Harvard University Press, 1980), pp. 171–73.

DAVID GORMAN

The Worldly Text:
Writing as Social Action,
Reading as Historical
Reconstruction

At the beginning of the 1960s, literary theory was an arcane subspecialty of literary scholarship comparable in status to, say, Anglo-Saxon philology. By the end of the next decade it had become a major field of research—and polemic—with a scope taking in all the human sciences. This transformation brought with it an amazing multiplication of methodologies available to interpreters of literature; an unlimited horizon of inquiry seemed, at the time, to open itself to critics making use of the new, theory-derived interpretive tools. Looking back from the late 1980s, however, it should be clear that the area of methodological innovation was in fact relatively confined: most of the new theories of criticism shared a basic theme, which was *language*. The novelty or radicality of the critical theorists' proposals for new directions in literary study usually hinged on some novel, radical claim about the nature of linguistic *signification,* or of allied terms (among them: *text, discourse, rhetoric, signifier, code, reading,* and *writing*). Perhaps this temporary fixation on the semiotic dimension of literature was helpful in advancing critics' understanding of signification, but the motives for a reaction were also inherent in it, as scholars began to remember how much more there is to culture and literature than language.

The now widespread recognition of this limitation of the new literary theory does not mean the end of the theoretical "moment" in the humanities; despite recent suggestions to the contrary, theory cannot—and should not—dissolve itself or shrink back to sub-disciplinary status.[1] The current trend, which will continue for the forseeable future, is rather an overall shift of orientation, as theorists attempt to carry the spirit of methodological innovation over into the many topics in literary and cultural study that are no longer felt to be merely *subsumable* under such concepts as semiosis or textuality. A new archipelago of key terms reflecting this shift has emerged during the past decade or so of theoretical writing: *history, society, politics, ideology, power,* the *body,* and *material culture* begin a list of them. These terms do not have all the same connotations in the work that has made them prominent, of course, but it is fair to say that, taken together, they symptomatize the advent of a second phase in literary and humanistic theory. For purposes of this essay I will use a single word to refer to this whole set, christening this the "worldly" phase of the theoretical enterprise. I utilize Edward Said's expression not only because of its happy generality, but because the borrowing is appropriate: Said was the first important literary scholar to criticize the linguistic preoccupations of theory, and my survey will start with his work.

My concern in what follows is narrower than "worldly" theory as a whole, however, since the topic is unmanageably wide for a chapter. I will confine myself to discussing prospects and problems for literary *history* consequent upon this change in theoretical perspective. For example, I will skim past questions of politics and criticism, which are the concern of other contributors to this volume. I will also have little to say about the so-called New Historicism in cultural studies: the name itself might suggest that this popular trend should be included, but I find the term misleading. What distinguishes the practice of New Historicists in, say, Renaissance studies (where the trend surfaced) is not a larger or smaller historical concern with Renaissance works than was demonstrated by previous students, but a distinctively sociological or anthropological focus. Though the New Anthropologism (as it could more aptly, if less elegantly, be called) is clearly affiliated with the broad movement of theory that I have sketched, toward problems of history, politics, and the rest, I have excluded it as rather marginal, then, preferring informativeness to comprehensiveness.

The following section on Said's thought is meant to introduce the three later sections of this essay, which deal with textual studies, the theory of social action, and the philosophical questions raised by historicism. These topics will be my central concerns, because I believe that current work in each suggests important new avenues of research in cultural history. Though most of the material I discuss is recent, some of it goes back to the 1880s. My criterion for including such material has been its potential usefulness for literary theorists, weighted against what the current generation of them seems most ignorant about, or least able to appreciate. The thought behind this is a simple one: the growth of theory in the 1960s and 1970s began when literary critics started to read around in unfamiliar disciplines—linguistics, anthropology, psychology, philosophy, and so forth; it is natural to suppose that the future of theory will depend on the continued openness of students of the humanities to ideas from other disciplines.

The Secular Prophet

Viewed in retrospect, Said's *Beginnings: Intentions and Method*, along with the concurrently and subsequently written essays mostly collected in *The World, the Text, and the Critic*, take on an almost paradoxical significance.[2] What seemed obvious about them at the time was how much they were part of the new, theoretical style of criticism; certainly they were greeted as such. J. Hillis Miller, in a well-known review of *Beginnings*, welcomed Said to the deconstructionist ranks of what he elsewhere called the "uncanny" critics, among whom he included himself, Jacques Derrida, Geoffrey Hartman, Harold Bloom, and Paul de Man.[3] No doubt Said's "meditative essays" (as he called them; *B*, 16) exhibited characteristically "theoretical" features, being strongly speculative in orientation, dense with allusion to European thought of the previous hundred years (and especially the previous two decades), and self-consciously difficult in style. Yet what seems most obvious now is the deep, unintentional irony of Miller's judgment; only a few years' distance has revealed the extent to which Said's thought worked *in reaction* to the trends of theory associated with the term "structuralism" and, soon, "post-structuralism." My previous comments on the development of recent theory have indicated how

the paradox is to be dissolved, for the route that Said followed
has been recapitulated by a whole movement of literary critics
since then. I mean that his work must be understood as operating
within *and* against the predominant type of theoretical analysis,
the formalistic or—as Said prefers to label it—"functionalist."[4]
While functionalist analysis provided an enabling, energizing matrix for Said's criticism, the force of of his meditations was inter-
rogative with respect to it. He did not at all question the workability
of formalism, but he asked what *purpose* it serves, and what the
relations might be between this kind of analysis and other sorts
of cultural work.

One aspect of Said's writing that illustrates this within/against
movement is his use of critical terminology: while employing the
same general vocabulary as, say, Hartman or de Man, Said tends
to attribute sharply different significance to its terms. Take, for
example, his use of the structuralist buzzword *text*. He adopts the
theoretical usage of the word (in which it supersedes "book" and,
often, "work") but criticizes the conception governing that use
because, he argues, it is a conception of something that is essentially
disembodied. The semiotic critique of the referential capacity of
signs, and the consequent reduction of textuality to a "pure" movement of signifiers, had in principle removed the text from the world,
for one thing. Much of *Beginnings* amounts to a relentless piling
up of examples to refute this inference. The production of texts—
writing—as it is characterized from chapter to chapter there has
almost nothing to do with representing the world through signs;
yet writing is held to be very much a matter of writers acting *in*
the world and adding something *to* it. In this social or activist
conception of textuality, someone might remark here, Said's position is a variant of the Marxist critique of formalism. However,
there is an additional dimension to *Beginnings,* since Said also
emphasizes the converse difficulty of the semiotic theory: not only
does this isolation of the sign from the world render texts socially
inert, powerless—an equally peculiar effect of this theory is to
make the text *invulnerable*. It becomes an ideal object, virtually
transparent to understanding, which floats over the messy, complex
opacity of the social and material world. Said is also much concerned, therefore, to emphasize the vulnerability of texts consequent upon their "situatedness" in material history. The pathos

of textuality, on Said's presentation of it, stands as a reminder that his thought has an existential as well as a Marxist component.

His general sense of what *criticism* means, as a word and a practice, likewise exhibits the salience of Said's position in the context of structuralist literary theory, and particularly of Hillis Miller's "uncanny," deconstructive approach to criticism. Just as he objects to any disembodied notion of the text, Said opposes any practice of criticism that reduces it to the routinized application of a method, or that reduces literature to a series of exemplifications of an all-embracing system. He sees, in fact, a close connection between routinized criticism and idealized textuality in modern theory: the structuralist emphasis on form and function in discourse, on the abstract, coded features of the sign, has produced a kind of criticism very susceptible to codification. The motivation for Said's hostility to methodologized critical practice, a leading motif in *The World, the Text, and the Critic,* is at least partly articulated by a recurrent figure in Said's writing, a figure of recognizably existential provenance—that of Mind in difficult or troubled confrontation with the world. It is not the Cartesian mind, however, since it is not treated as something apart from the world, looking into it; rather, it is a Vichian mind, a consciousness at first merely potential, literally buried in the human body, from which it must fight to emerge, to make itself. This self-production is the image of all intellectual activity for Said, who, in the final chapter of *Beginnings,* emphasizes how Vico presents himself in the *Autobiography* as an autodidact.[5] Moreover, though it is the foundation of culture and the source of spiritual values, the mind is a product of one material process—namely, its own self-creation— among others. It is to be understood not as a result of divine ordination but as arising from poor, uncertain, and indeed accidental circumstances. Moreover, before it becomes anything so sophisticated as intellection, consciousness is an affair of will (Vico's *conatus*); and, no matter how rarefied its activities become, its permanent condition remains one of struggle.

Said makes frequent use of the language of violence when describing the work of intellect in and upon a world that is vast, complicated, and essentially recalcitrant to it. The diverse modern projects of writing upon which he meditates in *Beginnings* are situated there within the constraints implicit in this figure or image.

Said identifies Vico's achievement in *The New Science* as the elaboration of a naturalistic, materialistic account of human culture along these lines; he adopts Vico's way of contrasting the conception of cultural evolution as a contingent process (in Vico's terms, a "gentile" one) with that of human history as an unfolding of events the form and meaning of which are given in advance and from above (Vico calls this the "sacred" or "Hebrew"—for which read Judeo-Christian—view of history). In Said's later essays, the former view becomes a model for "secular criticism," which he advocates (see *W*, 1–30) against the covertly or, often, overtly "religious criticism" in which the latter impulse recurs (see *W*, 290–92).

The upshot of Said's rethinking of literary theory is a turn toward history and politics. Against the many varieties of theory taken up with establishing generalities about the function of signs in discourse, Said argues for the study of signs in their embodied, historical individuality. Complementing this, particularly in his recent work, is a critique of the role and status of intellectuals in social institutions—this to counter the preoccupation with technical niceties and formal schemata at the expense of real thought, which he has deplored in much new theoretical criticism. For reasons indicated at the outset, I am interested here only in the historical part of Said's program. In turning from a retrospective view of his work to a brief consideration of it in prospect, therefore, I will omit discussion of his primarily political writings. But one point above all must be emphasized about Said's turn toward history and politics: in no sense is it a turn away from theory. Said's most enduring contribution to humanistic study is to have expressed a particular ideal of scholarly work as a combination of the most precise, detailed factual research with the broadest and most provocative speculation. This combination of superficially opposed qualities is shared by most of the thinkers whom Said celebrates, beginning with Vico, whose New Science was meant to embrace philosophy *and* philology, and including Nietzsche, Antonio Gramsci, R. P. Blackmur, Erich Auerbach, Raymond Schwab, and Michel Foucault. In his reflections on the work of these and other scholarly theorists and speculative scholars, Said has touched in important ways on themes that I believe will be basic in defining the historical study of literature and culture in the near future. As a way of adumbrating the topics in the remaining three sections of this essay, I will say something about Said's treatment of each of these themes.

PHILOLOGY.   Said does not especially intend to contrast "beginning" with "middle" or "ending"; rather, the correlated notion in his thought is *persistence,* and this notion moves to center stage in later essays, complementing his analyses of the former in *Beginnings.* Thinking about texts using these two categories virtually imposes a historical perspective on literary scholars. Said's point about persistence is that, just as no form or content is given for a text *prior to* its actually being written or "elaborated" (his frequent use of Gramsci's term highlighting the effort involved—W, 170ff.), so the text has no particular place or use reserved for it *subsequently.* Not only is a text's emergence marked by time and circumstance, the pressures of a writer's situation, and the changes, disruptions, or failures to which a writer's aims are subject during the production of a work; the text is in fact permanently exposed to every sort of vagary: neglect or sacralization, emendation, abridgment, translation, parody, and physical destruction—all this without even mentioning "interpretation and rewriting," to which it is *"essentially vulnerable"* (B, 205).

The stress previously noted here on the manifold fragility of a text is closely connected with Said's emphasis on its physical *materiality.* Against the tendency of most formalists, whether traditional (i.e., New Critical) or advanced (post-structural), Said insists on the extent to which a text is bound up with its physical embodiments and effects. This insistence imposes an obligation on critics to confront long-avoided issues of the editorial status of a work, and likewise suggests that textual criticism, far from being a discrete preliminary to interpretive scholarship, must be deeply implicated in any adequately historical practice of interpretation. Works are not created once and for all but *"must always be produced, constantly"* (B, 197). Here is one instance of how Said's philosophical position leads to philological commitments. The best illustrations of this are the fourth chapter of *Beginnings* (particularly the first two sections, 191–223) and "The World, the Text, and the Critic" (W, 31–53), where the historical task of critics is articulated in terms of both notions, beginning and persistence. What must be reconstructed or reimagined is both the writer's struggle to bring a text into articulation, and the ongoing efforts of readers that constitute the afterlife of a text, high or low as its career may be, usually intermittent, and always prone to decay and final disappearance.

SOCIAL ACTION.   The prevailing model in modern criticism is reading, or interpretation, in that the critic's task is held to be that of distilling some meaning from a text. Northrop Frye pointed out that this makes allegorists of a sort out of all critics.[6] While Frye seemed content to accept the situation, Said has not been. This is another face of his anti-systematic position: what I am calling the allegorist idea, that there is something—a meaning—inside, behind, or prior to texts that can be gotten out of them by a method of reading, encourages the creation of theoretical generalizations and their arbitrary application to texts regardless of circumstances. In this sense, Said's essays in *Beginnings* and elsewhere can be seen primarily as anti-allegorical in spirit. Texts are written, read, and then rewritten—whether by critics (in commentaries) or other writers (in that a literary work may influence or even provoke other works). One can, Said admits, view this process as a matter of "encipherment, decipherment, and dissemination. Yet this makes what I think is a fascinating, turbulent, and thick business sound like a bloodless mechanism" (*B*, 21).

Said's counterallegorical strategy for recovering the "thickness" of writing is a historical one. He proposes to treat the text, and everything involved in its elaboration and persistence, as forms of social action. "My position," as he sums it up, "is that texts are worldly, to some degree they are events, and, even when they appear to deny, it, they are nevertheless of . . . the historical moments in which they are located and interpreted" (*W*, 4). Many of Said's key terms are related to this concept of texts as events: *contingency*—that "literature" is not something "natural" or "inertly *given*" in canons of great books or authors, but "derives from a desire—to write—that is ceaseless, varied, and highly unnatural," and should be studied as such (*W*, 131); *emergence*—that ideas "are not best understood as if they were human beings born on a certain day" (*W*, 155), but derive from a concatenation of circumstances that include the forms of discourse available to articulate an idea, the existence of institutions supporting work on or with ideas, and communities of research receiving, promoting, or rejecting ideas; *exteriority*—the view Said finds exemplified in what is for him the best work of Derrida and Foucault, that the study of texts need not be conceived as the decoding of a secret, but is more fruitfully approached as the reconstruction of an activity.

GENEALOGY. Foucault has of course been the largest presence in Said's theoretical work, though a change is also evident there: earlier on, it is what Said agrees with in Foucault which he finds most interesting, whereas recently his concern has been with what he finds most troublesome and objectionable there. Since Said's criticisms are directed mostly at the political implications of Foucault's ideas, I will only say something about his historical views, which Said has found valuable. What is crucial in these ideas is "the special attitude to history"—one of "constitutive ambivalence"—that Foucault shares with Nietzsche. Their attitude toward their historical vocation is "antidynastic," as Said puts it: each sees himself as "carry[ing] on the work of his predecessors [in] . . . history or philology," but as chiefly "concerned with [relations] of *adjacency, complementarity,* and *correlation*" (*B*, 290). The technical term that Said most often uses to connote these concerns is "affiliation," which is meant to be quite close to Foucault's "archaeology;" meanwhile, Nietzsche's "genealogy" is connected with both. What intrigues Said about the Nietzschean approach adopted by Foucault (or by Gilles Deleuze: see *B*, 376–78) is its rejection of a purely linear, genetic image of cultural change over time; "what could be more Platonic (in a debased way) than seeing literature as a copy, experience as an original, and history as a line moving from origin to present? Once this type of linearity is revealed for the theology it really is, a secular reality for writing is enabled" (*W*, 139).

Said's fullest effort to carry out a piece of research along these lines is *Orientalism*, in which he examines how, over a period extending at least several centuries, Europeans were able to dominate and manage much of the Near and Middle East, less through any direct application of force than through the production and reproduction of a certain discourse about that region, its inhabitants, and their society and culture.[7] This discourse was not merely the byproduct of a progressive accumulation of the facts about them, of a sort which could be described in the "linear" or "Platonic" historiography rejected by Foucault. Instead, Said shows Orientalist discourse to have been something gradually constituted and sustained, where diverse interests contributed to the elaboration of an *image* of the Orient, and also the development of what was for a long time the *medium* within which this great area and its people could be discussed by those who had power or (in the Gramscian phrase favored by Said) hegemony over them.

Beginning with a Text

One of the most remarkable features of the institutional context of literary scholarship within which the theoretical revolution has taken place is the absolutely sharp division running through it— far transcending any division among specialties—between the studies concerned with the interpretation, criticism, and cultural history of literature, and those concerned with editing, bibliography, and philology. The primary factor in the separation of the discipline into two distinct fields of activity was, presumably, the rise of the New Criticism. At any rate, the separation of research is quite clearly implied in such standard methodological guides as *Theory of Literature* by René Wellek and Austin Warren (1949) and the MLA handbook entitled *The Aims and Methods of Literary Scholarship* (1963).[8] Most significant in the present context is that the rise of literary theory has had almost no effect on the division between editorial and interpretive studies in the humanities, being an event that has remained confined to the latter area. Yet it cannot be too strongly asserted that theoreticians must carry their efforts into the editorial area if their future goal is the creation of a new literary history. Such a history must be more than a chronicle of semiotic forms or discursive practices: it must also be a history of *documents,* and (as Said has reminded us) of persisting material objects.

In light of the present situation, there is an evident irony in the admiration professed by a number of contemporary theorists for such virtuosi of the Romance-philological tradition as Erich Auerbach, E. R. Curtius, or Leo Spitzer. The praise usually expressed seems, symptomatically, rather unfocused, as if Spitzer's importance lay primarily in his being a specially close and acute reader (like de Man?), or Auerbach's in a particularly comprehensive knowledge of his subject matter (comparable to Hartman's, perhaps). But certainly a defining common feature of their work is its focus on documents, and on the potential vulnerabilities and complexities associated with the fact that it is only possible for texts to pass through time by means of such vehicles. When we praise the integral quality of these scholars' methods and concerns, we should realize that this was more than a matter of their ability to situate the works they studied within an impressively wide background of linguistic, literary, and cultural history. They were all able to practice *textual* history and criticism as part of *literary* history and criticism. The task facing us today, to reintegrate these forms of historiography, meets two sorts of obstacles. One is that, with the new importance accorded to critical theory, there are more kinds of work to integrate. I do not see, however, that these additional perspectives necessarily obstruct critics from taking an interest in editorial problems, though of course the sheer ignorance of most literary theorists about bibliographic and editorial study presents a big contingent difficulty.

The other and more serious obstacle to the proposed unification of hermeneutic and editorial studies has to do with the fact that, until very recently, there was little interest in promoting such an effort. Textual editors seemed content to claim no more than had Fredson Bowers, the most distinguished contemporary figure in this sector of literary study, when he asked critics to take seriously the idea of sound and accurate texts, and to respect the efforts of those scholars who undertook to produce them.[9] Bowers's peers on the interpretive side of the discipline—Frye, Wellek, and Kenneth Burke might serve as representative figures—were presumably quite satisfied to accord textual studies the equal but separate status that its practitioners requested for it, and this cordial atmosphere of mutual oblivion remains largely undissipated today. I want to discuss briefly the work of three textual scholars who have begun—in different ways and for different reasons—to challenge this division of concerns by addressing matters of criticism and the theory of criticism directly. Though the initiatives of Hershel Parker, Jerome J. McGann, and G. Thomas Tanselle have not been unsupported, they have certainly been too little noticed by interpretive critics.

In what follows I will concentrate on the distinctive theses of each of these textual critics and the issues between them. I will simply assume as self-evident the claim on which they all agree, namely, that scholars of the future must take far more active interest in the documentary history of the works they study. It is not enough to say that philological critics like Curtius or Auerbach were chiefly occupied with ancient and medieval writings, and that problems of transmission and preservation hardly arise for the literature of the print era. The main significance of the work of Bowers and his associates and successors is to have shown that this assumption is grotesquely false, whether as applied to Shakespeare's work, or Hawthorne's, or even to a living writer such as Tom Stoppard. Moreover, an interpreter using an approach based, say, on rhetorical principles (whether in the New Critical or deconstructive manner) could produce good results (regardless of whether this means something more like "valid" or something more like "powerful") if the text being read were simply unsound—the product of arbitrary or inadvertent deformations to which every document is exposed during reproduction and use. Any interpretive critic or literary historian unconvinced of this point should consider the essays of Parker, McGann, or Tanselle essential reading, since each provides an eloquent defense of the relevance of textual scholarship, as well as unanswerable examples of the GIGO principle as it has manifested itself in the history of interpretation.

In his major publication, *Flawed Texts and Verbal Icons,* Hershel Parker mounts a critique of literary study which operates on two fronts.[10] On one front, Parker is questioning the interpretive procedures used by many literary critics. The "verbal icon" is, of course, the text as the New Critics conceived it: a fetishized object sealed off antiseptically from its producer, self-contained in a perfect formal unity. Against this, Parker has proposed a program for what he originally called the New Scholarship, which would call into play the evidence (often abundant in American literature, at any rate) of the compositional history of a work as a tool of interpretation and criticism.[11] Parker has repeatedly demonstrated how often such investigations will undercut traditional formalist assumptions about the unity and self-sufficiency of texts, and how many major works of American literature are either unfinished, or arbitrarily stitched together from drafts and fragments, or finished (or sometimes abandoned) only to be taken up later by the author and revised and published with quite different, inconsistent intentions. Moreover, he has pointed to the frequency with which authors have been forced to acquiesce to deformations of their work by publishing houses and other outside pressures. If Parker is correct about the extraordinary prevalence of "flawed texts" in the American canon, it would certainly force a considerable reorientation of current critical practice and would justify his contention that "better scholarship might lead to better criticism" (*FT,* xiv).

The other front along which Parker is mounting an attack is an internal one, directed against the dominant method for editing American literature, which he finds excessively narrow in focus. Partly this is just a matter of editors' lack of assertiveness about the significance of their work. Parker complains about the relative triviality of textual problems cited by scholars like Bowers—as if misprints were the only thing for critics to worry about, rather than the pervasiveness of "uncompleted texts, patched together texts, maimed texts, and meaningless texts" (*FT,* 16). At the same time, though, Parker has a deeper quarrel with the priorities of textual scholarship in American literature, and he proposes to rethink editorial theory in terms of two notions that he believes have been insufficiently considered within the received paradigm. The notions in question are those of *creativity* and *authority.*

Editors need to remind themselves, Parker contends, that an author's creative intentions are always multiple but not always coherent. The importance of this point relates to the aim of a scholarly editor to reestablish a text in accordance with an author's "final intention" (insofar as this can be reconstructed from evidence, of course). There is a tendency, according to Parker, for editors to attribute a neat set of intentions to an author and to postulate a precise moment when the author, in full control of those intentions, finalizes the text in light of them. Against this Parker emphasizes the contingent nature of composition and the emergent quality of the intentions involved as factors that may well leave traces on a text, even one published with no outside interference. Editors who idealize their texts are liable to efface what they should be most concerned to reveal: the "multitude of decisions made—and opportunities lost or seized—during each moment of the actual process of composition" (*FT*, 26). In this way, ironically, textual critics may be led into the same mistake as interpretive critics, that of reducing the historical reality of a flawed text to the (imagined) timeless status of a verbal icon.

An author's failure to render his or her intentions clear or coherent constitutes one of two ways in which a text can be flawed, according to Parker's theory. The other involves the case where there is some later distortion of an author's intention, and this is where the question of authority arises. Parker is particularly occupied by situations where such distortions are the product of "authorial second thoughts" (*FT*, 78). A well-known example of this would be Henry James's rewriting of his early fiction for the New York edition of his work, resulting occasionally in quite peculiar effects. Parker raises the extremely interesting theoretical question whether, and how, textual authority rests with an author. The answer to which his empirical studies have led him is that, while "all authority in literature comes from the author . . . that authority can be blurred or wholly lost and, paradoxically, it can persist even when the author thinks it has been removed" (*FT*, 16). The general rule of editing that Parker thus rejects is the one mandating the adoption of any later authorial revisions of a work. As Parker puts it, this principle confuses "correction and revision, the former restoring an original intention and the latter embodying what may well be a new intention" (*FT*, 60). The point being made is both aesthetic (that to revise is not always to improve) and historical (that the intermittency or provisionality that sometimes characterizes work on a text may fragment the writer's authority, so that instead of one text there may be two, or more, or possibly something in between). The ultimate suggestion is that aesthetic criteria must sometimes play a part in the historical judgment of editors.

Jerome McGann's program for what he originally called a New Historicism offers many parallels to Parker's New Scholarship—not least that it was articulated simultaneously, in *A Critique of Modern Textual Criticism* and in his collection of essays on English Romantic literature, *The Beauty of Inflections*.[12] Like Parker, McGann wishes to criticize the accepted practice of textual editing, as well as the practice of interpretation innocent of philological concern. Like Parker also, then, McGann views critical and scholarly work as closely connected. Thereafter, however, their opinions diverge acutely. In simplest terms, where Parker's focus is psychological, McGann's is social: for the former, the editor's efforts must be directed toward the author's creative process; for the latter, "the process of literary production" is the focus, a process for which McGann advocates a thoroughly "socialized" view, incorporating "the cooperative involvements" of the author with "his or her chosen (and sometimes fated) institutions of literary production" (*C,* 115). McGann also problematizes the concept of textual authority but comes to a conclusion diametrically opposed to Parker's: "Authority is a social nexus, not a personal possession" (*C,* 48).[13]

What has most impressed McGann in his research is the sheer multiplicity of evidence often available to editors of English literature. There may be several apparently equally authoritative versions of the "same" poem by Byron, due to the fact that composition seems to have been an ongoing and often collaborative process with Byron's social group (*C,* 51–54, 76–80).[14] McGann finds that the standard editorial aim of *deciding* on a particular version as being closest to definitive tends to misconstrue or dissimulate the case; the editorial task is better approached as one of presenting the relationships among different authoritative versions as clearly and accurately as possible. As a critic of recent editorial theory, McGann can be seen as another advocate of de-idealization: for him, the purity and simplicity of the received model of how authorial intention is embodied in writing must give way before the sheer heterogeneity that typifies the production and reproduction of a work. McGann's ultimate suggestion is that editors' historical judgments may depend in part on the transmission and reception history of a work.

A further distinctive feature of McGann's theory of textual criticism is the broad ideological and historical interest which informs his work. The political analysis of the history of Romantic studies which McGann started in *The Romantic Ideology: A Crit-*

ical Investigation and in various essays falls outside my discussion,[15] but some consequences that he draws from it are relevant for textual criticism. One is that the authority of the editor is a pertinent concern for editorial theory. This is not simply a point made in support of editorial self-consciousness, since McGann recognizes that "critical editors and theorists are normally quite self-conscious about their aims and purposes toward their received texts" (C, 100). The further implication is that the standard distinction between "modernized" and "definitive" editions is a misleading one at best, at least if the difference is supposed to be one between a text prepared to meet the particular needs of a current audience and one attempting to provide a full, permanent historical record of the text. In that sense, every text is necessarily "modernized" to the extent that its editor, however scholarly his or her aim, is responding to contemporary needs or interests; as these change, the criteria for what is "definitive" about the presentation of a text will, inevitably, likewise change. McGann does not view this inevitability as a problem, but he does see it as implying that all editors must consider their cultural and institutional situations. This consideration presupposes that textual editors will be able to situate their own work in the *history of scholarship,* and another consequence of McGann's historico-ideological framework is that a premium is placed on the need for editors to think historically, not only about the texts on which they work, but also about the methodological issues they have inherited.

What is perhaps most significant about McGann's conception is its largeness and exuberance. More than anyone else so far, he has articulated a believable vision of a reintegrated field of literary studies with textual criticism occupying a "central place" (C, 11). Like Parker, he has played the roles of scholar, interpreter, and theorist, and he has done respectable work in each area. Whether his memorable descriptions of the literary work as "a dynamic event in human experience" (B, 108) or of poems as "structures of social energy" (B, 129) will suffice, as he hopes, to provide a common locus within which to bind these critical activities remains to be seen—but it also remains indispensable to the consideration of theorists convinced of the need for a truly historical, historicized study of culture and its written artifacts.[16]

If Parker and McGann present themselves as dissidents within the ranks of contemporary editors, G. Thomas Tanselle's assigned role appears to be that of spokesman for the main tradition of editing associated with Bowers. Certainly Tanselle has built his reputation as heir apparent through the series of authoritative essays on every aspect of editorial and bibliographic study published annually since 1965 in Bowers's *Studies in Bibliography*.[17] Yet it would be a mistake to present Tanselle as the defender of some orthodoxy. Where Parker, McGann, and a number of other controversialists in the field have tended to articulate bold programs, Tanselle has preferred to bring out the complexities of textual study and to focus on the variety of options available to editors. His own position (in contrast with the others') appears elusive as a result. Nevertheless, a number of persistent themes run through Tanselle's writings on editorial procedure, themes that help lend them the admirable lucidity with which he is able to bring together and analyze so much material.

Tanselle is less interested than Parker or McGann in advocating a reunion of textual and interpretive criticism because he believes that the first is already part of the second: "a critical *edition* is, itself and of necessity, also a critical *study*."[18] Though not everyone may recognize the fact, he argues, an editor's work on a text is an effort of literary criticism, and the resulting edition— for those who know how to read it—is an interpretive statement by the textual scholar. This basic assumption has led Tanselle repeatedly to attack efforts to formulate all-purpose methods or systems of editing. What he finds objectionable in such programs is their suggestion that, with a good enough general theory, a scholar will be excused from having to use any judgment, because the program will automatically solve his or her editorial problems. "The job of a scholarly editor," as Tanselle defines it, is not the application of a method, whether derived from the work of Bowers or anyone else, but "the exercise of critical thinking in an effort to determine the final intention of an author with respect to a particular text."[19] A good editor cannot avoid thinking and must not avoid particulars.

This point, taken by itself, might make Tanselle seem an antitheoretical editor. This is not so, however: he has devoted as much energy to working through conceptual problems as have McGann or Parker—and possibly with sounder results.[20] While Tanselle seems flatly to dismiss the idea of textual theory as a search for one correct method, he is emphatic about the role of *principles* in editorial thought, as he shows in comments like this on another theorist: "His eagerness to emphasize the idea that one cannot edit by rules causes him to neglect certain basic principles or distinctions that are necessary for clear thinking on editorial matters."[21] The role of conceptual analysis, of defining procedural concepts and drawing distinctions between them, is another dominant theme in Tanselle's contributions. Moreover, it helps to explain the rather cold eye that he casts on the work of more radical theorists. He objects not to conceptual innovations, but to the confusions that can accompany them as to, for example, the differences between historical and aesthetic judgment, or between definitive and modernized editions.

One other notable motif in Tanselle's position is his advocacy of pluralism. He will not, typically, reject outright the line proposed by a revisionary editorial theorist, but will begin to search for its limitations, the sorts of cases to which it will not apply, the distinct concepts that it will blur together, and any inconsistencies or shortcomings in the arguments presented to justify it:

> There is a prima facie case for the legitimacy of more than one approach to the editorial treatment of historical evidence. . . . Acceptance of this multiplicity does not, and should not, end debate: for one still has to decide which approach is to be followed in a given situation, and many factors bearing on that decision can usefully be discussed. But the debate thereby moves to a different, and more productive level. Advocacy of one position then occurs in the context of valid alternative positions; and criticism levelled at a given argument springs not from the belief that only one approach is correct but from the detection of logical flaws in the argument.[22]

I do not propose to adjudicate the debates between Tanselle, Parker, McGann, or their colleagues, but only to point them out to critics who may not be familiar with this material. The level on which their theoretical debate is taking place is very high indeed, and one that should put many theorists of interpretive criticism to shame.

Linguistic Action as Social Action

I turn now to the field of political theory, to discuss recent work that I believe is of great potential interest to literary historians. I will focus on the methodical writings of one of the key innovators in the field, Quentin Skinner. He is usually associated with a number of historians of political thought, many of whom, like him, have affiliations with Cambridge University (including Peter Laslett, John Dunn, and John Wallace). Among those others I will make special reference to J. G. A. Pocock, whose methodical statements are no less important—though somewhat more diffuse— than Skinner's. Since their work is not well known among critics, a case will need to be made for its interest and future use in literary studies.

When Skinner and Pocock took up their work in the late 1950s and early 1960s, political theory was in a situation similar to that of literary criticism as I have described it in the 1980s: that is, it was a discipline typified by the availability of any number of sophisticated methods for the study of political concepts, and especially for reading political and social writings belonging to a canonized series of "classic texts" (from, say, Plato to Weber), but it was also a discipline lacking a fully historical outlook on its subject. This at least was the argument in early writings by Skinner and his associates, which were cast in polemical form because so many political theorists believed their procedures were perfectly historical. Skinner's most noteworthy publication in this vein is "Meaning and Understanding in the History of Ideas,"[23] a lengthy diagnosis of the varieties of pseudohistoricism afflicting the study of political thought; alongside this he published a number of essays on Hobbes as specimens of an adequately historical approach to "classic" writings. I will not go into the details of Skinner's polemic here; it is enough to say that he wants to repudiate acontextual and anachronistic treatments of past political writings when those are disguised as the historiography of political thought. Such errors are promoted by a curious feature of political theory, which has been labeled by John Gunnell "the myth of the tradition"—the idea that the received canon of major political works forms a real historical series, where the determining influences on each writer are held to be the works of his predecessors in the canon.[24] This conception was progressively demolished by the Cambridge group, who showed in many cases how, once the historical context of their discourse was reconstructed, various classic political writings were best understood as reactions to local features of that context far more than to Plato, Aristotle, or later figures in the purported but in fact largely retroactively projected "tradition" of political thought.

The aim of Skinner and his colleagues finds a clear echo in current controversies over the historical significance of literary canons. But I do not claim that this is the primary interest their work holds for critics, because I think debates over canons are relatively superficial. Indeed, far from reinforcing the current critical prejudice against canons, a review of this twenty-year-old episode in political studies should help anti-canonical theorists recognize the limitations of this issue. The upshot of Skinner's critique was not at all to denigrate terms like "canon" and "classic," as both Pocock and Skinner have often since affirmed. The application of the canon concept that they wanted to reject was to the *historical* study of discourse, where they argued that it inevitably has a distorting effect. Having articulated this important but hopefully rather obvious point, these theorists moved on to address the more difficult and more interesting problem of how any text (whatever status it eventually achieves) is to be understood in an adequately historical fashion. This is the work from which literary critics have the most to learn.

The central concept in Skinner's interpretive theory is that of *action*. During the 1970s he published essays developing a many-sided analysis of this notion, for which he has found several kinds of application. His starting point was the theory of speech acts (also called pragmatics), particularly as discussed in the work of J. L. Austin, H. P. Grice, and P. F. Strawson.[25] The notion of a speech act, and some of the terminology associated with it, has of course become commonplace in literary criticism, but Skinner's approach to it remains exemplary because he made a considerable effort to master its *technical* aspects: this in contrast to literary theorists, who have typically confined themselves to borrowing bits and pieces of it, or commenting highly selectively on certain discussions of it. Without a grasp of the technical issues, no researcher can hope to offer serious criticisms of speech act theory.

Skinner understood this well enough to have published two original contributions to the technical literature of pragmatics—something which, to my knowledge, has yet to be done by any literary critic.[26]

Skinner's first application of the speech-act conception to the historical interpretation of texts was to propose, as a methodological principle, that it is essential to understand not only what an author's text *says*, but also what he or she was *doing* in composing it. The general point was established by Austin with regard to utterances: the meaning of a sentence as spoken possesses not only a locutionary element (its literal sense) but also an illocutionary one, which is a matter of what the speaker is trying to do with those words. Skinner is fond of an example of Strawson's, "The ice over there is very thin." Interpreting this as a statement may involve more than understanding the descriptive content of the sentence. When spoken, for instance, by a policeman to someone skating across a frozen pond, it may constitute a *warning*. There is no indication of this illocutionary force in the words themselves: only attention to context reveals the intention expressed by this statement in this use. One goal of the historical interpreter who has adopted this principle, then, becomes the recovery of the author's intentions in writing.

The adaption of speech act theory to the historical interpretation of writing requires a number of qualifications, which Skinner has tried to make explicit. One is that an interpreter reconstructs not an intention, but intentions: there may be many answers to the question of what an author was trying to do in a work. Another is that the primary, intention-recovering task of the historical interpreter may depend on a reconstruction of the context of discursive conventions available at a given time; this preliminary job is particularly important, because such conventions tend to be implicit in direct proportion to their familiarity or standardization in a culture. A third qualification is that there is no guarantee that all illocutionary aims attributable to authors on the basis of available evidence are aims that they actually had, nor are we now in a position to establish all relevant contexts. The best claim that can be made for this aspect of Skinner's method is a negative one: it allows us to rule out intentions that, so far as we know, an author could *not* have been able to express.

The focus on intentions central to the speech-act analysis of linguistic action thus begins to give way to a concern with conventions governing such acts. The trajectory of Skinner's theoretical work in the 1970s is marked by this change of focus, bringing him closer in particular to Pocock, who, with a strong but eclectic interest in historical theory, was not much influenced by philosophers of language. The methodological issue that preoccupied him stemmed from his empirical work in the history of early modern European (and particularly English) political thought. Pocock's chief discovery was the specificity and persistence of certain modes of political discourse. Following an insight of Edmund Burke's, he noticed that there was, in the British tradition, a manner of political writing cast in the vocabulary and using the argumentative strategies of English common-law jurisprudence.[27] Pocock subsequently found that there were a good many such discursive modes in early modern writing, including those connected with scholastic political philosophy, the civic republicanism of the humanists, and the eschatological tradition, among others. He illustrated a number of these forms of political thought in *Politics, Language and Time*,[28] where he also attempted to theorize them, calling them "languages" or (borrowing from T. S. Kuhn) "paradigms." Neither term is entirely satisfactory, as Pocock has since noted. The latter is less misleading than the former, because it suggests a system of thought as well as a manner of writing, but both terms carry superfluous connotations (Kuhn's of a more technical sort). Pocock has since essayed substitutes like "vocabulary," "idiom," or "rhetoric," but he has found them all too lexical or formalistic. Perhaps "sublanguage" is his aptest choice of label for this phenomenon, the nature of which, despite terminological difficulties, he has made reasonably clear.

It should be apparent why this approach to the history of political thought via a description of its possible forms of expression foregrounds linguistic conventions rather than intentions. Such a conception takes each political actor to be committed to finding an appropriate role in a kind of language game (and Pocock has also sometimes tried out Wittgenstein's term as a label, though again it carries irrelevant associations). An agent's purposes are thus constrained by the options available to anyone playing that part in the game. Political actions carried out in a linguistic medium are to be understood, therefore, in terms of their function in such discursive-conceptual contexts. By alluding to "language games," Pocock signals his interest in adapting one Wittgensteinian idea for the purposes of historical research, which is that each mode of political discourse is constituted by an overlapping set of practices extending from purely verbal patterns to forms of life. Pocock also means to adapt an insight of Kuhn's theory of paradigms, that speakers of a political sublanguage may be almost completely unable to understand those who speak another sublanguage—which would explain the recurrent but otherwise baffling fact that parties disputing the same political issue sometimes fail completely to grasp each others' arguments, despite being citizens of the same nation and using the same (primary) language. Pocock also shares with Skinner a conception of texts as events, the production of which is one kind of action and the reception of which constitutes a further series of actions, all of which call for historical reconstruction.

At any rate, the reconstruction of sublinguistic contexts or language games as they operated in the early modern period of European history to make possible such linguistic events is the task undertaken in the major studies published so far by Pocock and Skinner. Pocock's *The Machiavellian Moment*[29] examines the formation of the "civic humanist" mode of political discourse in sixteenth-century Italy, and its great impact on seventeenth- and eighteenth-century British thought—including, ultimately, on the framers of the American Constitution. The two volumes of Skinner's *The Foundations of Modern Political Thought*[30] trace the interplay of a number of such "languages" of politics during the Renaissance (vol. I) and Reformation (II). The goal in each case is really twofold: to reinterpret "classic" texts from this era non-anachronistically, by situating them in their historical discursive context, and to redescribe each of those contexts as fully as possible in its own right, undistorted by preconceptions encouraged by subsequently established canons of "great" political writings. As Skinner puts it in the preface to *Foundations,* the idea is "to build up a more realistic picture of how political thinking in all its various forms was in fact conducted in earlier periods . . . to [produce] a history of political theory with a genuinely historical character" (xi).

Having sketched some elements of the theory, and before turning to its recent developments, I want to say something about its relevance to literary history. What I want to underscore is not the fact that Skinner, Pocock, or their associates deal with *political* writings, but the fact that they are trying to work out a method appropriate to a *historical* study of these texts and their ideological contexts. Skinner has pointed out recently that "the special techniques of the literary critic . . . ought to have a central place in the process of cultural criticism."[31] I want to make the converse suggestion: since political discourse is one topic of cultural historiography, and literary discourse is another, I believe the methods developed by the Cambridge historians for the "demythologized" study of political thought and its history can be carried over directly into literary history. Of course, it helps to emphasize the point that, as historical categories of writing, the political and the literary overlap. (Skinner has been interested in Thomas More, for example, and Pocock is working on a study of Gibbon; Machiavelli has been a key figure for both.) But the analysis of texts as events, and of writing as action, expressing intentions within contexts of linguistic and social conventions, would be adaptable to the case of literary works no matter how narrowly "literature" is defined.

At least two consequences of Pocock and Skinner's contextual approach make it significant for historians studying any sort of discourse in terms of sublanguages or traditions of argument (which need not be political, after all). One is that languages change, and accurate diachronic reconstructions presuppose accurate synchronic ones. It will often be an author's aim to modify or extend the available textual conventions: "the historian looks for ways," Pocock explains, in which the complex speech act that the text represents "may have rearranged, or sought to rearrange, the possibilities open to the author and his co-users of language." Moreover, this activity may become quite complex, because there is no reason why a sophisticated author might not be operating in several sublanguages or traditions simultaneously.[32] The other interesting point is that a language user's control over language is strictly limited: "Perhaps the key characteristic of tradition is that no single transmitter has complete control of the messages he either receives or transmits; there is always the element of the implicit and perhaps the contradictory, which must escape his attention at any single moment of transmission."[33] Literary critics should be particularly receptive to this observation, since it is one of the chief lessons to be learned from the rhetorical study of language.

On first encounter with Skinner's theory of linguistic action, with its emphasis on the centrality of an author's intention, literary theorists will think at once of E. D. Hirsch's program, which seems to resemble Skinner's closely. In his first theoretical writings, Hirsch certainly defended the appeal to authorial intention as a guiding principle of interpretation against the varieties of formalism prevalent in the New Critical era; and in later writings he has stressed the extent to which he means his theory to be employed as a guide to historical research.[34] The differences between Hirsch and Skinner are worth noting, however. Most generally, the philosophical basis for the latter's theory is sounder: Hirsch's peculiar, quasi-phenomenological idea of "meaning types" was not satisfactorily expressed in *Validity in Interpretation,* nor has he subsequently attempted to give it a better formulation. The basic problem is that a timeless, complete "meaning" is held to be imparted to a text by an author's intention, but this new entity, as well as the mechanism which engenders it, remains obscure. Skinner's modified speech-act analysis is more modest, by contrast: it simply aims to discover how many "redescriptions" in terms of function or purpose (as well as sense—Austin's locutionary meaning) a text will bear, given what is known about its context. The list of possible redescriptions is open-ended, in that there may be many intentions fairly ascribable to a writer, and loose-fitting, since a writer may conceivably have had fewer intentions than a full list would allow; Hirsch's account seems to entail a much more rigid methodology. A further, particular difference is that Skinner has suggested a way to negotiate the formalist/intentionalist dispute in interpretation that has made Hirsch's theory so unpersuasive to his opponents. A distinction needs to be drawn, Skinner explains, between the intentions of an author in a piece of writing—which is all that illocutionary redescription aims to recover—and the motives that induced the author to perform these linguistic acts. (To advert to the ice-skating example, the distinction is between *what* the policeman does in speaking to the skater—namely, warning him—and *why* he does so; in general, the Skinnerian interpreter will not look deeper than the agent's public role: e.g., that warnings are the kind of thing policemen offer.) Authorial motivation can be left out of the historical account as irrelevant or imponderable in just the way that the New Critics insisted. But there is a purposive residue directly implicit in the text, and in this narrower, illocutionary sense of "intention," theorists like Hirsch are quite right to say that a historically correct interpretation cannot dispense with it.

Skinner has made at least two additions to his theory that should be of special interest to literary and intellectual historians. His important article entitled "Hermeneutics and the Role of History"[35] conveniently summarizes his work on intention and convention, returning to the question of context, over which there is a sharp debate among literary theorists. The New Critical view, of course, is that texts can be understood largely on their own terms, given a close enough reading. Meanwhile, the traditional historicist view which it displaced, but which is now coming back into favor following the eclipse of the New Criticism, sees placing a work in its full context as vital to its correct interpretation. Though he generally endorses the second view, Skinner is again concerned to negotiate the debate here, rather than to take sides. He suggests that we distinguish between texts that are relatively "autonomous," or self-contained and self-interpreting, and those that are "heteronomous," where part of what their authors were doing was to make reference to other works, or to ideas or practices in the culture. Skinner notes that satiric or parodic texts tend to be heteronomous, as are those with polemical intent, whether this involves endorsing or attacking contemporary values. Even highly autonomous texts need to be approached historically, though, he concludes, since they draw on local idioms, genres, and beliefs. But he maintains that gross misinterpretation is much more of a danger for the unhistorical interpreter when the work in question is relatively heteronomous.

Skinner has also developed a new application of speech act theory to deal with one of the basic questions in the history of political discourse, that of the relationship between principles expressed by political figures and their actual practices. One kind of answer here is to say that there is no real connection, professions of principle being little more than thin disguises for the real—often sordid—motives of politicians; or to say (in the Marxist variant) that the political language of a social group simply reflects the

political interests that are determined for it at a deeper, infrastruc-
tural level. Skinner argues that such models do not fit the case
where proponents of some new social practice meet resistance and
need to find a way to legitimate their innovation. "If we . . . ask
how this central task of an innovating ideologist—that of legitimating untoward social actions—can really be performed, the theory of speech-acts immediately seems to provide an important clue
to the answer."[36] Part of any language is its "normative vocabulary," made up of those terms that are used to describe social
practices but that also carry connotations commending or condemning those practices. It is open to "innovating ideologists" to
try manipulating this vocabulary, changing the criteria according
to which such a term is applied, or the evaluative connotation
associated with it. Skinner cites Weber's classic analysis of how
the theological language of Protestantism was adapted by early
capitalists to justify their own commercial activities: what is being
contested in cases like this are, in effect, the kinds of speech acts
in which normative terms can be used, and what role they will
play in speech acts. To at least this degree, then, "our social vocabulary helps to constitute the character of [social] practices."[37]

The work of Skinner and his associates is salutary in another
way. Literary theorists who study this material stand to learn
something that is, so far, much better known to students of the
social sciences than those of the humanities. The lesson is that the
interpretation of texts is not a self-contained problem: it is one
part of the larger problem of the explanation of human behavior.
Again there is a methodological dispute here, which Skinner hopes
to negotiate in a manner described in his fundamental article,
" 'Social Meaning' and the Explanation of Social Action."[38] He
identifies one group of theorists of the "naturalist" persuasion,
who argue that all explanatory accounts are ultimately causal in
form, and that any valid hermeneutic theory should at least be
consistent with a causal-explanatory framework. (This is a revised
and newly influential version of the Logical Positivists' cruder claim
that interpretive theories should be reducible to causal ones.)
Against this is the "anti-naturalist" position, which holds that
interpretation is an entirely different mode of understanding an
entirely different range of phenomena (intentional phenomena)
than the causal analysis of natural phenomena that is characteristic

of natural science. Skinner's mediating strategy is to emphasize the notion of rationality: "to exhibit a social action as rational *is* to explain it," he argues. To see the importance of this idea, one must recall that the basic insight of the Cambridge historians is that linguistic action is a species of social action. "If we begin by assuming the agent's rationality," Skinner writes, "and find this assumption borne out, this will provide us with an explanation for the agent's apparent belief that he was acting rationally. . . . Conversely, unless we begin by assuming the agent's rationality, we leave ourselves with no means of explaining his behavior, or even of seeing exactly what there is to explain about it, if it should happen that he is not acting rationally."[39] Whether Skinner's attempt to reconcile these positions is successful involves complex philosophical questions far outside the present discussion. But his writings on the topic are important because he has grasped the fact that any thorough consideration of interpretation must involve thinking about explanation and rationality.

Historicism and Its Discontents

One of the most widely read works of literary theory has surely been Fredric Jameson's *The Political Unconscious*.[40] This book, along with a number of Jameson's other writings, has had as large an effect as Said's on the transition from a sign-oriented to a world-oriented style of theorization in the humanities. The general Marxist hermenuetics that Jameson advocates, being equally offensive to hermeneuts and to Marxists, has been extremely controversial but in any case falls outside the scope of my essay. However, Jameson begins his work with a statement he clearly assumes to be less contentious: "Always historicize! This slogan—the one absolute and we may even say 'transhistorical' imperative of dialectical thought—will ultimately turn out to be the moral of *The Political Unconscious*" (9). I think it fair to say that, in the current theoretical climate, a majority of theorists would accept this principle without much reflection. Yet the drift of the concluding portion of my essay will be that the philosophical task facing the next generation of literary historians is exactly to reflect on that principle, its possible limits, and the possible alternatives. *Can* one "always historicize"? If not, why not—and what then? The problematic here requires much thought, and I can only indicate some of its elements.

An obvious issue implicit in Jameson's slogan is that of what historicization involves. The classical answer to this question was, of course, elaborated in the milieu of German Romanticism starting in the late eighteenth century. The Historicist conception of history is a complicated one, but for present purposes an abstract statement will serve to isolate relevant features: (1) the appropriate relation of historians to their material ought to be one of complete *disinterest;* (2) to historians who assume such a contemplative stance, all periods of the past lie *equally open,* as it were—the ability of a historian to understand a past epoch is proportional to (and thus only limited by) the amount of evidence available; (3) achieving historical understanding is largely a matter of grasping objectively the *subjectivity* of historical agents, the traces of whose actions constitute historical evidence; and (4) the process of history is assumed to be essentially *cumulative,* the interpretive task of the historian with regard to an event being to establish a sequence of events leading up to it. From the late nineteenth century on, the general model of which these theses are facets has come under attack from a variety of directions. The term "antihistoricism" can serve as a generic label for the attack, so long as one remembers that the elements common to different critiques of historicism are mostly negative. Rather than review many specific alternatives to the historicist model, it may be useful to start with a generalization. Many of the most noteworthy attacks on historicism have been philosophically motivated (as opposed to having resulted from failures of empirical results), and I suggest that we can discern two large *types* of antihistoricism, deriving from the two main traditions of modern philosophy. Associated with the Continental or speculative branch of philosophy is what I call (using another generic label) *genealogy;* and with the Analytical branch, *rational reconstruction.* I will note some future implications of each in turn, beginning with the second.

The historical methodology of rational reconstruction is not very familiar to students of the humanities, because its practice thus far has been confined to the historiography of philosophy and the natural sciences. Its basic principle was expressed, with regard

to the history of mathematics, by the inaugurator of analytic philosophy, Gottlob Frege:

> The historical approach, with its aim of detecting how things begin
> and of arriving from these origins at a knowledge of their nature,
> is certainly perfectly legitimate, but it also has its limitations. If
> everything were in continual flux, and nothing maintained itself fixed
> for all time, there would no longer be any possibility of getting to
> know anything about the world, and everything would be plunged
> in confusion. . . . Often it is only after immense intellectual effort,
> which may have continued over centuries, that humanity at last
> succeeds in achieving knowledge of a concept in its pure form, of
> stripping off the irrelevant accumulations which veil it from the eyes
> of the mind.[41]

In setting aside traditional history as a legitimate but limited approach to the emergence of concepts, Frege also dropped the hint
for an alternative style of intellectual history that would be "normative" rather than simply "empirical," in the terminology of Imre
Lakatos, one of the philosophers of science who developed a
method of historical research fitting Frege's suggestion. It is normative because it interprets the sets of systems of belief professed
by past thinkers or cultures in light of relevant *modern* beliefs, and
the critical analysis of changing belief-patterns amounts to what
Lakatos calls an "internal history" of a field of belief. Its "external
history" is a matter of the context of social and psychological
factors affecting the formation and mutation of beliefs—the subjective world of historical agents that is the topic of traditional
intellectual history.

Rational reconstruction seems wide open to the charge of
anachronism; in its defense it can be said that it is at worst a
deliberate, controlled form of anachronism—not at all the same
as the inadvertent pseudohistoricism castigated by Skinner or Pocock. Rational reconstructions need to call upon traditional, "empirical," or non-anachronistic history in a very important way,
since the latter is needed to explain why the truths accepted today
were *not* recognized in the past. External history will chronicle the
"irrelevant accretions" of which Frege wrote, while the "immense
effort" with which they were overcome will provide internal history
with its themes. Richard Rorty has pointed out that contextual
interpretation in Skinner's style and normative interpretation in

Lakatos's are best seen as complementary methods: "Rational reconstructions are necessary to help us present-day philosophers think through our problems. Historical reconstructions are needed to remind us that those problems are historical products, by demonstrating that they were invisible to our ancestors."[42] The larger difficulty with the program is that it is hard to see how it applies to areas of cultural history less purely conceptual than philosophy or the sciences—hard to see, that is, how the normative/empirical distinction would apply to art, poetry, social mores, etc. I believe, however, that the attempt to elaborate an "internal" history for these fields of activity stands to be one of the more intriguing tasks open to future cultural historians.

Genealogy, in the loose sense in which I use it here, takes in ideas on historical method associated with Nietzsche, Walter Benjamin, and Foucault. As this (partial) list makes obvious, the concept of genealogy is much more widely disseminated in the humanities than is that of rational reconstruction; thus the problems connected with the two differ. Whereas we have yet to see whether "normative" history can be extended from science to the humanities, there is a growing body of theoretical writing on genealogy and there are several working examples of the genre, most notably Foucault's *Discipline and Punish*.[43] The genealogical approach, then, has passed the point where initial elaboration is needed; the priority is now evaluation and revision of the method in light of its first results. Critical theorists need to ask whether the method has proven itself a coherent alternative to historicism and, if not, whether it could become one. A complicating factor in all this is that, while genealogy as a self-conscious theoretical movement is a recent development, many of its key texts are fifty or a hundred years old: genealogy itself is then a reinterpretation of history based on a number of historical reinterpretations.

Nietzsche's major contributions to the critique of historicism were his second *Untimely Meditation*, "On the Uses and Disadvantages of History for Life" (1874), and *The Genealogy of Morals* (1887). The satirical criticism of historicist history in Nietzsche's early essay have of course become part of the stock of historical thought since. Yet the *Meditation* still presents unresolved challenges today. One is the dispute initiated by Nietzsche's attack on "antiquarian" or "Alexandrian" history as the accumulation of culturally inert facts, with its implied advocacy of a more engaged, partial practice of historiography. As much as rational reconstruction, genealogy has been open to the countercharge of willful anachronism, and literary theorists face a difficult job in adjudicating between positions that label the other "anachronistic" and "antiquarian," respectively. The general significance of Nietzsche's critique has also proven controversial. Does "Uses and Disadvantages" aim primarily to state a paradox—that any attack on historical consciousness is itself necessarily historical—or does it look beyond historicism somehow, toward a more socially and politically involved practice of history? These and other interpretations of Nietzsche's text have been offered.[44] Meanwhile, in the *Genealogy,* Nietzsche developed two further anti-historicist points which, though less immediately influential than the arguments in the *Meditation,* had immense delayed impact on post-structuralist theory. One is his attack on the notion of the *subject* as the fundamental one for research and writing (see especially I.13). This bit of metaphysics, Nietzsche claims, is one of several that historians tend to impose on the past without—and this is his second point—being able or willing to admit it. What historians believe to be objective descriptions of the past are only *interpretations* (see II.12, 13).

A recurrent motif in genealogy is that of the rejection of *origins,* where this concept underwrites a historical practice of narrating events according to an organic model or genetic principle. Somewhat confusingly, then, genealogy is antigenetic. We have already noted how Said has contrasted the principle of origins (assumed by critics who write as if the shape of later developments in cultural history or in an author's career where somehow concealed or contained, pre-formed, within earlier occurrences) with the principle of beginnings, reaffirming the aleatory quality of human action, unforeseeable in the future and shaped retroactively when past. Foucault, in his programmatic essay "Nietzsche, Genealogy, History," identified a similar pattern of concepts in Nietzsche's writings. He finds Nietzsche denigrating the search for the ultimate "origin" (*Ursprung*) of cultural practices, and promoting instead "effective history" (*Wirkliche Historie*), the interpretive—and nonobjective—reconstruction of the practice as something produced, bounded, and transformed by an array of contingent circumstances according to mechanisms of "emergence" (*Hernkunft*) and "descent" (*Enstehung*).[45] Interestingly, Benjamin also singled out *Ursprung* as a historical category in the "Epistemo-Critical Prologue" to another proto-genealogical work, *The Origin of German Tragic Drama,* where it is also contrasted with *Enstehung* (here translated "genesis"):

> Origin, though an entirely historical category, has . . . nothing to do with genesis. The term origin is not intended to describe the process by which the existent came into being, but rather to describe that which emerges from the process of becoming and disappearance. . . . That which is original is never revealed in the naked and manifest existence of the factual; its rhythm is apparent only to dual insight. On the one hand it needs to be recognized as a process of restoration and re-establishment but, on the other hand, and precisely because of this, as something imperfect and incomplete.[46]

Though the terms are reversed here, the opposition is the same: against the image of history as the objective record of the continuous movement of a historical object (in this case, the literary genre of the Baroque *trauerspiel*) from birth to dissolution, Benjamin emphasizes the "incompleteness" of the object and the way in which its "restoration" depends on the interpreter's "dual" (dialectical) intervention.

The suggestiveness of Benjamin's early monograph has only recently come to be appreciated and put to use. His final work, "Theses on the Philosophy of History," has been under active scrutiny for a longer time and has proven the most influential source of anti-historicist ideas after Nietzsche.[47] A larger appreciation of their significance has become possible, however, with the retrieval and publication of the great mass of writing on Baudelaire and nineteenth-century Paris which preoccupied Benjamin during the last twelve years of his life. This has made students of his work aware that the "Theses," along with a number of other published and unpublished writings of the 1930s, are affiliated with the so-called Arcades Project.[48] On any reading, though, the "Theses" can be seen to reject, point by point, the historicist assumptions reviewed previously. Against the contemplative stance toward the past endorsed by historicism, Benjamin insists that the task of the historian must be one of contestation—a struggle with the "victors" of past social and cultural conflict (see Theses VI, VII, XIV, XV). Against the belief that history forms a potential totality of moments equally available to the present, Benjamin puts forward his theory of "constellations"—that only certain moments of the past are vitally open for a particular present, and that historians must develop a de-homogenized sense of the past (V, XI, XIV, XVI, A). Against the individualistic subjectivity or empathy to which historicists appeal in justifying their interpretations, Benjamin defends the "materialist" view that historical knowledge is mediated by *class* formations (IV, XII). Finally, against historicist faith in the ongoing accumulation of knowledge, he relentlessly assaults the notion of "progress" underlying this faith (III, VIII, IX, XVII). Closely related to these theories, though not mentioned in the "Theses," is the interpretive concept of allegory, which is featured in many of Benjamin's other writings, early and late, and which almost inverts the standard notion of allegory which I mentioned in the discussion of Said as a genealogist. The complex itinerary of Benjamin's historical thought will certainly prove to be one of the major interests of literary historians searching for an effective alternative to historicist methodology.

Meanwhile, Foucault's oeuvre, transformed into a legacy by his recent death, will also serve as an ongoing provocation to genealogists, Foucault having been the catalytic figure within this tendency of thought, after all. But though he and Benjamin both died prematurely, Foucault suffered the even greater misfortune of premature canonization. The very neglect that Benjamin's major work underwent may help render its long-term effect on literary history more fruitful. Foucault's thought, in contrast, has been left wrapped in layers—partly of his own making—of revisionist commentary that accompanied each of his main publications after *The Archaeology of Knowledge*.[49] This distorting process elevated Foucault's legitimate though often unconvincing attempts at self-criticism to the status of oracular reinterpretations; endlessly parroted by modish disciples, these had the effect of defusing or discouraging intelligent response. A pertinent example of the confusions that resulted and await disentanglement involves Foucault's views on historical method, the most coherent of which he articulated during his "archaeological" period (roughly 1967–72), in writings that include the introduction to the *Archaeology* and his inaugural lecture of 1970, *L'Ordre du discours.*[50] The position is that there is no *inner essence* to the historical process, whether subjective, sequential, cumulative, or otherwise, but that much of intellectual and cultural history can be reconstructed in terms of an impersonal "knowledge" consisting of surface patterns of "discourse." This challenging but plausible development of Nietzschean themes is important enough to merit application, testing, and evaluation; but Foucault only distracted attention from such work when he introduced, during his later "genealogical" period, a series of new terms: "power/knowledge," "the will to truth," "ethics," "bio-power," "the history of the present." The notions correlated with these expressions seem to me more radical, vaguer, and less plausible, but in any case they are certainly *different* from the preceding ones and require separate analysis. This has proven impossible so far because of the Foucauldians' insistence that the master's later self-descriptions must apply retroactively to his earlier work. It may indeed be a distinctive feature of genealogy that its historical elements are intertwined with political ones; nevertheless, work on genealogy will be retarded if both these elements are used to obfuscate critical study of either of them.

NOTES

1. I allude to the notorious essay "Against Theory," by Steven Knapp and Walter Benn Michaels, *Critical Inquiry* 8 (Summer 1982): 723–42, reprinted in *Against Theory: Literary Studies and the New Pragmatism,* ed. W. J. T. Mitchell (Chicago: University of Chicago Press, 1985), pp. 11–30, along with a number of responses. I have presented some arguments *against* "Against Theory" in a review of the Mitchell volume in *Critical Texts* 3 (Winter 1986): 14–18.

2. Edward Said, *Beginnings: Intention and Method* (New York: Basic Books, 1975); henceforth *B,* and *The World, the Text, and the Critic* (Cambridge: Harvard University Press, 1983); henceforth *W.*

3. J. Hillis Miller, " 'Beginning with a Text,' " *Diacritics* 6 (Fall 1976): 2–7, esp. p. 4.

4. See Edward Said, "Roads Taken and Not Taken in Contemporary Criticism," *W,* p. 144.

5. Edward Said, "Vico in His Work and in This," *B,* pp. 345–81. See also Said, "Labyrinth and Incarnations: The Essays of Maurice Merleau-Ponty," *Kenyon Review* 29 (January 1967): 54–68, and "Am-

ateur of the Insoluble" (on E. M. Cioran), *Hudson Review* 21 (Winter 1968–69): 769–73.

6. See Frye's *Anatomy of Criticism* (Princeton: Princeton University Press, 1957), p. 89.

7. Edward Said, *Orientalism* (New York: Pantheon, 1978).

8. The latest edition of Wellek and Warren is the third (New York: Harcourt, Brace and World, 1970). James Thorpe, ed., *The Aims and Methods of Literary Scholarship,* 2nd ed. (New York: Modern Language Association, 1970).

9. See Bowers's *Essays on Bibliography, Text and Editing* (Charlottesville: University of Virginia Press, 1975), as well as "Scholarship and Editing," *Papers of the Bibliographical Society of America* 70 (1976): 161–88, and "Greg's 'Rationale of Copy-Text' Revisited," *Studies in Bibliography* 30 (1977): 90–161.

10. Hershel Parker, *Flawed Texts and Verbal Icons: Literary Authority in American Fiction* (Evanston, Ill.: Northwestern University Press, 1984); hereafter cited as *FT.* Some of the material that Parker presents is conveniently summarized in a short article, "Lost Authority: Nonsense, Skewed Meanings, and Intentionless Meanings," *Critical Inquiry* 9 (June 1983): 767–74, reprinted in Mitchell, ed., *Against Theory,* pp. 72–80.

11. See Parker's " 'The New Scholarship': Textual Evidence and Its Implications for Criticism, Literary Theory, and Aesthetics," *Studies in American Fiction* 9 (Autumn 1981): 181–97, and an essay written with Brian Higgins, "The Chaotic Legacy of the New Criticism and the Fair Augury of the New Scholarship," in *Ruined Eden of the Present,* ed. G. R. Thompson and Virgil L. Lokke (West Lafayette, Ind.: Purdue University Press, 1981), pp. 27–45.

12. Jerome J. McGann, *A Critique of Modern Textual Criticism* (Chicago: University of Chicago Press, 1983); hereafter cited as *C;* and *The Beauty of Inflections: Literary Investigations in Historical Method and Theory* (Oxford: Clarendon Press, 1985); hereafter cited as *B.*

13. Though McGann and Parker have not engaged each other's positions, Donald Pizer, using principles resembling McGann's, has criticized editorial work in which Parker has been involved: see Pizer's "Self-Censorship and Textual Editing," in *Textual Criticism and Literary Interpretation,* ed. McGann (Chicago: University of Chicago Press, 1985), pp. 144–61, as well as Parker's discussion of the controversy in ch. 6 of *Flawed Texts,* pp. 147–79.

14. For a parallel argument about Shakespeare, see Stephen Orgel's very

brief but much-cited opuscule, "What Is a Text?" *Research Opportunities in Renaissance Drama* 24 (1980): 3–6.

15. Jerome J. McGann, *The Romantic Ideology: A Critical Investigation* (Chicago: University of Chicago Press, 1983). I have gone into both aspects of McGann's work in an interview with him, "On Textual Scholarship as Literary History and Ideology Critique," *Social Epistemology* 1 (April 1987): 163–73. See also *Historical Studies and Literary Criticism,* ed. Jerome J. McGann (Madison: University of Wisconsin Press, 1985).

16. McGann has collected further relevant studies in *Social Values and Poetic Acts: The Historical Judgement of Literary Work* (Cambridge: Harvard University Press, 1988).

17. Some of these are gathered in Tanselle's *Selected Studies in Bibliography* (Charlottesville: University of Virginia Press, 1979) and in *Textual Criticism since Greg: A Chronicle, 1950–1985* (Charlottesville: University of Virginia Press, 1987).

18. "Textual Study and Literary Judgement," reprinted in *Essays on Bibliography,* ed. Vito J. Brenni (Metuchen, N.J.: Scarecrow Press, 1975), 355.

19. G. Thomas Tanselle, "The Editorial Problem of Final Authorial Intention," *Studies in Bibliography* 29 (1976): 169.

20. Tanselle has discussed their work in "Historicism and Critical Editing," *Studies in Bibliography* 39 (1986): 1–46; on McGann, see pp. 19–27, and on Parker, pp. 27–34.

21. G. Thomas Tanselle, "Recent Editorial Discussion and the Central Questions of Editing," *Studies in Bibliography* 34 (1981): 52.

22. Tanselle, "Historicism and Critical Editing," pp. 45–46.

23. Quentin Skinner, "Meaning and Understanding in the History of Ideas," *History and Theory* 8:1 (1969): 3–53. James H. Tully has provided a bibliography: "The Pen Is a Mighty Sword: Quentin Skinner's Analysis of Politics," in *British Journal of Political Science* 13 (October 1983): 489–509.

24. Gunnell debunks this myth in ch. 3 of his *Political Theory: Tradition and Interpretation* (Cambridge, Mass.: Winthrop Press, 1979), pp. 65–93; in the next chapter, however, Gunnell also turns to a criticism of the Cambridge intellectual historians (pp. 95–129). There followed a valuable exchange on this between Gunnell and Pocock: "Political Theory, Methodology, and Myth," *Annals of Scholarship* 1:4 (Fall 1980): 3–62. Literary historians will be interested by Marilyn Butler's outstanding essay, "Against Tradition: The Case for a Particularized Historical Method," in *Historical Studies and Literary*

Criticism, ed. McGann, pp. 25–47, which deals with the same sort of problem as it affects literary scholarship.

25. Austin's classic 1955 lectures were published as *How to Do Things with Words,* ed. J. O. Urmson and Marina Sbisà (Cambridge: Harvard University Press, 1962; 2nd ed., 1975); Grice's equally standard essay "Meaning" appeared in *Philosophical Review* 66 (1957): 377–88, and has been frequently reprinted; also important are Grice's "Utterer's Meaning, Sentence-Meaning, and Word-Meaning," *Foundations of Language* 4 (1968): 1–18, and Strawson's "Intention and Convention in Speech Acts," *Philosophical Review* 73 (1964): 439–60; both these essays are reprinted in *The Philosophy of Language,* ed. J. R. Searle (New York: Oxford University Press, 1971), with a useful introduction by Searle.

26. Quentin Skinner, "Conventions and the Understanding of Speech Acts," *Philosophical Quarterly* 20 (April 1970): 118–38; "On Performing and Explaining Linguistic Actions," *Philosophical Quarterly* 21 (January 1971): 1–21.

27. J. G. A. Pocock, *The Ancient Constitution and the Feudal Law: A Study of English Thought in the Seventeenth Century* (Cambridge: Cambridge University Press, 1957; enlarged ed., 1987).

28. J. G. A. Pocock, *Politics, Language, and Time: Essays on Political Thought and History* (New York: Atheneum, 1971). For the theory, see esp. essays 1 and 8; and see Pocock's further explorations in *Virtue, Commerce, and History: Essays on Political Thought and History, Chiefly in the Eighteenth Century* (Cambridge: Cambridge University Press, 1985), esp. "Introduction: The State of the Art," pp. 1–34. See also "The Reconstruction of Discourse: Towards the Historiography of Political Thought," *Modern Language Notes* 96 (December 1981): 959–80. For a bibliography of Pocock, see Iain Hampshire-Monk, "Political Languages in Time—The Work of J. G. A. Pocock," *British Journal of Political Science* 14 (January 1984): 89–116.

29. J. G. A. Pocock, *The Machiavellian Moment: Florentine Political Thought and the Atlantic Republican Tradition* (Princeton: Princeton University Press, 1975).

30. Quentin Skinner, *The Foundations of Modern Political Thought* (Cambridge: Cambridge University Press, 1978).

31. "The Idea of a Cultural Lexicon" (a discussion of Raymond Williams's 1976 book *Keywords*), *Essays in Criticism* 29 (July 1979): 223.

32. Pocock, *Virtue, Commerce, and History,* p. 15. See also the following page, where Pocock discusses the "ways in which a speech act in-

novates in and on a context consisting of several languages in interaction."

33. J. G. A. Pocock, "Political Ideas as Historical Events: Political Philosophers as Historical Actors," in *Political Theory and Political Education,* ed. Melvin Richter (Princeton: Princeton University Press, 1980), p. 147. Pocock sets out a full account of his theory of linguistic politics in "Verbalizing a Political Act: Toward a Politics of Speech," *Political Theory* 1 (February 1973): 27–43.

34. E. D. Hirsch, *Validity in Interpretation* (New Haven: Yale University Press, 1967), *The Aims of Interpretation* (Chicago: University of Chicago Press, 1976), and, among recent essays, "The Politics of Theories of Interpretation," *Critical Inquiry* 9 (September 1982): 235–47; "Meaning and Significance Reinterpreted," *Critical Inquiry* 11 (December 1984): 202–25; and "Back to History," in *Criticism in the University,* ed. Gerald Graff and Reginald Gibbons (Evanston, Ill.: Northwestern University Press, 1985), pp. 185–97.

35. Quentin Skinner, "Hermeneutics and the Role of History," *New Literary History* 7 (Autumn 1975): 209–32. See also "Motives, Intentions, and the Interpretation of Texts," *New Literary History* 3 (Winter 1972): 393–408.

36. Quentin Skinner, "Some Problems in the Analysis of Political Thought and Action," *Political Theory* 2 (August 1974): 243.

37. Skinner, "The Idea of a Cultural Lexicon," p. 222.

38. Quentin Skinner, " 'Social Meaning' and the Explanation of Social Action," in *Philosophy, Politics, and Society,* Series IV, ed. Peter Laslett, W. G. Runciman, and Quentin Skinner (Oxford: Basil Blackwell, 1972), pp. 136–57.

39. Skinner, "Some Problems," p. 295.

40. Fredric Jameson, *The Political Unconscious: Narrative as a Socially Symbolic Act* (Ithaca, N.Y.: Cornell University Press, 1981).

41. Gottlob Frege, *The Foundations of Arithmetic* (1884), trans. J. L. Austin, 2nd ed. (Oxford: Basil Blackwell, 1953).

42. Richard Rorty, "The Historiography of Philosophy: Four Genres," in *Philosophy in History,* ed. Richard Rorty, J. B. Schneewind, and Quentin Skinner (Cambridge: Cambridge University Press, 1984), pp. 67–68; see also pp. 49–56 of Rorty's essay, as well as the volume's introduction (pp. 1–14) and a number of other contributions to it. The major publication by Imre Lakatos on this topic is "History of Science and Its Rational Reconstructions" (1970), now in his *Collected Papers,* ed. John Worrall and Gregory Currie, Vol. I: *The Methodology of Scientific Research Programs* (Cambridge: Cambridge University Press, 1978), pp. 109–38.

43. Michel Foucault, *Surveiller et punir: naissance de la prison* (Paris: Gallimard, 1975), trans. Alan Sheridan, *Discipline and Punish: The Birth of the Prison* (New York: Pantheon, 1977). In addition, there are or will be four volumes to Foucault's unfinished *Histoire de la sexualité* (Paris: Gallimard, 1976–), trans. Robert Hurley, *The History of Sexuality* (New York: Pantheon, 1978–).

44. Friedrich Nietzsche, "Vom Nutzen und Nachteil der Historie für das Leben," trans. R. J. Hollingdale in *Untimely Meditations* (Cambridge: Cambridge University Press, 1983), pp. 57–123; for Nietzsche's critique of "antiquarian" history, see esp. pp. 72–77.

45. Michel Foucault, "Nietzsche, la généalogie, l'histoire," *Hommage à Jean Hippolyte* (Paris: Presses Universitaires de France, 1971), pp. 145–72, trans. Donald F. Bouchard and Sherry Simon in *Language, Counter-Memory, Practice: Selected Essays and Interviews*, ed. Bouchard (Ithaca, N.Y.: Cornell University Press, 1977), pp. 139–64.

46. Walter Benjamin, *Ursprung des deutschen Trauerspiels* (Frankfurt: Suhrkamp, 1974), trans. John Osborne, *The Origin of German Tragic Drama* (London: New Left Books, 1977), p. 45.

47. Walter Benjamin, "Über den Begriff der Geschichte" (pub. 1950), trans. Harry Zohn in *Illuminations*, ed. Hannah Arendt (New York: Schocken, 1969), pp. 253–64.

48. *Das Passagen-Werk* is now available as part V of Benjamin's *Gessammelte Schriften*, ed. Rolf Tiedemann (Frankfurt: Suhrkamp, 1982).

49. Michel Foucault, *L'Archeologie du savoir* (Paris: Gallimard, 1969), trans. A. M. Sheridan-Smith, *The Archaeology of Knowledge* (New York: Pantheon, 1972).

50. Michel Foucault, *L'Ordre du discours* (Paris: Gallimard, 1971), trans. (unsatisfactorily) by Rupert Swyer in *The Archaeology of Knowledge*, pp. 215–37, new trans. by Ian McLeod in *Untying the Text*, ed. Robert Young (Boston: Routledge & Kegan Paul, 1981), pp. 51–76.

MICHAEL CLARK

Political Nominalism
and Critical Performance:
A Postmodern Politics for
Literary Theory

The connection between literary studies and political action has been problematic ever since Matthew Arnold declared that criticism must remain "disinterested" and aloof from the philistine concerns of making a living and governing an empire. Reacting against what he saw as the self-indulgent narcissism of Romantic idealism, Arnold insisted that "Criticism, real criticism . . . obeys an instinct prompting it to try to know the best that is known and thought in the world, irrespectively of practice, politics, and everything of the kind." Noting the French penchant for getting a good idea and then immediately "running into the street with it," Arnold cited the Reign of Terror as the inevitable result of the Gallic mania "for giving an immediate political and practical application to all these fine ideas of reason" with which their Revolution had begun. "Ideas cannot be too much prized in and for themselves," Arnold said, "but to transport them abruptly into the world of politics and practice, violently to revolutionise this world to their bidding,—that is quite another thing."

Today, more than one hundred years after these remarks appeared in "The Function of Criticism at the Present Time," most criticism aspires to achieving this "other thing" that Arnold condemned. In books such as *Criticism and Social Change, The Political Responsibility of the Critic, The Politics of Letters,* and *The*

World, the Text, and the Critic, the transportation of the text into the world is described as the primary function of the critic. And if the goal is not always the violent revolution that Arnold feared, "practice" of a most worldly and pragmatic sort is usually prescribed as the point of departure for what real criticism must be in our own time. To be sure, Arnold himself presumed that criticism had a service to perform for the "practical man," but he deferred that effect to an auspicious moment in a distant future, when criticism "may perhaps one day make its benefits felt even in this sphere" of "political, social, humanitarian" concerns. The result, a vague trickle-down theory of cultural efficacy, claimed a social utility for the free play of the mind over ideas but premised the social importance of culture on its complete and inveterate separation from society. The careful redundancy of Arnold's cautions—criticism "may perhaps one day" have a beneficial effect on the world—indicates his own awareness of this paradox, but Arnold's insistence on the fundamental contradiction between criticism and direct social action made a choice inevitable. Consequently, the formalist—often aestheticist—cast of the Anglo-American humanism that derived from Arnold's work has reflected Arnold's own overt sympathy for "keeping aloof from what is called 'the practical view of things,'" and it has usually denigrated political concerns when it has not ignored them altogether.[1]

Despite periodic attempts to clarify the social function of cultural discourse within this tradition, the relation between humanism's political aspirations and its separatist aesthetics has remained troublesome. The first half of this century witnessed a number of literary and philosophical movements whose aims were primarily ethical and political. In the 1920s "New Humanists" such as Paul Elmer More and Irving Babbitt advocated a return to Neo-Classical ideals that would reunite ethics and beauty and redeem Western society from "the rise of a nightmare subject—aesthetics" that Romanticism had brought about.[2] On the Left, an uneasy alliance between social and aesthetic concerns was evident in the work of those associated with the *Partisan Review* and the *New Republic,* who were usually guided throughout the 1930s by what William Barrett called "the two M's": "Marxism in politics and Modernism in art."[3] The impact of the New Humanists was limited, however, by their often rabid anti-modernism and their Brahmin insistence on a literary canon even narrower and more exclusively "cultural" than that imagined by Arnold. The Marxist Left failed in America during the 1930s for much more complex reasons (most notably, of course, the success of the New Deal and the collapse of ties with the Soviet Union), but from the beginning the American Left had little interest in the simplistic identification between art and politics that fueled Socialist Realism, and it tended to ignore or even to celebrate the gap between its radical politics and modernist aesthetic, as Irving Howe has pointed out.[4]

Howe claims that this split is peculiar to American Leftist groups of the period, and it is tempting to find in this conflict between politics and art the vestiges of an Arnoldian humanism with its most debilitating paradox intact. Whatever the source of this incipient aestheticist strain in American Marxism, it had little impact on the way most literary critics conceived of their social and political responsibilities in the next two decades. Both Marxism and the New Humanism were eclipsed by the rise of the New Critics.[5] Based largely on a polemical rejection of history and human agency as determinative principles of literary interpretation, the New Criticism simply rejected most of the themes and ambitions of traditional literary discourse as irrelevant to the analysis of poetry, and for thirty years after World War II this rigorous formalism dominated literary criticism in the United States. Drawing upon the separatist aesthetics inherited from Arnold and refined in Eliot's notion of a "tradition" curiously insulated from historical change, the New Critics struggled to free art from the immediate pressures of everyday experience and to treat the poem as an autonomous, self-referential structure constituted within the discrete, formal "context" of the individual poetic work. As Richard Ohmann remarked in *English in America*, the New Critics saw art "as freeing man *from* politics by putting him above his circumstances, giving him inner control, affording a means of salvation, placing him beyond culture."[6]

The aestheticist tendency of New Critical formalism was apparent from the earliest days of the movement. In the early 1950s it was condemned as escapist by critics on the radical left, and more liberal commentators such as Robert Gorham Davis claimed that the formalist rhetoric hid a "reactionary position in politics and a dogmatic position in theology."[7] More recently, Ohmann and Frank Lentricchia have combined these two charges to argue that it was not so much a faulty politics but the actual political "disinterestedness" of the New Criticism that had the most pernicious effect on the character of American literary discourse. Rather than masking a reactionary political position or remaing aloof from worldly concerns, the New Criticism made it possible to read—and live—"as if deep politics did not exist."[8]

Charged with quietism on the one hand and collusion on the other, the New Criticism makes an unlikely candidate for the dominant form of political literary theory in the postwar years. Both of these charges are misleading, however, for they underestimate the explicit but unorthodox form of politics proposed by critics such as Allen Tate and especially Cleanth Brooks. The New Critics insisted on isolating the poem from the world, but they repeatedly argued that the poem, more than any other form of discourse, possesses the capacity to "make us better citizens," as Brooks put it.[9] Explaining this causal link between the formal autonomy of art and its social utility was the explicit ambition of most critics associated with this movement, and it demonstrates their evident debt to the same traditions of cultural humanism that underlay contemporaneous theoretical movements whose political concerns were more obvious.

If that similarity was not more apparent at the time, it was because the New Criticism was not simply politics as usual, at least not as usually imagined by American literary critics. The New Critics conceived of political efficacy and ethical action in Kantian terms, rather than through the modes of class conflict or liberal pragmatism that constituted the themes of more conventionally "political" criticism. According to Brooks, Tate, and their predecessor I. A. Richards, the regimented modes of ordinary political discourse simply restrict experience to preconceived categories that limit, and so falsify, the basis for action as well as for thought. Because the language of the poem resists such limitation by exploiting the full range of semantic possibility associated with each of its terms, it frees the reader from the categories prescribed by ordinary language, much as the capacity for aesthetic judgment frees us from the determination by nature in Kant's argument. Both for Kant and for the New Critics, this freedom restores the full range of complexity to human experience, though for the New

Critics it is now the experience of the poem and not the transcendental ground of Reason with which the reader is engaged. The poet, Brooks says, "must return to us the unity of the experience itself as man knows it in his own experience. The poem, if it be a true poem is a simulacrum of reality . . . by *being* an experience rather than any mere statement about experience or any mere abstraction from experience." Hence Brooks concludes an essay on "Irony as a Principle of Structure" by claiming that the poem makes us better citizens not because of what it says but because of what it *is*—an autonomous, autotelic linguistic form: "(One of the 'uses' of poetry, I should agree, is to make us better citizens.) But poetry is not the eloquent rendition of the citizen's creed. It is not even the accurate rendition of his creed. Poetry must carry us beyond the abstract creed into the very matrix out of which, and from which, our creeds are abstracted."[10]

An extended analysis of Brooks's argument is beyond the scope of this essay, but such passages make it clear that the New Critics took politics seriously, and that they took it into the realm of aesthetics in a innovative if inchoate form. The success of the New Criticism as a academic movement cannot be ascribed to such theoretical subtleties, of course, for the occasional and usually indirect articulation of this unorthodox notion of politics obscured its relevance to formalist analysis. It also left the impression of a rather conventional Arnoldian paradox that posited the aesthetic autonomy of art as the basis for its social utility. The dominance of the New Criticism as a broad social and cultural discourse is undeniable, however, and it did, in fact, achieve considerable political power in its earliest and in its latest stages. Considered together, these two moments in the evolution of the movement can suggest a possible explanation of how a new kind of politics emerged in literary theory in the United States, and how its changing ideological functions established a new kind of link between the realms of theory and politics in literary study after World War II.

The New Critics themselves had emerged from the curious politics of the Agrarian movement, which combined a utopian, anti-industrialist radicalism with a nostalgic faith in cultural continuity and local tradition (principally, of course, the antebellum South). The Agrarian movement itself was short lived and had little political impact, because its curious mélange of political attitudes crossed the conventional political affiliations of the time. The larger and more radical anti-industrial movements between the wars were usually Marxist and international in their orientation and materialist in their immediate ambitions and strategies. At the same time, most regional politics were based on populist sympathies that were resolutely anti-intellectual and usually hostile to the urban character of academic culture that motivated the Agrarians' pastoral fantasies of a new South.

Out of historical step as it was, Agrarian politics did make a certain kind of sense in Arnoldian terms. Like Arnold, the Agrarians identified industrialization with philistine pragmatism and posited the very possibility of social renewal on the critic's withdrawal from the world into a realm of absolute and universal cultural stability. That is why their regionalism did not eventuate in the cultural relativism and democratic populism that has characterized much anti-industrialist cultural theory since the late 1960s. Their decentralized, localized politics was counterbalanced by a faith in *cultural* homogeneity that served as the foundation for social stability; and this model of a monolithic literary tradition replaced the federalist authority of the industrialized state with the cultural authority of Western humanism. That faith was reinforced by the racial and economic homogeneity of the classrooms in which the Agrarians worked, and it was perpetuated by a method of reading that abstracted literary forms from their social and historical origins and validated that abstraction with a poetic "object" at once entirely unique yet universal in its formal integrity.

Eventually the New Criticism was articulated as a theoretical program for literary analysis, rather than as a political agenda; it retained only a vestigial and apparently arbitrary rhetoric of social utility in order to remind its practitioners of their origins. Furthermore, after World War II the educational benefits of the GI Bill and the heightened social aspirations inspired by the economic boom opened the universities to a wider variety of students—and, later, teachers—who came to school between the older generation of New Critics and the population of the late 1960s. This new group offered no significant challenge to the racial and gender homogeneity assumed by the earlier generations of critics, but it did introduce a greater diversity in terms of socioeconomic class and (perhaps even more important) in terms of educational background and cultural heritage. These new students did not see culture as a stabilizing basis for the status quo and a source of continuity with the past. Instead, they treated culture as a means of disrupting that continuity in the name of social mobility and individual aspiration. This instrumental attitude toward cultural forms was in no sense radical, since it took the efficacy of the forms for granted and embraced conformity rather than confrontation as its manifest strategy. It was also entirely compatible with the formalist methodology of the New Critics, which treated the structural properties of the poem as universally accessible to any careful reader and actually turned the autotelic poem itself into the ally of these new readers, who generally lacked the familiarity with cultural traditions necessary to perform the usual work of historical analysis and impressionistic appreciation.

In effect, and often in its explicit goals as well, at this later stage the New Criticism democratized literary study even as it reinforced the ethnocentric canon of literature itself. That is why the New Criticism could serve as the bridge between two entirely different populations of teachers and students with different values and goals. The New Criticism emerged within the cultural context of Arnoldian humanism, which treated cultural forms as stable points of continuity amidst a disintegrating social order. It reached its moment of greatest influence after the war, however, as the paradigmatic methodology of an instrumentalist attitude toward culture. This shift accounts for the increasing rhetoric of participatory democracy and a public citizenry that marks the work of many New Critics in the 1950s, in contrast to the patrician elitism of the Agrarian movement. Such differences indicate that, despite the methodological continuity between these two periods, "close reading" meant something very different politically for critics before and after World War II.

This capacity to serve entirely opposite political ends did allow New Critical formalism to retain its dominance despite drastic changes in the social contexts in which it functioned. When that context shifted again in the late 1960s, what counted as "politics" outside the classroom was no longer compatible with the Kantian political claims of the New Criticism, and the New Critics again incurred charges of elitist escapism and collusion with the status quo. Throughout the 1960s and early 1970s, the New Criticism remained the single most influential critical paradigm through which English departments prepared students to take their place in society. The problem was that society had changed dramatically. When the Vietnam war ended, the economic prosperity sustained by the grotesque expansion of the defense budget was slowing down, and the ideal of social mobility that prosperity had inspired began to fade, along with the instrumental notion of culture as a neutral tool accessible to everyone.

As a result of these changes, the political rhetoric of the New Criticism finally faced a world of incompatible social practice. The formalist values of coherence, balance, and ironic disengagement were challenged by a politics of confrontation and engagement. Students who had been taught to rewrite aesthetics with each poem they encountered found themselves confronting a "real world" outside the classroom, a world intent on enforcing tradition in its most naked forms: as police power in the streets of Chicago, and as state-sanctioned murder on the campus of Kent State University. The plodding empiricism of most literary historians, like the simplistic materialism of most U.S. Marxists of the time, could not resolve this contradiction between literary notions of the political and social practice beyond the text. (The only other significant methodological alternatives to the New Criticism at the time—the Aristotelian formalism of the Chicago critics and the mythopoetic paradigms of Northrop Frye—tended toward a structural model for literary analysis that was even more abstract and autonomous than that proposed by the New Critics.)

Lacking a cultural concept of the political that could be applied outside the classroom, many students and their teachers rejected the very possibility of a theorized politics, instead celebrating a spontaneous practice that ignored or parodied more conceptual forms of political action. Turned desperate by an abusive and unresponsive government, enraged by events in Prague, and inspired by May '68, university students in the United States abandoned traditional forms of political protest and embraced a cultural radicalism that subordinated economics to expression. Their own transient alliances ranged from the surrealist anarchism of Yippie street theater and the Situationists to the subversive violence of radical groups such as the Weather Underground and Vinceremos.

The effectiveness of this challenge to cultural isolation in the name of social relevance remains debatable, and its influence on the shape of literary theory in United States was oblique. The link between literary studies and political action is easier to trace at the level of institutional policies, where the proliferation of political alternatives and competing ideologies obviously opened the traditional literary curriculum to works by a wider range of writers. However, aside from noting the ethnic and racial identities of these new authors—and, later, their gender—radical politics did little to change the way literature was taught. Slave narratives and Native American myths were studied and praised for their formal properties and aesthetic complexity as written texts; black novelists were included in the tradition as equal partners, while the ethnic specificity of their works was subordinated to cultural universals. A number of teachers advocated and, briefly, practiced a variety of pedagogical techniques designed to open the classroom to a diverse range of equal participants from many social classes. Nevertheless, the texts these teachers taught tended to be linked to their social context with simplistic mimetic or expressive terms that made even the crudest reflective models of socialist realism seem insightful.[11] The theoretical inadequacy of these politicized pedagogies became painfully apparent under the simplest questioning, and they quickly faded. Utopian aims gave way to institutional convenience, and separatist rhetoric yielded to the pragmatic careerist aims of racial assimilation and financial aspiration.

The failure of these enthusiastic but simplistic programs of radical aesthetics tended to reinforce the dominance of American formalism in literary studies, if for no other reason than because their failure demonstrated the lack of a viable alternative. They did have a lasting rhetorical effect, however, because they introduced a rhetoric of political activism and cultural heterogeneity into the study of literature that was quite different from the more general universal values of citizenship and independence associated with the New Criticism. The result was a conflict between materialist assertions of what literary study *should* do for society and formalist theories of what literary critics *could* do within the narrow domain of literary language. One consequence of this conflict was a new split between the text and its context, one that derived not so much from Arnoldian optimism about their ultimate reconciliation as from a profound skepticism about the relevance of literary study to political action in a nuclear world. What counted as "political" in literary theory simply no longer worked as a model or as a motive for social practice. Ironically, at the very moment when the discourse of literary criticism was becoming more political in the traditional senses of that term, politics was moving quickly toward an emphasis on spectacle and image that resembled nothing so much as the modernist aesthetic from which American formalism had emerged. This paradoxical exchange of rhetoric and values between aesthetics and politics in the late 1960s seemed only to exacerbate their strategic and institutional incompatibility, however. Not until the advent of structuralism and post-structuralism did politics and literary theory find a common discourse in the United States, and by then the Arnoldian tension between cultural and political experience had been replaced by an entirely new paradigm that made the conjunction of these two realms deceptively easy.

The speed with which the New Criticism was supplanted by post-structuralism is by now a commonplace among historians of literary theory, and the conflicts between these two loosely defined movements are too diverse and subtle to enumerate here.[12] At least some of those differences may have been exaggerated by the polemical context in which they were often argued. But American and continental formalisms tend to share an interest in close reading, tropological analysis, and a paradoxical or dialectical self-consciousness that elevates theoretical generalization over the more descriptive discourse of traditional empirical historicism.[13] Predictably, given these similarities, the work of structuralists and even post-structural theorists such as Foucault, Lacan, and Derrida incurred the same charges of elitist abstraction and arcane preciosity that were levied against the New Critics. Several recent commentators such as Frank Lentricchia have simply dismissed deconstructionists as the "newest generation of New Critics" intent on what Lentricchia describes as "the political defusion of writing and the intellectual life." Earlier, Ohmann had claimed that the abstract formalism of the New Criticism not only failed to oppose pernicious political attitudes but actually reflected the general cultural assumptions that allowed them to flourish. Similarly, Gerald Graff finds in the theoretical principles of deconstruction exact analogues to the economic values of late capitalism, which perpetuate an oppressive hierarchy of social relations, and to an ethic of consumerism, which subordinates human need to the exigencies of the marketplace. At best, according to Edward Said, the hyperprecision of deconstructive analysis is simply pointless. He condemns it for what he calls the idealist thrust of its "ideology of refinement," an obsession with increasingly subtle and precise analytic methods that are apparently motivated by nothing beyond the intellectual vanity of their authors. Hence Said claims that "contemporary critical discourse is worldless, in a frequently numbing way."[14]

These parallels between political objections to the New Critics and to post-structuralism tend to portray the tension between literary theory and politics as a Manichaean struggle between proponents of the word and the world, and they tend to conflate the very different social contexts in which the two movements evolved and the different ideological needs that they met. However, the liberal ethos of individual aspiration, social mobility, and economic expansion that supported the rise of the New Criticism bears little resemblance to the conservative doctrine of a competitive economy and the inevitability of social inequality in a zero-sum society that nourished deconstruction. That distinction is important to our understanding of how these two methodologies constituted literary analysis as a concrete practice compatible with the institutional and social relations in which readers read. To explore—and to argue for—a single kind of connection between literary theory and political action assumes that these terms mark a permanent opposition between *kinds* of experience that remain discrete, even as the specific forms of those experiences change. This assumption perpetuates the idealist opposition of action to thought, and it sustains the most simplistic distinctions between theory and practice even as it argues for their union. As I have already suggested, what deconstruction and the New Criticism really shared as modern formalisms was not isolation from social and political commitment as "theory"; rather, it was the aim of conducting the reading of literary texts in terms that recognized reading not as an alternative to social action but as a paradigmatic practice that conceived of literary study (or, more generally, tropological analysis of any text) as the passage from thought to action within the world. This is why Cleanth Brooks claimed that a poem is not about experience but *is* an experience, one that plunges us into the very matrix out of which political action is derived. It is also why J. Hillis Miller has argued that "In literary study the first material base is the words on the page in the unique, unrepeatable time of an actual act of reading," an act that engages us in the material world as fully as any other form of human action.[15]

The suggestion of a fundamental continuity between literary theory and social practice at the level of the act goes beyond the charge of a complicity between theory and politics. It opens the possibility for a direct identification between literary analysis and political intervention, and for a deconstructive politics that is the inverted, post-structural counterpart to the Kantian freedom attributed to art by the New Critics. This possibility inspired one of the earliest efforts to establish the political dimension of deconstructive criticism, Michael Ryan's *Marxism and Deconstruction*.[16] Ryan agrees that contemporary modes of economic exchange function according to the same principles as the textual properties of literary expression defined by deconstructive readings. But Ryan goes on to claim that this parallel—which is in fact a fundamental continuity among textual, academic, and social organizations—constitutes the common ground of literary insight and political intervention. Noting the formidable capacity of deconstruction to lay bare the metaphorical character of literary effects and philosophical "truths," Ryan argues that deconstructive analysis possesses an equal capacity to demystify ideological formations beyond the text and so elevates deconstruction to what Marxists used to consider the "scientific" status of dialectical materialism. To be sure, in Ryan's argument text and world are joined through a functional homology, rather than linked with a transcendent historical law, and the results of deconstructive analysis are defended on strategic rather than epistemological grounds. Nevertheless, for Ryan the deconstructive method possesses a universal character that elevates the critic to the perspective of the objective seer, one whose vision transcends the ontological barriers between text and world as well as the political boundaries between the university and the marketplace.

Ryan's case for the political import of deconstruction resembles the contextualist defense against charges of aestheticism thirty years earlier. Just as Brooks argued that the poem *is* an experience that engages us in the full complexity of human experience, Ryan insists that writing and reading the poem are institutional practices governed by the same logic that determines social relations at large. Ryan's more subtle and more sophisticated concept of ideology avoids the ontological pretension of Brooks's less careful proclamations, but the enabling assumption behind both arguments is that of an "act" or "experience" common to both literary analysis and social relations. Literary analysis grants a more direct access to that experience and so resists the distortions and limitations of ordinary language and the symbolic forms of everyday life. Whether it takes the form of textual insight or revolutionary action, this resistance derives from the same critical stance and constitutes the political dimension of literary theory.

The contention that the world and the text share a common ground on which literary analysis and political action meet directly contradicts Arnold's insistence that culture and politics must be kept separate. Yet, even for Arnold, that separation was only temporary, an operational caveat that looked forward to the resolution of their conflict "some day." Temporalizing their union in that way marks Arnold's debt to the emphasis on historical evolution characteristic of German idealism, just as Ryan's claims about the binary character of ideological formations and social hierarchies indicates the centrality of discourse and semiotic analysis to the human sciences in the twentieth century. Despite its discursive nature, however, Ryan's union of literature and society takes place at a level of abstraction and generality that resembles Arnold's teleological deferral as an argumentative strategy if not as a philosophical claim. Edward Said has attacked the political pretensions of both deconstruction and the New Criticism for sharing this idealist tendency. Claims to extend the authority and power of literary analysis to the political realm are merely rhetorical gestures, Said argues; they have no basis in theory and no effect beyond the narrow confines of the brotherhood that preaches them. The New Critics and deconstructionists alike have often adopted the rhetoric of opposition and radical political commitment, Said says, but this "oppositional manner . . . does not accurately represent its ideas and practice, which, after all is said and done, further solidify and guarantee the social structure and the culture that produced them."

This charge echoes Ohmann's criticism of the implicit and usually inadvertent collusion between literary theorists and the status quo in the 1950s and early 1960s, but Said's charge here goes beyond accusing post-structuralism of a numbing worldlessness or a hypocritical complicity with the status quo. Instead, he argues that literary theory itself now masquerades as political sensitivity and radical action—that politics has, in effect, been absorbed by literary theory and reduced to theoretical conflicts among institutional or professional affiliations that are abstract mockeries of real social conflict. Thus he says, "We find that a new criticism adopting a position of opposition to what is considered to be established or conservative academic scholarship consciously takes on the function of the left wing in politics and argues *as if* for the radicalization of thought, practice and perhaps even of society by means not so much of what it does and produces, but by means of what it says about itself and its opponents." Graff charged deconstruction with a different kind of hypocrisy, one that accused the theory of escapist abstraction while condemning the practice for not being disengaged enough from its social context. Said's complaint is more subtle, for he sees deconstruction as attempting to subsume practice into and *as theory*, thereby not only cutting itself off from society but disguising that isolation as engagement: "What distinguishes the present situation is, on the one hand, a greater isolation than ever before in recent American cultural history of the literary critics from the major intellectual, political, moral, and ethical issues of the day and, on the other hand, a rhetoric, a pose, a posture (let us at last be candid) claiming not so much to represent as *to be* the affiliations entailed by true adversarial politics."[17] According to Said, even when the theory does assume the postures and categories of political practice, that assumption is purely rhetorical and conceives of politics strictly in the terms of literary theory, rewriting the world *as* text, rather than connecting them through a truly "critical" practice.[18]

This rhetoric of opposition that Said condemns as merely rhetorical opposition is perhaps the most familiar manifestation of politics in literary theory today. It presents itself as a bridge across the gap between theory and practice that remains as one of the unfortunate vestiges of the rhetoric of Arnoldian humanism. Rather than exposing the obvious fallacy in Arnold's distinction between criticism and practice, though, it takes that distinction as its point of departure and posits politics either (1) as the present but invisible significance of "pure" theory, or (2) as the ideal project toward which theory must be led. Politics thus serves as the "Truth" of literary theory in the most traditional hermeneutic sense. The project of making theory more political is conceived in conventional heuristic terms that seek to establish a true discourse that will lift the political meaning of criticism into the language of its theory. The result is a form of political nominalism that understands the connection between theory and politics as one of interpretation and naming, and that equates Knowledge, the idealized form of those discursive practices, with Action, the equally idealized form of political practice.

Political nominalism may well be the single most pervasive form of politics in current literary theory. The simpler forms of radical literary theory in the late 1960s were often associated with a vulgar Marxism that restricted the political dimension of criticism to manifest content or theme. Political nominalism, however, relies on a subtle understanding of the phenomenon of signification that not only tolerates but actually requires a high level of theoretical sophistication and analytic precision. One of the best examples of such work is Jim Merod's *The Political Responsibility of the Critic.*[19] Merod offers a detailed and astute introduction to the full range of currently influential literary theories with a political orientation, but he also considers those theories as means toward the end designated by his title. The book is eclectic in the best sense, for it establishes common bonds among quite different positions, carefully delineating their differences but consistently bringing their compatible points to bear on a definition of the critic's political responsibility.

Merod defines that responsibility entirely in terms of a political nominalism. His point of departure is a critique of contemporary literary theory that combines accusations of engagement and disengagement in the familiar paradox: "criticism in North America inevitably serves a political role of one sort or another" (4), Merod says, but he adds a few pages later that "criticism is all but closed to the institutional basis and institutional consequences of its work" (8). On the one hand, "The intellectual production of critical writers is politically unaffiliated with any segment of American society. It is an academic event" (48); on the other, "the work of criticism is unavoidably interrelated with a social and political context" (11). The problem with much contemporary literary theory, Merod argues, is that it obscures that relationship, leaving critics "without the vision, will, or commitment to intersect the world as citizen-activists" (172). That intersection is thus already there as the truth of critical work and at the same time serves as the objective of that work. The logical difficulties of this position become apparent in many passages such as the following one, where Merod sets out to define what the critic *should* do as an account of what the critic inevitably does do: "Criticism at root is a clarification of intellectual positions. . . . It is first a self-clarification that prepares for an unending reclarification. . . . Therefore criticism is not work *on* texts. It is work *with* texts, an effort to demonstrate through them the lines of institutional force which connect texts and intellectual practices to one another. One way to put this is to say that criticism moves *from* the world toward texts and *through* texts back again into the world. Another way, more accurate, is to say that criticism and texts never leave the world" (132).

Merod's difficulty is that he invokes the rhetoric of a crude materialist separatism—texts vs. world—in the name of a much more subtle political nominalism. This nominalist argument does not describe the association between these two domains in terms of a geographical metaphor of "here" vs. "there" or an ontological opposition of "material" vs. "intellectual." Rather, it links text and world as an association of sign and meaning. At times the simple materialist side of Merod's book leads him to the predictable rhetoric of preparation and exercise as the critic's only job: "the main effort of oppositional criticism right now can be directed only at the critical institution itself. Before intervention into the world of public consciousness can take place in any significant way, it will have to gain strength in the university as a debate about intellectual identities" (124). More often, however, Merod invokes the more subtle nominalist equation of word and work, knowledge and action, and he portrays the critic's job as one of discovery through interpretation and naming. In these cases, the relation between the text and the world is assumed to exist but is also assumed to be hidden, and "the work of making criticism a viable activity for students requires the teacher to show how that relationship works" (11). "No matter how politically acute any particular theory may take itself to be," Merod says, "the only way it can avoid an idealistic retreat from the actual conditions of social life is by *naming* as accurately as it can the relation between intellectual work and the organized forms of power" (93, my emphasis). How does one struggle against the "political horrors of one's time"? "I think the individual teacher and critic does just that by making affiliations between knowledge and power an explicit topic, a demonstrable institutional context for interpretation" (131). Here, critical knowledge is treated as political action, not because of an idealistic reduction of the world into the word as Said suggests—Merod remains acutely sensitive to that tendency among contemporary theorists—but because the world and the word are construed in terms of a traditional hermeneutic practice that joins them through interpretation and naming.

Merod thus avoids the reductive positions of either simple materialism or linguistic idealism. Nevertheless, the nominalistic politics of Merod's literary theory requires a form of agency that can both "know" and "act," and so privileges a conventional notion of individual subjectivity as the domain in which the political dimension of literary theory is realized. Although Merod objects to "contemporary ideologies of the fettered but indignant self" (175), he asks "of the humanities and of theory generally, in what way they increase human agency" (174). "The teacher's purpose," Merod claims, "especially the oppositional teacher's purpose, is to promote an intellectual identity in students. . . . The teacher or critical theorist who takes it [i.e., that aim] seriously seeks to spark an anomalous individuality in students, a freely constituted, self-directed desire . . . that leads them, in the process of questioning received assumptions and conventional practices, to challenge authority not by temporary (and mostly futile) rebellion but by working wherever they work in the long-drawn-out effort to create resistance to domination and cultural indoctrination" (129). Merod notes that such an "idealistic projection of the individual as an intervening force" argues against the Marxist insistence on a collective movement for social change, and that it contradicts what common sense tells us about the futility of personal resistance to authoritarian power. But he asks, in a nation such as ours, "Where does the will to change rituals, expectations, habits, and policies that constrain such imagination come from if not from individuals trained to exercise intellectual courage, people encouraged by critical training to exert their intellectual and moral force" (131)—presumably by naming the forces that constrain their imaginations.

In this way political nominalism establishes critical practice— the "act" of naming—as the hinge between the text and the world. Merod avoids both the idealistic conversion of world into text and the crude materialistic reduction of text into world by inserting between these realms the critic's "individuality." The gesture of naming then bonds the two realms together to equate knowing and acting. This recourse to individual agency is problematic, how- ever, as Merod admits. Not only does it echo the romantic rhetoric of existential revolt, but it also contradicts the strategic common sense of a Marxist emphasis on collective action. Nevertheless, this antiquated humanism is crucial to the political dimension of literary theory as Merod defines it, because the individual is the agent of the name and the ethical armature of the critic's responsibility. For Merod, and for political nominalism in general, the imbrication of text and world is both motive and project. It serves as the "meaning" of an interpretive gesture that functions largely within a logocentric model of subjectivity, one that links knowing and acting as expressions of an *idea* of the world conceived in terms of individual experience, whether it is the "maimed individual" described by Fredric Jameson or the "idealistic projection" of Mer- od's critic.

In *The World, the Text, and the Critic,* Edward Said situates the critic between the world and the text much as Merod does. For Said, however, that position does not require a nominalist locution that joins text and world. Instead, it depends on a strategic dislocation of the text's being in the world that will open up what Said calls a "potential space inside civil society."[20] In this space, the critic can act "on behalf of those alternative acts and alternative intentions whose advancement is a fundamental human and in- tellectual obligation" (30–31). Texts "are always enmeshed in circumstance, time, place, and society—in short, they are in the world, and hence worldly," Said says (35), but as texts they are not simply determined by that place. As texts, "they place themselves . . . and indeed are themselves, by soliciting the world's attention" (40). Noting the long tradition of Western novelists who present themselves as the "editors" of epistolary works by describing the contexts from which the letters are ostensibly taken, Said describes this device as an effort "to turn the text back, if not directly into speech, then at least into circumstantial, as opposed to meditative, duration" (44). The text's place in the world, then, is a product of its own textuality, an event that decants its world-liness as the condition of its existence *as* a text. Said identifies this link between world and text as the same relation between texts and their circumstantiality assumed by the "Zahirite notion of meaning," which is quite different from the hermeneutic model that governs political nominalism. What ought to strike us about Zahirite interpretation, Said says, "is that it represents a consid-erably articulated thesis for dealing with a text as significant form, in which . . . worldliness, circumstantiality, the text's status as an event having sensuous particularity as well as historical contin-gency, are considered as being incorporated in the text, an infran-gible part of its capacity for conveying and producing meaning. This means that a text has a specific situation, placing restraints upon the interpreter and his interpretation not because the situation is hidden within the text as a mystery, but rather because the situation exists at the same level of surface particularity as the textual object itself" (39).

The task facing a critic confronting such a text in this way is therefore "the presentational problem of historically recreating or reconstructing the possibilities from which the text arose" (175). In part, this reconstruction consists in the critic's effort to "recreate the bonds between texts and the world . . . to make visible, to give materiality back too, the strands holding the text to society, author and culture" (175). Said's reconstructive historicism thus goes be-yond nominalism with a presentational gesture that attributes worldliness to the text, rather than simply naming it. The world is not something the critic "knows," but an event that the critic stages as the condition of possibility for the text's existence—a response to the appeal, to use Said's terms, by which the text exists in the world. So Said claims that critics "embody in writing those processes and actual conditions in the *present* by means of which art and writing bear significance" (53). This "bringing of literature to performance" (53) firmly situates the critical consciousness in the world of the present (16), but it presents that world in a theatrical sense, rather than as a truth or meaning to be discovered in the text or projected as its political consequence. This is why Said insists that the critic's attitude must be "frankly inventive" (53), and why he argues that "criticism creates its subject matter—there are no problems simply lying about to be dealt with" (154).[21]

To bring literature to performance in this way is to stage one's own relation to the world as a *critical* consciousness that is made in, but not entirely of, the culture in which it exists. "To stand between culture and system," Said says, "is therefore to stand *close to* . . . a concrete reality about which political, moral, and social judgements have to be made and, if not only made, then exposed and demystified" (26). Such an attitude places the critic at what Said characterizes as a "sensitive nodal point" that he names simply "criticism" (15), a "distance" that ensures the "individual consciousness is not naturally and easily a mere child of the culture, but a historical and social actor in it" (15).

Said's account of the political importance of the critical "act" thus avoids the reductive determinism of materialist schemes that insist on the critic's place *in* the world. It also avoids the idealist projections of the nominalist's faith in an autonomous subjectivity that is free from material determination and so capable of identifying the "real" or "true" political meaning of a literary text. For Said, the political dimension of criticism lies in its performative nature, in both the theatrical and the linguistic senses of that term. Like any performative utterance, the critical act is, for Said, primarily a speech act that depends upon the critic's position within his or her world and invokes that position as the condition of possibility for the utterance itself. The historical context of the text is not something that the critic *names* but something that is *staged*, a production of the critic's own moment that enacts political responsibility as the historical possibility of speaking, both in the "then" of the text and the "now" of the reading.

The critic's being "close to . . . concrete reality" as Said claims—subject to, yet not determined by, the material world—resembles what Kant called the "freedom" that protects humans from natural determination and so establishes the possibility of a choice among their actions. Said says this is the basis for the critic's political responsibility, and Kant claimed that this freedom is the basis for ethics and a sign of our "higher destination." For Kant, ethics is a product of that freedom; it is a cause and consequence of our capacity to represent the world *as if* it operated according to the principles of Reason. That is why Kant closely associated ethics with the aesthetic. Although he insisted that the aesthetic judgment was entirely autonomous and disinterested, Kant also argued that it gained its importance only in reference to the destination that governed our spiritual evolution and that in fact motivated both the aesthetic judgment and artistic creation. "Beauty" thus becomes a "symbol of the morally good" at the end of "The Critique of Aesthetic Judgment." It is evidence of our desire for something more than nature offers, and the ground on which we communicate that desire to others. The aesthetic thus served Kant as an indication of an ultimate unity to take place in the spiritual domain and as a source of immediate community in the material domain where we live.

In this way the aesthetic takes on a crucial ethical importance for Kant, despite the necessary autonomy of aesthetic judgment. It is inspired by our need for community and guides our actions in the world, not despite its deliberate "disinterestedness" in the world but *because* it is free from worldly concerns and deals with a representation of the world, the fiction of the "as if." The centrality of this fiction to Kant's ethics presages Said's emphasis on the creative function of the critic, but it raises an important methodological question for Said's aesthetic. His methodological aim of reconstruction does not theorize exactly what criticism is supposed to do to achieve its paradoxical proximity to the world, nor does it explain how that proximity can ground the critic in the history that is reconstructed for and with the text in the "frankly creative" act of the critical performance.

The methodological complexity of a historical criticism motivated by political responsibility in the present yet situated somewhere to the side of immediate engagement in material action is the central topic of Fredric Jameson's *The Political Unconscious*.[22] Jameson takes as his point of departure a Marxian emphasis on utopian thought, rather than a Kantian emphasis on the fictive basis of critical judgment, and he argues for a dialectical reciprocity between deconstruction and reconstruction that links the critic to the world through the medium of History. Anticipating Said's challenge for an account "of what there is to be done *after* deconstruction is well underway" (193), Jameson conceives the text as the intersection of two contrary discourses: ideology, with its tendency to obscure contradictions lived in the material world where the text is produced; and utopian fantasy, with its tendency to represent those contradictions in the text as resolved through the image of a unified society. The critic's job, Jameson says, is to deconstruct the ideological mystifications that obscure the text's place in the world—in short, to demystify the text's pretensions to an idealist autonomy. Following that, however, the critic must restore to the text the "repressed and buried reality" of the "collective struggle to wrest a realm of Freedom from a realm of Necessity" (19, 245). The result is a "dialectical" reading that reconstructs the past as a figure of the future and so gives shape to History through the medium of a deconstructive narrative.

By situating the individual texts within the narrative of this collective struggle, Jameson claims that critics not only restore the historical context to the text but also position themselves within the historical moment in which they write. The worldly affiliations of particular texts cannot be left to the antiquarians or the modernists, Jameson says. "The [historical] matters can recover their original urgency for us only if they are retold within the unity of a single great collective story; . . . only if they are grasped as vital episodes in a single vast unfinished plot. . . . It is in detecting the traces of that uninterrupted narrative, in restoring to the surface of the text the repressed and buried reality of this fundamental history, that the doctrine of a political unconscious finds its function and its necessity" (20).

From the perspective of a crude materialism that privileges the world as the reality of the text and the sole ground for political action, Jameson's ambition to restore that reality to the "surface of the text" smacks of linguistic idealism, the drive to convert the world into the text and so to support the critic's delusions of political significance. But Jameson dismisses the objections of such materialist determinism and claims that History and the material conditions of existence that constitute it are distinct from the text, yet inaccessible through any other means than the symbolic act of narration. So Jameson can argue "that history is *not* a text, not a narrative, master or otherwise, but that, as an absent cause, it is inaccessible to us except in textual form, and that our approach to it and to the Real itself necessarily passes through its prior textualization, its narrativization in the political unconscious" (35).

To measure the effects of this "absent cause" on the text, the critic must situate the text within three interpretive contexts that constitute the "semantic horizons" of the text's relation to history. The first is the "political" context in which the text is read as an "imaginary resolution of a real contradiction" (77). The critic's job is to deconstruct or demystify that resolution by exposing the resistance of political and social conflicts to full incorporation within the ideological coherence of the narrative. The second phase of interpretation takes place on the "social horizon" of the text, where the narrative is situated within the antagonistic network of competing ideologies of its time, and its apparent autonomy is read against the silence of subordinated discourses. The third semantic horizon of the text is that of History itself, and where "the texts emerge in a space in which we may expect them to be crisscrossed and intersected by a variety of impulses from contradictory models of cultural production all at once" (95). This "space" constitutes a new object of study for the critic, which Jameson calls *cultural revolution.*

> The concept of cultural revolution, then—or more precisely, the reconstruction of the materials of cultural and literary history in the form of this new "text" or object of study which is cultural revolution—may be expected to project a whole new framework for the humanities, in which the study of culture in the widest sense could be placed on a materialist basis. . . . The task of cultural and social analysis thus construed within this final horizon will then clearly be the rewriting of its materials in such a way that this perpetual cultural revolution can be apprehended and read as the deeper and more permanent constitutive structure in which the empirical textual objects know intelligibility. [95, 97]

Jameson's notion of history as a semantic horizon of the text thus insists on the importance of the critic's chronological point of view to the determination of the text's place on that horizon. The historical meaning that emerges within this vision of history is not, however, the product of a materialist objectivity or the disengaged insight of an autonomous subject that underlies the nominalist's argument. Jameson claims that these alternatives dominate most of the criticism done today; he says they are based on a "model of immanence" that assumes the "phenomenological ideal—that of some ideal unity of consciousness or thinking and experience or the 'objective' fact" (282). The idealized theoretical aim of such criticisms is that of a "cure" to ideological mystification. This cure recalls the common treatment of politics as the truth of the text and the project of a political literary theory, and it occurs within "the vision of a moment in which the individual subject would be somehow fully conscious of his or her ideological conditioning by sheer lucidity and the taking of thought" (283). Jameson rejects this position as a retreat from the Real into an illusory domain of "intellectual comfort," and he argues that that vision has neither an object—the truth it seeks "in the world" is inaccessible—nor a subject. Such "transparency" is possible, he says, only from within the "collectivity" that will emerge "at the end of what Marx calls prehistory" (293). Until that time, the individual's relation to the social whole, his or her "place in the world" can only be experienced as a "painful 'decentering' of the consciousness of the individual subject, whom it [i.e., the relation to society] confronts with a determination . . . that must necessarily be felt as extrinsic or external to conscious experience" (283–84).

To press Jameson's metaphor, the relation between text and world might be considered a parallactic effect of the critic's own position in the present as he or she examines the text against the background of history. The hermeneutic effect of ideological or deconstructive analysis, which would establish the text's "affiliation" with the world of its own time, depends upon a proleptic or what Jameson calls a "typological" reading of the text as a prefiguration of the utopian future that orients the critic as well as the text within the historical process that generates meaning. The historical context of the text is made visible only in and as the vision of a reader located at a particular time and place; that vision is measured not so much for its accuracy as for its status as a revolutionary gesture that anticipates "the logic of a collectivity which has not yet come into being" (286).

In Said's terms, Jameson's critic "performs" the text on the stage of History. The setting is real and determines the critic's performance, but it is accessible only through the representational forms that constitute the scene of reading. The "consciousness" that is situated historically through such a performance therefore is neither determined by the material conditions of its existence, nor is it disengaged from them in a realm of autonomous individuality. The critical act registers the effect of its historical stage— both as time and as setting—through the narrative forms that engage it. The place of the text on that stage, however, and its relation to the reader and the world constituted through that act, can only be a projection—or what Jameson calls a "figure"—of an idealized or utopian vision, one that looks forward to its realization rather than outward toward a world beyond the text.[23]

The political claims of Jameson's typological model of historical interpretation has come under attack from several sides. Marxists have condemned the idealist strain of his insistence that History is inaccessible except through narrativization, and many others have criticized Jameson's invocation of a Marxian telos as what Hayden White has called the "master-narrative" of world history. It may be, White argues, "that the doctrine of 'History' is . . . ready for retirement along with the 'politics' that it helped to enable. The problem may be not how to get into history, but how to get out of it."[24] Many of these objections may be relegated to ideological squabbles among firmly entrenched camps competing for power upon the critical scene. The antipathy that has made Jameson's work so controversial today no doubt derives in equal parts from the rightist swerve in contemporary politics and from professional envy at the ascendancy of Marxism as a critical method in the academy. But White's remark touches upon a more subtle conjunction between history and politics that the works of Said and Jameson illustrate. Both of these critics avoid the simpler forms of nominalism and materialism that pervade most political readings of literary texts today because they are skeptical of any immanent link between the text and the world. Still, they both insist on that link as inherent in the historical reconstruction that is the critic's principle goal. History thus insures the link between the world and the text and supports rather traditional hermeneutic analysis while rejecting any possibility of its ontological justification (materialism) or its epistemological verification (nominalism). This is the way interpretation has been politicized by many critics in the United States. If we were to "retire" history, as White suggests, the political dimension of literary theory (at least as it has been conceived to this point) would necessarily disappear along with it.

White's critique of Jameson's project thus presents a challenge to the future of literary theory. Can the "political" be conceived beyond the limits of a conventional materialism without invoking the "Historical" as a transcendental telos to justify the critical act? And can that act be conceived as something other than the hermeneutic gesture of an autonomous interpreter, however sophisticated and self-conscious? If so, literary theory might well become the force for social change demanded by critics such as Lentricchia and Said, but its political function may be unrecognizable from the material and historical perspectives in which that force is imagined today. White's challenge to imagine a new kind of "political" realm has begun to be answered by a number of writers over the past decade, but this new politics has less to do with the world imagined by the materialists than with the representation of that world as spectacle. In our time, Jean Baudrillard has written, politics

> is not a question of the expanded reproduction of capital and of the capitalist class; it is a question of the production of a caste by the collective grace of a play of signs, and of the production of these signs by the destruction of economic value. . . . Everywhere the magic of the code, the magic of an elective and selective community, fused together by the same rules of the game and the same systems of signs, is collectively reproduced, beyond economic value and on the basis of it. Everywhere this process comes to penetrate class conflicts, everywhere . . . it acts to the advantage of the dominant class. It is the keystone of domination.[25]

Baudrillard's emphasis on the determinative power of signs explicitly denies the primacy of the material world that has dominated most political theory as well as literary theory on the political left. For Baudrillard, "the structure of the sign is at the very heart of the commodity form. . . . It makes little difference whether the contents of material production or the immaterial context of signification are involved; it is the code that is determinant" (146). Rejecting the scientist pretensions of simple materialisms, Baudrillard claims that distinctions between the sign and the world are fiction, and they can only lead to science fiction (152). The "real" and the "referent," the respective projects of materialist and nominalist politics, are only the "simulacrum" of the symbolic, Baudrillard says (162), its "reference-alibi" (120). Inverting the complaints of Said and Graff, who object to much contemporary theory for its tendency to collapse the world into the text, Baudrillard argues that even the illusion of reference to a world beyond the text leads to a hermeneutic gesture that replicates the structures of domination characteristic of ideological hegemony and political oppression: "Signification is in some ways kin to the notion of reification. It is the locus of an elemental objectification that reverberates through the amplified systems of signs up to the level of the social and political terrorism of the bracketing [*encadrement*] of meaning. All the repressive and reductive strategies of power systems are already present in the internal logic of the sign" (163).

In fact, Baudrillard says, what Marxists call reality is simply an effect produced by the system of signs as its idealized point of reference. "Use value," he adds, "and the signified do not constitute an *elsewhere* with respect to the systems of the other two; they are only their alibis" (137). Baudrillard's critique of use value and the materialist theory of a world immanent in the text has its corollary in his attack on the humanist notion of an individual subject who experiences that world as the object of his needs. Quoting Marx "in substance," as he says, Baudrillard claims that "production not only produces goods; it produces people to consume them, and the corresponding needs" (136). In an essay entitled "The Ideological Genesis of Needs," Baudrillard summarizes his argument by saying that these needs "can no longer be defined adequately in terms of the naturalist-idealist thesis—as innate, instinctive power, spontaneous craving, anthropological potentiality. Rather, they are better defined as a *function* induced (in the individual) by the internal logic of the system. . . . In other words, there are only needs because the system needs them" (82).

For Baudrillard, then, the political—the arena of social domination and hierarchical order—is defined primarily in terms of artifice or representation, not the categories of historical materialism. Its goal is not the production of commodities but the reproduction of the code, and the object of its power is not the slave or the worker but a new kind of being: "the saturated consumer

[who] appears as the spellbound avatar of the wage laborer" (83). The time of this new being is now "free," but its desire is carefully organized to produce "a new kind of serf," "the individual as consumption power" (85). And just as the object of production and the target of power have changed, so, too, have the mechanisms by which power and production are disseminated and perpetuated. Baudrillard claims that industry and even corporate organizations have been replaced by "media," understood not as an economic force or even as a source of ideological mystification, but as an organizational practice that governs all forms of exchange. It is "not as vehicles of content, but in their form and very operation," Baudrillard says, that "media induce a social relation" (169). Rather than being a "technical problem"—i.e., a technology in the hands of the elite that governs the messages being broadcast— "media ideology functions at the level of *form,* at the level of the separation it establishes, which is a *social* division" (169). The fundamental distinction thus induced, according to Baudrillard, is simple but crucial to the construction of the individual as consumer:

> the totality of the existing architecture of the media founds itself on this latter definition: *they are what always prevents response, making all processes of exchange impossible* (except in the various forms of response *simulation,* themselves integrated in the transmission process). . . . This is the real abstraction of the media. And the system of social control and power is rooted in it. . . . The same goes for the media: they speak, or something is spoken there, but in such a way as *to exclude any response anywhere.* [170]

Thus all of the traditional manifestations of economic and political concerns are collapsed into the political economy of the sign, and revolutionary action, or even democratic participation, is transformed into a veritable theater of consumption. Baudrillard thus claims that consumer goods themselves constitute a mass medium, and the most beautiful mass medium of all is the electoral system. Hence for the time being, Baudrillard says, "we live in the era of non-response—of irresponsibility" (170).

Within such a world, the political dimension of representational forms is neither their truth nor their reality. It is the forms of representation themselves that constitute the political, along the traditional lines of social discrimination and economic exchange that are usually taken as the origin or infrastructure of those forms. Representation is treated as the organizational principle of the social order, and the reification of that principle in art becomes a central mechanism for reproducing that order. Baudrillard claims that the "truth" of modern art is no longer the "literality of the world, but the literality of the gestural elaboration of creation . . . that which was representation—redoubling the world in space—becomes repetition—an indefinable redoubling of the act in time" (106). What the art "repeats" is not the world, but the performance that brought the work into being. In works by artists such as Pollack and Rauschenberg, *"Subjectivity triumphs in the mechanical repetition of itself"* (106). But that triumph is pyrrhic at best because, to survive, subjectivity must take the form of the same reproductive technology that rejects it. This is the limiting condition of modern art, Baudrillard says: "that of a subjectivity fascinated by a technical world that denies it, fascinated by the positivity of that world but which paradoxically can only absorb this world by repeating itself across serial diffractions" (109). Hence he concludes that modern art can only be an *"art de la collusion"* with the contemporary world: "It can parody this world, illustrate it, simulate it, alter it; it never disturbs the order, which is also its own" (110).

This tendency toward formalist parody of historical "content" has led Jameson and many others to denounce postmodernism for its aestheticist trivialization of history and its collusion with the status quo of consumer capitalism.[26] In his introduction to Lyotard's *The Postmodern Condition*, Jameson remarks that "the dynamic of perpetual change" is not a "natural" rhythm or imaginative flux free from determination by the social order, but "is the very 'permanent revolution' of capitalist production itself: at which point the exhilaration with such revolutionary dynamism is a feature of the bonus of pleasure and the reward of the social reproduction of the system itself."[27] That charge is crucial to many current defenses of literary theory as a political force, for it assumes that a proper theoretical perspective can expose that complicity of art with the social order against a more properly historical horizon on which the text can be interpreted, theory "correcting" art by restoring its political dimension. Such an aim is implicit in the titles of books such as *Criticism and Social Change* and *The Political*

Responsibility of the Critic, which emphasize the role of the critic rather than what the nineteenth century might have considered the political responsibility of the artist.

But if Baudrillard is right, and if the hierarchical order of the modern state is determined not by the reproduction of industrial relations but by the endless production of semiotic distinctions (the reproduction of the code, Baudrillard says, is "the keystone of domination"), then the historical and materialist aims of such projects may be anachronistic. In a recent article in the *American Quarterly,* John Carlos Rowe has observed that in the politics of the postmodern state, "the utopian project of modern literature has been perversely realized." The fictionality and textuality of history implicit in works such as Pound's *Cantos* has become the working order of consumer capital, and "the old forms of modernist art—novel, poem, play—have helped dream the postmodern world into existence and are reproduced in the lives we are compelled to lead."[28] If this is the case—if, in Baudrillard's terms, the modern state has "extend[ed] the aesthetic to the entire everyday world" and dissolved the "segregation between the beautiful and the useful" (186)—then the political projects so prevalent in literary theory today may be curiously beside the point. While theorists have been busy politicizing literary analysis in the name of history and the material world, politics has become aestheticized, retaining the rhetoric of history and materialism as what Baudrillard calls an "alibi" for the sign. The anachronistic agenda of so many political literary theories may therefore be well on the way toward restoring the literary text to a world that no longer exists.

The aesthetic character of postmodern politics has already undercut the significance of more conventional forms of political action. On the most obvious level, the overwhelming importance of television in the processes of election, governance, and international diplomacy has transformed "act" into "performance" of the most theatrical sort. The election of an aging actor as President of the United States confirms this transformation, as does the prominence of speculative and simulated disaster in international diplomacy and economics. Unlike the international treaties ratified after World War II, which were written and signed in the terrible light of Hiroshima and Nagasaki, contemporary negotiations regarding global issues such as oil resources, nuclear arms, and the militarization of space are couched in the curious rhetoric of proleptic horror. They constitute an effort to represent what does not and has never existed, and to negotiate on the grounds of that representation in the hope of the referent being forever deferred. At the end of a long meditation on the nature of contemporary political forms, Baudrillard thus concludes that many postmodern political "events"

> *never began,* never existed, except [as] artificial mishaps—abstracts, ersatzes of troubles, catastrophes and crises intended to maintain a historical and psychological investment under hypnosis. All media and the official news service only exist to maintain the illusion of actuality—of the reality of the stakes, of the objectivity of the facts. All events are to be read in reverse, where one perceives . . . that all these things arrive too late, with an overdue history, a lagging spiral, that they have exhausted their meaning long in advance and only survive on an artificial effervescence of signs.[29]

In such a world the referent is replaced by simulacra, and spectacle supplants the actual in a parody of conventional historical argument. Yet here the parodic character of the simulacra takes on a distinctly subversive effect. "History" appears only through the retrospective vision of a curious anticipatory logic, one that discards the idealist forms of historical inevitability or even simple causality in favor of a speculative pluralism that situates the present at the origin of several different futures. None of the futures is inevitable. Each is incompatible with the others: we cannot have a nuclear free world *and* have a nuclear war. And each is linked with the past through a different form of the present: disarmament now will produce a future that verifies human compassion, whereas a continuation of the arms race will demonstrate the opposite. The fact that these alternatives are represented as equally possible, if not equally probable, dramatizes the pluralistic and speculative— and, necessarily, the spectacular or representative—quality of such "historical" argument. These alternatives also illustrate the extent to which both continuity and causality have been replaced by a radical heterogeneity as the primary mode of historical discourse in the society of spectacle that Baudrillard describes.[30]

This notion of the present as a kind of relay or switching yard through which any number of historical narratives may be actualized resembles Jean-François Lyotard's analysis of social relations in what he calls the "postmodern condition." Describing the " 'atomization' of the social into flexible networks of language games," Lyotard claims that the postmodern world no longer abides by a single coherent narrative that organizes social relations according to a fixed hierarchy of values or a continuity with the past. The illusions of such continuity may persist, Lyotard says, but they derive not from "history" in the traditional sense so much as they are constituted by the narrative form of their own representation: "a collectivity that takes narrative as its key form of competence has no need to remember its past. It finds the raw material for its social bond not only in the meaning of the narratives it recounts, but also in the act of reciting them. The narratives' reference may seem to belong to the past, but in reality it is always contemporaneous with the act of recitation."(*PC*, 22). Thus, in *Au juste,* Lyotard argues that the repetition of popular narratives need not, as Western culture has always supposed, "turn them into what we call history, and to think that it progresses because it accumulates." Rather, the repetitions of such narratives "cause the forgetting of what is being repeated and they make for a nonforgetting of time as a beat in place. . . . Narratives must be repeated all the time because they are forgotten all the time. But what does not get forgotten is the temporal beat that does not stop sending the narratives to oblivion."[31] Rather than hypostatizing time in the form of history, narratives of this sort splinter history into a collection of instants, each a temporal pulse that is joined to the others only through its form of address, or what Lyotard calls (after Levinas) the obligation to pass on the tale to another time (*J,* 35).

Stripped of its historical continuity but shot through with this endless series of narrative engagements, the social bond is established in and through language, Lyotard claims; but in *The Postmodern Condition* he insists that the bond is not governed by a single semiotic principle, as Baudrillard claimed in *The Political Economy of the Sign*. Instead, Lyotard says, "The social bond is linguistic, but it is not woven with a single thread. It is a fabric formed by the intersection of at least two (and in reality an indeterminate number) of language games" (*PC*, 40). In this world, legitimacy is not measured by a transcendent standard, nor is it governed by what Niklas Luhmann called the "normativity of laws." Rather, each "move" in these games is judged by the criterion of "performativity," which Lyotard defines briefly as "the best possible input/output equation" (*PC*, 46), i.e., a form of behavior that facilitates the production of further performance. Thus, each use of these languages "is subject to a condition we could call pragmatic: each must formulate its own rules and petition the addressee to accept them" (*PC*, 42). Identifying all forms of social relations as "language games" in this way recalls the idealistic equation of text and world underlying the political pretensions of most formalist literary theories, but for Lyotard those games are not governed by a uniform text. They take shape within the "pragmatic context" of the moment and are indistinguishable from the use to which they are put. That is why Lyotard insists that every language game "necessarily has an effect on the world, whatever it may be"; each move is "tactical," Lyotard says, and "it is in this sense that I do not believe myself to be a philosopher . . . but a 'politician'" (*J*, 55).

Lyotard's sense of politics derives from the effect of such tactical prescriptions. Rather than naming a condition to be known—the nominalist definition of action—Lyotard's politician establishes a new form of social relation between or among the participants in the "pragmatic context" that motivates and governs the utterance. "Even if the prescription is not followed by an effect, in the usual sense," Lyotard says, "it is nonetheless the case that its recipient finds himself in a state of obligation, the obligation to reply, or not to reply, to do as he wills, but still he is in a state of obligation" (*J*, 52). This obligation has a rhetorical or discursive base—that of the "address" that joins the author to his or her audience—but it is not simply an obligation to reply or even to understand. It is simply the obligation to retell, to repeat the address and reproduce the social bond it forms. I am not necessarily obligated to reply to the one who has addressed me, Lyotard says, "but I am obligated in the way of a relay that may not keep its charge but must pass it on." Lyotard claims that this obligation is "older, much more archaic" than the role of the lawgiver in classical politics, and he claims that it not only structures social relations but constitutes the very ground of their inevitability: "No maker of statements, no utterer, is ever autonomous. On the contrary, an utterer is always someone who is first of all an addressee, and I would even say one destined. By this I mean that he is someone who, before he is the utterer of a prescription, has been the recipient of a prescription, and that he is merely a relay" (*J*, 31). Thus, society "finds the raw material for its social bond" in the act of reciting its narratives. The obligation to retell the story constitutes what Lyotard calls "the ephemeral temporality inhabiting the space between the 'I have heard' and the 'you will hear'" (*PC*, 22). The moment of forgetting cancels history, only to resurrect it as the temporal beat that constitutes the possibility for politics in a post-modern age, where "this relation to time that is so astonishing that it has led us to make the most preposterous statements about societies without history, gets translated into a pragmatics whose chief effect is that no discourse presents itself as autonomous, but always as a discourse that has been received" (*J*, 34).

Lyotard's concept of pragmatics and his proposition of nar-rative obligation as the basis of the social bond suggest a sense of the political that has an obvious resonance for literary theory today. His emphasis on the pragmatic context of narrative address re-sembles the issues raised by speech act theory and by reader-response criticism, both of which have stimulated considerable interest among politically oriented literary theorists. Lyotard's in-terest in the discursive character of the social bond also recalls Foucault's work during the late 1960s and early 1970s, which has inspired not only the politicized antiquarianism of the New His-torians but also a wide range of social and cultural analyses fo-cusing on contemporary issues in mass culture and political discourse. But Lyotard's unremitting insistence on the absolute heterogeneity of discrete language games, his definition of history as a forgetting of the past linked to a prescription for the future, and his identification of politics with the "pragmatics" of narrative address confute the nominalist ideals and the materialist ambitions that continue to characterize the political for most literary critics today. If literary theory is to move beyond those vestigial forms of nineteenth-century dualism, it will have to abandon its attempt to revive such outmoded themes of political discourse as history, the subject, and even "politics" itself. It must give up its attempt to politicize aesthetics and recognize instead that today the systems of exchange that underwrite the social order are less economic than semiotic, and less semiotic than narrative and "pragmatic" in the sense described by Lyotard.

The specific shape of this postmodern turn toward aesthetic politics is difficult to predict, simply because it will not look like a "political" theory in the conventional sense. Nevertheless, as postmodernism increasingly dominates the public scene through architecture and advertising as well as the more overtly political arenas of economics and international diplomacy, we can occasionally glimpse new forms of the political already at work.[32] Most dramatically, postmodern architecture has assumed an overwhelming role in the organization of daily urban life. In part, its prominence derives from the concentration of wealth in the hands of a few landowners (whether individuals or corporations) over the past two decades. These windfall years have enabled them to replace the buildings built during the last great period of capital accumulation earlier in this century, and postmodernism is simply the style of the day. But the attitude toward history implied in the postmodern "quotation" of styles, motifs, and tastes characteristic of earlier periods also embodies and quite literally shapes a new kind of social space, one that is organized by the pragmatics of performance more than by the traditional themes of political control.

A step toward understanding this new form of social organization has been sketched by Linda Hutcheon in her essay "The Politics of Postmodernism: Parody and History." Hutcheon argues that postmodern art "offers a new model for mapping the borderline between art and the world," and she calls this model "parody." Directing her remarks specifically to the work of several postmodern architects, Hutcheon rejects the charge that postmodernism trivializes history by reducing it to the form of a playful pastiche. Rather than marking its ahistorical superficiality, Hutcheon says, the ironic quotations of historical forms in postmodern architecture are in fact "all resolutely historical and inescapably political precisely because they are parodic." Postmodernism does refuse to grant the past (and its metonymic counterpart, the future) any status as the referent of aesthetic form. But rather than "cannibalizing" the past, as Jameson accuses postmodern architecture of doing, this playful inscription of older forms "teaches and enacts the recognition of the fact that social, historical, and existential 'reality' is *discursive* reality when it is used as the referent of art, and so the only 'genuine historicity' becomes that which would openly acknowledge its own discursive, contingent identity. The past as referent is not bracketed or effaced [by postmodern art], as Jameson would like to believe: it is incorporated and modified, given new and different life and meaning." [33]

That life, according to Hutcheon, is lived in the present, which is occupied by a subject whose very subjectivity is constituted within the parodic reference itself. According to Paolo Portoghesi, one of the architects Hutcheon discusses, the historically gratuitous references of postmodern buildings—that is, anachronistic incorporations of architectural formulas from previous ages that break up the formal coherence of a contemporary structure—engage the audience in the processes of signification because such references demand interpretation by the very fact of their formal perversity. [34] Historical significance becomes a function of formal closure as both history and form are predicated on the viewer's active participation on the scene of the work. Hutcheon claims that this is the motive for the "increased accessibility and didacticism" of postmodernism, as distinct from modernism, and she argues that this participatory or performative dimension of the postmodern scene constitutes its social and political dimension: "Postmodernist parody . . . uses its historical memory, its aesthetic introversion, to signal that this kind of self-reflexive discourse is always inextricably bound to social discourse"(204). Parody thus restores the political dimension of the text without invoking either the world or history as its truth or meaning. In fact, both world and history are staged by the formal properties of the postmodern structure as effects of the viewer's living within—by making sense out of— the shifting collocation of formal cues and historical references that engage the viewer in work and situate him or her in the world of that moment.

The difference between the parodic postmodern politics Hutcheon describes and the literary or textual effects of more conventional political issues was dramatized in the controversy surrounding Jacques Derrida's article on the term "apartheid," which was translated in *Critical Inquiry*. [35] Derrida's essay was originally published as part of the catalog for a traveling exhibition called "Art contre/against Apartheid." This exhibit was organized by the Association of Artists of the World against Apartheid, and it opened in Paris in November 1983. Under the title "Le Dernier Mot du Racisme," (translated as "Racism's Last Word"), Derrida opens his essay with a plea: "APARTHEID—may that remain the name from now on, the unique appellation for the ultimate racism in the world, the last of many" (330). The utopian foresight of this plea, which is carefully couched in the optative mood for this opening statement, then immediately is lifted out of mere chronological sequence and grounded in the rhetorical posture of representation itself. The result is a concept of memory that has less to do with the past than with the future. It dwells in events such as those Baudrillard describes, speculative gestures in which the future is performed—or, here, "exhibited"—as an obligation to retell the story of racism another time. Here is the entire opening section of the essay:

> APARTHEID—may that remain the name from now on, the unique appellation for the ultimate racism in the world, the last of many.
>
> May it thus remain, but may a day come when it will only be for the memory of man.
>
> A memory in advance: that, perhaps, is the time given for this exhibition. At once urgent and untimely, it exposes itself and takes a chance with time, it wagers and affirms beyond the wager. Without counting on any present moment, it offers only a foresight in painting, very close to the silence, and the rearview vision of a future for which *apartheid* will be the name of something finally abolished. Confined and abandoned then to this silence of memory, the name will resonate all by itself, reduced to the state of a term in disuse. The thing it names today will no longer be.
>
> But hasn't *apartheid* always been the archival record of the unnameable?
>
> The exhibition, therefore, is not a presentation. Nothing is delivered here in the present, nothing that would be presentable—only, in tomorrow's rearview mirror, the late, ultimate racism, the last of many. [330]

Derrida continues to emphasize the paradoxical temporality of the collection. Discussing the planned "trajectory" of the exhibition, he remarks, "Its movement does not yet belong to any given time or space that might be measured today. Its flight rushes headlong, it commemorates in anticipation—not its own event but the one that it calls forth" (332). If the exhibit finally does succeed in winning its place in the state of South Africa, Derrida concludes, "it will keep the memory of what will never have been, at the moment of these projected, painted, assembled works, the presentation of some present. Even the future perfect can no longer translate the tense, the time of what is being written in this way— and what is doubtless no longer part of the *everyday current*, of the cursory sense of history" (337). The silence of these works resists incorporation into the Western-European discourse that underwrites the persistence of *apartheid*, Derrida claims; it is the silence of an accusatory gaze that "keeps watch on that which is not, on that which is not yet, and on the chance of still remembering some faithful day" (338).

The response to the publication of Derrida's essay in *Critical Inquiry* was immediate and predictable. In "No Names Apart: The Separation of Word and History in Derrida's 'Le Dernier Mot du Racisme,'" Anne McClintock and Rob Nixon attacked the "strategic value" of Derrida's method and claimed that "Derrida's protest is deficient in any sense of how the discourses of South African racism have been at once historically constituted and politically constitutive." They then propose to compensate for that deficiency in a detailed analysis of the "successive racist lexicons" that preceded and followed the use of the term *apartheid* by the Nationalist party's victory in South Africa in 1948, and they offer this discursive genealogy as a corrective to Derrida's "blindness to the unfolding of the racial discourse in their historical context." Stressing the strategic importance of a "historical eye" capable of integrating "discursive, political, economic, and historical analyses," Nixon and McClintock insist on grounding our understanding of racism in the historically specific details of the "dense everyday life of South Africa." They then conclude with a call to abandon the "favored monoliths" and "bulky homogeneities" of post-structuralism because their excessive abstraction make them of "limited strategic worth." In short, this response to Derrida invokes reconstructive historicism for its political efficacy and limits the "strategic force" of textual commentary to the discursive features of concrete detail and historical specificity. Knowledge is invoked unambiguously as power, and analysis is proposed as a means of "releasing that pariah of a word, *apartheid*, from its quarantine from historical process" that was brought about by Derrida's "severance of word from history."[36]

Derrida's response to McClintock and Nixon makes it clear that what is at stake in their differences on the issue of the term "apartheid" is neither historical accuracy nor relative degrees of ontological sophistication regarding the term's referent. The argument is, in fact, over the operation of the term itself. For McClintock and Nixon, the political dimension of the word "apartheid" is determined by the discursive network in which it functions (or does not function) within the discourse of domination that organized and controlled the movement of people across geographical boundaries at a certain moment in history. Within this Foucauldian argument, the power of the term as a political tool depends on that network, which is why the "effect" of apartheid can persist without the use of the term itself. For Derrida, "apartheid" cannot be reduced to a function of a discursive network situated within a particular historical moment, because it possesses a signifying potential beyond its capacity to produce social discriminations within the "affiliative" network of relations that constitutes its historical context. Appropriating the term as a proleptic marker of political liberation—it "will have been" racism's last word—Derrida's own discourse responds to the discursive function of the term by dislocating it from history, turning it back upon the hierarchy of domination it once supported, in order to undermine the very discriminatory practices that it "names."

Derrida's essay thus incorporates the history of the term parodically, more as a quotation than as the referent or truth of the term itself. Predicating his reading of "apartheid" neither on the historical context of its past nor upon the repressive politics of the present, Derrida literally rewrites the term within a reading that calls attention to its own moment and to the historical stage on which the reading is performed. His insistence on the specific circumstances of his essay as part of the catalog for a traveling exhibition is more than a defensive gesture against charges of ahistorical universalization. It is a recognition of the performative basis of his or any reading, and a justification of that performance as the ground for whatever political force the word "apartheid" might have.

If Baudrillard and Lyotard are right about the narrative or semiotic character of contemporary politics, then performative acts such as Derrida's may be the only form of political action feasible in a postmodern world. Noting the repressive tendency to exclude the capacity for response that characterizes the discursive organization of social power today, Baudrillard has observed that this is why "the only revolution in this domain—indeed, the revolution everywhere: the revolution *tout court*—lies in restoring this possibility of response. . . . No other theory or strategy is possible."[37] It may well be that the political future of literary theory depends on our ability to develop just such a strategy. To do that, we would have to begin by taking seriously the revolutionary potential of response. We would have to seek, in the act of reading and writing, not access to some higher authority, whether it be history or the material world, but the very basis of authority itself and the fundamental principle of social action. To conceive of the critic's political responsibility in hermeneutic terms as the revelation of truth, or even as the reconstruction of a world of meaning immanent in a text, cannot meet this challenge. Those aims merely perpetuate the illusions of reference and subjective autonomy that occlude the repressive authority they would resist, and they condemn the critic to dream of the future within the nightmare of the past. If, however, we can recast the political in performative terms, there is a chance that we may yet be able to fulfill the "obligation to reply" that Lyotard describes as the impulse to justice and the origin of the social bond.

NOTES

1. Matthew Arnold, *Essays in Criticism, First Series* (1865, rev. 3rd ed. 1875; rpt. Chicago: University of Chicago Press, 1968), pp. 17, 14, 22, 18. See Matthew Arnold, *Culture and Anarchy,* ed. J. Dover Wilson (1869; rpt. Cambridge: Cambridge University Press, 1969), p. 70, where Arnold proposes a much more direct link between culture and society. See also Edward Said, *The World, the Text, and the Critic* (Cambridge, Mass.: Harvard University Press, 1983), p. 11, for a critique of Arnold's notion of culture and society.

2. The phrase is Babbitt's and is from Ch. 5 of *Rousseau and Romanticism* (Boston: Houghton Mifflin, 1919). The title of the chapter is

"Romantic Morality: The Real," which takes on a special irony in the light of subsequent materialist efforts to develop an ethically responsible aesthetics. Babbitt's attraction to Arnold's culture as a *social* force reinforces the hegemonic thrust of Arnoldian "disinterestedness."

3. William Barrett, *The Truants* (New York: Doubleday, 1982), p. 11.
4. Irving Howe, *The Decline of the New* (New York: Harcourt, 1970), p. 218.
5. The sixth volume of René Wellek's *A History of Modern Criticism* covers this period in American letters in detail. For a concise analysis of the rise of the New Criticism and its triumph over competing theoretical approaches of the time, see Part Two of William E. Cain's *The Crisis in Criticism: Theory, Literature, and Reform in English Studies* (Baltimore: Johns Hopkins University Press, 1984). The notes to Ch. 5 of Cain's book contain an extensive list of histories relating to this period in the development of American criticism.
6. Richard Ohmann, *English in America: A Radical View of the Profession* (New York: Oxford University Press, 1976), p. 78.
7. Robert Gorham Davis, "The New Criticism and the Democratic Tradition," *American Scholar* 19 (1949–50): 9–19. See also Ohmann, *English in America*, p. 85, where he sets the stage for more recent commentaries. Ohmann discusses Davis on p. 78.
8. Ohmann, *English in America*, p. 316.
9. Cleanth Brooks, "Irony as a Principle of Structure," in M. D. Zabel, ed., *Literary Opinion in America* (1951; 3rd ed. rev., New York: Harper and Row, 1962). See my essay "The Genealogy of Coherence and the Rhetoric of History in American New Criticism," in Richard Fleming and Michael Payne, eds., *Criticism, History, and Intertextuality* (Lewisburg: Bucknell University Press, 1987), pp. 17–60, for a consideration of the utopian undercurrent in humanist thought indebted to Coleridge's reading of Kant.
10. Brooks, "Irony," pp. 1040, 1048. The ontological questions raised by this ambivalent account of the poem's relation to reality are vexing. For comments on this issue, see Murray Krieger's *The New Apologists for Poetry* (1956; rpt. Bloomington: Indiana University Press, 1963), Gerald Graff's *Poetic Statement and Critical Dogma* (Evanston, Ill.: Northwestern University Press, 1970), and Frank Lentricchia's *After the New Criticism* (Chicago: University of Chicago Press, 1980).
11. For a sample of relatively sophisticated essays related to such teaching, see *The Politics of Literature: Dissenting Essays on the Teaching of English*, ed. Louis Kampf and Paul Lauter (New York: Random

House, 1972), and the NCTE proclamation "Students' Right to Their Own Language," *College Composition and Communication* 25 (1974): 1–32.

12. One of the most subtle and polemical arguments against deconstruction from the perspective of a sophisticated American formalism can be found in Murray Krieger's *Theory of Criticism* (Baltimore: Johns Hopkins University Press, 1976).

13. These two movements even share a polemical context, for both American and continental formalisms arose in reaction against an ossified historicist tradition that was firmly entrenched as the institutional norm in the university. For an early account of this debate in France, see Serge Dubrovsky, *Pourquoi la nouvelle critique: critique et objectivité* (Paris: Mercure de France, 1966).

14. Lentricchia, *Criticism and Social Change* (Chicago: University of Chicago Press, 1983), p. 39; Gerald Graff, *Literature Against Itself: Literary Ideas in Modern Society* (Chicago: University of Chicago Press, 1979); Said, *The World, the Text, and the Critic*, pp. 167, 151.

15. See J. Hillis Miller, "Presidential Address 1986: The Triumph of Theory, the Resistance to Reading, and the Question of the Material Base," *PMLA* 102 (1987): 281–91, noting especially his view that "the concept of the material is therefore not a solution but a problem" (289).

16. Michael Ryan, *Marxism and Deconstruction* (Baltimore: Johns Hopkins University Press, 1982).

17. Said, *The World*, pp. 159, 160.

18. As David Gorman points out elsewhere in this volume, Said's objection to the rarefied nature of much post-structural analysis assumes a profound sympathy with many of its most radical philosophical critiques of logocentrism and Western metaphysics. That sympathy is most apparent in Said's *Beginnings* (New York: Basic, 1975), as Gorman notes. More recently, however, Said has moved toward a more conventional historicism that relies on many of the methods of traditional historiography.

19. Jim Merod, *The Political Responsibility of the Critic* (Ithaca: Cornell University Press, 1987). Pages cited in the text.

20. Said, *The World*, pages cited in the text.

21. Said's emphasis on the inventive dimension of this historical reconstruction distinguishes it from more traditional reconstructive arguments such as those proposed by Hippolyte Taine in his *Histoire de la litterature anglaise* (1863, 1867). For other contemporary alternatives to the naive empiricism of nineteenth-century reconstructive historiography, see Gorman's essay in this volume.

22. Fredric Jameson, *The Political Unconscious: Narrative as a Socially Symbolic Action* (Ithaca: Cornell University Press, 1981).

23. "At the end of what Marx calls prehistory," Jameson says, "the problem of the opposition of the ideological to the Utopian, or the functional-instrumental to the collective, will have become a false one" (293). At the end of *The Political Unconscious,* Jameson briefly alludes to the work of Walter Benjamin, whose "Theses on the Philosophy of History" foresaw much of this current interest in the revolutionary potential of performative history. In Gorman's essay in this volume, this aspect of Benjamin's work is discussed at greater length.

24. Hayden White, "Getting Out of History," *Diacritics* 12:3 (1982): 13. This whole issue is devoted to Jameson's work. For another collection of essays on *The Political Unconscious,* see the *New Orleans Review* 11:1 (1984).

25. Jean Baudrillard, *Pour une critique de l'économie politique du signe* (Paris: Editions Gallimard, 1972), p. 119. Translated as *For a Critique of the Political Economy of the Sign,* trans. Charles Levin (St. Louis: Telos Press, 1981). I have used published translations of texts by Baudrillard and (below) by Lyotard whenever possible. All other translations are my own. Pages are cited in the text.

26. See Jameson, "Postmodernism, or the Cultural Logic of Late Capitalism," *New Left Review* 146 (1984): 53–92. Also see Terry Eagleton, "Capitalism, Modernism and Postmodernism," *New Left Review* 152 (1985): 60–73, where Eagleton argues for a postmodernism that would take its relation to modernism more seriously and so be able to offer a political critique of contemporary capitalism that is unavailable within the limits of the present age.

27. Jean-François Lyotard, *La Condition postmoderne: rapport sur le savoir* (Paris: Editions de minuit, 1979). Translated as *The Postmodern Condition: A Report on Knowledge,* trans. Geoff Bennington and Brian Massumi, with a foreword by Fredric Jameson (Minneapolis: University of Minnesota Press, 1984). Cited as *PC* in the text. Quote is from p. xx.

28. John Carlos Rowe, "Modern Art and the Invention of Postmodern Capital," *American Quarterly* 39 (Spring 1987): 158, 172.

29. Jean Baudrillard, *Simulacres et simulation* (Paris: Editions Galilée, 1981), p. 71. Part of this collection has been translated as *Simulations,* trans. Paul Foss, Paul Patton, and Philip Beitchman, Foreign Agent Series (New York: Semiotext[e], 1983).

30. I have borrowed this phrase from Guy Debord, whose analysis of contemporary society parallels Baudrillard's. See Debord's *Société*

du spectacle (Paris: Buchet/Chastel, 1967), translated as *Society of the Spectacle* (Detroit: Black and Red Press, 1977).

31. Jean-François Lyotard, *Au juste* (Paris: Christian Bourgois, 1979). Translated as *Just Gaming,* trans. Wlad Godzich, with an afterword by Samuel Weber (Minneapolis: University of Minnesota Press, 1985). Cited as *J* in the text.

32. See Michael Schudson's *Advertising, the Uneasy Persuasion: Its Dubious Impact on American Society* (New York: Basic Books, 1984) for a discussion of the way advertising promotes a "capitalist realism" that reinforces the repressive social forms described by Baudrillard.

33. Linda Hutcheon, "The Politics of Postmodernism: Parody and History," *Cultural Critique* 5 (Winter 1986–87): 180, 182.

34. See Paolo Portoghesi, *After Modern Architecture,* trans. Meg Shore (New York: Rizzoli, 1982).

35. Jacques Derrida, "Racism's Last Word," *Critical Inquiry* 12:1 (1985); rpt. in Henry Louis Gates, ed., *"Race," Writing, and Difference* (Chicago: University of Chicago Press, 1986), pp. 329–38. All references are to this edition. The response by McClintock and Nixon discussed below is from pp. 339–53, and Derrida's response to that response is from pp. 354–69.

36. Anne McClintock and Rob Nixon, "No Names Apart: The Separation of Word and History in Derrida's 'Le Dernier Mot du Racisme,'" in Gates, ed., *"Race,"* pp. 339, 346, 353, 340.

37. Baudrillard, *For a Critique,* p. 170.

FERMENT: THEORY, CULTURE, INSTITUTIONS

SUSAN R. HORTON

The Institution of Literature
and the Cultural Community

I can only say what things "out there" in the institution
of literature and the cultural community look like from "in here"
in my own study. But if my experience writing this essay can stand
in synecdochically for what we all may be feeling, I'd say we just
might be living in the "interesting times" referred to in the ancient
Chinese curse: "May you live in interesting times." The major
product of my struggle to describe our future is a stack of over
three hundred pages of rejected draft: seven distinctly different
beginnings, each written in an entirely different vocabulary and
for a different audience. That alone reveals a lot about the extent
to which we may not yet be a—let alone *the*—cultural community.
One sample from a rejected beginning:

> Every word of my title here, even—and maybe especially—the
> definite articles, enters my discourse in citation and thoroughly prob-
> lematized, and that, to ventriloquize Derrida, must be my subject.
> We can learn something about what we in "the" "institution" of
> "literature" and "the" "cultural" "community" might do in the
> future if we take each of those words to be instances of catachresis
> generating a moment of interruption in which our discourse is
> brought to crisis, forcing us to produce, as Gregory Ulmer says,
> "with the same materials new rules for exchange, new meanings."[1]
> "Future" offers such an occasion for a catachretical reading, since
> it is of course always already present. Thus any notion of a present/
> future dialogic is both oxymoronic and monologic. But as Richard
> Ohmann said in 1976, "Problems are problems *for* somebody; there
> are no problems in nature."[2] My aim here, then, is to move us from

the presently problematized to the pragmatized or pragmatizable; from the *in citation* to the *incitation*.

In lots of ways I still think that particular rejected beginning is pretty nifty. At the same time, because it reproduces general problems present in our profession, it might be worth some study. As a matter of fact, this piece has ended up doing exactly what that introduction predicted: defamiliarizing all the central words of my own discourse. By highlighting their metaphorical base, I've hoped to propel us beyond the hand-wringing of the recent past to a place where we can begin to consider how we might really see ourselves, and then where we might want to move next.[3] Throwing my own discourse into "crisis" (in the *generative* sense of that word, and not the kind of "crisis" Jürgen Habermas cites as one hallmark of a failed modernism[4])—allows a host of useful questions to begin to intrude themselves: What does it say about our profession, for instance, that I have just put my own discourse on citation in citation? It would appear that our "future present" is from one point of view nothing more than what my own discourse is here: a succession of moments of interruption (even of my own interruption here of my discourse on interruption), tracing a series of trajectories on which I have launched myself and from which I have reeled myself back in, in part because of my own awareness that whatever I say is destined to be simultaneously folded into the discourse of one "cultural community" (which by definition doesn't want or need to hear what I say because it "already knows" those things), and rejected by others (who are those I would most like to reach but, because of the terms of my discourse, those most unlikely to read me). Must I inevitably arrive *en abîme* because by now, like so many of us in the profession, I have come almost instinctively to do the kind of "dual or multiple tracking" I do here, producing discourse even as I try to situate myself relative to that discourse, perpetually performing what Gilles Deleuze calls "auto-critique"?[5] Each draft I wrote displaced another at least as compelling; each narrative seemed arbitrary or partial; each attempt offered evidence that I had been seduced by one or another philosophical or theoretical system. Each draft was interrupted in mid-trajectory, driving me and it *en abîme* one more time. But as Jane Tompkins notes, *en abîme* is itself a place at which one arrives not from some neutral or un-self-interested place, but from the place of theory. As such, it is neither better nor more honest and "true" than any other place.[6]

I begin with this account of the writing of this essay not to elicit sympathy or impatience, but to suggest that the only way I have been able to map the terrain of our future is by letting my experience of trying to provide that mapping do three things: first, interrogate the notion of "future" itself; second, not write "about" that "future" so much as participate in what Ulmer calls its *scripting*, helping to actualize what I pretend only to describe; and, finally, letting my own experience of trying to script that future stand in synecdochically for the moment in which I believe we may all be secret sharers. By confessing my own frustrations and inabilities here, for instance, I simultaneously suggest and represent a future in which each of us begins any conversation with our fellows in or out of print by raising the visor, as it were, declaring our own position. Each discourse so launched might then be seen as hanging in midair, somewhat like a strip of flypaper. If enough passersby stick, then we have the makings of at least one—though hardly "the"—cultural community.

Here, then, is my strip of flypaper.

I cannot talk about the "institution" of "literature" because I see both as instances of catachresis. Both the institution(s) in which we do our work and the literature we teach there are not "things," but sets of discursive practices and processes; as such, both need to be read. This work has already begun, and is often to be found in readings done by people outside our profession. Peter Uwe Hohendahl, for instance, argues for "denaturalizing" the notion of literature as an institution. We tend to split off consideration of the institution from its works, he says, subjecting the latter only to aesthetic or psychological analysis.[7] The consequence is a serious displacement resulting in what Habermas sees as a kind of cultural inertia created by the absence of an ongoing critique of the relation between what we teach and where we teach it. Jean-François Lyotard also recommends that we avoid an overly reifying view of what is institutionalized, seeing our institution instead as an arena in which "the limits [of discourse, of the language "moves" available to us] are . . . both the stakes and provisional results of language strategies, both within the institution as they are without."[8]

The sociologist Niklas Luhmann also describes an institution not as "a thing so much as a process designed to stabilize," by institutionalizing particular forms of experience-processing (habits of perception, interpretations of reality, values).[9] Hohendahl, Lyotard, and Luhmann's view of the institution sounds much like Foucault's, especially in his *Discourse on Language*. Less evident is that they reflect Derrida, who has defined the university as "that onto-and-auto-encyclopedic circle of the State."[10]

If we see the "institution" as an ongoing process of institutionalizing and stabilizing separate discourses, then the "institutionalizing" of "literature" is always emergent in a particular historical moment; it is what Foucault would call "an event." Most recently Sam Weber draws a distinction between *institutional* functioning, which corresponds to Paul de Man's notion of "error correction," and *instituting*, which is what thought does when it proceeds blindly, to cut a path "where none was before."[11] Exactly this kind of thinking can give us a vision of a more salutary future in which we no longer "merely" teach literature but study at the same time what Ulmer calls its "enframing": the entire cultural, political, social, and economic context in which it comes to be written and read. "Literature does not end," says Ulmer, "but the classification 'literature' becomes irrelevant."[12] We have already begun to re-examine the notion of literature as a series of sovereign texts. Throughout *Literature among Discourses: The Spanish Golden Age*, for instance, a "masterpiece" is regarded as "the nexus of themes, motifs, verbal devices, narrative models, etc. present in other texts, of whatever status in the epoch," those "other texts" seen as "the intertext."[13] If what "literature" means differs from one epoch to another and from one cultural milieu to another, then it might also be (as Terry Eagleton suggests) that "English literature" itself is yet another catachresis: something created and institutionalized as a displacement of socially engaged criticism.[14] Here Eagleton and his erstwhile nemesis Derrida share the same ground, both insisting upon an ongoing study of the relation between the reading and writing of texts, and the operations of the institution(s) within which those texts are written and/or read. A major task of Derrida's GREPH (Group for Research on the Teaching of Philosophy) is a critique "not only formal but effective and concrete . . . of all existing hierarchies, of all the criteriology, implicit and explicit, that privilege certain evaluations and classifications ('major' and 'minor' texts)." His recipe for such a critique is far-reaching and complete: we should be studying *how* certain texts get to be seen as canonical and how others are shunted to the peripheries; how our evaluative procedures for credentialing students and for determining what shall and shall not get published are constituted.[15] These and other recommendations are contained in "The Age of Hegel," in which "Hegel" refers not primarily to a historical personage so much as to a particular attitude of watchfulness which, for Derrida, Hegel represents: a watchfulness directed in particular toward the "seemingly extraphilosophical content" of what we do within the institutions where our work is carried out. This same admonition that we watchdog what we do appears in Dominick LaCapra's work, where he notes that recent doubts about exactly what should count as literary, or about what is relevant for literary studies are indications that we may need ever more critical concepts if we are ever to understand the present (not to mention the future) of our discipline.[16]

These admonitions would seem unnecessary but for the fact that it is all too easy to slide into an essentialism or romanticism, even when and where we least expect it. J. Hillis Miller's 1986 Presidential Address to the MLA urged vigilance against foundationalism or essentialism, yet in his Fall 1986 MLA Newsletter piece, "The Joy of Writing," Miller describes writing as "in fact intrinsic to the vocation that begins with the more or less private joy of reading. Writing . . . remains rooted in that solitary transaction with the words on the page," he says, and all the pressures we feel to publish are merely "the extrinsic and in a certain sense contingent institutionalization of our separate 'interior,' 'private,' 'solitary' actions."[17] This position is largely enlightened and cautious, but at the same time, to read it closely is to see that it teeters on the edge of essentialized visions of both institution and self. It seems wisest to accept Sam Weber's recommendation that our better future depends on our "within and without the Academy, admitting and accepting the fictionality of what [we] assume to be real, as well as the reality of [our] fictions."[18]

271

Despite my desire to write straightforwardly of the future of the institution of literature and the cultural community, so far I have done no more or better than throwing up for grabs the words "institution" and "literature." But "future" must be interrogated as well. We seem obsessed with discourse on the future, disingenuous as it is of me to say such a thing in a book on precisely that subject. Paul de Man, for instance, saw Nietzsche's hatred of history as a consequence of Nietzsche's seeing history as a generative chain that "fatally" linked present, past, and future, a reading of history that the Darnton/LaCapra debate recapitulated: reading the past to understand present and future ensures that past will contaminate whatever future we create.[19] In "The Taste of the Future" Denis Hollier expresses what instinctively we all know: once we have made a "goal" of the future, it cannot be distinguished from the present.[20] This is something feminist theorists are in advance (as usual) in recognizing, as the subtitle and title of two representative essays indicate: "The Past Before Us," and "Forward into the Past."[21] Frank Lentricchia, among others, warns us against any notion of "future" that is nothing more than a product of intellection "artificially separated from praxis," because such a notion "cannot any more than the autonomous past bring pressure to bear on the present moment as a critical alternative." Such a future, he says, "is too remote to be touched by our will."[22]

My discussion of "future" here begins by citing Lentricchia's warnings because he, like Nietzsche—like Derrida, like Edward Said, and like me—believes in the importance of the exertion of will and purpose over present and future, against and instead of more intellection and problematization of that term. I will say more about the importance of will (and desire) later, but for the moment I proceed here in two ways: by insisting that our present be defined as Lentricchia recommends, as "nothing but the intersecting moment of past and future," and as "an aggregate of survivals and possibilities, of retentions and innovations"—a conception echoing Derrida's description of the sign itself, as "a crossed structure of intentions and protentions." When Derrida noted, in *Of Grammatology,* that the future could only be "anticipated in the form of an absolute danger . . . [something that] breaks absolutely with constituted normality and can only be proclaimed, *presented,* as a sort of monstrosity," I take his definition to be a strategy designed to dramatize what any future not conceptualized *as a process* would look like.[23]

My essay here hangs in midair, then, partly because it wants to participate in a future-in-process, but also because it emanates from a present in which we are all living, as Richard Rorty says, "between the repudiated past and a dimly seen post-Philosophical future." Suspended in this moment, I see traces of at least two futures; my choice here is to set in motion one or the other every time I pick up a pen or step up to a podium. In actualizing one future I could, for instance, cite here the characteristically scrupulous warnings of Gayatri Chakravorty Spivak in her 1985 MLA paper "Post-Modernism, Post-Structuralism, Post-Marxism, Post-Analytic Philosophy, Post(e) Pedagogy: Where Is the Post Coming From?" She warns that all discussions of "future" may be thinly disguised attempts to colonize that future as white, First World males have colonized past and present. I could continue to enumerate other constraints that militate against talking about any "future" for "the" "institution" of "literature" and "the" "cultural" "community" because theory has thrown all those terms into citation. Or I could attack theory for my dilemma.

Instead, I choose to take positions. Partly I do so by defining my task as Richard Rorty defines philosophy: as "a study of the comparative advantages and disadvantages of the various ways of talking which our race has invented,"[24] or by defining philosophy as Adorno does, as merely "thinking breath." I see my own philosophizing here as Lyotard defines it; as the speaking of *petits récits* against and in preference to the master narratives of our times, even though I am aware one of our difficulties now is that we seem to be doing nothing *but* telling stories to one another—about how things are, about how texts and their contexts are to be read—in an arena whose characteristic and defining feature is what Sam Weber calls its "exclusion of exclusion" that renders us reluctant to pass judgment on anyone's stories or in any way to prefer one over any other.[25]

Despite the dangers of colonizing the future, or of contaminating it with the present, or of instituting a future not entirely pure, I prefer to see "future" here as a horizon against which fruitful speculation (or "conversation," in Rorty's sense of the term) and then maybe even action might be taken. I would like, for instance, to set in motion a dialogue in which we ask ourselves some version of the Lacanian question, What have we been getting out of putting the future "up ahead"? In part we get access to the kind of millennial thinking that went on in too many rooms of the 1986 MLA convention, where all the talking about what "must be done" functioned primarily as deferral and deflection from the daily work—in the classroom, for instance—that we might be doing now. Gayatri Spivak comments in her new book, "I think less easily of 'changing the world' than in the past. I teach a small number of the holders of the can(n)on male or female, feminist or masculist, how to read their own texts, as best I can." That is an eminently appealing sentiment and an antidote to the "up ahead" discussions that remind me of nothing so much as of Habermas's warnings that our "forward gropings" and our "anticipation of an undefined future and the cult of the new" can never eventuate in anything but "the exaltation of the present."[26]

Every future is born in what Walter Benjamin calls the *Jetzzeit:* the moment of revelation.[27] My own came at the moment when I felt most weighed down by the demand to give a complete reading of the problems in our profession. If the charge I was given was that of surveying the present/future seam in our profession, I might do so in ways that would not merely highlight debates and disagreements, but might instead help push us some small step closer to consensus. In my own discourse here, then, my pivotal (and, I hope, exemplary) move is not only *upward,* to a more and more meta-discursive space where I endlessly critique my own position (though it does not exclude that); or only *sideways,* to the kind of lateral and autotelic discourse that makes up so large a part of what we produce today (though it does not exclude that); or only *backward,* to the kind of "archival fetishism" Terry Eagleton abhors (Mark Krupnick on Lionel Trilling; William Cain on nearly everybody; Jonathan Arac on F. O. Matthiessen; a later Edward Said on an earlier Edward Said on an earlier and then a later Michel Foucault; Michael Ryan on Marx and deconstruction, Terry Eagleton on Michael Ryan on Marx and deconstruction, Gayatri Spivak on Terry Eagleton on Michael Ryan on Marx and deconstruction—though it does not exclude that, either).[28] Paradoxically, a genuinely *forward-looking* future might in part be somewhat backward-looking: engaging in a genealogical project of the sort that Foucault recommends and that Jonathan Arac has begun.[29] We might simultaneously trace the history of our enterprise and critique that history including its most recent moments, interrupting the trajectory of that history wherever doing so seems efficacious, since (as Rorty rightly notes) "our time" is really ever no more than "our view of previous times."[30] At their best, Hayden White suggests Marxists study the past not to reconstruct what happened, but to derive the laws of historical dynamics in order to preside over systematic changes in the future.[31] That same kind of genealogical project is a necessary part of our "future" work as well.

Creating a future in such a present moment is surely anxiety producing, but we can take comfort in Dominick LaCapra's suggestion that we *not* try to eliminate the anxiety caused by "the elusiveness of a clear and distinct object of inquiry that lends an identity to one's field or discipline," instead allowing our anxiety to work productively: "to affect institutional practice and discourse in ways that enable people to pursue issues into eccentric spaces or disconcerting temporalities."[32] Obviously, if anything at all can be said with conviction about our future work, it is that we will increasingly be occupying our time and attention not with the study of literature as it has historically been construed, or even with the theory out of which our practices of reading, writing, and teaching have grown. No one has marked this present/future seam more succinctly than J. Hillis Miller, in his MLA Presidential Address mentioned earlier. There he notes the sudden and almost universal shift *away* from theory "in the sense of an orientation toward language as such," and the simultaneous turn toward "history, culture, society, politics, institutions, class and gender conditions, the social context, the material base in the sense of institutionalization, conditions of production, technology, distribution, and consumption of 'cultural products,' among other products." It's difficult to find a book in "our field" any longer that doesn't have in its title or subtitle some word like *history, politics,* or *culture.* This sudden turn from theory has grown out of "an impatience to get on with it, that is, not to get lost in the indefinite delays of methodological debates but to make the study of literature count in our society"; it came in response to a demand from within the academic community itself "to be ethically and politically responsible in our teaching and writing, to grapple with realities."[33]

I want to explore exactly how such a turn from theory happened, for a number of reasons. First, I'm uneasy about burying theory before we've come to some agreement over exactly what "theory" is, what it can or ought to do or has already done. Second, with Gayatri Spivak, I believe theorists have a responsibility to become what she calls "as vulnerable" to the gaze of theory as we have made the texts we deconstruct, accepting our critical texts' vulnerability. We should not expect Marx to be an impeccable feminist, Derrida an impeccably accurate historian, or ourselves to be as purely free from all imbrication with capitalist modes of production and consumption in our own production and consumption of theory itself. Third, it is important that those in the profession who have remained adamantly "anti-theory" be denied the comfort of believing that, now that theory is "dead," we will revert—or have already reverted—to some pristine, prelapsarian state of affairs. In fact, the "death of theory" is often taken to be evidence of the *triumph* of theory:[34] the perpetual critique that theory generates has become habitual. Without thinking, we now critique both theory itself and our own discourse about it, as I do here.

But if "theory" has got me into a tight spot where I watch over my own shoulder as I write every sentence, I hope it is evident I don't believe theory to be the "enemy" its detractors on both the right and the left have suggested. Theory is surely not the enemy of tradition, for instance. To the contrary, I would argue that established forms of literary study that *neglect* the traditional theoretical questions about the ends and social functions of literature and criticism are themselves "the enemy." Gerald Graff sees theory simply as what "breaks out" whenever our presuppositions and tacit agreement about such terms as *text, reading, history, interpretation, tradition,* and *literature* can no longer be taken for granted.[35] Far too much time and energy has already been wasted in internecine warfare between pro-theorite and anti-theorite. As Christopher Norris suggests, issues of politics are rarely very far from the surface in any debate between "theory" and "commonsense" pragmatics, the terrain my own discourse maps here.[36]

Theory might most productively be seen as Frank Lentricchia sees it: as a type of rhetoric, neither true nor false, imposing or forcing nothing at all, but simply offering certain ways for us to see what it is we do, and to be judged well or ill depending on the extent to which that rhetoric does or doesn't contribute to the formation of community.[37] Among other things, what deconstructive theory has done is remind us that "theory" and "practice" are metaphors: one is not above the other, nor does one encompass the other. Theory and practice are simply different registers of narrative. We do best to regard all antagonisms that *oppose* theory to practice as deceptive, and to regard theory, of whatever stripe, as the constructing of various narratives meant to legitimate what we do in our everyday working lives as teachers and scholars. At its best, theory works exactly as Peter Hohendahl describes it working in the 1960s in West Germany: taking the role of a "catalyst stimulating and provoking various ideological camps to articulate their positions."[38] At its best, theory works the way Baudrillard suggests in a footnote to *Forget Foucault*: it is the place "where terms lose their meaning."[39] This is Baudrillard's way of indicating that whenever we question the very terms of our discourse—*institution, criticism, culture, community*—as I do here, we clear a space in which we can gain perspective, stretch, grow, and change. Sam Weber's long and salutary list of questions for us in his *Institution and Interpretation* were clearly generated by theory: What are the ends of the humanities, and where are the questions about ends coming from? What values do we serve and hold, and what functions do we serve? What *good* are we and are we doing? What is the institutional role of the humanities? What in fact constitutes the humanities themselves? Is the institution simply the skeletal framework that holds us up? The walls within which our work is contained? Are *we* it, or are we not? What forces of power and desire are affirmed or questioned by the institutional role of the humanities today?[40]

But at the same time we need to acknowledge that, if theory inspires important questions, theory's effects have *not* always been altogether salutary. Two things combine to make theory itself the culprit. Taking its cue from continental philosophy, theory makes us wary of any conviction that we have access to anything like higher truth. Thus it walls us off from the "higher" realm of universal or shared assumptions and goals. At the same time, it makes us wary of our own imbrication with power, thereby making us suspicious of the "lower" realm of common practice and *Real-politik*. Thus, as the contributors especially to the Spring 1985 *Critical Exchange* so persuasively argue, theory has had the consequence of leaving us feeling "marooned" between those two spheres.[41] That we are finding ways to while away our time while we are marooned here goes a long ways toward explaining the wheel-spinning dialogue we carry out in print and at conferences over questions like whether "the discourse of political action is the same as a political action." No one describes this phenomenon with more impatience or accuracy than Terry Eagleton; he chides us for remaining "marooned between a hostile academia and a dream of a public sphere" and for trying to relieve our discomfort by seeing ourselves as somehow "meta-political," and our role as that of "invigilat[ing] the political domain in the name of the 'human' without entering it."[42] We believe and say we want to teach values, yet we teach that all values are invented: "human fictions; relative." Caught between twin exclusive beliefs, we do nothing at all. If we take from contemporary philosophy its position that all truth is inaccessible, all meaning contingent, all intention irretrievable, and all interpretation arbitrary, we have only ourselves to blame if we have as a consequence nothing to offer to our students who come into our classrooms already fully aware of those things. (Not only do they live in the same ambient culture we do, but they no doubt know even more than we about many things, including science, technology, politics, and sex.) Faced, then, with a lack of a "saleable commodity," it has been too easy for some of us to wield the specialized vocabulary of theory as a badge of expertise, giving the illusion that we have something to offer when we might "sell" something far better: strategies for beginning to answer the questions Gary Stonum hears them asking: "in the face of the arbitrariness or apparent arbitrariness of existence, *how do I live my life?*"[43] This is precisely the kind of question Cornel West insists the humanist must help others to answer, calling for a "theoretical mechanism that sustains hope and generates praxis in the present moment of the historical process," and chiding especially deconstructive theorists for worrying about the *philosophical* bankruptcy of the bourgeois humanist tradition without worrying about the far more important fact of the *political* bankruptcy of that tradition.[44]

Fear of a confrontation with this kind of issue has led us to various actions explicable only as defensive or holding actions. Insofar as we see ourselves as marooned between two spheres, we seem to have begun to fulfill Habermas's prophecy (Lyotard's as well) of the conditions under which the postmodern world was born: we have begun to create a solipsistic world in which "theory" is nothing but a topos played out by isolated self-absorbed theorists engaged in what Paul Bové aptly calls "navel gazing."[45] Derrida warned us in 1982 and before that whatever we produce in literary studies could and would always be used: "even if it should remain useless in its results, in its productions, it can always serve to keep the masters of discourse busy: the experts, professionals of rhetoric, logic or philosophy who might otherwise be applying their energy elsewhere."[46] More recently Derrida's warnings have become stronger, most particularly in "The Age of Hegel."[47] Far from being the decadent or apolitical theorist that his detractors have taken him to be, Derrida has *always* advocated a concern with the political and the pragmatic—even in *Of Grammatology*, for instance, where he insisted that we "must begin wherever we are," even though "it [is] impossible to justify a point of departure absolutely: in a text where we already believe ourselves to be."[48]

Again I step aside from my own exposition here to point out that, in "scripting" a future for the institution of literature and the cultural community, I have become involved in exactly the kind of genealogical project that I suggested will constitute a part of our future work, since our future will be seen as it is largely as a consequence of how we construe our *past* moments. Although LaCapra advocates this same kind of writing of the history of our discipline as a way of directing its future, at the same time he recognizes the difficulties of writing a history of such a "radically heterogeneous and internally dialogized 'object'" as literary studies. The temptation will always be "to simplify one's story. . . . The present 'time of troubles' may be perceived as an aberrant, babble-like era of confusion—a time of transition from a purer past to a repurified future." In his 1987 English Institute paper, "Oppositional Professionals," Bruce Robbins noted even more strongly the tendency of critics and theorists, as they write their own histories, to construct various meta-narratives of "the fall from grace": referring to some "better times" when intellectuals were more engaged, more political, more moral than they are now. LaCapra's contribution to this enterprise is a reminder that, while different critical perspectives will necessarily convert this "plot" into different stories, they will all share "not only a convenient reduction of the complexities of the current critical scene, but an avoidance of inquiry into the sociocultural and political conditions that may actually be common to heterogeneous modes of criticism."[49]

In my own narrative of our recent past here, the story of our discipline as a sequence of various holding actions designed to stave off the necessity for action, I consider even Jonathan Culler's plea (in *Structuralist Poetics*) that we attend not so much to the meanings of texts as to "the conditions under which meaning becomes possible" as what Peter Hohendahl would regard as a *displacement* of the legitimation crisis in which we find ourselves. The analysis Culler advocated, far from walling the humanist off from considerations of value and walling him or her into a "safe" world of textual analysis, instead has the effect of thrusting the humanist willy-nilly into an assessment of the whole cultural system within which anything comes to have meaning and value. That same thrust into the world of *Realpolitik* brings with it the risk that criticism itself "may well lose its privileged position," not to mention whatever power base it has. That danger has been recognized by theorists both in the "radical" wing of the profession (Terry Eagleton and Fredric Jameson), and in the "conservative" (Stanley Fish).[50]

In my narrative of the recent history of our profession we find ourselves in a present moment of crisis where we are no longer sure exactly what our product is, and what (if anything) we ought to be doing to protect our credibility and maintain some usefulness to the society upon whose sufferance we depend. At the same time, we are in crisis not only because we have begun to fear we will lose our power base if we begin to critique culture at large from within that same culture, but also because we have begun to recognize the extent to which we are and have always been imbricated in precisely those cultural values we had thought ourselves safely outside of and immune to. Even our critical methods for reading literary texts can be seen to be "contaminated" by the consumer society we dream of counteracting. Much of such a critique remains to be done. For now I will only suggest, for instance, that reader-response criticism, which arrived in the early 1970s with a liberating "power to the people/readers" whiff about it, can in retrospect more easily be seen as a subtle version of consumerism. The inevitable result of the application of the Fish-ian question "What does that X *do?*" is not primarily a description or affirmation of some personal emotion or psychological response to a work of art so much as it is the enactment of one of the economic principles of a late-capitalist society: If it doesn't *do* anything, it's not *worth* anything. Or, to push a bit harder, "my" response becomes an enactment by one member of a privatized society carefully taught both inside and outside the academy that a *private* anything, including response, is the only kind of thing worth having.

Part of the resistance to deconstructive theory originates, I think, in a recognition that it is not easily turned into a product. If it is not an intellectual "fast food" easily digested and passed from hand to hand, then it's eminently attackable. But my own critique here needs critique, since it perpetuates at least two inefficacious oppositions that deconstruction warns against: an opposition between "them" and "us," which drains away energy for collaborative effort that might be directed toward transforming teaching and the institutions in which we work; and the opposition between "inside" and "outside," which tempts us to forget that we in the institution of literature are in fact *inside* the consumer culture we serenely presume we are *outside*. At this point I must allow my own post-structuralist narrative to become "vulnerable" to my own deconstructive gaze.

My first impulse was to nod assent when Derrida, in his footnote at the end of Chapter 1 of his *Memoires for Paul de Man*, chastises people like Walter Jackson Bate or René Wellek for attacking theory, seeing them as "part of a campaign certain professors with lots of prestige and power" wage while trying to defend that power against perceived threats to their discourse, "its axiomatics, its procedures, its theoretical and territorial limits." He accuses them of forgetting "the elementary rules of reading and of philosophical integrity in whose name they claim to do battle." "Did Wellek read Paul de Man?" he asks. "Was he capable of it?"

"Will he have the honesty to admit his haste and superficiality?"[51] Hillis Miller raises the same issue in *The Ethics of Reading*. One would *think* a book could have no effect unless it is read, "unless it is used as a missile or falls on the head of someone who walks by the shelf on which it is stored." In fact, somehow books— especially books of critical theory—seem capable of producing a great many effects without ever having been read at all.[52]

The humor is refreshing but obscurative. In fact, those anti-theory articles are not primarily being written by people with "power and prestige," and one of the most interesting things about Derrida's attack on attackers of theory is that he responds so far as I know only to those who *do* have power and prestige. Coming from anywhere else, those attacks are by definition inconsequential: no more than the temper tantrums of those who find reading Derrida "too hard," or taking "too much time or effort." Elizabeth Bruss's narrative of recent theory in *Beautiful Theories* suggests an alternative explanation. She describes us in the 1960s as living in a time of "subsidized and expanding faculty, producing scholarship at an unprecedented rate"—a situation that allowed us to "achieve an equally unprecedented degree of specialization." All that might be seen as desirable, except its end result has been that of "making a 'community of scholars'—with access to the same information—all but impossible."[53] It's easy enough to see that today the subsidizing (via sabbatical leaves and generous grants) for some scholars at major universities, and the lack of the same for many others working at the important but exhausting work of teaching, does several things. It forces us to regard the notion of a singular "institution" of "literature" or "cultural" "community" as in yet another way an instance of catachresis. But in this instance catachresis generates a revelatory moment of interruption—a moment caused by nothing more elaborate than the carrying out of an individual empirical audit. When one looks at one's own experience of one's colleagues at other institutions, it becomes clear that there *is* no "cultural community," in part because the "institution" of "literature" reproduces exactly the same divisions into socioeconomic classes that exist outside the university, even if our salary highs aren't quite as high, or our lows quite as low, as those outside our walls. What is produced is a hierarchy reinforced every day in the simplest and most direct ways: separating those who can pay $50 for the *Glas* translation from those who cannot; those who can pay for the ticket to the MLA convention from those who cannot; those who can pay $500 (or whatever it is now) for a Harvard library card from those who cannot. And, since time is one of the most valuable commodities in Western culture and is in consequence also a value reproduced in the academy, it perpetuates hierarchies by separating those who have *time* to read and digest theory from those who do not. Some dim recognition of these economic disparities is without a doubt behind some of the often inchoate rage in essays written by some who attack theory, and at the very least some dim recognition of the cause of that rage ought to be present in those (including Derrida) who attack those who attack theory. Assuming that the hierarchies within the cultural community are purely intellectual ones (which tend soon enough to become equated with moral hierarchies) rather than accidental ones created as a result of lack of access to time, materials, and information is inexcusable. Such an assumption reproduces unexamined the rationale that the "haves" have always used to justify and explain the outsider status of the marginalized and the excluded. Stanley Fish asserts that "theory can have no consequences" since it cannot succeed in what it purports to do (which, as he sees it, is to do what theories are always designed to do: predict future directions). On the contrary, I would say one of the most powerful consequences theory has had is the perpetuation within the cultural community of just such hierarchies that serve to split its members from one another in postures of mutual antagonism that affects any action we might take as a community either inside or outside the university. Denying that this is so, as Foucault says in another context, can "never be anything but play, utopia, or anguish."[54]

What struck me with most force when reading Peter Stallybrass and Allon White's *The Politics and Poetics of Transgression* was the extent to which our MLA conventions might usefully be seen as operating as classic instances of the fair seen not simply as the place and space of social inversions and free play (as Bakhtin does), but as a crucial nexus between commerce and culture, both high and low. Insofar as the MLA convention is economically, socially, and professionally useful, it is "civilizing." Insofar as it is "low, playful, decadent," it is "the locus of vagabond desires," an epistemological hybrid that "undermines oppositions between play and work," reflecting as a consequence our bourgeois "uneasy oscillation between high and low, business and pleasure, and consequently retaining a potent imaginative charge in the culture of those who increasingly define themselves as above its gaudy pleasures." It is a "point of economic and cultural intersection" evident not just in the obvious place: in the hotel exhibition hall, where we advertise, display, sell, and buy one another's products at the book exhibits. More crucially, the convention is a place where the "low" (those who "merely teach" at "lesser known" institutions) mingle with the "high" (those with more name recognition and status). As such, it can be seen as a potentially powerful place for transformation: the place where the "highs," isolated as they often are from too much of the important daily work in the trenches of teaching, might make contact with the pragmatic concerns of the majority of their colleagues. But instead of this happy convergence, what happens resembles exactly what Stallybrass and White describe in their analysis of the fair: the "lows" tend to be seduced by the newfangled wares of theory, and though those wares *could* constitute a powerful rhetoric, a scene for collaboration and a means for transforming our work and our vision of ourselves if theory were effectively introduced to those "lows," instead theory is offered as nothing but a mystifying new vocabulary. "Part of the transgressive excitement of the fair for the subordinate classes," say Stallybrass and White, "was *not* its 'otherness' to official discourse, but . . . the disruption of provincial habits and local tradition by the introduction of a certain cosmopolitanism, arousing desires and excitements for exotic and strange commodities."[55]

Many oppositional theorists place their hope in exactly this space of desire—and, in my own way, so do I. If those of us with time and leisure to read and comprehend theory and its implications could *tap* that desire; if, for instance, we could regard ourselves as *brokers* of theory, taking time to talk about it with those who haven't the time to read it and think through its implications; and if at the same time, and equally importantly, we were to *listen* to the concerns of people in the profession who teach in different circumstances and more difficult conditions, then perhaps we might manage to bring about a more salutary and communal future for us all. The broker of theory might talk not only with his or her fellows in higher education, but with fellow teachers from kindergarten through high school. Among other things, brokers sell futures. And so might we. If, on the other hand, we insist upon regarding theory as some commodity we "own," its vocabulary as some currency we spend to gain influence, jobs, or status, then we are surely busy actualizing a future exactly like the one the deconstruction-bashers describe: we are producing nothing more than a "strategy for self-preservation" that can do nothing more than "fuel the institution with its own impotence."[56]

I could fill the rest of my essay here with more analyses of attacks on theory or with defenses of theory, but here, too, I prefer to actualize a different future. Instead, I offer myself as one representative of the kind of "brokering" I recommend. By laying out as fairly as I can the range of positions held by those who regard themselves as oppositional critics, I may serve to highlight the range of possible places from which each of us might launch whatever work we do in the profession.

The most conservative see our job as continuing to read texts and to teach the reading of texts, as they believe we have always done. A few points along the continuum are those who agree that our main work should remain the teaching of texts, though they expand the range of texts to include the non-traditional, non-canonical, non-Western. Further to the left are those who regard our most important work not as the reading of literary texts so much as the reading of culture at large, and teaching students to acquire the critical reading skills that will enable them to become critical readers of their culture as well. Leftward still more are those who propose that our best work must include the reading of ourselves and the institutions within which we work, as well as an examination of our role as transmitters of culture. Leftward still more are those who suggest we need to see ourselves not only as transmitters or consumers of, or spectators at, culture, but as people directly involved in the *writing* of culture, as shapers of ethics, morals, and behavior whose best work is teaching those who come into our classrooms to see themselves in the same way. Furthest left we might put those who take "culture" itself as yet another instance of catechresis: not a thing to be transmitted at all, but as another arena where forces not yet under dominion of the state might be identified, tapped, and unleashed. (See the essays in the *Yale French Studies* volume entitled *Everyday Life* for representative instances of such a critique.)

Many of those whose work gives every indication of being important are not professors of English, and even those who are can hardly be said to be producing the kind of thing we recognize as "literary studies." It is hardly an accident that the people whose names are most often invoked in discussions of these issues are involved in an activity that we don't yet quite know how to name, working in a strange (to us) terrain variously named "cultural studies" or "textual studies." They might best be regarded as the "post-Philosophical philosophers" whom Rorty describes so well, who study "the comparative advantages and disadvantages of the various ways of talking . . . our race has invented," cultural critics comfortable riding a kind of "literary-historical-anthropological-political merry-go-round." They are what Rorty calls "all-purpose intellectuals" who "feel free to comment on anything at all . . . in order to get something done." "Name droppers," talking about Foucault here, Deleuze there, Baudrillard somewhere else, Marx and Freud sprinkled throughout. They drop names not in some display of mental virtuosity but "as a kind of shorthand for referring to different symbol-systems, or ways of seeing."[57]

Much could be said about the kind of future we can expect as a consequence of this state of affairs. Any member of our cultural community who feels helpless in the face of all that theory, theory that there is not enough time to read now, is destined to feel even more helpless when confronting the prospect of our "field" becoming even less easy to comprehend than it is already, its boundaries expanding or dissolving into politics, history, ethnography, and anthropology as they have already expanded into psychology and history. The gap between the "haves" and the "have nots" of the profession can only widen, and the need for "brokers" can only grow.

Back to my own "brokering." In the first position on our critical continuum, among those who insist that our most important work is and should remain the teaching of texts, it is easy to find people whose politics—and here we are referring only to *academic* politics—are both of the left and of the right (though it would be useful at some future time to consider the extent to which the two senses of politics do and do not coincide in individual instances). On the left, which in this case happens to be both a political and an academic left, we can place Richard Ohmann, whose most recent work, significantly, addresses more "popular" criticism. Ohmann has long argued that our best work will always lie in teaching the classic texts, since all of them have always been "inherently revolutionary in content."[58] In *Criticism and Social Change* and *After the New Criticism* Frank Lentricchia takes something like the same position, as when, in reacting to Marx's eleventh thesis on Feuerbach, he suggests that to interpret either the world or texts is at the same time, and necessarily, to change them. For Lentricchia as for the Kenneth Burke he so admires, "all intellection is a form of political action." Although Lentricchia believes academic intellectuals *may* protest the happenings in El Salvador, we produce our most powerful political effects when "we do what we are trained for, in the context in which we work and for which we were hired: teaching, reacting, teaching one another." For him the inside/outside distinction that presumes that the university somehow is not *of* the world "is killing us." He insists that there is a politics both *in* the classroom and *of* the classroom, and he suggests our power might best be wielded as we teach, operate in departmental meetings, and fight over such things as curriculum. He sees literary theory, like Marxist theory, as "a kind of rhetoric, a reading of the past and present [which] invites us to shape a certain future: an invitation to practice, not epistemology."[59] In this respect his position is very close to that of the participants in the Society for Critical Exchange and in the GRIP (Group for Research Into the Profession) enterprises, with members of both insisting upon a theory-praxis continuum leading to classroom practice and beyond.[60]

Bill Cain, for instance, insists that "political change, if it comes at all, will come through specific acts of work," and the work to which he refers is always the day-to-day work in the classroom and in departmental struggles over issues like curriculum.[61] Lentricchia differs from Cain in insisting that, although effective work in meetings is necessary, those "meetings won't help unless we talk and theorize those people who speak and act in those departmental meetings."[62] I share this position.

On the academic right are to be found not just those whom

we would place on the political left, like Lentricchia or Ohmann, but those who might regard themselves as uncomfortable in that leftist company, such as Eugene Goodheart or to a large extent Gerald Graff. Also found there are some who advocate that we continue to teach in the traditional way not because we want to transmit traditional values, but because that ground upon which we teach in fact constitutes the professional power base without which we have no authority to do anything at all. Outside of that ground no values *can* be taught, precisely because it determines what shall and shall not be said to have value in the first place. In the forefront of this latter group—those who advocate an academically right position for politically right, rather than left, reasons—one would have to place Stanley Fish and most of the others who have engaged the issue of "professionalism" in recent years, most notably in the pages of the two issues of *Critical Inquiry* devoted to that subject and the issue of *Critical Exchange* devoted in part to the same debate, this time carried out by Fish and James Sosnoski.[63] For Fish, for instance, the term "oppositional professional" is redundant. We cannot *help* but be "oppositional," because intellectual debate is what *constitutes* and defines the work we do. For Fish, then, it is useless to advocate that we be oppositional because we cannot be otherwise. The difficulty is that, in Fish's universe, the word *opposition* has become a victim of the kind of "semantic slide" he described at work in texts in his earlier reader-response phase: what Fish means by "opposition" and what, say, Ohmann means are two very different things.

If we move along the continuum to a position where oppositional critics (in Ohmann or Lentricchia's sense of oppositional, rather than Fish's) begin to suggest that something in addition to the reading of texts may be our major work, the first and most persuasive person encountered is Edward Said, and to some extent Frank Lentricchia again. For Said especially, theory joins with practice to create the notion of what he calls a "critical consciousness" encompassing four distinct practices: practical criticism (journalism and reviews), the practice of academic literary history, the appreciation and interpretation of literature, and the activity of theorizing itself. Said sees this critical consciousness "mov[ing] skeptically in the broader political world where such things as the humanities or the great classics ought to be seen as small provinces of the human ventures, to map the territory covered by all the techniques of dissemination, communication, and interpretation, to preserve some modest (perhaps shrinking) belief in non-coercive human community." Included in Said's vision of critical consciousness is a notion Hillis Miller shares, that theory's best work is to resist theory: to offer theory what I have called an "empirical audit" at each point of contact between it and our own experience of the world, "to point up those concrete instances drawn from everyday reality that lie outside or just beyond the interpretive area necessarily designated in advance and thereafter circumscribed by every theory."[64] In fact, this description of the place where theory and practice meet and serve as a system of checks and balances over one another sounds like nothing so much as Fredric Jameson's description of criticism itself, which he sees as situated somehow in a space of theoretical reflection midway between narrative and meta-narrative, where the end result of the interaction is a kind of totalizing "meta-critique" shedding light on our entire cultural system and our understanding of its operations.[65]

This same critical consciousness that Said recommends leads to the next position on the continuum, where we could position all those who recommend that we use our close-reading critical skills to read not only literary texts but also our own institution(s) and our relations to the institutions of power "outside" ourselves within which we work. Said expresses dismay that we tell our students and our general constituency that we defend the classics, the virtues of a liberal education, and the pleasures of literature, "even as we also show ourselves to be silent (perhaps incompetent) about the historical and social world in which all these things take place."[66] Reading our own imbrication in the institutions in which we work is no easy task, especially since the end product of such a critical reading must surely be a consideration of teleological issues: a straight-ahead look at the cultural politics from which our present obsession with the endless deferral of at least a particular reading of post-structuralist theory has given us a temporary reprieve. But deconstruction, when it is most usefully construed, insists that we pay attention not just to "the scene of writing" that Derrida talks about, but to the "scene" of *all* our works: teaching, writing, research, cultural transmission.

I have already given two small indications of what this kind of reading of the "scene" of our work might look like when I challenged the theorist to become a "broker" of theory, rather than hoarding his wares, and in my brief critique of the MLA convention scene itself. Later I will offer something more. For now I simply point out that much of our "future" work is already beginning to take shape as a critique of the various "sites of assembly" where we do our cultural work, since each constitutes a nucleus of material and cultural conditions that regulate what may and may not be said, who may speak, how people may and may not communicate, and what importance is given to what is said within each space. The history of all political struggle, as Stallybrass and White suggest, echoing Foucault, is in fact the history of attempts to control significant sites of assembly and spaces of discourse.[67]

If in the future we will need to be well read in what we have always thought were "other" disciplines, it is also true that the issues with which the literary scholar concerns him or herself will be the same ones confronting those in other disciplines. Each cultural community's need to critique the ground from which it speaks is one issue already well in the forefront of other disciplines—in John Clifford's collection of essays on anthropological theory, *Writing Culture,* for instance, which insistently asks for "the specification of discourses": "Who speaks? Who writes? Where or when? With or to whom? Under what institutional and historical constraints?"[68] Here again, feminist theory and criticism is in advance of the rest of our profession in pointing out that perspectives, stances, and readings are always motivated by the positions from which we speak and question.[69] Such an exploration of the struggle for control over the sites of assembly at which our work occurs is an ongoing concern in Terry Eagleton's work, especially in *The Function of Criticism;* it was prefigured in Richard Ohmann's *English in America* in 1976, is a central concern in Peter Hohendahl's work, and will undoubtedly play a large part in Pierre Bourdieu's new *Homo Academicus,* which promises to "examine the social background and practical activities of his fellow academics—their social origins and current positions, how much they publish and where they publish it, their media appearances, political involvements and so on. . . . construct[ing] a map of the intellectual field . . . and analys[ing] the forms of capital and power, the lines of conflict and the patterns of change which characterize the system of higher education."[70]

Hohendahl constructs his own list of questions we must answer if we want to operate with any integrity and self-awareness within the spheres in which we work. By now those questions begin to look awfully familiar: "Who is assigned the right to criticize? What institutions assume the guardianship of criticism? How do those institutions defend their guardianship in competition with other institutions? How are those who are to criticize selected, trained, and supported? To whom is the criticism communicated, and on what occasions is criticism required?"[71] Hohendahl refers regularly to "the consciousness industry," which he sees as struggling for people's taste. To some extent he blames academics for the fact that "culture" has become "mass culture," consumerized precisely because it has not been mediated through a public sphere. Terry Eagleton also blames intellectuals for the huge gap between those of us in "the culture industry" and the people it is our work to teach and serve. In Eagleton's narrative, however, this failure of the academic humanist occurs because of the historical shift in the position and role of the cultural critic. If author and audience are close, as in earlier centuries, no critic is required. He traces a progression from the "man of letters" in the eighteenth century, who actively and regularly involved himself in writing for ordinary people about culture, to the "sage" of the nineteenth century. With this progression came a gradual change in the role of the critic: from one who shared in the making of culture to one who arbitrated and determined taste. While the sage of the nineteenth century was a "middleman," "shaping, regulating, and receiving a common discourse," the academic humanist who replaced him by 1900 had become fully ensconced in the university—isolated there, in Eagleton's "fall" narrative. Consequently criticism became "a transaction only *within* academia rather than one between the academy and society."[72] This vision of our academic community, as consisting of people who do not transmit cultural values but who thrust culture and values upon people in consequence of our power, is not one with which we are entirely comfortable. Yet it requires analysis and exploration that will be some of our future work, work we will be sharing with those in other disciplines. In psychology, for instance, Tullio Maranhao has been asking hard questions: "What is it that cures? Is it a science of the psyche, or a rhetoric of communications?" He describes therapeutic discourse exactly as we have begun to describe our own discourse of theory recently: as "a complex of knowledge, power, and rhetoric wielded by the healing social institutions . . . a cultural system . . . shaping westerners' world view of all levels of life. . . . standing side by side with its co-cultural systems, such as philosophy, religion, science, and politics."[73]

In our immediate future and beyond we will find ourselves with obligations—of both intellect and morality—extending beyond the terrain to which we have become habituated. Terry Eagleton, for instance, has always maintained that the institution of criticism "is only ever significant when it engages in extra-literary issues," when, for instance, in speaking about a literary work it "emits a lateral message about the shape and destiny of a whole culture."[74] Both Eagleton and Said regularly invoke the name of Raymond Williams as a model to be emulated insofar as Williams's work crosses the frontiers between the academic institution and the political society at large; Said admires Williams in particular because he put in motion a reading of the institution that *uses* theory to carry out that reading.[75] In my judgment this work is being done most directly in this country by members of the GRIP project and the Society for Critical Exchange, in England by the CCCS (Center for Contemporary Cultural Studies) at Birmingham University, the Open University, and the Council for National Academic Awards, and, in France, in the work Derrida and others are doing under the sign of GREPH.

The relation of our daily work to questions of politics and the world at large is a concern never far from the center of Lentricchia's, Said's, Ohmann's, and, most recently, Jim Merod's work as well, in his *Political Responsibility of the Critic*.[76] The difference between, say, Frank Lentricchia and Edward Said on the one hand and Terry Eagleton on the other is largely a difference of opinion about strategy or direction. The first two advocate bringing the world of politics into the books we teach in the classroom (or they insist that the world of politics already inheres in the books we teach). The latter would take the close-reading skills we foster in the classroom out into the world at large. Paul Bové, for instance, suggests that to talk about literature as if it were outside or beyond questions of power and authority, "a kind of semi-autonomous field . . . outside of politics," is a delusion—false, dishonest.[77]

The sociologist Pierre Bourdieu shares that position, suspecting the academic intellectual of being guilty of a kind of "cultural power, half conscious, that advances by denying we are attached to any immediate political ends, thereby allowing us to accumulate 'symbolic capital.' "[78] Such an indictment has a fairly long and continuous history in our profession. In 1983, for instance, Said was citing with approval Richard Ohmann's "devastating observation" of 1976, that English departments themselves represented "a moderately successful effort by professors to obtain some of the benefits of capitalism while avoiding its risks," by way of our "reluctance to acknowledge any link between how we do our work and the way the larger society is run."[79] Studying those links would be part of a new field of study that Bourdieu calls "the sociology of cultural production" and that Peter Hohendahl sees as "turning literary criticism into a new discipline" which will be a kind of critical sociology of the institution of literature in a capitalist society. This is also a goal currently advocated by everyone from conservative humanist to radical theorist. In fact, a study of the complex social and political factors outside the university that motivate our present critical stances is advocated now by the Modern Language Association itself.

This work, too, has already been initiated by people outside our discipline. The philosopher W. F. Haug's *Critique of Commodity Aesthetics* offers a reading of commercials and a study of the impact of advertising on "high" culture. Cornelius Castoriadis's *The Imaginary Institution of Society: Creativity and Autonomy in the Social-Historical World* is a critique of Marxism and a study of the relations between action and social institutions and of the role of symbolism on both individual and social levels.[80] Jürgen Habermas's *Philosophical Discourse on Modernism* and Pierre Bourdieu's *Homo Academicus* will both inevitably turn the tools of close reading on those of us who maybe ought best to be doing that reading ourselves. Paul Bové's may be the most complete recipe yet offered by an academic humanist of what we will need to do in order to read the institution and our place in it. He asks that we study how the institutions for producing and circulating cultural representation work in our society; how certain parts of the intellectual elite understand our society; how the cultural apparatus in general works. Bové sees the "hallmark" of the postmodern as inherently anti-hegemonic in its belief that it is an "alternative to established beliefs and values of mass culture and the cultural practices that legitimate those values." In his view, the postmodern scholar necessarily stands in opposition to the institutions in which he/she works and the culture those institutions support. The postmodern he defines as what is constituted out of all that is repressed by mass culture or by "modernity," or, alternatively and more positively, as "a generative mythmaking response to the shallow egotism of late modernism and its anomie," or, yet again, as an ongoing attempt to reconnect literature and criticism with political, sociological, anthropological, psychological, historical, or philosophical interests.[81]

Bové's promise of a better future through a triumph of the postmodern is, of course, not the only current view. Eagleton, for instance, takes the postmodern to be a prime enemy whose "depthless, styleless, dehistoricized, decathected surfaces" he finds incapable even of signifying alienation, "for the very concept of alienation must secretly posit a dream of authenticity which [it] finds quite unintelligible."[82] Oppositional critics have of course interpreted postmodernism and its effects in very different ways, but since that cannot be my subject here I will simply say that the central question that Bové suggests constitutes the postmodern debate is the question of how one can (or in fact *if* one can) carry out an oppositional role from within the institution, and the correlative question of whether the literary critic is the best person to do that job. Addressing at the same time the question of how we can avoid "losing our center" or our "power base" in doing that work, Bové illustrates again the extent to which critics of the left and the right tend often to share the same concerns. Lentricchia and Said also, for instance, have concerns that once we begin to read culture and ourselves "in the absence of an enclosing domain called 'literature,' there is no longer an authorized or official position for the literary critic."[83] This question of how we can go outside both our disciplinary boundaries and the sheltering institutions in which we operate without losing our authority and definition (experiencing thereby, I suppose, true "dissemination") is a more urgent issue when we include the radical oppositional critic's further suggestion that we resist the temptation to perpetuate the divisions of labor—specializing in "medieval literature" only, say, as well as thinking of ourselves as "writers/thinkers" rather than as teachers. Such divisions of labor Bové takes to be not only the hallmark of the academy's general subservience to hegemony, but at the same time maybe the prime block in the way of the academic's joining his or her own work with that of other oppositional forces in a society "struggling against both hegemonic manipulation and state violence."[84]

Bové's call, like Lentricchia's and Said's, is a call for individual acts of change and resistance: new attention to how we teach the classic texts (Lentricchia, Ohmann, Said); a call to reconsider which ones we teach (the issue for academic feminism); a call to study our own imbrication in power (Eagleton and Bové); a call to teach students to think critically about themselves and the society in which they live (the most recent Spivak, and Merod); and a call to extend our critical capacities and maybe even our physical bodies into the world outside the academy in oppositional ways (Elaine Scarry and Cornel West).

This last and most radical position on the continuum is, as often as not, occupied by those within our cultural community who have most often been marginalized, outside the centers of power. Women seem most adept at crossing the line between the academy and the world, between discourse and action—perhaps, as Cornel West suggested in his 1987 English Institute paper entitled "Theory, Pragmatism, and Politics," because feminism is a continuous movement carried out by women both within and without academe. Elaine Scarry's work on nuclear feminism at the 1986 MLA convention seemed to me to promise just the right mixture of philosophical and theoretical sophistication and possibility for genuine action in the world at large; Lynn Hanley's persuasive article in *Radical Teacher,* "Demilitarizing Literature and Literary Studies," offers another model for crossing that boundary.[85] At the same time Gayatri Spivak, who artfully creates and then occupies that perfect representational space of the trebly displaced or marginalized, has most recently been calling for that most simple and direct, and therefore most radical, of actions. In response to the scrupulously "pure" question of a radical who asked how she could teach a Bengali novel since she did not speak Bengali and therefore could not teach it fairly, Spivak's response was simply that one could *learn* Bengali, or at the very least could recognize that one's position, politically correct as it may appear to be, might be suspected of being ultimately a self-serving one.[86]

It would seem, then, that at the most radical end of the continuum, the *most* oppositional critic is the one who suggests that three things may be in style once again: body, action, and teaching—the last representing, not coincidentally, one of the finer marriages of body and action. In fact, one thing academic humanists might want to confront in the immediate future is the awareness that we earn our salaries by *teaching* culture; not by those activities of theorizing, interpreting, or doing research by which so many of us identify ourselves, activities for which in largest part we are not paid. I find hope in our renewed interest in pedagogy, and in the transportation of the more salutary observations of literary theory and continental philosophy into our work in the classroom. Some attention, for instance, to some version of the deconstructive question: not just "What does [our] writing write?" but *What does our teaching teach?* would be helpful.[87] Until very recently people like Mary Louise Pratt have been absolutely accurate in noting the complete silence in our profession around the goals not only of literary criticism, but of pedagogy as well.[88] The *Yale French Studies* volume entitled *The Pedagogical Imperative* was one step in a right direction, as was (and is) Cary Nelson's edited collection of essays entitled *Theory in the Classroom*.[89] Both Bill Cain and Tony Davis, on opposite sides of the water, have been addressing the widening gap between those who do theory and those who teach.[90] Greg Ulmer's *Applied Grammatology*, too, devotes its entire latter half to issues of pedagogy.[91]

But more needs to be done. What is most promising in all these efforts is that the attention they turn to teaching is different, both in quality and in kind, from what we have seen in the past. As Peter Widdowson suggests in *Re-Reading English*, we are no longer engaged only in debates over what approach to take in teaching particular literary works, but we are beginning to engage instead in forming more far-reaching questions about "what English is, whether it should have a future as a discrete discipline, and if it doesn't, in which ways it might be reconstituted."[92] Pierre

Bourdieu's work addresses these same kinds of questions, and the reincarnated *Glyph,* now *Glyph Textual Studies,* at least in its premier issue seems to promise to address pedagogy in the substantive philosophical way in which it deserves to be addressed.[93] If part of our post-structuralist pedagogical future will find us reading not only our classrooms but also ourselves as we operate within those classrooms, one model for doing so will remain Roland Barthes' "Writers, Intellectuals, Teachers," in which he urges that teachers "auto-critique" their work, watching their own discourse in the classroom, becoming what he calls "peaceable speakers" who adopt a kind of "floating discourse."[94] Lyotard's concern with pedagogy takes the form not only of calling attention to teachers' power (since increasingly "modes of information," rather than "modes of production," will determine access to power) but also of calling for more teamwork among teachers. Teamwork will be needed not only in teaching (or the reproduction) of knowledge, but in research (or the production) of knowledge as well, especially across disciplinary boundaries.[95]

Still, I cannot help feeling a bit of *déjà vu* about all this. I was inspired recently to read again a few of those works written in the wake of the Vietnam war by scholars whose social consciences had been galvanized by that war. Richard Ohmann's *English in America,* Noam Chomsky's *American Power and the New Mandarins,* and Lionel Trilling's *Beyond Culture,* all published between 1967 and 1969, all explored what they then saw as the "crisis" in the humanities. Like Said, Lentricchia, Eagleton, and Cain among others today, they saw a failure of humanists not only to connect their work of research and publication with their work of teaching in the classroom, but also to connect their work as intellectuals with their work helping to improve the world at large. It now seems as if the ideas of oppositional critics of the 1980s have been born parthenogenically, without forefathers; this sometimes leads me to think that, whatever the enterprise in which I am engaged as a teacher and member of the "institution" of "literature" or "a" "cultural" "community" might be, it surely is not a cumulative one. The feeling is distressing. It is also distressing to discover (as I have more than once) that anyone who suggests we might reopen the question of how we teach and what we are teaching is likely to be accused of a desire to "return to the '60s."

As we work to incorporate marginalized cultures into our teaching and criticism, we will need to be conscious of our motives. To some extent the emphasis on expanding canons, while necessary and right, may paradoxically eventuate in our serving even more than we have to date those in power outside the university. Insofar as we continue to teach what is usually thought of as "high" culture, we need to remain aware that the locus of that high culture, as Terry Eagleton reminds us, is "in liberal humanistic discourse in late monolopoly capitalism." As such, it is "neither decorative nor superfluous, but a properly marginal presence, marking the border where that society both encounters and exiles its own disabling absences." Bourdieu and Passeron makes this same point. Eagleton sees us as having been largely "incorporated into the culture industry," providing nothing much more than "a type of unpaid public relations, part of the requirements in any large corporate undertaking."[96] Teaching "marginalized" cultural texts only aids the state by "proving" to everyone how "liberal" and "free" we are.

Lyotard sees our work in a far more hopeful way, envisioning a future in which the increased access to information on the part of more people, including access to more culture "high," "low," and "other," holds out the promise for a genuine breakdown in the structures of authority and the promise of a free circulation of ideas that can bring about a leveling between high or elite and low cultures. Such a move, Lyotard believes, might be capable of producing a "delegitimation process," something that will become clearer later when I talk about Habermas's notion of a "legitimation crisis."[97]

Lentricchia believes that, because the "dominant" culture doesn't yet cover or suffuse all of society, there are realms of other cultures outside the dominant in which and from which the intellectual can work—all the more so precisely because the "dominant" culture believes it has all the territory covered. In Lentricchia's scenario, an oppositional critic might choose the community, institution, culture, and criticism from which to launch a critique of the dominant. This is something Stanley Aronowitz recognizes too when he calls for the critic to find that "apogee of critical science" which for him "resides in specifying the non-subsumable."[98] But at the same time for me an old question from

Paul Ricoeur recurs: What will happen to us when the dominant culture (which we see ourselves as the defenders of) meets other cultures without the "benefit" of the kind of automatic appropriation of which we have been guilty in the past? If we move out into "other" cultures instead of taking those others into us, how will our dominant culture remain dominant?[99]

Pop and mass culture are often seen as potential launching sites, as in the work of Bové, Bourdieu, or Aronowitz. But at the same time another piece of our future work will involve subjecting our own assumptions about what constitutes "high," "elite," "low," or "pop" to some critical study. Bourdieu's *Distinction*, for instance, is a fascinating study, complete with statistics, charts, and graphs that might make the "elite" intellectual feel more than a bit foolish. Bourdieu's apparently inescapable conclusions are that the hallmark of what we consider to be "great" art is the extent to which it disguises its appeal to the body: the distance it puts between reader, perceiver, or auditor and anything like a gut emotion. Educated people find a photograph of tree bark far more edifying than a photograph of a child in first communion dress; educated people at least pretend to find a tastefully decorated minuscule portion of *cuisine minceur* preferable to a hearty plate of spaghetti. In each case the former succeeds better in giving us what Bourdieu calls "the pleasure of denying pleasure." Both in *Distinction* and in his earlier study of education Bourdieu insists that "the" cultural community of academic humanists needs to pose the question of how and why we have failed to see that what we take to be "objective truth"—or for that matter "better" art (more uplifting, more inspiring, more sophisticated)—is in fact "the imposition of a cultural arbitrary . . . objectively misrecognized."[100] Ulmer and Lyotard, among others, insist we cannot ignore the ways in which new media are bringing about radical cultural transformations. Those students we teach can become a source of information if we learn to listen as well as talk to them.

In fact, "center" and "margin," like "high" and "low," "elite" and "pop," are all instances of catachresis. Laurie Finke argues persuasively that deconstruction, for instance, even with its constant reminders of the necessity for paying attention to the margins, has in fact effectively "marginalized us all," since it is "institutionally part of the 'center' which we know as literary studies."[101]

We may want to consider the dependent relationship between not only "center" and "margin," but also "high" and "low" culture. Precisely *because* high or elite culture defines itself as that which is in the business of denying pleasure, those of us who advocate high culture might in fact *need* the vulgar or the low so we can assure ourselves of regular "hits" off those bodily or emotional pleasures from which our own high culture has cut us off. Evidence of this is all around: many of my male colleagues publicly attend the opera while privately tuning their car radios to AM country music stations.[102]

There lurks beneath my analysis here something more than a simple matter of competing tastes. Some of our current interest in "other" cultures—our interest, say, in Cape Verdean linguistics or contemporary feminist poetry of the Dominican Republic—may have as much to do with our need to generate new product lines (or, as they say in business, with our need to "obsolete" old ones) as it does with any socially or politically conscious attempts to invite appreciation of previously excluded cultural forms. Our integration of other cultural forms into "the" cultural community must necessarily include exquisite attention so we can avoid merely turning those cultures into more commodities for our own consumption.

In our future, then, attention to pedagogy, its content, and its workings will hardly be as simple as it was in the past. Far from being a matter of introducing non-canonical texts to students in the classroom, we will need at the same time to offer a critical analysis of our own motives. Beyond that, we must consider reading those cultural works themselves as Mark Poster suggests Lefebre and Deborth and other Marxists of the '60s did: to "study how subordinated groups suffer domination and lose control over their communal life."[103]

All this self-assessment—constant attention not only to content, and pedagogy, but also to motives—seems a large order. And with all of our terms being themselves up for grabs, no wonder people have begun to talk of our profession in terms of the rhetoric of "crisis." Many blame theory, especially post-structuralist, deconstructive theory, for "causing" this "crisis." But if contemporary theory is viewed through postmodern rather than modern eyes, it might be seen not as a problem or as the cause of a crisis so much as part of the solution to present difficulties, and we might, with Hillis Miller, see our present not as one of "crisis" but as one of "challenge."[104] At the very least, we can see "crisis" itself as just one more instance of catachresis. A good place to start here is with a short genealogy of our use of the word *crisis* over the past few decades. To some extent the presence of that word in our vocabularies might have something to do with the work of Jürgen Habermas, who in the early 1970s described a "legitimation crisis" which he saw as perhaps the inevitable consequence of the passing of "personal testimony" or "individual erudition" as adequate, or even available, grounds for our work.[105] Theorists such as Jameson or Lyotard, who call for a reactivation of narrative in theory, are addressing just this notion of crisis. But Habermas's view was even bleaker, and the problems he saw were far less easily corrected. For him, during a "liberal" age the idea of aesthetic autonomy and the possibility that art could have a revolutionary component existed precisely because art was not needed for the support of the prevailing economic or political system. As a consequence, art could nurture residual needs that were not being fully met by or integrated into the system of needs. In late-capitalist society not only does this revolutionary component to art fade away, but all of the socio-cultural system, including literature, loses even its capacity of "reproduc[ing] the privatistic syndrome necessary for the existence of the system."[106]

The crisis Habermas identifies then occurs, because literature is no longer a site of potential revolutionary changing of consciousness that teachers could tap, or one place for the fulfilling of human needs not met by the prevailing socio-political-economic system. Indeed, it ceases even to be useful to the system that it aspires to critique, modify, mollify, or overturn. Simply put, the system no longer finds art necessary to legitimate itself.

This is hardly the only narrative that exists regarding the birth of the notion of "crisis" (I discovered with some dismay that there is an entire recent book that does nothing but survey theories of crisis theories[107]), and others may be at least as useful. In his introduction to *Postmodernism and Politics,* for instance, Jonathan Arac suggests the word *crisis* appeared in our rhetoric most recently in the 1920s, "set in motion by the modernizing wing of the academy." I suspect he has in his mind's ear here Habermas's notion, expressed in "Modernity—An Incomplete Project," that the modernist adopted the notion of crisis when he began to foresee the failure of the Enlightenment dream: that dream of developing science, morals, and art, all "scientifically," each according to its own "inner logic" that would ultimately result in some master discourse upon which we could all agree.[108] The crisis that followed from the recognition that this project was doomed to fail, Habermas suggests, is the hallmark of a failed modernism—but a notion it hangs onto nonetheless, because it *needs* that notion to ward off its own enervation.

In *Prophets of Extremity* Allen Megill traces the beginning of the notion of crisis to the same era and to "the death of faith in historicism" as well. Romantic thinkers had believed that all process moves forward and rounds back, but those whom Megill calls "prophets of extremity" discovered instead a circuitous journey without return, "a crisis without resolution, a dialectic without reintegration."[109] Given this narrative, Paul Bové is correct to say that our current situation should no longer be described in terms of crisis rhetoric at all, since crisis is a permanent feature of our society, and "critics have no right or reason to assume it will pass away."[110]

Still other versions of crisis are being played out in the profession today. Sam Weber suggests that the crisis in the humanities can be understood as the inevitable outgrowth of our "aporetic ends." By nature, English studies is involved with aesthetic judgments "in which the singularity of the object" of study "resists all attempts to subsume it under general concepts." Thus our founding aims themselves preclude "the establishment of a discipline of literary studies or literary criticism."[111] If I read Weber correctly, the title of the first *Glyph Textual Studies* volume (*Demarcating the Disciplines*) must be an elaborate joke, because precisely what defines us as a "field" is our inability, or in fact our principled refusal, to demarcate ourselves as a discipline.

Put all these descriptions of crisis together and one can hardly imagine any more profound state of irrelevance for the "institution" of "literature" and "the" "cultural" "community" than the ones that Habermas—or Hohendahl, or Eagleton, or Weber—describe. We are without a "field," without "authority," without consensus: we have no shared beliefs about exactly what our work is or how it ought to be done.

My own sense is that the most recent flurry of crisis rhetoric might have begun harmlessly enough, with our intramural debates in the 1970s over whether we could agree on the meanings of our texts, the Hirschean debate that always seemed to me a minor and an insoluble one because it always had at its heart a kind of psycho-religious base: those who needed to believe in a rigorously restricted and determinable set of meanings were those who believed man's fallen nature would, if not kept in check by rules and restrictions, burst out in aggressively individual and eccentric assertions of meaning that posed some danger I have never quite been able to come to fear. That debate has subsided, undoubtedly because, as both the Society for Critical Exchange dialogues and the members of the GRIP project suggest, critical positions are not by their nature "correctable" knowledge so much as they are the result of the imposition of some kind of raw power.[112] Critical debates are won not on the basis of "reason" but by reference to some authority presumed to be held by the arguer and the site from which he (usually) launches his argument. Positions emerge victorious because of their denominalization value: How transportable is it? What is its use for power and advancement? How teachable is it? How easily can it acquire disciples?[113]

If, then, our most recent "crisis" seems to have begun in a debate over the limits of interpretation, it has grown into the larger one we now face: the need to address the whole question of the role of the academic in society. This question is by its very nature a community project, and if there is one refrain heard regularly now, it is that nothing like a genuine sense of an intellectual community yet exists. Gerald Graff and Reginald Gibbons's collection of essays on *Criticism in the University,* for instance, opens with a plea that interpreters, researchers, and theorists begin to ask "how their work contributes to an intellectual community."[114]

Possibilitarian that I am, I am convinced that the strong sense of the *absence* of such a community can't help generating a strong *desire* for such a space. As anyone who reads theory knows, the space of desire (or will and purpose) is the one place thought to hold out the possibility for better times. It is not impossible to find even this space deconstructed by some—Dean MacCannell and

Juliet Flower MacCannell and Jean Baudrillard, most notably—
but I insist on remaining hopeful, and one does have to stand
somewhere.[115] Foucault believes this, too, and he retains his optimism by constructing a narrative I find very appealing. Twentieth-
century man, he says, inserted into the dialectic of production,
finds himself with needs and hungers that go far beyond what the
commodity culture that generated those needs can gratify. These
unfulfilled needs then have the potential to generate a space of
desire that he, like Bové, Aronowitz, Deleuze, and Weber, among
others, sees as a potential site for the hammering out of consensus
and the beginnings of community.[116] Lentricchia, Said, and
Derrida, following Nietzsche, see that same potential for community and then communal action generated not so much in the
space of desire but in a will and purpose capable of imposing
meaning on the world and of inspiring a faith that doing so can
make a difference.

Jürgen Habermas offers the most promising vision yet of exactly how an intellectual community, ideally one encompassing far
more than just the academic community, might be forged. In contrast to Hans Gadamer, who believed we can never escape the
hermeneutical circle and that understanding must always be nothing more than "pre-understanding," Habermas is convinced that
there is always a possibility for fruitful, rational social critique of
the ground on which we stand, with such a critique ideally ending
in something like a hard-won consensus. This critique would become possible by way of the carrying out, in what in *Structural
Transformation of the Public Sphere* (1962) he first referred to as
the "public sphere," that place where, among other things, a full
discussion of the workings of the regressive social institutions of
which we are a part could be conducted in what he calls an "ideal
speech situation." This situation occurs in what Habermas identifies as the third of three spheres, the other two being the state
and the "intimate," which includes family and household. For
Habermas, literature occupies a "privileged space" that makes it
a "third sphere midway between the depth of the autonomous
subject and the institutional life of political society." In 1976 Habermas suggested that ordinary language contained within it the
possibility of a "truth criterion" that might hold out the possibility
not only of generating communication, but of a place where a

genuinely democratic politics might be forged, the goal of such a public sphere being an intersubjective agreement on values and standards that could be used to resolve very practical questions.[117] Habermas sees institutionalized in this public sphere individuation, emancipation, extensions of communication free of domination. Peter Hohendahl finds this attempt to introduce the possibility of communication appealing, even though he is well aware of the criticisms of this model and offers probably the most articulate and complete discussion both of the model and of its inherent difficulties.[118]

For me, this "public sphere" is not necessarily best seen either as a geographical or a temporal "space." It exists rather as a sequence of particular moments for doing particular things with and for particular people: colleagues, students, one another. Finally, "public sphere" is catachretical, too; remembering that will help us behave less like the child on a car trip who, in constantly asking "Are we there yet?," loses the pleasure of the ride in contemplation of the arrival. We are always already *in* that public sphere, and remembering that fact can help us stop the infinitely regressive search for an "elsewhere" where we can be politically and socially useful.

Among others who find Habermas's vision appealing is Terry Eagleton, who, even while admitting its controversial nature and its vulnerability to charges that it is nostalgic or idealistic, nonetheless sees its aim as a re-connection of language and power.[119] Even as he advocates the academic humanist's participation in Habermas's public sphere, Eagleton anticipates objections that it is "too radical" by insisting that such a goal is not radical at all, but a return to our own historical beginnings. At this point the genealogy Eagleton provides is much like the one offered in Graff and Gibbons's *Criticism in the University*.[120] Up until the eighteenth century, "criticism" was not something that happened in a university at all, but what journalists and men of letters did as a matter of course. "Literature," in the sense of some kind of "high culture," was not separate from any other kind of writing that some men wrote and some other men critiqued. Hohendahl sees the whole modern notion of literary criticism as a "field" as closely tied to the rise of the liberal bourgeois public sphere. Literature, he says, originally had no elite status, but served "the emancipation movement of the middle class as an instrument to gain self esteem and to articulate its human demands against the absolutist state and the hierarchical society."[121] Bourdieu, Williams, Eagleton, Graff, Hohendahl, Webster,[122] Lentricchia, and Foucault have all written about the consequences that follow from this beginning of literary study as a discipline within an institutional framework. Much of Foucault's work, for instance, reminds us that the disciplinary mechanisms not just in our own field but in all the key institutions of society—the schools, the army, hospitals and prisons—came to "normalize" and "fix" those institutions. Lentricchia suggests that, if we join the historical understanding of Raymond Williams with that of Foucault, we will come out with something like the following: the late eighteenth century intellectual "refined" the concept of the "literary" to mean only imaginative writing, and in so doing provided an inadvertent service "on behalf of the coercive and even totalitarian tendencies of modern society." Academic humanists, that is, managed to concoct the perfect mechanism for "supervising and containing the 'literary' by keeping it enclosed in its own space, a modern mode of self-policing, as it were."[123] This self-policing, its mechanisms and the particular ways in which it is carried out, are the subject of some present and I presume future work, asking, as Foucault has, "What is an educational system after all . . . if not a ritualization of the word: if not a qualification of some fixing of roles for speakers, if not the constitution of a (diffuse) doctrinal group; if not a distribution and an appropriation of discourse, with all its learning and its powers?"[124]

"Scripting" our future will involve more exploration of the ways in which this past has created a future whose progress we might want to interdict: in part by interrogating that past, in part by deconstructing our own work in the classroom,[125] and in part by beginning to think of the possibility of engaging our work with that of people outside our profession in that public sphere Habermas envisions.

None of this sounds easy. I am also aware of the reservations of many people on both the left and the right about Habermas's public sphere. Eagleton and Hohendahl both worry that what we might accomplish when we academics enter that public sphere is not consensus but something closer to what Clifford Geertz first labeled *dissensus*. Success in the public sphere will depend upon our own skill, ability, and willingness to engage in persuasive straight talk—first among ourselves, and then with members of society at large. I'm inclined to say that the *ideal* ideal speech situation will have to be one in which academics will recognize that the social, economic, and in fact even intellectual status of the participants will be determined not by our positions within the academic culture, but by *how well we perform* within that sphere. That, in turn, will depend in part on the attitude with which academics enter that sphere. If we do so with insufficient belief in the basic intelligence of the general public, if we enter it with a dismissive air, unwilling to listen, prone to preach and pronounce, if (as Eagleton says) we perceive the "public" of the public sphere as "the masses," then the possibility for a classic public sphere will disintegrate before our eyes.[126] Perry Anderson sees this ideal speech situation as inherently pedagogical: "the forum becomes a classroom."[127] But it will not be a classroom over which academics will necessarily preside; it will be instead one in which we ought to see ourselves called upon to do far more listening than talking.

Despite the fact that, like Gadamer, Lyotard is convinced that Habermas's public sphere and ideal speech situation are impossible dreams (because, outside of a particular cultural context, any discussion that takes place within it would necessarily be unintelligible to its participants), and despite the fact that Lyotard is convinced there's no way to reach consensus (because language games and social meaning must inevitably dissolve into a babble of conversations eventuating in no more than the triumph of the seductive "idea" of communication, rather than its actuality), Lyotard's *own* visionary project seems not altogether distinguishable from that of Habermas. When, in his *Postmodern Condition,* Lyotard advocates our going beyond attention to "knowing how," or beyond "knowing that" to the far preferable states of "knowing how to live" and "how to listen," and when he suggests that these proper kinds of knowing eventuate in "the consensus that permits such knowledge to be circumscribed [making] it possible to distinguish one who knows from one who doesn't," and when he suggests that this same knowledge is "what constitutes the culture of a people," Lyotard sounds very like Habermas.[128]

A major difficulty in talking about Habermas's vision of a

public sphere where consensus and community can be achieved is that critics who attack his vision seem at times to be arguing *one* Habermas, when in fact there are many. Early and late Habermas look very different. Paul Rabinow, for instance, urges us to prefer Richard Rorty's New Pragmatism, his "consensus" view of truth in which the goal is "conversation" in which we all ask one another not ultimate philosophical questions that lead us round and round the same old oppositions, but pragmatic questions like Rorty's favorite, "Why did you find what you just said so appealing?" Rabinow prefers Rorty's version of conversation because he believes it lacks the "foundationalism" he sees in Habermas.[129] But I see two problems here. First, as Hohendahl notes, the later Habermas is no longer after some absolute or transcendent truth, but after attempts to identify and tap into what he calls "knowledge-constituting interests."[130] This later Habermas is also not the one Perry Anderson criticizes as "the curious innocence of Habermas' vision," calling the consensus to which Habermas aspires nothing but a "salve."[131]

A second difficulty with Habermas's public sphere is the same one Lentricchia sees in Rorty's New Pragmatism—which is not surprising, since increasingly in the 1970s Habermas borrowed from the American pragmatists from William James to Rorty himself. If the notion of "conversation" freed of the monologism of power and of master discourse is, as Lentricchia says, not a conversation at all, but a "pluralism that is no more than the babble of many tongues," then I suppose there is little hope for a communal future.[132] But it's unnecessary to get harpooned on either of those horns, where the only two options are seen to be either a "master tongue" or the "babble of competing and mutually incomprehensible individuals." It also does not necessarily follow, as Christopher Norris suggests in *The Contest of Faculties* and Michael Ryan in *Marxism and Deconstruction,* that if we behave as some version of a pragmatist we are necessarily operating in the realm of blind, unexamined "commonsense." Perhaps my dream is one of being a pro-theory pragmatist, something Charles Sanders Peirce, at least, would have said is possible. Worrying about whether such a pragmatism might collapse ultimately into an earlier Habermasian realm of pure ideas, or about how it might yield nothing but a naturalized or commonsense ideology, is so far down the road that I cannot worry overmuch about it, partly because I suspect such worry is another instance of that kind of millennial thinking that spares us having to do anything here and now.

Even if we can no longer believe in the kind of "truth criterion" that Habermas used to imagine (and Michael Ryan is right to warn that such a belief would need to be deconstructed and, once deconstructed, would no doubt reveal itself to be a suppression of difference and of the margins), I can't see why we can't nonetheless aim for consensus and the "bloc politics" that both Bové and Aronowitz advocate. What Eagleton calls the "counter-public sphere" might hold out hope for our future, since it represents a place and space where "previously repressed or inarticulate needs, interests and desires can find symbolic form—a place where repressed or censored forms can find articulation."[133]

This sounds like a program everyone on the left in the profession could embrace, but this is not always true. Mark Poster, like Perry Anderson, prefers Foucault to Habermas because Foucault is suspicious of all systems; Poster is dubious about the possibility of genuine communication because, unlike Habermas, he questions the relation of reason to democracy, seeing reason as "nothing but a form of power" and communication as having a "contaminating impact on our lives ... such things as electronic technologies, consumer ads especially," all of which he sees as contaminating not just our speech but our whole mode of perception as well.[134]

But at points like this I feel uncomfortable. Insisting *nothing* is possible does not necessarily reveal more integrity or wisdom than hoping does. It is easier for me to side with Habermas or Lyotard, because the former rejects a necessary power/knowledge relation and holds out instead for a belief in the power of reflection, moving critical theory and all of us who practice it closer to a point where language and action might intersect; the latter believes all those new technologies that Foucault and Poster worry about will not just "contaminate" but may instead give everyone access to information in our postmodern society, a phenomenon that can lead to a democratization of knowledge such as we have never yet seen.

I posit this possibilitarian future in the face of suspicions about it that emanate not only from the "radical" wing of the profession, but from the "conservative" as well. I have already said Stanley

Fish finds the notion of consensus among professional academics absurd and destructive, because we operate on a model that is conflictual rather than cooperative.[135] But this view relies on several assumptions open to challenge: one, that the only "work" academics might want to do is to interpret texts; another, that "belief" is something one cannot get outside of, change, or adjust in the face of a desire for collaboration that is stronger than, and can therefore win out over, a desire to retain one's personal beliefs.

The philosopher Nancy Fraser suggests we can look at our philosophical stances as revealing what she calls "emblems of value."[136] One "emblem of value" of the pragmatist is that of "using common sense" to "get things done." Ultimately a collaborative future may rely on getting others in our profession to adopt such pragmatist "emblems." My own reading of academic humanists today is that we are uncomfortable with collaborative work. To some extent Fish is right to suggest that our whole history, unlike that of scientists in some situations at least, has been one of competition and conflict. Add to that our long history of Romantic consciousness—Paul de Man's insistence, for instance, that "collectivity" is always a "dodge" from the "problems of individual consciousness"—and such a vision insures that we will remain locked or marooned in our separate spaces. Nothing in deconstruction or post-structuralist theory, as I read it, necessarily calls for such isolation. Derrida's letter of May 18, 1982, for instance, was nothing if not an open, international call for suggestions, advice, participation: collaboration.[137] And even if Foucault insists that all communication systems are restrictive, limiting, determinative of what can and cannot be said, at the same time he is careful to insist that exchange and communication are "positive forces at play within complex but restrictive systems." If discourse functions as ritual, as he suggests, *fellowships* of discourse still preserve and reproduce discourse. Despite the "strict regulation" it must undergo, it *does* circulate, "without those in possession being dispossessed by this . . . distribution."[138] In an ideal speech situation, then (like that of the ancient poet, for whom a telling or retelling of the poem to a new audience hardly deprived him of his wares), the academic humanist might become a broker of theory, a sharer of his wares, a listener to others outside the academic community, one who places him or herself in the same context with other oppositional forces outside the university in a public sphere, in order to help theorize what Bové calls "the counterhegemonic in the light of . . . local struggles."[139]

This future I would like to see us "script" is one in which we all engage in collaboratively writing a "text" for our "cultural community," one that would resemble Stephen Tyler's eloquent description of an ideal postmodern ethnography: "A cooperatively evolved text consisting of fragments of discourse intended to evoke in the minds of both reader and writer an emergent fantasy of a possible world of commonsense reality, and thus to provoke an aesthetic integration that will have a therapeutic effect. It is, in a word, poetry—not in its textual form, but in its return to the original context and function of everyday speech, [which] evoked memories of the ethos of community and therefore provoked hearers to act ethically."[140]

We need, of course, to remain wary lest that dream turn out to be one more kind of monologism or triumph of a shared but unexamined "rationality" doomed to fail, as Habermas suggests the dream of modernism failed. The antidote to such a future might be the coupling of our dream of collaboration and shared discourse with a full understanding that the sharing might be largely a *local* sharing, and the consensus at which we arrive the beginning of what Bové and Aronowitz call "bloc politics," "specific intellectuals engaged in the struggle of autonomous groups in their local situations" working in what Adorno refers to as "constellations."[141] If, as Lyotard suggests, we can achieve the dream of the "break up of the grand narratives," we might begin again to privilege "corridor talk"—not the aimless talk we have come to refer to as "recipe sharing" of pedagogical "tricks" to get us through a composition class, but a sharing that might lead us closer to forming something that could replace our "interpretive communities" with "interpretive federations."[142] Among other things, such "federations" could help to usher in what Kenneth Frampton calls an age of "critical regionalism." If all art tends to gravitate toward pure entertainment, pure commodity, or pure technique (as in modernism), then such interpretive federations might collaborate with the community at large in reinventing what Frampton refers to as an *arrière-garde* art having "the capacity to cultivate resistant, identity-giving culture."[143]

SUSAN R. HORTON

My "scripting" here can be misconstrued as a call for a nostalgic return to simpler times. It can be misconstrued as the first tentative steps toward a new monologism. Representing the space of the broker of theory as I have here can surely be taken to be disingenuous, since obviously I have hardly revealed myself to be reluctant to take positions relative to the theory I have pretended only to broker. Still, I see what I have done here not as *representation* so much as *evocation* of one possible scripting of our future. Evocation "presents no objects and represents none, yet it makes available through absence what can be conceived but not presented."[144] My essay evokes here no specific program but my own desire for a more genuinely communal future, and my own will to help bring that about.

If that future is one in which we will all be more self-effacing, more involved in listening to others (students, people in the community, "marginal" peoples) than in displaying our wares, more engaged in the brokering of theory than in mystification of theory, it is at the same time a future that will reward us for our self-effacement by offering us the prospect of a future where we will be more connected not only with one another but also with the political, defined as Alicia Ostriker so aptly defines it, as that which contains "wit, grace, passion, eloquence, playfulness, compression, vitality, and freshness."[145]

It is a future I welcome.

NOTES

1. See Gregory Ulmer, *Applied Grammatology: Post(e) Pedagogy from Jacques Derrida to Joseph Beuys* (Baltimore: Johns Hopkins University Press, 1985), p. 33.
2. Richard Ohmann, *English in America: A Radical View of the Profession* (New York: Oxford University Press, 1976), p. 178.
3. Again, see Ulmer's *Applied Grammatology.*
4. See Jürgen Habermas, "Modernity—An Incomplete Project," in *The Anti-Aesthetic: Essays on Postmodern Culture,* ed. Hal Foster (Port Townsend, Wash.: Bay Press, 1983).
5. See Michael M. J. Fischer, "Ethnicity and the Post-Modern Arts of

Memory," in *Writing Culture: The Poetics and Politics of Ethnography,* ed. James Clifford and George E. Marcus (Berkeley: University of California Press, 1986), p. 201.

6. Jane Tompkins, "Indians: Textualism, Morality, and the Problem of History," *Critical Inquiry* 13:1 (Autumn 1986): 101-17.

7. Peter Uwe Hohendahl, *The Institution of Criticism* (Ithaca: Cornell University Press, 1982), p. 38.

8. Jean-François Lyotard, *The Postmodern Condition: A Report on Knowledge,* trans. Geoff Bennington and Brian Massumi, foreword by Fredric Jameson (Minneapolis: University of Minnesota Press, 1984), p. 17.

9. Niklas Luhmann, cited in Samuel Weber, "Caught in the Act of Reading," in *Demarcating the Disciplines: Philosophy, Literature, Art, Glyph Textual Studies I* (Minneapolis: University of Minnesota Press, 1986), p. 195.

10. Jacques Derrida, "The Age of Hegel," in *Demarcating the Disciplines,* p. 33.

11. See especially Wlad Godzich's introduction to Samuel Weber, *Institution and Interpretation* (Minneapolis: University of Minnesota Press, 1987), pp. 156-57.

12. Ulmer, *Applied Grammatology,* p. 128.

13. See *Literature among Discourses: The Spanish Golden Age,* ed. and intro. by Wlad Godzich and Nicholas Spadaccini (Minneapolis: University of Minnesota Press, 1986), p. xiii. See also the works of Peter or Christa Bürger, both of whom emphasize the social aspect of literature by using Walter Benjamin's model for a definition of literature as an "institute." See also Peter Hohendahl's citing of Peter Burger's *Theorie der Avant Garde* (Frankfort, 1974) and Christa Bürger's *Der Ursprungder burgerlichen Institution Kunst* (Frankfort, 1977) in Hohendahl, *The Institution of Criticism.*

14. Terry Eagleton, *The Function of Criticism: From the Spectator to Post-Structuralism* (London: Verso, 1984), pp. 76-77.

15. Derrida, "The Age of Hegel," p. 33.

16. Dominick LaCapra, "Writing the History of Criticism Now?," in *History and Criticism* (Ithaca: Cornell University Press, 1985), p. 111.

17. J. Hillis Miller, "The Joy of Writing," *MLA Newsletter* (Fall 1986): 4.

18. Weber, *Institution and Interpretation,* p. 152.

19. Paul de Man, *Blindness and Insight: Essays in the Rhetoric of Contemporary Criticism,* 2nd ed. rev. (Minneapolis: University of Minnesota Press, 1983), pp. 148, 150.

20. Denis Hollier, *The Politics of Prose: Essays on Sartre*, trans. Jeffrey Mehlmann, foreword Jean-François Lyotard (Minneapolis: University of Minnesota Press, 1986), p. 45.

21. See Nancy F. Cott, "Feminist Theory and Feminist Movements: The Past Before Us," in *What is Feminism?*, ed. Juliet Mitchell and Ann Oakley (New York: Pantheon Books, 1986), and Sandra Gilbert and Susan Gubar, "Forward into the Past," in *Historical Studies and Literary Criticism*, ed. Jerome McGann (Madison: University of Wisconsin Press, 1985).

22. Frank Lentricchia, *Criticism and Social Change* (Chicago: University of Chicago Press, 1983), pp. 118–19.

23. Ibid., p. 118; Jacques Derrida, "Difference," in *Speech and Phenomena and Other Essays on Husserl's Theory of Signs*, trans. David B. Allison (Evanston: Northwestern University Press, 1973), pp. 142–43; Jacques Derrida, *Of Grammatology*, trans. Gayatri Chakravorty Spivak (Baltimore: Johns Hopkins University Press, 1974), p. 5.

24. Richard Rorty, *The Consequences of Pragmatism* (Minneapolis: University of Minnesota Press, 1982), pp. xxi, xl.

25. Weber, *Institution and Interpretation*, p. 138.

26. Gayatri Chakravorty Spivak, *In Other Worlds: Essays in Cultural Politics* (London and New York: Methuen, 1987); Habermas, "Modernity—An Incomplete Project," p. 5.

27. Walter Benjamin, "Theses on the Philosophy of History," in *Illuminations*, trans. Harry Zohn (New York: Schocken Books, 1969), p. 261.

28. For one of the harsher evaluations of our cultural community and especially its theorists, one can always look to Terry Eagleton, especially *The Function of Criticism*.

29. See Jonathan Arac, *Critical Genealogies* (New York: Columbia University Press, 1987), as well as Paul Bové, *Intellectuals in Power: A Genealogy of Critical Humanism* (New York: Columbia University Press, 1986).

30. Rorty, *Consequences of Pragmatism*, p. xl.

31. Hayden White, *The Content of the Form: Narrative Discourse and Historical Representation* (Baltimore: Johns Hopkins University Press, 1987), p. 142.

32. LaCapra, "Writing the History of Criticism Now?," p. 110.

33. J. Hillis Miller, "The Triumph of Theory, the Resistance to Reading, and the Question of the Material Base," *PMLA* 102:3 (May 1987):283.

34. Ibid., p. 286.

35. See Gerald Graff, "Taking Cover in Coverage," in *Profession '86* (New York: Modern Language Association, 1986), p. 41.

36. Christopher Norris, *The Contest of Faculties: Philosophy and Theory after Deconstruction* (London and New York: Methuen, 1985), p. 6.

37. See Lentricchia, *Criticism and Social Change,* pp. 12–13.

38. Hohendahl, *The Institution of Criticism,* p. 30.

39. Jean Baudrillard, *Forget Foucault* (New York: Columbia University, Semiotext(e), 1987), p. 38.

40. Weber, *Institution and Interpretation,* pp. 134–35.

41. See especially *Critical Exchange # 18* (Spring 1985), as well as "Institutional Issues in the Humanities," *Critical Exchange # 19,* 1986. Both in format and in content this journal, published by the Society for Critical Exchange under the general editorship of James J. Sosnoski, is in the forefront of critical debate in our profession. Its articles are as often as not transcriptions of dialogues that take place among colleagues over issues of concern in the humanities, including most especially questions of the role of the humanist in today's society.

42. Eagleton, *The Function of Criticism,* p. 78.

43. See this exchange in "Institutional Issues in the Humanities" *Critical Exchange,* p. 34.

44. Cornel West, "Ethics and Action in Fredric Jameson's Marxist Hermeneutics," in *Postmodernism and Politics,* ed. Jonathan Arac (Minneapolis: University of Minnesota Press, 1986), p. 126.

45. Paul Bové, "The Ineluctability of Difference: Scientific Pluralism and the Critical Intelligence," in *Postmodernism and Politics.*

46. Jacques Derrida, "The Conflict of Faculties," in *Languages of Knowledge and of Inquiry,* ed. Michael Riffaterre (New York: Columbia University Press, 1983). See also Derrida's "The Principle of Reason," pp. 12–13.

47. Here I urge a careful reading of Derrida's "The Age of Hegel" in *Demarcating the Disciplines.*

48. Derrida, *Of Grammatology,* p. 162.

49. LaCapra, "Writing the History of Criticism Now?," p. 99.

50. See Hohendahl, *The Institution of Criticism,* p. 42.

51. Jacques Derrida, *Memoires for Paul de Man* (New York: Columbia University Press, 1986), p. 42.

52. J. Hillis Miller, *The Ethics of Reading: Kant, de Man, Eliot, Trollope, James, and Benjamin* (New York: Columbia University Press, 1987), p. 106.

53. See Elizabeth Bruss, *Beautiful Theories: The Spectacle of Discourse*

SUSAN R. HORTON

in Contemporary Criticism (Baltimore: Johns Hopkins University Press, 1982), pp. 16–17.

54. Michel Foucault, *The Discourse on Language,* in *The Archaeology of Knowledge and the Discourse on Language* (New York: Harper Colophon Books, 1972), p. 220.

55. Peter Stallybrass and Allon White, *The Politics and Poetics of Transgression* (Ithaca: Cornell University Press, 1986), pp. 31, 37.

56. Harsh words aimed at theory and theorists are not difficult to find. The most cogent are Edward Said's in *The World, the Text, the Critic* (Cambridge, Mass.: Harvard University Press, 1983); Eagleton, *The Function of Criticism;* Lentricchia, *Criticism and Social Change;* and the essay from which this quotation was taken, Donald Pease here being quoted by Paul Bové in "Variations on Authority" in *The Yale Critics: Deconstruction in America,* ed. Jonathan Arac, Wlad Godzich, and Wally Martin (Minneapolis: University of Minnesota Press, 1983), p. 6.

57. Rorty, *Consequences of Pragmatism,* pp. xl–xli.

58. See especially early chapters in *English in America.*

59. Lentricchia, *Criticism and Social Change,* pp. 10, 7, 13.

60. See any of the volumes produced by the Society for Critical Exchange and any of the drafts of the GRIP reports as well.

61. William Cain, "English in America Reconsidered: Theory, Criticism, Marxism, and Social Change," in *Criticism in the University,* ed. Graff and Gibbons, p. 92.

62. Lentricchia, *Criticism and Social Change,* p. 110.

63. See Stanley Fish, "Profession Despise Thyself: Fear and Loathing in Literary Studies," *Critical Inquiry* 10:2 (December 1983), as well as the subsequent debate and responses in later issues of that journal, and various issues of *Critical Exchange* as well.

64. Said, *The World, the Text, the Critic,* pp. 247, 242.

65. See Fredric Jameson, *The Political Unconscious* (Ithaca: Cornell University Press, 1981).

66. Said, *The World, the Text, the Critic,* p. 2.

67. Stallybrass and White, *The Politics and Poetics of Transgression,* p. 80.

68. See Clifford, ed., *Writing Culture,* p. 13.

69. See especially the "Men in Feminism" issue of *Critical Exchange* #18 (Spring 1985).

70. Copy taken from advance advertisements for Pierre Bourdieu's *Homo Academicus* (Cambridge, Mass.: MIT Press, forthcoming).

71. Hohendahl, *The Institution of Criticism,* pp. 235–36.

72. Eagleton, *The Function of Criticism,* p. 67.

73. Tullio Maranhao, *Therapeutic Discourse and Socratic Dialogue* (Madison: University of Wisconsin Press, 1986), pp. xi–xii.
74. Eagleton, *The Function of Criticism*, p. 108.
75. Said, *The World, the Text, the Critic*, p. 241.
76. Jim Merod, *The Political Responsibility of the Critic* (Ithaca: Cornell University Press, 1987).
77. See especially Bové's *Intellectuals in Power,* but also his earlier essays, most particularly "The Ineluctability of Difference."
78. Pierre Bourdieu and Jean-Claude Passeron, *Reproduction in Education, Society, and Culture,* trans. Richard Nice, foreword by Tom Bottomore (London and Beverly Hills: SAGE [Studies in Social and Educational Change], 1977).
79. Said, *The World, the Text, the Critic*, p. 229.
80. See Haug, *Critique of Commodity Aesthetics* (Minneapolis: University of Minnesota Press, 1986), and Cornelius Castoriadis, *The Imaginary Institution of Society: Creativity and Autonomy in the Social-Historical World,* trans. Kathleen McLaughlin (London: Polity Press, and Cambridge, Mass.: MIT Press, 1987).
81. Bové, "The Ineluctability of Difference," p. 4.
82. See Terry Eagleton, "Capitalism, Modernism, and Postmodernism," in *Against the Grain,* p. 132.
83. Said, *The World, the Text, the Critic.*
84. Bové, "The Ineluctability of Difference," pp. 6–7.
85. Lynne Hanley, "Demilitarizing Literature and Literary Studies," *Radical America* 20, pp. 17–28.
86. Gayatri Chakravorty Spivak, conversation following a lecture at the Harvard Feminist Studies Theory Group, Spring 1987.
87. For one demonstration of the kind of information that kind of question can offer, see my "Response to Robert Scholes" in *Critical Theory and the Teaching of Literature,* Proceedings of the Northeastern University Center for Literary Studies, ed. Stuart Peterfreund (1985), pp. 51–57.
88. See Mary Louise Pratt, "Interpretive Strategies/Strategic Interpretations: On Anglo-American Reader-Response Criticism," in Arac, ed., *Postmodernism and Politics,* p. 34.
89. See *The Pedagogical Imperative: Teaching as a Literary Genre, Yale French Studies* 63 (1982), and Cary Nelson, ed., *Theory in the Classroom* (Urbana: University of Illinois Press, 1986).
90. See William Cain, *The Crisis in Criticism: Theory, Literature, and Reform in English Studies* (Baltimore: Johns Hopkins University Press, 1984), and *Re-Reading English,* ed. Peter Widdowson (London and New York: Methuen, 1982), especially Tony Davies's essay

in that collection, "Common Sense and Critical Practice: Teaching Literature," pp. 32–43.

91. See especially Ulmer's chapter entitled "The Scene of Teaching," in *Applied Grammatology*.

92. Widdowson, introduction to *Re-Reading English*.

93. Bourdieu and Passeron, *Reproduction in Education, Society, and Culture*, p. 91. I have in mind here especially David Punter's extremely interesting essay "University English Teaching: Some Observations on Symbolism and Reflexivity," in *Demarcating the Disciplines*, in which he offers readings of the power relations inherent in, and the rewards attendant upon, teaching in a seminar format, large lecture, private conference, etc.

94. See Roland Barthes, "Writers, Intellectuals, Teachers," *Tel Quel* (Fall 1977), discussed also in Vincent Leitch's "Deconstruction and Pedagogy," in Nelson, ed., *Theory in the Classroom*, pp. 49–50.

95. See Lyotard, *The Postmodern Condition*, pp. 52–53.

96. Eagleton, *The Function of Criticism*, p. 92, quoting Peter Hohendahl. See also Stallybrass and White, *The Politics and Poetics of Transgression*, quoting Georges Balandier's *Political Anthropology* (p. 14).

97. Lyotard, *The Postmodern Condition*.

98. Stanley Aronowitz, *Crisis in Historical Materialism* (New York: Praeger, 1981), p. 96. See also Aronowitz, *Education under Siege*, with Henry Giroux (South Hadley, Mass.: Bergin and Garvey, 1985).

99. Paul Ricoeur, "Universal Civilization and National Cultures" (1961), rpt. in *History and Truth*, trans. Charles A. Kelbey (Evanston: Northwestern University Press, 1965), p. 283.

100. Pierre Bourdieu, *Distinction: A Social Critique of the Judgement of Taste*, trans. Richard Nice (Cambridge, Mass.: Harvard University Press), p. xi.

101. Laurie Finke, "The Rhetorics of Marginality: Why I Do Feminist Theory," *Tulsa Studies in Women's Literature* 5:2 (Fall 1986): 251–72.

102. See Stallybrass and White, *The Politics and Poetics of Transgression*, p. 25.

103. Mark Poster, *Foucault, Marxism, and History* (London: Polity Press, 1984), p. 18.

104. See Miller, "The Triumph of Theory."

105. See Jürgen Habermas, "Does Philosophy Still Have a Purpose" (1971), rpt. in *Philosophical-Political Profiles*, trans. Frederick G. Lawrence (Cambridge, Mass.: MIT Press, 1983), pp. 1–3.

106. See Hohendahl, *The Institution of Criticism,* p. 38.

107. See James O'Connor, *The Meaning of Crisis: A Theoretical Introduction* (London: Basil Blackwell, 1987).

108. Arac, ed., *Postmodernism and Politics,* p. xxiv; Habermas, "Modernity—An Incomplete Project."

109. See Allen Megill, *Prophets of Extremity: Nietzsche, Heidegger, Foucault, and Derrida* (Berkeley: University of California Press, 1987), p. 19.

110. Bové, "The Ineluctability of Difference," p. 22.

111. Weber, *The Institution of Criticism,* pp. 141–44.

112. See the *GRIP Report,* 2nd Draft, Vol. I, especially p. 37.

113. For an extended discussion of this issue, see *Critical Exchange #15* (Winter 1984).

114. Graff and Gibbons, *Criticism in the University,* p. 11.

115. See Dean MaCannell and Juliet Flower MacCannell, *The Time of the Sign: A Semiotic Interpretation of Modern Culture* (Bloomington: Indiana University Press, 1982), p. 28, and Jean Baudrillard, *Forget Foucault and Forget Baudrillard* (New York: Columbia University Press Semiotext[e], 1987).

116. Michel Foucault, "Preface to Transgression," in *Language, Counter-Memory, Practice,* ed. and trans. Donald F. Bouchard (Ithaca: Cornell University Press, 1977), pp. 49–50.

117. Jürgen Habermas, *Communications and the Evolution of Society,* trans. Thomas McCarthy (Boston: Beacon Press, 1976; London: Heinemann, 1979).

118. Hohendahl, *The Institution of Criticism,* especially "Jürgen Habermas and His Critics," pp. 242–80.

119. See, e.g., Terry Eagleton, *The Function of Criticism,* p. 14, where he sees that the public sphere holds out the promise of "cement[ing] a new power block at the level of the sign."

120. Graff and Gibbons, *Criticism in the University,* p. 8.

121. Hohendahl, *The Institution of Criticism,* p. 52.

122. Grant Webster, *The Republic of Letters* (Baltimore: Johns Hopkins University Press, 1979).

123. Lentricchia, *Criticism and Social Change,* p. 54.

124. Foucault, *The Discourse,* p. 227.

125. In this regard, again I would recommend David Punter's essay in *Demarcating the Disciplines* as one model, Vincent Leitch's essay in Cary Nelson's *Theory in the Classroom* as another, and maybe even my own short response to Robert Scholes referred to earlier as another.

126. Eagleton, *The Function of Criticism,* p. 80.

127. Perry Anderson, *In the Tracks of Historical Materialism* (London: Verso, 1983), p. 66.
128. Lyotard, *The Postmodern Condition*, p. 19.
129. Rabinow, "Representations Are Social Facts," p. 239.
130. See Hohendahl, *The Institution of Criticism*, p. 271, and the writing of Habermas from which he quotes: "The knowledge-constitutive interests take form in the medium of work, language, and power" (Jürgen Habermas, *Knowledge and Human Interests*, trans. Jeremy Shapiro [Boston: Beacon Press, 1971], p. 314).
131. Anderson, *In the Tracks*, pp. 66, 64.
132. Lentricchia, *Criticism and Social Change*, p. 16.
133. Eagleton, *The Function of Criticism*.
134. Poster, *Foucault, Marxism, and History*, pp. 13, 32.
135. I am basing my assessment here not so much on a particular piece of Fish's work as on a general understanding of the course of his work over the past fifteen years or so, and on private conversations in which we have engaged during that time.
136. Nancy Fraser, "Social Critique: Stories or Theories," English Institute paper, August 1987.
137. See Derrida, letter reprinted in *SubStance* 35 (1982): 80–84.
138. Foucault, *The Discourse on Language*, p. 225.
139. Bové, "The Ineluctability of Difference," pp. 6–7.
140. Stephen Tyler, "Post-Modern Ethnography: From Document of the Occult to Occult Document," in *Writing Culture*, pp. 125–26.
141. Bové, "The Ineluctability of Difference," p. 20; Theodor Adorno, cited in Rainer Nagele's excellent essay "The Scene of the Other: Theodor W. Adorno's Negative Dialectic in the Context of Poststructuralism," in Arac, ed., *Postmodernism and Politics*, p. 92.
142. Lyotard, *The Postmodern Condition*, p. 15; Rabinow, "Representations Are Social Facts," pp. 253, 256.
143. Kenneth Frampton, "Towards a Critical Regionalism: Six Points for an Architecture of Resistance," in *The Anti-Aesthetic*, ed. Hal Foster, p. 20.
144. Tyler, "Post-Modern Ethnography."
145. Alicia Ostriker, "Dancing at the Devil's Party: Some Notes on Politics and Poetry," in *Critical Inquiry* 13:3 (Spring 1987): 584.

Notes on Contributors

RICHARD A. BARNEY is completing his doctoral work at the University of Virginia. He has published essays in *Genre* and the *James Joyce Quarterly*, a bibliography on deconstructive criticism in a supplement of *Society for Critical Exchange Reports* (1980), and an essay surveying American deconstruction in *Tracing Literary Theory* (1987). He is currently writing on the sociopolitical basis for the emergence of the novel of education in eighteenth-century Britain.

MICHAEL CLARK is associate professor of English at the University of California at Irvine. He has published books on Michel Foucault and Jacques Lacan and articles on literary theory, American literature, and popular culture, as well as editing a special issue of the *New Orleans Review*.

EDWARD DAVENPORT is associate professor of English at John Jay College of Criminal Justice. His articles have appeared in *Mosaic, Et cetera,* and *Philosophy of the Social Sciences,* as well as in Paul Hernadi's collection, *What is Literature?* He is currently studying how Spinoza's theory of a scientific method of interpreting scripture has influenced modern criticism.

DAVID GORMAN teaches in the Humanities Department at Fordham University. He has published essays and reviews dealing with literary theory and the history of literary scholarship in *Diacritics, Poetics Today, Critical Texts, Annals of Scholarship,* and *Social Epistemology.* He is working on a study of historicism and its rivals in modern literary and intellectual history.

SUSAN R. HORTON is professor of English at the University of Massachusetts at Boston, where, having been persuaded by her own arguments voiced in her chapter here, she has become chair of the English Department. She is the author of *Interpreting Interpreting, The Reader in the Dickens World, Thinking through Writing,* and various articles on Dickens, critical theory, women's literature, and composition theory. She is currently working on the 1989 Dickens survey for the *Dickens Studies Annual,* an exploration of the fair in Dickens and Hardy, and further essays on cultural politics and the university.

WILLIAM A. JOHNSEN is professor of English at Michigan State University. Johnsen publishes in the areas of British, Irish, and comparative literature, as well as critical theory, and is completing a book on the crisis of modernization revealed in the texts of High Modernism.

JOSEPH NATOLI is English & American literature bibliographer at Michigan State University, where he also teaches in the Humanities Department. He has published "heterogeneously": from textual criticism, phenomenology, psychology, and literary theory to Blake, Shakespeare, Joan Didion, and Walker Percy. He has just completed *Re-presenting the Later Dickens* and *Disorder's Literary Presence.*

ELLIE RAGLAND-SULLIVAN is professor of English at the University of Florida in Gainesville. Her books include *Rabelais and Panurge* and *Jacques Lacan and the Philosophy of Psychoanalysis.* She is now completing *From Freud to Lacan* and is also working on *A Lacanian Poetics.* She is the editor of the newly founded Lacan journal, *The Newsletter of the Freudian Field (NFF),* and has written over fifty articles in journals such as *SubStance, The Literary Review, Romance Quarterly, James Joyce Quarterly, Gradiva, Hartford Studies in Literature,* and the *Journal of Higher Education.*

Index

Index

Index

Index

mimesis, and Girard, 116–44 *passim*;
cultural, 119; of appropriation, 124;
and rivalry, 126, 134; and mode, 131;
conflictive, 132

mind, Cartesian, and Said, 185; Vichian
and Said, 185

Mitchell, Juliet, 65, 175

mode, and myth, 128

Modern Language Association, and feeble
democratization, 172; convention, 283–
84

modern temper, 17

modernism, 17; in 1930s art, 223;
contrasted with postmodernism, 256,
294; and Habermas, 268, 302; its
failure, 311

monologism, 20

More, Paul Elmer, 222

More, Thomas, 204

Muller, John, 39, 62

myth, 24; and ritual, 116–44 *passim*; and
history, 128; and mode, 128

La Mythologie blanche, 42

Nabokov, Vladimir, 151, 153

Naletov, Igor, 156–57

Nancy, Jean-Luc, 40

narrative, and history and Lyotard, 252–
55; and society, 254

Natoli, Joseph, 165

Nelson, Cary, 296

Nelson, John, 173

Neumann, Erich, 122

New Criticism, 136, 190, 205, 206, 223–
33 *passim*; and de Man, 96; and Said,
187; and politics, 223–25; and Kant,
227–28; and deconstruction, 230–31;
and post-structuralism, 230–31

New Critics, and the verbal icon, 192

New Historians, and Lyotard, 254

New Historicism, as a New
Anthropologism, 182

New Humanists, 222–23

New Pragmatism, 308

New Republic, 222

New Science, 186

Nietzsche, Friedrich, 167; and Said, 186;
and Foucault, 189; and genealogy, 211;
and de Man, 272

Nineteen Eighty-Four, 136–44

1965 Colloquium in the Philosophy of
Science, 162

Nixon, Rob, 258–60

noise, and Serres, 23

nominalism, 6; and materialism, 231–60
passim; political, 231–260 *passim*; and
critical practice, 238

normal science, and Kuhn, 162–72 *passim*

Norris, Christopher, 61, 99–97, 308;
politics, theory and common-sense, 276

observer, psychological, sociological,
literary, 154

Oedipus, 124–25

Oedipus Tyrannos, 125

Of Grammatology, 272, 279

Ohmann, Richard, 223–24, 230, 234,
290, 293, 297; and teaching of texts,
287

Open University, 292

opposition, in Fish and Ohmann, 288

oppositional critics, and politics, 292–97

order, of the state, and the production of
semiotic distinctions, 250

L'Ordre du discours, 214–15

Orientalism, 137, 170, 189–90

Origins of German Tragic Drama, 213

Ornicar?, 38

Orwell, George, 131, 137–44

panopticism, 8, 12, 18, 19–21, 18, 19,
24, 26; and cultural critique, 21; and
will-to-power, 22; and surveillance, 22;
and de Man's rhetorical structure, 107

paradigms, 163–64

parasite, and Serres, 25

Parker, Andrew, 99

Parker, Hershel, 192–94

parody, postmodern, 255–56

Partisan Review, 222

past, and future, 279

pedagogy, and metaphor in John Locke,
105–8; renewed interest in, 296; post-
structuralist future of, 297; and
Lyotard, 297; and future, 300; and
ideal speech situation, 307

Peirce, Charles Sanders, 308

performance, critical, 239–41; of art in
Baudrillard, 249; and act, 250–51; and
postmodernism, 256

Index

psychoanalysis, 16, 33–81 *passim*, 116–44 *passim*, 123; and literature, 40; and Habermas and physics, 154; as dialogue, 154–55
Psychoanalysis and Feminism, 175
Psychoanalytic Politics, 73
psychology, and theory, 183
public sphere, 278; and Habermas, 304–11 *passim*; counter-, and Eagleton, 309
Purloined Poe, 62

Rabinow, Paul, 308
Ragland-Sullivan, Ellie, 5
Rapaport, Herman, 2
rational reconstruction, 209–11
rationality, 158; and social acts and linguistic acts, 208
reader, and constituting the text, 188
reader-response theory, 154; and consumerism, 281
reading, deconstructive, 86–89; and systematic method, 88; and the allegorist idea, 188; dialectical, 242; typological, 244; performative basis, and Derrida, 259–60; and writing, in performative terms, 260
Reading Lacan, 39
Real, in Lacan, 33, 40; in Jameson, 243–44
Real Life of Sebastian Knight, 153
reason, 24
referentiality, 16
religion, 24, 160
representation, forms of, and politics, 248–51
Re-reading English, 296
Resistance to Theory, 86
Responses: On Paul de Man's Wartime Journalism, 114n41
rhetoric, 83, 84; and literary inquiry, 172; and postmodernism, 173; and social science, 174; feminist political, 174–75; and science and learning, 175; and science, 176–77; of opposition, in deconstruction and New Criticism, 233–34
Rhetoric of Romanticism, 86, 101
"Rhetoric of Temporality," 101
Rhetoric of the Human Sciences, 173
rhetorical analysis, and testing, 173

Richards, I. A., 12, 152, 165, 224
Richardson, William, 39, 62
Ricoeur, Paul, 65, 166, 299; and Freud, 65–66; and Lacan, 65–67; and science and Marxism, 160–61
ritual, and myth, 116–44 *passim*
rivalry, and Girard, 116–44 *passim*
Robbins, Bruce, 279–80
Romantic Ideology: A Critical Investigation, 195–96
"Rome Discourse," 38
Rorty, Richard, 12, 21, 156–57, 308; and "Passing Theory," 22; and pragmatism, 23; and de Man, 93–98; and deconstruction, 93–98; and Derrida, 94, 96; and epistemology, 94; and post-structuralism, 94; and conversation, 94–95; and Derrida and epistemology, 96–97; and interest and edification, 97; and Kuhn, 165, 170; argumentation and positivism, 170; and literary language, 172; and storytelling, 174; and rational reconstruction, 210–11; defining philosophy, 273; the post-philosophical future, 273; and culture critics, 286, and Lentricchia, 308; and Habermas, 308
Rose, Jacqueline, 65
Rosmarin, Adena, 94
Rowe, John Carlos, 250
Russian Formalism, 157
Ryan, Michael, 72, 99, 232–33, 274, 308; and deconstruction, 103–4; and Arnold, 233

Said, Edward, 6, 72, 116, 122, 208, 237, 245, 246, 272; on beginnings, 21; and Girard, 136–37; and worldliness, 137; and criticism, 137, 185; as Popperian and Kuhnian, 170; and worldly theory, 182–90; and structuralism, 183; and post-structuralism, 183, 187; and text, 184–85, 187; and functionalist theory, 184; and Marxist critique, 184; and existentialism, 185; and Vichian mind, 185; and humanistic study, 186; and politics, 186; and history, 186; and culture and literature, 186–87; and intellectuals in social institutions, 186; and signs, 186; and theorists he

334

Index